Advances in Adolescent Psychology

Claudio Violato
LeRoy Travis

Detselig Enterprises Ltd.
Calgary, Alberta

© 1995

Claudio Violato
  University of Calgary
LeRoy Travis
  University of British Columbia

Canadian Cataloguing in Publication Data

Violato, Claudio, 1952-
  Advances in adolescent psychology

  Includes bibliographical references.
  ISBN 1-55059-102-9

  1. Adolescent psychology. I. Travis, LeRoy Douglas. II.
Title.
BF724.V56   1995   155.5   C95-910520-4

Detselig Enterprises Ltd.
1220 Kensington Rd. NW, Unit 210
Calgary, Alberta T2N 3P5

Printed in Canada   SAN 115-0324   ISBN 1-55059-102-9

Preface

While there are many textbooks on adolescent psychology, none of them provide an advanced treatment of the subject. Most of these books are designed for senior undergraduate courses in adolescence and consequently fail to provide much more than the usual survey of the conventional area of "adolescent psychology." Such books and courses by necessity emphasize breadth over depth and therefore, are not very suitable for advanced studies. In teaching advanced and graduate courses in adolescent psychology, we have been limited by the lack of an advanced text. Accordingly, this book is an attempt to fulfill this need.

In writing this volume, we have tried to provide detailed and in depth analysis of central issues. By not attempting to "cover" the whole area of adolescent psychology, we were able to pursue issues, topics and concerns much more thoroughly than is typical in adolescent texts. At the same time, we have tried not to lose sight of some of the conventional and socially relevant topics in the area.

Our discussion and analyses are frequently irreverent, critical and, we hope, iconoclastic. Few areas in psychology are fraught with so much misunderstanding, folklore and purposeful obfuscation than is adolescent psycholgy. We have tried as much as possible to write clearly and pointedly. At the same time, we have tried to invoke as much empirical evidence bearing on the topics and issues as possible. Wherever applicable we have sought to conduct empirical research employing advanced multivariate procedures such as factor analysis and structural equation modeling. Indeed, some of our research is sufficiently advanced to justify the title of this book.

In adolescent psychology as in much of psychology, there is more theory and opinion than empirical evidence. We have tried to emphasize the latter. We believe this book fulfils the need for an advanced text in adolescent psychology.

Claudio Violato
LeRoy Travis

Detselig Enterprises Ltd. appreciates the financial assistance received for its 1995 publishing program from the Department of Canadian Heritage and the Alberta Foundation for the Arts, a beneficiary of the Lottery Fund of the Government of Alberta.

ALBERTA Lotteries   **The Alberta Foundation for the Arts**   **Alberta** COMMUNITY DEVELOPMENT

COMMITTED TO THE DEVELOPMENT OF CULTURE AND THE ARTS

Contents

Tables

Figures

General Introduction

What is adolescence? This seemingly simple question has a surprisingly complex and inconclusive answer. At the outset we can say that this book makes no attempt to provide a definitive answer to this question. Rather we have attempted to address and explore this question from a variety of perspectives, methods and subject matter. To a great extent this book reflects an attempt at integrating much of the research, theory and writing that we have done either individually or collaboratively over the past fifteen or so years. As well, we have tried to employ the broadest possible methods and theory drawing on historical, socio-political and empirical research to elucidate the meaning of adolescence. Our collective efforts in the study of adolescence have yielded this book, *Advances in Adolescent Psychology*.

Adolescence is at least as much a socio-political phenomenon as it is a psychological one. Accordingly, the concept, subject matter and experience of adolescence change and shift with time, culture and place. Adolescence is a multiplicity of events, experiences, behavior, people and cultural meanings. Psychologists of nearly all stripes ignore culture, history and the political economy at their own peril in understanding their phenomenon of interest. This is particularly true of adolescent psychologists, however. The particular features, characteristics, manifestations, and psychological experiences of adolescence are determined by the particular culture, time and place in which it is situated. Yet, is there something that is general and that encompasses the particulars in a way that has not yet been delineated? Notwithstanding the contextual specificity of adolescence, is there something universal about it?

Adolescent psychologists must attend to features of the political economy, cultural longings, commercial culture, mass media entertainment and information, the nature of schooling and the intrapsychic and biological aspects of development. We have tried to adhere to this imperative in this book. Most text books on adolescent psychology (e.g., Adams, Gullotta & Markstrom-Adams, 1994; Conger, 1991; Dacey & Kenny, 1994; Muuss, 1988; Santrock, 1993) emphasize intrapsychic theories and thus either create the impression indirectly, or state the claim directly, that adolescence is essentially an intrapsychic phenomenon. Such books frequently emphasize the theories of Erik Erickson, Jean Piaget, Sigmund Freud, Peter Blos, G. Stanley Hall, Lawrence Kohlberg, James Marcia, and to a lesser extent the theories of Albert Bandura, B.F. Skinner, Margaret Mead and Urie Bronfenbrenner. Frequently, such text books pay lip service to the social-cultural context of adolescence and its history, but these are regarded more as ancillary topics than central ones. We believe that adolescent psychologists, more than other psychologists, need to take into account history, the political economy, the contents and effects of mass media, the commercial culture and scientific approaches to human development.

To tackle this broad range of subject matter, methods of research and theory, we have organized this book into four sections. Each of the four sections comprising in total of 20 chapters, are attempts to thematically connect papers that deal with the panoply of subject, method and theory that we have set before the reader. In section one, we address "Fundamentals of Adolescent Psychology." The five chapters in this section detail perspectives and theories of our subject, as well as historical accounts, and discussions on the nature of human nature. We also provide a reconceptualization of the adolescent experience (chapter 3) and provide some guidelines for future research. This section contains "fundamentals" insofar as the topics, ideas and critiques are fundamental to much of psychology as a whole; we have emphasized their relevance for understanding adolescence. Two of the chapters (1 and 5) have Skinner and his approach to the science of human behavior – a name and topic not usually associated with more conventional accounts of adolescence – as their topics. In these chapters we wished to both provide an understanding of the history and position of natural science approaches to psychological phenomena, and their limitations. B.F. Skinner arguably the most influential psychologist of modern times, has taken the ideas of scientific materialism and monism – philosophies traceable to the philosophies of Aristotle and Democritus – to their apogee as approaches to understanding human behavior. In so doing, he also challenged us to expose the limitations and short comings of operant behavior in arriving at satisfactory explanations and predictions of human behavior (cognitive, affective as well as instrumental).

The other three chapters in this section deal with more conventional adolescent topics. So in chapter two, we discuss the meaning of "theory" for understanding adolescence and the variety of perspectives from which it can be addressed. In the reconceptualization chapter (3), adolescent phenomena are recast as resulting from lacunae or gaps in experience. These lacunae result in young people's psychological unpreparedness for the new social, cognitive and interpersonal events and demands. This, accordingly, requires responses without the benefit of experience.

Section two, "Context of Adolescence" consists of chapters 6-10 which examine various aspects of socio-cultural contexts in which humans are reared and grow. In these chapters we define and utilize the concept of context in its broadest sense. Accordingly, we examine context as commercial culture and mass media depictions of youth (chapter 7), as images of adolescents in English literature from Chaucer to Dickens (chapter 8), as stereotypes of adolescence in television portrayals (chapter 9), and as cross-cultural differences and similarities of adolescent concerns (chapter 10). Chapter 6, "Truths, Concerns and Consequences," sets the tone and provides the background for the other chapters which follow. In general this tone is critical of the cultural context in general and addresses how the insipid commercial culture of modern times creates a "youth culture" which is then misattributed to adolescents as its creators, for purposes of flattering the ignorant and thereby providing markets for its wares.

"Nature of Adolescence," section 3, consists of six chapters that, together, reflect an attempt to probe basic elements of the nature of adolescence. Chapter 11 reports the results of an empirical study of four factors that underlie adolescent concerns. Primary infant and childhood attachments are examined in chapter 12 for their role in organizing emotional experience and interpersonal relations during adolescence and beyond. In chapter 13, the basic coping mechanisms of adolescents for dealing with negative life events are outlined and the results of an empirical study of such coping mechanisms are reported. Chapter 14 is a report of a national survey of prospective teachers that we conducted, with particular interest in their adherence to prominent stereotypes of youth. We found that our subjects generally endorsed the validity of several dimensions of youth stereotypes (which were fictions given widespread and massive visibility in mass media). Equally interesting, we found that those subjects who were heavy users of superficial television fare tended to more readily believe the stereotypes than subjects who used more serious mass media fare. Subsequently, we replicated the study with veteran teachers who had much more classroom experience with young people than did our undergraduate sample. The results of this study are reported in chapter 15. Astonishingly, the more experienced subjects (teachers) adhered to the stereotypes even more vigorously than the undergraduates. We provide several possible explanations for this in chapter 15. The final chapter (16), outlines the basic argument that much of education and serious learning runs counter to the will of the student who tends to lack self-control, sustained effort, discipline and focus – all factors which are necessary to serious learning but which are glorified and encouraged in popular culture. Instinct (impulse, immediate gratification, hedonism) runs counter to civilization (serious learning and education) as Freud noted several decades ago.

The final section (4), "Problems in Adolescence," consists of some of the "hot" topics of adolescence and those favored in mass media depictions. Thus we discuss adolescent suicide (chapter 17), delinquency (chapter 18), sexual abuse (chapter 19), and the relationships of intelligence, creativity, and achievement in preadolescents (chapter 20). These problems are obviously real but have been "normalized" as part of adolescence by both psychological theory and the emphasis placed on them in serious and mass media discussions. Accordingly, we address them from a critical and empirical perspective to complete our broad spectrum analysis of adolescence.

Taken together we hope that our 20 chapters organized within four sections educate, provoke, and inspire our readers to serious and critical reflection and meaning of the concept of adolescence. Finally, we certainly hope that our exposition gives our readers a sense of the nuances, complexity and multiplicity of our subject matter – adolescence. Any single aspect theory of adolescence (cognitive, affective, self, etc.) is bound to be hopelessly inadequate as comprehensive explanation of the adolescent experience.

References

Adams, G.R., Gullotta, T.P., & Markstrom-Adams, C. (1994). *Adolescent life experience* (3rd ed). Belmont, CA: Brooks/Cole.

Conger, J.J. (1991). *Adolescence and youth* (4th ed). New York: Harper-Collins.

Dacey, J. & Kenny, M. (1994). *Adolescent development*. Dubuque, IA: WC Brown.

Muuss, R.E. (1988). *Theories of adolescence* (5th ed). New York: Random House.

Santrock, J.W. (1993). *Adolescence* (5th ed). Dubuque, IA: WC Brown.

Introduction
Section One: Fundamentals

This section, the first of the four, consists of five chapters that focus on matters fundamental to our understanding of adolescents. At the level of surface particulars, each of these five chapters has its own topic; but at a deeper level all are addressed to the matter of perspective and how our observations are affected by the perspective from which they are made. These fundamental matters include the question of how we think about human nature; the history of the object of our thoughts, adolescence, and the history of thoughts about that object; and issues of theory and theorists' beliefs about what is important and how such important matters are related in their attempts to make sense of adolescent phenomena.[1]

Also included in this section devoted to discussions of fundamentals, is an essay that describes a perspective from which adolescent experience has been reconceptualized. In setting forth the outlines of this reconceptualization of adolescent experience, the essay raises the question of how adequately "aspect theories" (theories that address only one or another of the aspects or provinces of adolescents' mental or psychological life) serve our understanding of all adolescents; and it sets out a direction for making a new synthesis that can encompass the entire mental ensemble of feeling, thought, and will which, in congress, are the constituents of the everyday, working imagination – that focus of life that composes, arranges, conducts, and even sings, the song of a given life. The first and last chapters in this first section focus on the work of the distinguished behaviorist, the late B.F. Skinner. At first glance this may surprise some readers because Skinner's name is not usually associated with adolescence, the subject of this book. Both chapters reflect an admiration for Skinner's work. Like so many psychologists, we recognize the profundity of Skinner's influence, even on many who, perhaps, would deny he had such influence on themselves. However, even as we share an appreciation for his work, we appraise it differently as the two papers reveal.[2]

The first chapter discusses Skinner's influence on the way people think about human nature. Obviously, the way we think about human nature is a fundamental consideration with regard to how people orient to and think about adolescents. Skinner is placed in the very select company of Copernicus, Galileo, Darwin and Freud, a group whose members had unparalleled impact on the way we think about human nature – and hence about the nature of adolescents. The claim that Skinner is among those who "naturalized" humankind is not the only basis for placing him in such select company. For his insistence on the exclusion of inner-life phenomena from the subject matter of human psychology forced people to consider the limits of what materialist science can incorporate and address. Few have been able to jar significant numbers of humanity to do this sort of thing.

But this bold and noble stance offended many who refused to concede that exclusion of inner-life phenomena would improve human psychology. Frequently, those who objected, failed to appreciate Skinner's subtlety or the service he rendered by forcing people to examine closely what was to be excluded.

In the last chapter of the "fundamentals" section, Skinner's work is assessed in the light of just such examination. In this chapter, "Skinner, Behaviorism and Adolescents," Skinner's work is appraised for both what it wins us and what acceptance of his exclusive address to performance costs us. In the latter case, the educational enterprise receives attention. Here, we point out the costs that may arise from an agreement among educators that humans are essentially captured by, or their psychology is adequately summed up by, their performances. In effect, this position counters the laudatory tone of the first paper – even as it is written from a stance that is sympathetic with the materialist prejudice. All the same, it underscores the need to recognize the primitive and very severe requirements of considering humans as just more matter-in-motion. Clearly, the sixteenth century model of man-as-billiard-ball, set forth by Thomas Hobbes in *The Leviathan,* is not as subtle as Skinner's sense of our nature.

However, when the unit of analysis is the human individual who is not confined to binary choices in desperate situations, we have to wonder about the adequacy of a view that assumes that humans just perform and that the performances described in the metrics of frequency and duration say all that matters. This last consideration is particularly pertinent to the adolescent situation in which choices of a complex sort are pressed on adolescents. Here, what can't be seen can matter most from the adolescent's (or parent's, or teacher's) view. Conflicts and other inner-life phenomena in imagination, arise from the interplay of the mental provinces, and are central to the experience of adolescence. Leave these aside and what do we have? What of affection (sensation, appetite, feeling, emotion, mood – the varieties of affect); what of cognition (memory, knowledge, reasoning, comparison, contemplation – the varieties of thought); what of conation (striving, choosing, deciding, resolve, volition – the varieties of will)? Together (and with some particulars of content or substance assumed) these define the stuff of adolescent troubles because feelings and thoughts; memories and resolve; choice and reason; striving and thought; mood and knowledge, can (and sometimes do) collide. While ecological description and behavior analysis reveal much about adolescent life, they reveal little of what is involved in an identity crisis; they show nothing of what instigates too little or too much social anxiety for a young person's long-term advantage.

Considerations such as these inform the other four chapters in this section on fundamentals. Each of these papers takes as its focus, matters just as fundamental as how we think about human nature and what needs to be considered. Accordingly, the second chapter deals with theory. This chapter describes a variety of perspectives that arise from the involvements, knowledge, cares and desires of different groups who share an interest in adolescents. It also sets forth some issues and problems that have been, and continue to be, of interest to students of adolescence. In addition, it describes contrasting emphases given by theories that arise from attention to and emphasis on particular aspects of the adolescent psyche; and it suggests that adolescent psychology consists of a collection of various isolated works that tend to be monophonous in character. That is, adolescent psychology has been an aggregation of single-aspect theories which fail to give adequate recognition to the polyphonous character of the human psyche. The wide-spread adoption of the behaviorist prejudice of avoiding anything deep, interferes with the recognition of public maneuvers, masks, contrivances that hide and mislead observers who take observable surface appearances for all that matters. Thus, in a troubled world, adolescents have been depicted as being untroubled even as their prospects worsen. The age-old sense of adolescence as a time of trials and tribulations, of extreme earnestness that alternates with high whimsy, is nowadays denied by those who take surface appearances to be total reality.

These matters lead to a reconceptualization of adolescent experience that encompasses a polyphonous model of the human mind and that favors life analogues (like music) over mechanical metaphors for analysing and describing experience. Given the multiple provinces of mental life, each of which has a voice to express the tones, rhythms, pitches, and melodic themes of a given aspect of life as embodied in a given person; the soul, psyche, or mind of each human is represented as an ensemble or chorus made up of multiple voices that may sing in unison, that may harmonize, that may express discordance. The various provinces of one's mental life are linked to our sense of beauty, our sense of truth, our sense of goodness, as well as our sense of lacunae or holes, shortfalls, or deficiencies in our experience. This sensitivity to lacunae is seen to be especially acute during adolescence due to a concatenation of factors including the marginal status, the biological readiness for reproduction, the socio-cultural demands, and the relative inexperience of people who live simultaneously on the margins of childhood and adulthood without permission to enter or dwell in either zone of life.

This set of circumstances and that mental orientation maximize conflicts which call forth coping efforts. A variety of patterns are set forth as a more reasonable way of conceptualizing adolescent experience since differences in temperament, intelligence, culture and so on make highly implausible any singular characterization that does not allow for the full range of human response to trouble and triumph. At the same time, denial of the reality of conflicts and turmoil during this time requires more than a little wishful thinking and myopia. We might recognize that some youngsters hide, disguise, deny or repress any sort of trouble that they have. Others trumpet their troubles to the world. Just because the latter may be outnumbered by the former does not justify claims that for the former, life is serene and lightheartedly lived. For perhaps only those of unusual strength and those who suppose they have nothing to lose or fear, give undisguised expression to their life of trouble. The more numerous may feel too vulnerable or be too threatened to allow anyone direct, conscious apprehension of their troubles. Rudimentary knowledge of what aggregation entails should allow the elementary insight to anyone who is otherwise not over-invested in a position, theoretical preference, or commitment, that in data reduction and aggregate analysis, the mass at or near the middle of a distribution will overwhelm the others who deviate notably from the mid-point. Crowd behavior, furtive vandalism and so on, speak to this possibility as does close scrutiny of affect and will in interviews.

These latter observations raise the subject of the other chapter in this section on fundamentals of adolescence. This chapter brings an historical perspective to bear on adolescence. Historical scholarship has been increasingly fruitful in enhancing our understanding of adolescence as a period of life, and adolescents as people living in particular periods or in specific circumstances that are particular to a given period and place. Since past circumstances may not persist, research methods of historians are needed. So in the fourth chapter, the history of adolescents is explored. These then, are the fundamentals that are addressed in the first five chapters that comprise section one: "Fundamentals of Adolescence."

Notes:

[1]A new name has emerged for adolescent studies that reflects the interdisciplinary nature of the subject. The name is "adolescentology." The First International Congress of Adolescentology was convened in October, 1993, at Assisi, Italy.

[2]These two chapters are revised drafts of invited papers that were given in a symposium on Skinner, at the Northwest Communications Conference at Couer D'Alene, Idaho, in April, 1991. A similar version of the chapter on Skinner by Professor Travis, appeared in *The Canadian Journal of Special Education*, 1993, under the title "Voice versus message: On the importance of B.F.Skinner."

1

On The Nature of Human Nature

Freud remarked more than once that in the history of scientific thought, his psychoanalytic theory represented the third great outrage against humanity (Gay, 1989, p. xvii; Vivas, 1965). With this remark Freud was suggesting that his theory offended not only the sensibilities and conventional wisdom of his epoch, but mankind's megalomania as well. Therefore this represented an "outrage" against humanity. (In a similar vein, Neitzche characterized the work of scientific materialism in the following manner: "All sciences today work for the destruction of man's ancient self-respect.") The preceding two great outrages that Freud was referring to were Charles Darwin's theory of natural selection and the Copernican/Galileo revolution in physics. Like Freud's own challenge to the prevailing views of human nature itself, the work of Darwin and Galileo shook the conception of human nature and humanity's place in the universe to its very foundation. Each of these great ideas – psychoanalysis, natural selection and the earth's motion – elicited great controversy and consternation from their own epoch's. The latest such great idea coming in the final century of the second millennium of recorded history is B.F. Skinner's behaviorism. In the tradition of Galileo, Darwin and Freud, Skinner has produced the fourth great outrage against humanity. His work has challenged the foundations of the beliefs about the very nature of humanity and what governs behavior. Skinner took the implications of scientific materialism – that matter is the source of everything in the universe including life and consciousness – to its logical conclusion when he expelled "mind" from human behavior.

The main purpose of the present chapter is to trace the evolution of thought about the nature of humanity and our role in the universe from Galileo to Skinner. These thinkers have been selected for analysis because they have come to represent each of the four great outrages.[1] While many others in history have professed scientific ideas that were controversial in their time (e.g. Pasteur and the "germ theory"), the present scientists that have been selected are clearly associated with a revolutionary point of view (Kuhn (1962) might call it a paradigm) that is the result of the application and explication of scientific materialism. There are two main reasons for the vehemence of attack that these great theories and views of humanity elicited during their epochs: (1) as Freud said, each was a blow to humanity's megalomania, and (2) perhaps even more importantly, each of these four "outrages" challenged the legitimacy and political authority of the major institutions of their day. Copernicus and Galileo as well as Darwin directly challenged the relevancy and authority of the Church, Freud went further and asserted that a belief in God was either a form of neuroses or a childish fixation. By this time, however, the Church's authority in explanations of nature was already seriously undermined though it still claimed authority in matters of human affairs. Freud's greater threat was to the legitimacy and authority of important institutions such as medicine, education and government. Moreover, he exposed the "true meaning" of conventional social and moral customs of the family, interpersonal relations, and sexual behavior. Skinner similarly criticized many institutions of the twentieth century including government, legal systems, psychotherapy, education, and economic structures. In the tradition of his predecessors (Galileo, Darwin, Freud), Skinner also attacked the Church and its practices. The main thesis of the present chapter, then, is that these thinkers and their ideas received such strident criticisms (and frequently abuse) because (1) they promulgated unpopular accounts of humanity, and (2) they challenged political authority of their day. We begin with an examination of scientific materialism.

Origin and Rise of Scientific Materialism

No discussion of scientific materialism can be adequate without acknowledgement of recent developments in the philosophy of science. Since the 1960s there has been debate among historians and philosophers of science on the nature of "scientific progress." Kuhn (1962) introduced a provocative thesis wherein he postulated two distinct types of activities, "normal science" and "revolutionary science." Normal science proceeds within the framework of a "paradigm" which consists of a variety of ontological, epistemological and methodological principles, laws and assumptions. The history of science can be understood as the succession of paradigms which disrupts normal science during the revolutionary phase as a new paradigm – which essentially defines reality – succeeds the old paradigm which has outlived its usefulness. Kuhn (1962) has argued moreover, that paradigms are incommensurable – there are no common basis for comparison across paradigms. The implication of this is that no paradigm is necessarily superior to another and that science must deviate from the "narrow path of rationality" if progress is to be made. Knowledge is relative according to this view.

Kuhn's views have not been accepted without criticism. Masterman (1970), Popper (1970), and Lakatos (1970, 1978) are among Kuhn's most notable critics. Masterman (1970) has argued that Kuhn's concept of "paradigm" is far too vague to be useful since at least twenty-two different uses can be found in Kuhn's work. Popper (1970) has charged Kuhn with irrationalism, grossly over-emphasizing discontinuities in the history of science thereby obscuring the cumulative and rational nature of progress. Lakatos (1970, 1978), perhaps the most incisive of these critics, has argued that it is more appropriate to speak of a research program which involves a succession of theories rather than a paradigm. What Kuhn has called a scientific revolution, Lakatos has described as the defeat of one research program by another. Laudan (1984) has provided a similar critique of Kuhn.

Gholson and Barker (1985) in reviewing the works of Kuhn, Lakatos, Laudan and others and their applicability to physics and psychology, concluded that "it is now possible to give a sophisticated account of the development of scientific disciplines that avoids the problems of incommensurability and retains a clear sense in which a science may be said to progress, even when fundamental commitments are modified" (p. 767). One of the central contentions of the present paper is that science has progressed because knowledge is to some extent cumulative, notwithstanding the popularized Kuhnian ideas of incommensurability and extreme relativism which have been readily embraced by social scientists (Gholson, Shadish, Neimeyer & Houts, 1989; Krauser & Houts, 1984). Our contention is that thought about human nature has been cumulative from Galileo, finally culminating in Skinner's behaviorism.

There is no attempt in the present chapter to discuss the "four great outrages" from the perspective of paradigms (Kuhn, 1962), research programs (Lakatos, 1970), or research traditions (Laudan, 1984) since to do so would be to invoke a confused and irrelevant (for present purposes) argument. Moreover, Kuhn's ideas have by now been so widely popularized, misread and misapplied (Peterson, 1981), that to use them would be to introduce confusion rather than clarity. Rather than saltatory developments, the outrages are seen as progressive applications of scientific materialism which has its origins in antiquity.

Plato (428 B.C. - 347 B.C.) developed a rather extensive theory of human nature with a dualism assumption as the cornerstone of his theory (Field, 1930). His famous dictum, *soma sema* sums up the division of body and soul. While the body is the seat of the soul, it also fetters it. The soul can achieve high rational and critical thought but it must triumph over the pull of the body. The Platonic School encouraged mysticism and dualism.

Democritus (460 B.C. - 370 B.C.), a contemporary of Plato, anticipated much of 19th and 20th century science including the idea of the unity of nature which was forcefully argued by Charles Darwin much later. This idea – that there is nothing unique and different in humanity's constitution from any other matter in the universe – forms the underpinnings of scientific materialism. Democritus believed that all things are made up of "atoms" – tiny particles of many sizes and shapes moving at different speeds. Humans were composed of "soul" atoms which were more spherical but otherwise did not differ from any other atoms. Thus Democritus put forth a monistic theory of human nature (Robin, 1928).

Aristotle, (384 B.C. - 322 B.C.) one of Plato's most successful students, diverged from his teacher and agreed with Democritus on the point of dualism or mind-body separation. He began with a doctrine of monism or the unity of the physical and mental worlds. Like modern material psychologists such as Skinner and Freud, Aristotle saw the soul as the function of the body which provides the structure. This then is the origin of a materialist interpretation of humanity – mind or soul does not exist independently from the body and matter (Charles, 1984).

Plato's dualism however triumphed during the first and part of the second millennium of history since Christ. Particularly during the epoch called the Medieval Period, for nearly one thousand years the view of the world and human nature was based largely on Christian theology and religious dogma. From the total collapse of the Roman Empire in the 5th century to the 15th century and the Renaissance, the dualistic view of humanity prevailed.

The Renaissance or rebirth after the Middle Ages marked a sharp break with Medieval ideals and practices, particularly in the arts, in literature, in science and in the concept of human nature. These changes began in Italy primarily during the 15th and 16th centuries and later spread throughout the world. The major break of Renaissance thought with Medieval doctrine was over the doctrine of dualism. As this was the cornerstone of religious dogma, the Church was challenged directly. Monism, the central theme of scientific materialism, was embraced by many thinkers during this period and reached its apogee late in the 19th century and early in the 20th with the works of Marx, Darwin and Freud. Skinner – embodying behaviorism with its origins in the work of St. Thomas Aquinas, John Locke, I.M. Shecenov, V. Bekhterev, J.B. Watson, E.L. Thorndike (McLeish, 1981) – took to its natural conclusion the materialist philosophy when he declared "mental life" to be irrelevant to behavior (Skinner, 1990).

Modern scientific materialism may be characterized as consisting of four interrelated postulates (Novack, 1965, p. 4-5).

1. Matter is the primordial substance, the essence of reality.
2. Mind or consciousness is a manifestation of matter and arises from it. Mind can never exist apart from it.
3. Nature exists independently of mind, but mind cannot exist apart from matter. As Feuerbach observed, "Thought springs from Being, but Being does not spring from thought."
4. The foregoing three postulates preclude the existence of souls, spirits, deities or other immaterial constructs in the operations of nature, society and human behavior.

Materialism can be brought into sharper focus by contrasting it with its polar opposite, idealism, which can be also be summarized by four postulates (Novack, 1965, p. 4-5).

1. The basic element of reality is mind or spirit.
2. The material world has been created by a spirit or mind.
3. Spirit or mind preceded matter which is no more than a passing phase or illusion.

4. The immaterial emanates from the supernatural or divine which governs nature, society and human behavior.

Materialism and idealism have been, and are, the two dominant points of reference in philosophy although of course, there are other view-points. The history of philosophy exhibits many combinations of this idea which occupy a spectrum of positions between these extremes (Feyerabend, 1963, 1978; Malcom, 1964)[2]. Each of the four great outrages represent a victory of scientific materialism over idealism and the social institutions which derived their legitimacy and authority from the latter. The first major challenge to idealism embodied in the dogma of christian theology came from the work of Galileo Galilei who provided supporting data for the mathematical model of the universe developed by Nicolaus Copernicus.

Copernicus, Galileo and the First Great Outrage Against Humanity

Copernicus was born in Poland in 1473 and studied law and medicine in Italy. In 1543 after many years of dedicated service to the government and Pope, Copernicus published his mathematical description of the heavens, *De Revolutionibus Orbium Coelestium* wherein, the sun – rather than the earth – was placed at the centre of the solar system (Kuhn, 1957). Copernicus died that same year and never witnessed the impact of his ideas.

The final blow to the Ptolemaic model of the solar system (the earth at the centre with the planets revolving around it) came from Galileo more than half a century later. When in 1608 Galileo made his first telescope, he was already a renowned and famous scientist throughout Europe (Stillman, 1970). He soon perfected the instrument and turned it skyward to make several sensational discoveries – the satellites of Jupiter and the topography of the moon – which he published in *Sidereus Nuncius* (1610). As his data accumulated, Galileo became convinced that Copernicus was right and the Ptolemaic solar system of the Roman Catholic Church was wrong. This challenge mounted by Galileo was disastrous to himself of course, but was the first main triumph of scientific materialism over dogma and superstition. Galileo naively assumed that the truth would prevail over doctrine (Stillman, 1970), but the issue was not one of doctrine but of authority.

The Catholic Church had felt embattled by the Protestant Reformation and in the 16th century, it mounted a Counter-Reformation. So when Galileo proposed his tendentious view of the universe, the Catholic Church was in no mood to accept it. It believed that the Church's authority should dominate while Galileo believed that truth should prevail. In espousing his view of epistemology, Galileo revealed his commitment to scientific materialism:

I think that in discussions of physical problems we ought to begin not from the authority of scriptural passages, but from sense-experiences and necessary demonstrations. (Bronowski, 1981, p.130)

Galileo, of course, was silenced and lived out the remainder of his life in imprisonment after his trial in 1633. His legacy to humanity was the triumph of reason and data over dogma and idealism and hence a victory of materialism over idealism.

When Freud referred to the Copernicus/Galileo revolution as the first great outrage against humanity (Gay, 1989), he was suggesting that human nature was henceforth altered forever and that humanity's position in the universe was diminished. In the Ptolemaic system of the Catholic Church, the earth was the centre of the universe. And since according to Christian theology, humans are above all other living things just below God and the angels, humans are *de facto* the centre of the universe and God-like. Humans, after all, had been characterized in the Old Testament as follows: "What is man that Thou art mindful of him . . .Thou hast made him a little lower than the angels, and hast crowned him with glory and honour" (Psalm 8). Galileo changed the perceptions of humanity's place in the universe forever.

More important than proposing an alternate and less flattering view of humanity than had been maintained by the Church, however, was Galileo's direct challenge to the legitimacy and authority of the Vatican. Had Galileo not pressed the confrontation by publishing his highly offensive book (to the Pope), *Dialogue of the Great World Systems,* in which he characterized the Pope as *un scioco* (a dunce), the trial would probably never have taken place. Indeed, the Vatican was able to accept Galileo's views themselves as non-threatening. It was Galileo the upstart, the megalomaniac, and the arrogant who had to be repressed and silenced. So vehement was the Church's reaction to Galileo that it was not until 9 May, 1983 – 450 years after the trial – that Pope John Paul publicly declared that Galileo was correct after all. But more telling than this was the Pope's observation about the Church that the "Galileo affair and after it has led to a . . . more accurate grasp of the *authority proper to her*" (emphasis added) (Grove, 1989, p. 154). The second Great blow to humanity's dignity and challenge to idealism came in the middle of the 19th century.

Darwin and the Second Great Outrage Against Humanity

In the wake of the Copernican revolution completed by Newton, humanity made its peace with its diminished stature and the Church adapted to its undermined authority. When *The Origin of Species* was published in 1859, it was an instant sensation and a best-seller which still reverberates through time to the present. Darwin, of course, had anticipated how deeply shocking the theory of natural selection would be to his contemporaries and indeed, had delayed publishing it for more than 20 years (Stebbins, 1971). As Darwin (1872) himself said in the sixth edition of *The Origin of Species:*

> That many and grave objections may be advanced against the theory of descent with modification through natural selection I do not deny. I have endeavoured to give to them their full force. Nothing at first can appear more difficult to believe than that the more complex organs and instincts should have been perfected, not by means superior to, though analogous with human reason, but by the accumulation of innumerable slight variations, each good for the individual possessor. (p. 435)

Darwin's masterpiece transformed attitudes toward God and humans. The criticisms from the Church on the grounds that Darwin's theory contradicts the story of creation in Genesis, led to vituperative polemics which continue to the present. Darwin's idea that evolution proceeds by natural selection from *accidental* variations holds in it the denial of purpose and thus the irrelevancy of a Deity. By an accidental and natural selection, variations and differences favoring survival would be preserved. Survival of the fittest based on natural variation thus provided a completely mechanical and material system by which to account for the changes in living forms.

There was no need for purpose either from a Deity or even a single individual other than survival or reproduction in this view of the world. Mind and consciousness were byproducts of evolution, gradual, incremental and very recent and unimportant in Darwin's system in which he proclaimed *"Natura non facit saltum"* (Darwin, 1872, p.435). In this *modo di vedere* even the most sublime phenomena – mind and consciousness – were reduced to a material explanation. Scientific materialism thus reached its apogee in the middle of the 19th century.

Notwithstanding the reaction to Darwin's "mechanistic" universe, Darwin himself saw not soulless, ugly, mechanistic and bleak results. Rather he marvelled at the processes and results of "natural selection from accidental variation." He concluded his *magnum opus,* which he regarded as "one long argument," with grandiloquent prose:

> Thus, from the war of nature, from famine and death, the most exalted object which we are capable of conceiving, namely, the production of higher animals, directly follows. There is grandeur in this view of life, with its several powers, having been originally breathed into a fewer forms or into one...from so simple a beginning endless forms most beautiful and most wonderful have been, and are being, evolved. (Darwin, 1872, p. 459-460)

The objections to natural selection and evolution by Darwin's contemporaries and many since were numerous. In order for evolution to have occurred the Earth had to be much, much older than many people assumed. Moreover, nature and its products – living forms – were highly dynamic and ever-changing; not static and fixed since the beginning of time. And finally, humans – the pinnacle of life – were not separate and above other life forms, but were part of them, governed by the same natural laws. No purpose and no Deity was necessary in

Darwin's universe. Life had no purpose and no meaning; it was pointless change – a cycle of birth and death without a guiding Providence.

The reaction by the Church to the theory of evolution by means of natural selection was fierce. It was the last major battle between materialism and theological idealism. The legitimacy and authority that had remained for the Church after the Galileo–Copernican victory, was now threatened. According to materialist view the story of Genesis was wrong and no God or purpose was necessary in creation. Thus the Church, its teaching, ministrations, and even authority on moral matters, became superfluous. In one last but futile attempt to maintain authority over explanations of nature, the First Vatican Council of 1870 proclaimed the infallibility of the Pope, and reasserted the unshakable opposition of the Church to evolution, "Darwinism" and liberalism. Nevertheless, idealism in the form of theological doctrine had forever lost its authority over explanations of nature. By the time that Freud was formulating the third great outrage, however, idealism had re-emerged in new forms: the idea of the absolute had been rejected. A new reign of consciousness, purpose, teleology, relativity and pluralism was born with the new century. Knowledge itself was relative. Both of Skinner's and Freud's battles, therefore, were not with the old familiar foe of materialism, the Church, but with the new idealism.

Freud and the Third Great Outrage Against Humanity

Sigmund Freud was born in 1856, three years before Darwin published *The Origin of Species*. By the time Freud entered the University of Vienna to study medicine in 1873, evolutionary ideas had saturated intellectual life in Europe (Gay, 1989). Biological determinism, instincts, homeostasis and other biological principles are strongly reflected in Freud's theory of the psyche.

No single book or publication can be readily pointed to as capturing and representing all of Freud's ideas or even his main ones as his output was prodigious. He spent nearly fifty years developing his ideas and theories, but his first major work which essentially laid out the whole framework of his psychoanalytic theory (and the book he considered his best) was the misleadingly titled, *The Interpretation of Dreams* (1900). Initially this book was largely ignored but his *Three Essays on the Theory of Sexuality* in 1905 aroused animosity from Freud's contemporaries. Psychiatrists and neurologists assailed these (and later) works as ludicrous, filthy and more a matter for the police than scientific congresses (Jones, 1953).

What is it about Freud's theory that has so offended and outraged many? Freud's theory of humanity is so comprehensive and original that it is difficult in a brief space to identify all that is controversial about it. In brief, however, there are at least 9 main elements of his theory that arouse indignation and controversy.

Freud adhered to the principle of determinism. All behavior and mental states are determined by hidden causes in the mind. This includes slips of the tongue, memory loss, dreams, feelings, thoughts and all of mental activity and behavior. Therefore, nothing a person does or says or feels or thinks is accidental, haphazard or without a cause; everything can be traced to its origin in principle (Freud, 1900, 1910a). Many have objected to this principle of determinism on the grounds that it denies humanity's "free will" (Vivas, 1965). As we shall see, this is also a profound objection to B.F. Skinner's radical behaviorism.

The second main element – the unconscious – arises from the first principle of determinism. By definition, the unconscious aspects of the mind cannot become knowable under normal circumstances. But the unconscious is the main part of the human mind which exerts it influence on the conscious mind (Freud, 1900). Virtually everything that humans do, then, is governed by unconscious desires which cannot be explained rationally (or even known) to the self or others. Indeed, much of the functions of the conscious mind is to justify or rationalize (partially through defense mechanisms) behaviors which are irrational and governed by the unconscious. In this characterization, then, humans are slaves to unconscious impulses (Freud, 1900, 1910b).

The unconscious impulses are comprised of instincts and drives. In his later work (1920 on) Freud classified all the instincts of the unconscious into two categories: (1) Eros or "life" instincts (sexual, self-preservation), and (2) Thanatos or "death" instincts (aggression, self-destruction). The third point in this theory which many find offensive, then, is that human behavior is essentially instinct driven but particularly by base instincts: sexual and aggressive.

If this were not enough, Freud asserted that the sexual theme predominates and exists from birth. In this way Freud introduced the concept of infant sexuality (1910b). The main theme governing life even for seemingly "innocent" appearing neonates, is that they are sexual just as they surely are later on even though at first sexuality is expressed in infantile modes (i.e. oral, anal and phallic). Infant sexuality is a fourth point of offensiveness.

The fifth point of contention and controversy, is the prepotency of early childhood experiences (Freud, 1900, 1905). According to psychoanalytic theory, the prototype for later personality development is complete by about age five. Thus all later behavior, development and personality must be understood on the basis of early childhood experiences (particularly traumatic ones). Many find this early childhood determination objectionable.

One of the main conflicts of that all human children must face is the Oedipus complex (for males) and the Electra complex (for females). With this idea – and the sixth point of offense – Freud asserted that all children have incestuous feelings for their parents. Moreover, the male child has murderous feelings and impulses for the father as he sees him as a rival for the mother's affection. Freud outraged Victorian sentiments (and modern day ones as well) with these dual impulses of sex and murder of children for their parents.

Theologians and religious people have also been outraged by Freud because of his characterization of religion. Freud was an avowed atheist (Jones, 1953) who asserted that a belief in God and an afterlife reflected not a truth about the universe, but a human neurotic response to the fear of death. Thus humans created God and an afterlife as a way of neurotically coping with death. While corporeal death is undeniable and inevitable, humans have invented a "soul" or "spirit" to deny death (Freud, 1912, 1927) which shall live on in perpetuity. The God of Judaism and Christianity for Freud was paternalistic and reflected a regression of humanity in the face death to a childish stage and the need for a protective father (Freud, 1912). Such assertions represents a seventh point of offensiveness.

Freud has been referred to as the greatest pessimist in history (Gay, 1988). This of course comes about because of his bleak depiction of humanity and contemporary life. In *Civilization and Its Discontents* (1930), Freud depicted a gloomy picture of humanity ever destined to misery because unconscious drives could never be satisfied due to the constraints of civilization. The individual could never be happy because of the restrictions and impositions of civilization on the gratification of human "needs" and drives. By the time Freud wrote this essay, he had lived through World War I and was witnessing the Nazi rise to power together with their persecution of political enemies and particularly Jews (Freud was to flee Austria when the Nazis invaded and settle in London where he died in 1939). Thus Freud depicted humanity as not only at war with civilization but also with itself (Eros vs. Thanatos). In the concluding paragraph of *Civilization and Its Discontents,* Freud proposed that: "The fateful question for the human species seems to me to be whether and to what extent their cultural development will succeed in mastering the disturbance of their communal life by the human instinct of aggression and self-destruction" (p. 92). Freud went on to argue that humans must struggle for self-preservation. The outcome, however, was anything but clear: "But who can foresee with what success and with what result?" (p. 92). This pessimism about the future of humanity is the eighth point of objection to Freud.

Finally, a more recent condemnation of Freud has come from feminist critiques (e.g. Gilligan, 1982). Many have objected to Freud's characterization of women. Freud asserted that "anatomy is destiny" and, therefore, one's psychic life can never transcend one's gender. Some feminists have argued that women in psychoanalytic theory are depicted as inferior, defective and degenerate male forms who suffer from penis envy (Ruble, 1984). This point of outrage, then, is Freud's putative sexism and unfavorable depiction of women vis a vis men.

In addition to the contentious views of humanity, Freud also directly criticized important institutions of his day such as the family, government, religion and education. Civilization as a whole he saw as too repressive thus condemning humans to a perpetual state of misery (Freud, 1930). Freud attacked religion as "distorting the picture of the real world in a delusional manner" (1930, p. 31). The pretensions surrounding the family came under attack since its primary goal was to satisfy the "need for genital satisfaction." For the male, the family functioned to keep "the female . . . his sexual objects, near him" (p. 46). For the female it provided shelter, protection and help with child-rearing. Freud (1930) also criticized education:

> . . . the education of young people . . . conceals from them the part which sexuality will play in their lives . . . and does not prepare them for the aggressiveness of which they are destined to become the objects . . . education is behaving as though one were to equip people starting on a Polar expedition with summer clothing and maps of the Italian lakes. (p. 81)

Unsurprisingly, many people responded with hostility to Freud's descriptions and criticisms for he was challenging directly the legitimacy and authority of these institutions.

Despite Freud's "outrage" towards humanity, he still left humans with a mental life, notwithstanding a dark one. It was the 20th century behavioral psychologists who committed the fourth great outrage against humanity by dismissing mental life as a causal or significant factor in human behavior.

B.F. Skinner and the Fourth Great Outrage Against Humanity

B.F. Skinner was born in 1904 at the time when Freud was formulating and refining his essential principles of psychoanalysis. Skinner's psychology, however, took a radical turn away from psychoanalysis or other mentalistic psychologies and he championed behaviorism over the course of 50 years of professional activity. Two weeks before he died in 1990 and in his final public address, Skinner unwavering to the end, still dismissed mentalistic explanations of behavior and perfunctorily rejected cognitive science as "the creation science of psychology" (Skinner, 1990, p.1209). During the course of his career Skinner published more than 175 papers and a dozen books and yet was still widely misunderstood and attacked. He was called "the new Machiavelli," "a Nazi," "a high priest," "a parochialist" and so on (Epstein & Skinner, 1982, p. 5). What is it about Skinner's work that can arouse such hostility?

The most crucial and fundamental point of Skinner's behaviorism which elicited "outrage" and hostility from his critics, was his dismissal of mental life as unimportant and irrelevant to an understanding of human behavior. This of course was not original with Skinner – J.B. Watson among others wanted to ban consciousness – but he became the champion and most forceful, persuasive and prolific spokesperson for this radical view. Skinner never tired of reiterating this point. Thus, throughout numerous works he said: "mentalistic explanations explain nothing" (1953, p. 33; 1971, p. 145; 1974, p. 224). This rejection of mental life as an explanatory entity was crucial to Skinner. This was the only way to establish a science of behavior which was the proper subject matter of psychology as Skinner saw it. The eternal search for explanations of behavior via mental states for Skinner was a waste of time. Thus, he said:

> When the important thing is a relation to the environment, as in the phylogeny and ontogeny of behavior, the fascination with an inner system becomes a simple digression . . . We have not advanced more rapidly to the methods and instruments needed in the study of behavior precisely because of the diverting preoccupation with a supposed or real inner life. (Skinner, 1975 p.46)

Skinner did not deny the existence of a mental life; he asserted only that it is in the realm of private events and thus has no special significance to the explanation of human behavior. In contrast to Freud who, though he had characterized humanity in very unflattering terms nevertheless put great importance on mental events, Skinner re-classified the role of mental life into a subordinate position. In this way, Skinner broke from the early behaviorism of Watson and included mental activity as a repertoire of covert private events or private behaviors.

Three essential postulates about the nature of human nature can be identified in Skinner's system. First, and as we have seen, mental life is unimportant. It is, therefore, unnecessary to look inward to discover "mental states" that cause behavior. Skinner simply assumed that "the organism behaves" (Skinner, 1953, p. 284). A second postulate is that humans learn from the interaction with the environment and that behavior is selected by consequences (Skinner, 1981). Indeed, Skinner (1987) regarded his analysis as a natural extension of evolutionary theory where "there is no longer any need for a creative mind or plan, or for purpose or goal direction" (p. 783). The third postulate which derives from the second, is that behavior is under the control of the environment and not individual mental life (Skinner, 1953, 1960, 1975, 1977, 1981, 1990). Thus he replaced creation with the principles of variation and selection. In these postulates, Skinner depicted humanity in a way that eliminates what most religions, philosophies and psychologies have always held to be sublime (consciousness and mental life). By asserting that mental life is unimportant and its pursuit a mere "digression," Skinner dismisses the work of modern day cognitivists, personality theorists, psychoanalysts and any other psychologists who also focus on mental events, not to mention most philosophers, theologians, poets and other writers, as a waste of time. As far as understanding human behavior is concerned, Skinner saw these activities as frivolities. Indeed, in one of his last systematic statements, Skinner (1987) identified humanistic psychology, psychotherapy and cognitive psychology as major obstacles to psychology becoming a science of behavior:

> . . . the antiscience stance of humanistic psychology, the practical exigencies of the helping professions and the cognitive restoration of the royal House of Mind have worked against the definition of psychology as the science of behavior. (p. 784).

Is it any wonder that his views are met with indignation, hostility and vituperation?

If this characterization of humanity weren't enough, Skinner proposed applying principles of operant conditioning to controlling human behavior for particular purposes. In order to do this, Skinner first criticized and attacked several institutions of society and the people who work in them. He maintained a relentless and systematic criticism of education over a forty-year period for example. In the *Technology of Teaching* (1968), operant conditioning was to be applied to the classroom to improve American education. Skinner acknowledged that this would be difficult because those responsible for education continued to discuss "learning and teaching in the language of the layman. It is almost as if those who are concerned with improving medicine and public health were to talk about disease as a lack of balance among the humors" (p. 259). Moreover, "the teachers are not competent" and there ". . . is a shortage of good teachers" (p. 250). Skinner went on to assert that teaching "does not attract or hold good teachers. At times the profession has been tolerable only to weaklings or those who enjoy treating others aversively." (p. 99). Finally, on pedagogy Skinner said "the subject has . . . fallen into disrepute (1968, p. 255). It is not surprising that the educational establishment and teachers reacted with hostility.

In *Beyond Freedom and Dignity,* Skinner (1971) proposed a program for improvement of society. This had to begin by a direct challenge:

> Governments are said to promote justice, security and peace, religious piety and salvation, economic wealth, educational knowledge and skills, and psycho-therapeutic mental health . . . There is no absolute truth in value judgements . . . these values are now being challenged. (p. 176-177)

Skinner (1971) proposed the elimination of autonomous man as the first step in achieving his program since "he has been constructed from our ignorance" (p. 200). The legal system came under criticism for inefficiency and punitiveness, religion for maintaining illusions and superstition, and child-rearing practices as misinformed and damaging. The main problem as Skinner saw it, was that major institutions such as governments, religions, and economic systems, and to a lesser extent educators and psychotherapists exert a powerful and often troublesome control (1974, p. 190).

This control is troublesome because it is aversive. Skinner's program for social change was political and revolutionary in nature.

How a better society might be developed was hinted at in a work of fiction, *Walden Two* (1948). These ideas of control are based on the proposition that "a person's behavior is controlled by his genetic and environmental histories rather than by the person himself as an initiating, creative agent" (Skinner, 1974, p. 208). Skinner realized fully, however, the force of reaction that such assertions elicit: "but no part of the behavioristic position has raised more violent objections" (p. 208). Such objections have included accusations of totalitarianism, advocating use of punishment, suffering from megalomania, extreme environmentalism, and naivete about human behavior. Arthur Koestler called behaviorism "a monumental triviality . . . [having] returned psychology into a modern version of the Dark Ages." Peter Gay spoke of the "innate naivete, intellectual bankruptcy, and half-deliberate cruelty of behaviorism" (Skinner, 1971, p. 158-159).

Skinner has received much great condemnation. But like every great idea – especially the other three great outrages – Skinner's view shakes humanity's conception of itself to the very core. Mental life has for centuries been considered the quintessence of humanity. Any denial that it lacks importance is likely to outrage many. Possibly the most serious objection to Skinner's approach is the positing of humans as empty organisms; "Skinner's error, of course, is the empty organism" (Hershberger, 1988, p. 823). This was also one of the main objections to behaviorism of Carl Rogers who saw the inner life as all important and that behavior is consistent with the internalized notions of self (Rogers & Skinner, 1956). Noam Chomsky was also a frequent critic of Skinner's especially over issues of verbal behavior and language development. Jerome Bruner as well frequently clashed with Skinner on central issues of psychology. Much of the attack came from so-called humanists. Ironically, Skinner has been frequently referred to as a great humanist by many (Mahoney, 1991) and when queried about his own view on this, Skinner gave the following response:

> I often wonder whether I am a humanist. If it means someone concerned with the maximization of freedom and dignity, I am not. If it means someone who is concerned about the fate of the human species in the not so distant future, I certainly am." (Note 1)

Skinner's behaviorism is the logical outcome of scientific materialism with its central assumption of the unity of nature and the principle of monism. Skinner himself regarded his operant analysis as the natural heir to evolutionary theory which itself has been the subject of so much controversy and debate (Skinner, 1981, 1987). Perhaps what is surprising is that Skinner's radical behaviorism did not emerge earlier in human history but seems to be a peculiarly 20th century phenomenon.

Summary and Conclusions

Scientific materialism has its origins in the work of the early Greek philosophers, particularly Democritus and Aristotle. For more than 1500 years, however, Plato's dualism was favored as an explanatory mode of human nature. This dualism found its authority not only in Plato but also in the Scriptures and Christian dogma. The first real great challenge to this view of humanity came from Copernicus and Galileo – the first great outrage – who rejected the Ptolemaic view of the universe. This was a great blow to human dignity as humans no longer occupied the centre of the universe. Charles Darwin and his theory of natural selection represents the second great outrage against humanity. Once again, humanity had to rethink its nature and its role in the universe. Freud provided the next great blow to humanity's megalomania. He depicted humans as slaves to unconscious libidinal impulses. Finally, Skinner took the next logical step in the spirit of scientific materialism when he banished mental activity as an explanatory factor in human behavior.

In the first two outrages, the struggle was between materialism and idealism in the form of Christian dogma. With the triumph of evolutionary explanations over the account in Genesis, scientific materialism reached its apogee. By the close of the nineteenth century, however, it had degenerated into "mechanistic materialism" or "crude" materialism and had fallen into disfavor. Some of the strongest proponents of earlier materialism such as Huxley and Spencer had doubts and closed their careers with statements of scientific uncertainty. Alfred Wallace actually declared himself a believer in God.

Developments in a number of fields were setting the stage for a new idealism. William James in psychology dismissed "simple-minded evolutionists" like Spencer. Nietzche had re-introduced relativism in truth among philosophers. In economics, Veblen anointed ideas as *causative* factors. In physics the quantum theory of Planck and Einstein's relativity theory undermined simple mechanistic materialism. The principle of uncertainty formulated by Heisenberg became a matter of popular culture and seemed to indicate that nothing was precise, knowable or fixed. The absolute was dead and relativism ruled. This new idealism of the twentieth century was the environment in which Kuhn's (1962) relativism and incommensurability thesis could eventually thrive.

Freud was still partially engaged with the old foe of materialism (religious dogma) but was fighting a more serious battle with the new idealism. Skinner though was fully engaged with the new idealism first manifested as clinical psychology, then as humanistic psychology and finally as cognitive science. While Skinner's behaviorism had prevailed for a time in American psychology, the pendulum has now swung back in favor of idealism. In his last years, Skinner felt he was suffering the anti-scientific attacks of cognitive, clinical and humanistic psychologists (Skinner, 1987, 1990). The place of scientific materialism in modern psychology is far from secure.

Skinner has championed scientific materialism and the idea of the unity of nature for more than 50 years. He saw mental life and consciousness as nothing more than byproducts of material processes: "mind is what the *body* does . . . it is behavior" (p. 784). In the past five hundred years, scientific materialism has won some tentative victories over ignorance, superstition, mysticism, religion and speculative philosophy. The decisive victory, however, has still eluded us. Novack (1965) has observed that materialism and idealism in our time "stand arrayed against each other in mortal combat for complete possession of the provinces of rational thought and scientific knowledge" (p. 16). Skinner showed unwavering confidence in his great idea but can it endure under the onslaught of the new idealism?

Reference Notes

Note 1. B.F. Skinner, Personal Communication, Sept. 28, 1988.

References

Bronowski, J. (1981) *The ascent of man.* London: Futura Press.

Charles, D. (1984) *Aristotle's philosophy of action.* Ithaca, New York: Cornell University Press.

Darwin, C. (1872). *The origin of species (6th edition).* New York: Arvell Books.

Epstein, R. & Skinner, B.F. (1982) *Skinner for the classroom: selected papers.* Champaign, Illinois: Research Press.

Feyerabend, P.K. (1978). *Science in a free society.* London: NLB.

Feyerabend, P.K. (1963). Materialism and the mind-body problem. *The Review of Metaphysics, 27,* 49-66.

Field, G.C. (1930). *Plato and his contemporaries.* London: Oxford University Press.

Freud, S. (1900). *The interpretation of dreams.* Standard edition, vols 4, 5. London: Hogarth, 1953.

Freud, S. (1905). *Three essays on the theory of sexuality.* In P. Gay (ed), *The Freud reader.* New York: Norton, 1989, p.239-292.

Freud, S. (1910a). *The origin and development of psychoanalysis.* New York: Gateways edition, 1965.

Freud, S. (1910b). *Theory of infant sexuality.* New York: Norton, 1961.

Freud, S. (1912). *Totem and taboo.* In P. Gay (ed), *The Freud reader.* New York: Norton, 1988, p.481-513.

Freud, S. (1927). *The future of an illusion.* In. P. Gay (ed), *The Freud reader.* New York: Norton, 1988, p.685-722.

Freud, S. (1930). *Civilization and its discontents.* New York: Norton, 1961.

Gay, P. (1988). *Freud: A life for our time.* New York: Norton.

Gay, P. (ed) (1989). *The Freud reader.* New York: Norton.

Gholson, B., & Barket, P. (1985). Kuhn, Lakatos, and Laudan: Applications in the history of physics and psychology. *American Psychologist, 40,* 755-769.

Gholson, B., & Shadish, W.R., Neimeyer, R.A., Houts, A.C. (1988). *Psychology of science.* New York: Academic Press.

Gilligan, C. (1982). *In a different voice: Psychological theory and womens' development.* Cambridge, Mass.: Harvard University Press.

Grove, T.W. (1989). *In defense of science.* Toronto: University of Toronto Press.

Hershberger, W.A. (1988). Psychology as a cognitive science. *American Psychologist, 43,* 823-824.

Jones, E. (1953). *The life and work of Sigmund Freud.* London: Hogarth Press.

Krasner, L., & Houts, A.C. (1984). A study of the "value" systems of behavioral scientists. *American Psychologist, 39,* 840-850.

Kuhn, T. (1962). *The structure of scientific revolutions*. Chicago: University of Chicago Press.

Kuhn, T. (1957). *The Copernican revolution*. Cambridge, Mass: Harvard University Press.

Lakatos, I. (1970). Falsification and the methodology of scientific research programs. In I. Lakatos and A. Musgrave (Eds.). *Criticism and the growth of knowledge*. Cambridge: Cambridge University Press.

Lakatos, I. (1978). *The methodology of scientific research programs*. Cambridge: Cambridge University Press.

Laudon, L. (1984). *Science and values*. Berkeley: University of California Press.

Mahoney, M.J. (1991). B.F. Skinner: A collective tribute. *Canadian Psychology, 32,* 628-635.

Malcom, N. (1964). Scientific materialism and the identity theory. *Dialogue, 3,* 115-125.

Masterman, M. (1970). The nature of paradigm. In I. Lakatos & A. Musgrave (Eds.). *Criticism and the growth of knowledge*. Cambridge: Cambridge University Press.

McLeish, J. (1981) *The development of modern behavioral psychology*. Calgary: Detselig.

Novack, G. (1965). *The origins of materialism*. New York: Pathfinder Press.

Peterson, G.L. (1981). Historical self-understanding in the social sciences: The use of Thomas Kuhn in psychology. *Journal for the Theory of Social Behavior, 11,* 1-30.

Popper, K.R. (1970). Normal science and its dangers. In I. Lakatos, and A. Musgrave (Eds.). *Criticism and the growth of knowledge*. Cambridge: Cambridge University Press.

Robin, L. (1928). *Greek thought and the origins of the scientific spirit*. New York: Russell and Russell.

Ruble, D.N. (1984). Sex-role development. In M.C. Bornstein and M.E. Lamb, *Developmental Psychology: An advanced textbook*. Hillsdale, NJ: Erlbaum.

Skinner, B.F. (1948). *Walden two*. New York: Mcmillan.

Skinner, B.F. (1953). *Science and human behavior*. New York: Mcmillan.

Skinner, B.F. (1960). Pigeons in a pelican. *American Psychologist, 15,* 28-37.

Skinner, B.F. (1968). *The technology of teaching*. New York: Appleton-Century-Crofts.

Skinner, B.F. (1971). *Beyond freedom and dignity*. New York: Knopf.

Skinner, B.F. (1974). *About behaviorism*. New York: Knopf.

Skinner, B.F. (1975). The steep and thorny way to a science of behavior. *American Psychologist, 30,* 42-49.

Skinner, B.F. (1977). Hernestein and the evolution of behaviorism. *American Psychologist, 43,* 455-484.

Skinner, B.F. (1981). Selection by consequences. *Science, 213,* (July), 501-504.

Skinner, B.F. (1987). Whatever happened to psychology as the science of behavior. *American Psychologist, 42,* 780-786.

Skinner, B.F. (1990). Can psychology be science of mind? *American Psychologist, 45,* 1206-1210.

Stebbins, G.L. (1971). *Processes of organic evolution* (2nd edition). Englewood Cliffs, N.J.: Prentice-Hall.

Stillman, D. (1970). *Galileo studies*. Michigan: University of Michigan Press.

Vivas, E. (1965). Introduction In S. Freud, *The origin and development of psychoanalysis*. New York: Gateway Editions.

Notes

[1]To use the five names associated with the four great outrages is not to suggest the "great man" view of history. This is done more for convenience than to imply single-handed creation. The mathematician Keppler and subsequently the physicist Newton obviously contributed to the Copernican/Galileo revolution. Darwin's work drew from his own grandfather's ideas, in part from the work of Lamarck and was assisted by others like Spencer and Huxley. Moreover, the theory was proposed independently at about the same time by Alfred Wallace. Freud's ideas for the development of psychoanalysis, of course, were influenced by Charcot, Janet and Breuer. Many colleagues such as Jung, Adler, Jones, and others helped refine and propagate psychoanalysis. Skinner in his work with behaviorism owed a great deal to the foundations laid by others such as Pavlov, Watson, Thorndike and Guthrie. No person alone obviously establishes and propagates such important and profound ideas, methods and movements as embodied in the four great outrages.

[2]There are a number of important philosophical traditions that occupy a middle-ground between the polar opposite of pure materialism and pure idealism. These include the American Pragmatists such as William James and John Dewey, Existentialists such as J. Paul Sartre and phenomenologist such as Husserl.

2

Theories of Adolescence

Introduction

In the years between childhood and adulthood, a stream of life for each of us is formed from the trickles and showers of childhood, and each stream soon reaches a place where it acquires a character and a more or less general direction. This character and that direction set the range of possibilities that a given stream will subsequently have; they select the ground through which the remainder of its course will flow, and they affect the breadth and depth of flow. When a life reaches this place, and as it takes on the task of finding direction for the duration of its course, certain choices and commitments have to be made, and certain tasks have to be accomplished. For such timely accomplishments, commitments and tasks make the waters of a given life flow clearly, freely and in a contained and pleasing form. In the absence of these developments, there is little chance that such a life will be serene enough and strong enough to be of benefit to the rest of creation, or manifest the qualities or graces required to face and surmount the floods and droughts that come in the fullness of life's course. The span of time when life acquires this character and direction is called adolescence. The various bodies of thought which attempt to explain the formation of the varieties of character and direction that lives take at this time, and which try to account for the differences in difficulties that are experienced in forming such character and taking such direction, comprise the theories of adolescence.

Motives For the Study of Adolescence

As Muuss (1988) says, "numerous theories have been advanced to explain the phenomena of adolescence" (p.3). These theories address phenomena that are the subjects of concern and interest for a variety of groups. So we ask: What has moved people to wonder about, observe, study and, more generally, be interested in, the young people known as adolescents? The practical motives of the interested differ from group to group: parents seek assistance, insight, comfort and reassurance and desire successful coping and adjustment for their offspring. Teachers want insight too. They want to minimize interference with learning and teaching so they can aid and abet the development of competence, sensibilities, taste, and knowledgeability in their pupils. People in the world of commerce seek profit. Young people comprise a significant market; they have much influence on the spending patterns of their parents and others with whom they regularly spend time. Politicians also have an avid interest in the young. Apart from their nobler motives for understanding the populace whose interests they represent, politicians seek influence, support and assistance. They also want to harness youthful energies and enthusiasms in pursuit of electoral success – attractive youngsters are always welcome as animate props at ceremonies and commonplace pseudo-events. So they need to be understood to be engaged. Scholars who seek enhanced understanding of human development also study adolescents. They sense that insight into the mysteries of human development can be derived from studying children during this period.

Finally, adults generally prefer peace to strife. So this too moves people to study those who have the wherewithal to make trouble. In sum, the troubles of adolescents and troubles with adolescents draw people to seek understanding of adolescence. People seek knowledge to cope with, and possibly preempt, the appearance of adolescent troubles; sometimes they have epistemic motives that serve commercial, political and humanistic ends. What all share is a need for good theory to make sense of what is seen and what is common.

Adolescents and Adolescence

This chapter addresses that need for theory. However, as prelude to the direct address of that matter, some basic particulars of the subject can be reviewed with advantage. We begin with the identification of adolescents, and an exploration of adolescence and adolescent phenomena.

Everybody knows that teenagers are adolescents. Fewer know that some who are not yet teenaged are adolescents too (because sometimes puberty or reproductive maturity arrives before the teen years). Perhaps even fewer know that some people beyond the second decade of life are also adolescents because they have not yet been accorded, or have not yet assumed, the full panoply of adult burdens and benefits. Even so, no theory is needed to clarify these matters since only a question of definition is involved. Thus, from the foregoing, we see that adolescents are those people whose childhood has, with puberty, come to an end, but whose adult life has yet to begin for want of full adult status with its duties, obligations, and responsibilities – and with its prerogatives, privileges, power.

As a concept then, adolescence is multi-dimensional because its onset markers are biological phenomena – the signs of reproductive readiness – and its termination is marked by sociological, economic, cultural and legal indicators – the evidence of *de facto* and *de jure* independence and responsibility. In the socio-cultural sense, and in the contemporary legal sense, adolescence is a transitional status, a marginal status, that separates the status of childhood (with its condition of dependency, and its formal or codified as well as informal protections) and the status of adulthood (with its ascribed self-sufficiency and responsibility which get formal recognition in law, and less formal but forceful recognition in social customs and economic arrangements). In the legal and sociological perspectives then, adolescence is a public or social phenomenon marked by public signs of status and legal standing.

Adolescence in a Psychological Perspective

In the psychological sense, adolescence is somewhat less easily delineated than it is in law or in social and behavioral sciences like sociology, anthropology, ethology and economics. This difficulty arises in part because psychologists try to take account of the inner life which is not directly observable. While some psychologists' interests are restricted to the level of matter-in-motion and so share the behavioral focus of the other social and behavioral sciences, the character of the inner life of adolescents is recognized as indispensable to an adequate understanding of adolescent psychology.

In psychology, human beings are not just animate objects, humans are animate objects that feel, think, choose, and act. We act and choose, think and feel, in a material world that includes powerful forces that are indifferent to humans' existence or fate. As animate objects that are vulnerable to the powerful and uncaring forces of the material world, sustained existence for humans requires that we be mindful of how circumstances vary in what they offer or portend. Survival requires that we partake of the provenance of the objective world under hazardous conditions. This means that we must pay attention, feel, notice, remember, compare, anticipate, plan, choose and act. We must objectify and subjectivize. Of special significance for adolescents, is the fact that, as Isaiah Berlin said, "we are doomed to choose and every choice may entail an irreparable loss" (1991, p. 13).

Human experience then, entails a busy trade or traffic between the two realms in which each person has a life: the inner or subjective sphere of sensations, feelings, wishes and thoughts and the outer or material world of objects, relations, conditions and events. At any given time for any given person, reality is what that person's imagination or mental powers compose from the stock of the internal life and those features of the outer world that the person is disposed to notice and assimilate. This "reality" is the effective situation for the person and comprises the psychological context for his or her experience. Organized in language, it can be "a metaphor to live by" (Lakoff & Johnson, 1980).

From a psychological perspective, human experience is context bound. That is, at any given time, a person's thinking, feeling and striving are related to a situation the human apprehends with imagination. The situation, as imagined by the person, is the context of affect, thought and will as they constitute present experience. Sensations and appetites and emotions have meaning in relation to the situation. So too for memories, wishes, and plans, just as is the case with resolve, choice, action and resignation.

Given all this, it remains for those who assume that adolescence is a phase of life that is psychologically distinctive, to show how adolescents differ from children on the one side, and adults on the other. This is no mean feat given the range of variability in all three groups.

The Adolescent Situation and Psychological Perspective

From this psychological perspective, a human is to be understood in relation to what that person takes to be his or her situation. However, a situation is not merely a subjective matter, nor is it merely an objective matter. It is both. Moreover, people have smaller and larger situations; the former can be nested in, or otherwise be related to the latter. Sometimes people relate situations, sometimes they don't. Certainly the patterns are not clear. Adolescents, from a psychological perspective, occupy a marginal situation in which childish ways are to be left behind while corresponding adult ways are still forbidden. This is the common, objective feature that we may call the adolescent situation. In brief, if adolescence, from the sociological perspective, is a marginal status, it is from a psychological perspective, a marginal situation. And it is this "situation" that is transformed by personal meanings, emotions and strivings as each adolescent in imagination, subjectivizes it and re-forms himself or herself as he or she will. While not all theorists would subscribe to the foregoing conceptualization, considerations of a kind ensure that inner-life constructs are given a heavy explanatory burden in most psychological theories that would account for adolescent phenomena. Illustrations include G. Stanley Hall (1904) who stressed emotional lability; Sigmund Freud (1905/1975) who pointed to "sexual excitation"; Allison Davis (1944) who dwelled on "socialized anxiety"; Otto Rank (1945) who made much of "the will"; Eduard Spranger (1955) who relied on "value direction"; Erik Erikson (1959) who proffered the "sense of identity"; and Jean Piaget (1967) who emphasized "egocentrism" and reasoning. All such constructs are intended to bear an important or significant explanatory burden in dealing with the respective theorist's concerns and involvements.

The Generalization Gap

Adolescents are an identifiable group: we know who they are. But what non-trivial generalizations can be made about them? What can be said about them that sets them apart from children and adults? After all, this is a group whose members' ages range over more than a decade of life, and this is not just any such span of life. On the one side, generalties emanates from puerility and the protections of childhood, and on the other, it merges with the experience of adults who may know first hand, adult responsibilities and rewards: the costs and benefits of compromise, the price and the worth of duty; the burdens and indispensability of loyalty; the dangers and necessity of authority, the personal indifference of contingency, the omnipresence of expediency, and the persistent moral squalor within which each adult must steer a course. In simpler terms, some adolescents know little more than the life of play and school while older others know something of the world of work and other features of adult life.

So we repeat the question: What generalizations apply to adolescents, to a group whose ranges of age and experience alone ensure the existence of remarkable human diversity within it? The point of the question is underscored when one notices that in addition, the adolescent population encompasses both sexes, the full range of intelligence, all types of character, all sorts of personality, all socio-economic classes, all temperaments and body types, and every cultural and ethnic and national division.

Moreover, the fullness of human differences within this population, as great as those within the populations of adjacent age-spans of a similar breadth, is immense and assured because, as Scarr says "the psychological character of . . . situations is influenced by inherited characteristics" (1993, p. 46) such as temperament. And these are no less important in adolescents than in any other human population. Nearly two decades ago, Adelson drew attention to this problem which he called "the generalization gap." He set forth the reasons why the conventional lore about adolescents and the generalizations of the time were unsatisfactory: they were based on observations of unrepresentative samples of the adolescent population. He concluded that a consequence of the habitual practice of relying on visible, easily accessible youth for a vision of the young is that "our general theory of adolescence" is misleading and in need of reconceptualization (Adelson, 1979, pp. 34-35). While interest in adolescents generated a large volume of studies of adolescents in the ensuing years, the problem of theory has persisted. This state of affairs deserves further attention.

Adolescent Phenomena:
What is Common to Adolescents Generally?

Since this chapter addresses questions of theory in adolescent psychology, there is advantage in setting forth a description of what adolescents share before theory per se is discussed. Accordingly, a brief account of the sameness, of what is common to or shared by adolescents, precedes an exploration of basic questions about the nature of theory.

The fact that a special name has been given to this population suggests that they have much in common. That commonality or sameness may or may not comprise the basis for stereotypes or images of youth that are so readily seen (Travis & Violato, 1981, 1985; see also chapter seven). In any event, these simplified representations provide a common sense of what or who is the subject of the lore about adolescents that has accumulated over the years. Adolescents share with all others who partake of the mass-mediated information environment and the consumption of that farrago of lore and stereotypes of adolescents.

While these simplifications and that lore can be mischievous as a basis for defining reality, forming expectations, and developing a sense of what is needed, wanted, or required from teachers or parents or others who gather with them regularly, there is a commonality, a shared reality that parents and teachers can know and understand. Such knowledge and understanding can provide a grounding for meeting adolescents in a spirit of care, concern and support; can serve as a foundation for confident guidance, instruction and example; and can constitute a basis for providing adolescents with circumstances and opportunities that afford the discovery and development of their powers to find their own way, make their own discoveries, and direct their own lives.

Perhaps the most obvious matter that is shared by adolescents is the basic adolescent situation discussed above. In meeting that situation , each adolescent is faced with some important questions: how is one to behave, how is one to live (to feel, to think, to strive, to imagine, to choose and to act, and to make one's way in the world on one's own) when one is put on notice that the standards and paths of childhood are now inappropriate, while adult alternatives are untried, unhoned and frequently not allowed or available for some time? In the absence of clarity with regard to behavioral expectations, adolescents sometimes seem bewildered, confused and impatient. The frequently seen, exaggerated strivings of adolescents create waves. When such waves swell, the anxieties of adults become evident. The ensuing expressions of adult emotion can add to adolescents' difficulties. The adolescents' expressed frustrations with the problems of handling all the competing demands presented in their situation, in turn, complicate life for both the adolescent and the adults in his or her life. (e.g. see Douvan & Adelson, 1966; chs. 10, 11) The common tasks of adolescence also warrant some attention. The following series of questions point to these tasks: How does one cope with what the mature body suggests to others – and to oneself? How does one prepare for life apart from one's family of origin? How does one decide what matters most in life? How does one choose among compelling alternatives?

As Isaiah Berlin said, "collisions of values are of the essence of what . . . we are." (1991, p.13) But this is not a realization that comes readily or quickly to adults much less adolescents. So we must make choices and commitments. In so doing, the mature and experienced adult may know that such choices and commitments entail trade-offs and create new needs and problems; but the inexperienced youth is often little prepared for such discoveries. He or she may embrace spontaneity as a general principle of virtue and pay the price exacted by failure to plan.

Since making choices and commitments is central to so much that adolescents must face, the tendency of inexperienced youth to be "totalistic" and to be naive about the availability of perfection, beckons trouble and frustration. The following questions represent common task demands in the experience of adolescents, that often give force to this issue: What commitments must one make to ensure that one can live with pride, confidence, energy and integrity? What must one do to ensure that the person one was, is and will be, remains the person others see and respect? On what basis does one decide which values or goods are to be sacrificed for the attainment of other goods? (For example, how much liberty is to be sacrificed for how much equality – and vice versa?) The task demands that these questions represented are a significant component of the commonality or sameness adolescents share. But there is more.

Perhaps the most obvious of the qualities shared by adolescents are youth and the concomitant readiness for biological reproduction. While recent work points to (apparently biological) limitations on fertility in the early teens (e.g., Bogin, 1993), and a modicum of observation and reflection suggests that wisdom and some other mental graces come only with considerably more time and experience than two decades afford, adolescents are conventionally represented as being at the height of their physical and mental powers. Youthful maturity is not, however, a singular and unmixed blessing. Usually, in the degree of his or her youth is a person immature in both sensibilities and judgment. By virtue of age, the adolescents are inexperienced with regard to grown-up life. Hence, they are prone to the errors of the inexperienced and ignorant. Frequently too, adolescents exaggerate their virtues (often betrayed by an unrestrained self-righteousness that can grate), manifest extreme behavior, and affect extravagant postures and appearances. But not always; patterns are not very clear or predictable. Hence, there is need for explanation, for theory.

Theories: What are they and what do they do for us?

Two elements are needed to form a truth – a fact and an abstraction. (Gourmont)

When something intrigues or puzzles us, or when we face some problem or difficulty, we observe, reflect, speculate and try get a better understanding of whatever is involved. We imagine order in the puzzle, structure in the problem, regularities or recurrences in the conditions of difficulty. In other words, we try to discern what is important and how these important things are related in the sphere of interest. In any given realm of scholarship, this is what scholars do. In pursuit of matters that interest us, we form beliefs about what is important and how these putatively important things are related. In our attempts to make sense of such matters we contemplate them, we examine them to discern regularities. When we give formal expression to the conceptions or formulations that we believe summarize the putative order of things, we theorize.

A theory then, is a statement of belief about what is important in a realm of interest, and how those things deemed to be important are related. Such statements or claims direct attention or guide observation, and they may be influential in building expectations about what is the case.

Theory and Fact

> It is the theory that decides what will be observed. (Einstein)

Non-trivial theories embrace everything factual in the domain of interest so that coherent sense can be made of what is observed. But, as Bertrand Russell said, "a fact, in science, is not a mere fact, but an instance" (Auden & Kronenberger, 1962, p. 259), and all instances are variants. Accordingly, we notice, as did the German poet-scientist, Goethe, that "everything factual is, in a sense, theory." (ibid. p.101) Theory confers meaning on fact because it identifies observed fact as an instance of a class that is identified as significant; it places fact in a framework of relations between whatever the theory's author supposes are important matters. Patterns or orders of fact confer meaning on theory when they correspond with what the theory has implied or suggested – when they correspond with what the theory leads one to expect.

In sum, a theorist imagines an order of objects, conditions, relations and dynamics that define, describe and explain what is important in a realm of interest. To the extent that matters of observed fact correspond with the imagined order, the theory helps us understand those matters.

Idea and Observation

> Concepts without percepts are empty; Percepts without concepts are blind. (Kant)

Since there is no immaculate perception, observation is theory-laden. That is, we observe through the templates of ideation. Ideas, as it were, both allow us to see order, and impose order upon ourselves and the realms we observe and consider. Unfortunately, not all ideas are good ideas. Fortunately, from time to time, a member of the aristocracy of intellect among us (whose status issues from the grace of concision, contemplative temperament, and informed judgement) notices the inadequacies of an idea and insists that the particulars of Nature do not correspond with or support it. So any given theory, like everything this side of Paradise, is imperfect. Discerned imperfections in the correspondence between idea or expectation and observations require that the theory be revised or discarded. In a word, Nature has a say in what is fact, and if intellect notices that thing and theory are discrepant, intellect articulates, Nature's critical powers.

Advantages and Hazards of Simplification

Theories then, are like maps: they show important features of realms with which we may have commerce, but they are not the territories themselves. They are, rather, simplifications which select and represent whatever is believed to be important given the concerns and involvements of the theorist. But this selection and simplification, undertaken to distinguish and give emphasis to what is important (given a particular perspective), do not capture all that is true. Accordingly, a given theory may disregard or place in the background some matter that is of great significance to people of markedly different concerns and involvements (and even knowledge) than the theorist. In adolescent psychology, this is often the case. Thus, some theorists seem to be more concerned with and involved in studying the troubles of adolescents as opposed to the troubles with adolescents that are the principal concerns of others. Each discipline and occupation has its own categories and ideas about what matters most. Each has a focus and a characteristic manner of simplifying matters with theory.

A Biological Focus: Endocrinology

Medical people most characteristically, have a biological focus. Accordingly, adolescent phenomena are issues of the body in context. Interest in the so-called "raging hormones" of adolescence arises from and illustrates work with this focus . It is interesting to note in this connection, that Offer, a medical reviewer of recent work that speaks to the impact of pubertal hormones on adolescent turmoil, moodiness and emotionality, drew the conclusion that "current . . . findings . . . contradict [the putative] relationship between puberty and disturbance, and instead suggest that the effects of pubertal hormones are neither potent nor pervasive." (Offer & Schonert-Reichl, 1992, pp. 5-6).

Clearly, there is more to the body than hormones; the work under review does not dispose of their importance in explaining some adolescent phenomena. For example, the changes in body size and appearance that we see during adolescence are linked to the hormonal changes of that period as well as to the dynamics and difficulties one sees in the "dating-mating complex" of teenagers. However, the problem of coming to terms with what the mature body suggests to others and to oneself is not just a body problem, nor is it solely a biological problem in the more encompassing sense.

A Psychoanalytic Focus

The emotional concomitants of that problem are so well documented in literature and other arts, in diaries and letters, in clinical cases and parental testimony, it is curious and perhaps very significant, that the linkage of emotional turmoil and pubertal hormones is denied or downplayed, and that memories of such emotional experiences are repressed as in "adolescent amnesia" (Douvan & Adelson, 1966). Perhaps questionnaire research (e.g, Offer, Ostrov, Howard, & Atkinson, 1988) often overlooks the possibility that adolescents and adults tend to repress and forget (and there is so much people would want to forget), and so perhaps questionnaire research under-reports emotional experience during adolescence. This may also be the case with the Experience Sampling Method (Csikszentmihalyi & Larson, 1984; Wong & Csikszentmihalyi, 1991) whereby respondents record their experience in a context when they are cued to do so by a radio signal. While there is much to appreciate and admire in this procedural innovation, it is no less vulnerable to observational error, due to events and states within respondents, than the questionnaire method.

A psychoanalytic focus does not emphasize the body or its anatomical or physiological aspects so much as it brings to the fore what a body's history has wrought. In particular, the unconscious defenses that, in a given case, have been developed in childhood to manage the tensions and troubles encountered in that period, come into play during adolescence when there is a "recrudescence" of archaic struggles and conflicts occasioned by the onset of puberty, by the social repercussions of that development, and the other tasks of adolescence (not least of which is that of making choices and commitments under pressing conditions and so re-forming an identity that has authenticity given one's background or past, that has integrity given one's present situation, and that has viability in the adult future that one desires).

A virtually universal defense that appears in childhood is denial. The widespread existence of and reliance on this work-horse of defenses together with the customary practice of putting on a "cool" face as a public manoeuvre, should raise suspicions about the reliability and completeness of retrospective self-reports of emotional experience during adolescence (and perhaps during adulthood too). The manifestations of avoidance manoeuvres and repression of emotional experiences were so common in the large-scale interview study reported by Douvan and Adelson (1966) that the researchers explicitly drew attention to and dwelled upon the conventional pattern which consists in "the stubborn burial and isolation of affect" (p. 3).

Of course, this is not to say that life is thereby made serene for adolescents. On the contrary, the cool face one sees frequently, disguises "too passionate a period: hot, angry, sentimental, lustful, guilt-ridden, sullen, anxious, bitter, elated, tormented" (p.3). Accordingly, we might be wise to be wary of the sunny accounts of adolescent experience that have become the conventional version of reality set out by so many investigators over the past 30 odd years. The portrait of serenity that Offer and his associates (1988, pp. 110-113) call a "portrait of the 'universal adolescent'" (p.110) is implausible and depends upon a myopic view of the world, as well as a superficial sense of the psyche. Barber's (1992) assessment of the forces that oppose one another in the world today – conflicts between local loyalties and intimate ties on one side, and the forces of "McWorld," of "globalization," of the New World disorder on the other – is more able to accommodate the reality of youth in Tehran, in Baghdad, and in other centres where the "jihad" resists the soft takeover, resists conquest by the pop guns of diversion or amusement culture. Offer's questionnaire is utterly blind and insensitive to the shared anger that moves adolescents to speak with contempt of the poorly paid "McJobs" that await them as their most likely employment prospects beyond school. The forces and entities which Offer and company portray as the creators of a putative "universal self," a "collective personality and a collective consciousness" shared by "today's teenagers," also destroy work prospects and living standards (e.g. see Hacker, 1993) where many teenagers live; and this seems to get noticed in Germany, in Somalia, in Bosnia and elsewhere – including the USA (e.g. see *World Press Review,* 1993).

Moreover, while perhaps the "normative adolescent tends to avoid overt conflict with his or her family" (Douvan & Adelson, 1966, p. 352), conflict doesn't necessarily cease to exist for such adolescents: it may be displaced or transferred to the interior or covert life, and submerged as unconscious conflict or transformed into a semi-conscious resentment. Or it may be displaced to inflate aggression in sports or driving, to intensify arguments with peers or siblings, or to provoke vandalism, delinquent actions, or acting out in school. In the psychoanalytic view, the importance of "the erotic intrusion" is stressed along with aggressive drives and the social agencies, cultural arrangements and personal efforts that are directed at controlling and restricting such instinctive impulses. Biology is in conflict with civilization from the start; and the accrued experience an individual has of that conflict informs the (adolescent's) address to current manifestations of the unending struggle. Accordingly, the psychoanalytic perspective assumes that "adolescent behavior is over-determined" (p. 7).

Research methods that incorporate aggregation procedures are bound to do violence to the variety of insight and truth that this perspective can yield. At the same time, such cautions don't preclude frequency counts. Thus Douvan and Adelson were able to contrast "the normative response to adolescence" that they observed nearly 30 years ago, with those " at the extremes" or " opposing ends of the [American] social class continuum." Said these researchers:

> . . . one cannot generalize these [adaptive] processes to the adolescent population at large. The adolescent at the extremes, responds to . . . [inner and external] upheaval . . . by disorder, by failures of ego-synthesis, and by a tendency to abandon earlier values and object attachments. In the normative response to adolescence, however, we more commonly find an avoidance of inner and outer conflict, premature identity consolidation, ego and ideological constriction, and a general unwillingness to take psychic risks. (Douvan & Adelson, p. 351)

Observations of these sorts draw attention to the social realm and the focus of sociological theory.

Sociological Focus

A sociological perspective focuses on what society does to a body (i.e., how society organizes a person's experience) and so focuses attention on a body's status in society. Social position is reckoned in relation to centres, agencies, groups or persons with more or less power, prestige, wealth, popularity, or authority. Gradients of these factors are organized to grasp the nature of relations, or understand the fluctuations of association. So the nuances of custom, the differential recognition of mores, the application of laws, and the dynamics or stability of other features of social life and its organization receive attention when adolescent phenomena are studied. Social forces focused on adolescents of marginal status are taken to be of central importance in explaining adolescent phenomena. Difficulties with school achievement, for example, tend to be analyzed in terms of social-class interests, gradients of social opportunity, relations to hegemonic entities, or incongruence or incompatibility between the values or beliefs of an individual or group and those of teachers or officials. This last mentioned factor shades into another widely noticed perspective that is focused on adolescence. This is the cultural focus which contrasts most notably with the biological perspectives that range from a focus on body chemistry to the psycho-sexual dynamics of psychoanalysis.

The Cultural Focus

If the biological perspective focuses on the body, its chemistry, its maturation, and its sexual significance in social contexts, as principal factors in the manifestations of adolescent phenomena; and if psychoanalytic thought focuses on a recrudescence of early childhood struggles with the management of aggressive and sexual impulses that, with puberty, have gained unprecedented urgency; the cultural focus looks outward to features of a society's way of life to explain manifestations of adolescent phenomena. Above all else, the way of life, the culture, is presumed to shape adolescence.

Several decades ago, when cultural relativism was at its zenith, cultural anthropology was a notable influence on students of adolescent psychology. The plasticity in human nature was emphasized, and observed contrasts of particulars were sought to show that variations in cultural patterns shaped the adolescent experience and that there are few universal or shared features of adolescence. It is fair to say that the ethnographic enthusiasm has decidedly waned in more recent times as the evidence has accumulated against strong cultural determinism (e.g., Scarr, 1993).

Nowadays, biological questions concerning adolescents are explored by anthropologists like Bogin (1993) who links factors in reproductive biology during the teen years to cultural preparation for parenthood. In noting that the growth spurt for the sexes don't coincide, Bogin speculates on the evolutionary significance of this state of affairs:

> My argument . . . is this. Girls best learn their adult social roles while they are infertile but perceived by adults as mature; boys best learn their adult social roles while they are fertile but not yet perceived as such by adults. Without the adolescent growth spurt this unique style of social and cultural learning could not occur. And this is why adolescence deserves to stand alongside our large cerebral cortex, bipedality, and unique sexual behavior as a factor in defining us as human . . . .(Bogin, 1993, p. 38)

This illustration of recent work in anthropology should not be taken as indicative of a general abandonment of interest in a cultural focus. On the contrary, there is a lively interest as we will shortly see. However, the critics (e.g., Ausubel, 1977) who said that the cultural anthropologists of the first five decades of this century underplayed biological factors and overemphasized the socio-cultural environment seem to have made their point among anthropologists. Even so, among those who see in economic conditions, powerful forces that shape experience, there is a recognition that the cultural environment deserves close attention.

The Economic Focus

After the recent upheavals and transformations of what was the officially Marxist sphere of eastern Europe, the only visible subscribers to viewpoints that assume economic determinism are aggressive conservatives. However, certain cultural patterns are nowadays, generally recognized as central to an economic focus on adolescence. These patterns are readily discerned when they are set forth in historical narratives like one finds in textbooks (e.g., Santrock, 1990, pp. 18-22). The excesses, inaccuracies and parochialism that mark some such narratives do not cloud the pattern of economic forces at work.

There is even a conventional name for this perspective: "the inventionist view." What is common to the various versions of this view, is an emphasis on the importance of changes in the base and system of production in creating the phenomena we now recognize as adolescence. In outline, this view emphasizes the following: as the industrial revolution gained momentum, economic life changed for the great bulk of people (who had been country people living in an economy of subsistence agriculture). This meant that urbanization accelerated; the division of labor became increasingly elaborate; reliance on mechanization grew; home and work became separated as never before; the medieval crafts, guilds and apprenticeship systems were debased and transformed; and traditional social support systems were unable to meet the emergent reality of increased homelessness and misery in the towns. In the face of the fears of impending social calamity, legislatures passed "child-saving" and "youth" legislation that curtailed the exploitation of child labor and eventually instituted compulsory, age-graded, "universal" schooling. These were the economic and legislative roots of the "moratorium" on adulthood that we now associate with adolescence.

In societies that afford a more or less protracted moratorium on productive participation in the economy of paid work, homemaking and other adult pursuits, children of adolescent age are funnelled into two streams of involvement. One is schooling and education (what could be and sometimes is an involvement in coming to know and work out the tensions between serious or durable culture and amusement or toss-off culture). The other is immersion in the flow of detritus that is the usual issue of consolation culture – popular culture's entertainments for those who cannot or will not face their condition (e.g. see Buhle, 1987; Postman, 1986; Rybezynski, 1991; Twitchell, 1992; and chapter 7). Well-meaning but under-educated "progressive educators" not infrequently – even if unwittingly – substitute disguised versions of the latter for the former

(Partington, 1987).[3] These connerbations for youth have been explored from time to time (e.g., Thomae & Endo, 1974; Csikszentmihalyi & Larson, 1984; Travis & Violato, 1989, 1985, 1981). However, theoretical advancement has been slow.

Meanwhile, the economic focus has drawn attention to the fact that some adolescent phenomena are directly connected to the arrangements made for the management of labor markets, the manipulation of consumption and the use of custodial strategies (i.e. using schools for warehousing youngsters) for maintaining law and order when a large segment of the population is institutionalized as "superfluous humanity." This matter of serving time is increasingly problematical in countries that have been undergoing de-industrialization, since employment prospects are bleak, living standards are falling and costs of schooling are rising for the individual.

McQuaig's (1993) recent analysis of the Canadian situation and Hacker's (1993) brief but vivid description of the American scene drive this last point home. For these are difficult times, and they have been getting more difficult for more and more people. Several years ago Uhlenberg and Eaggebeen (1986) drew attention to "the declining well-being" of American adolescents – and matters have clearly deteriorated since then. Such thoughts bring the time focus to mind.

The Time Focus

Time is a more complex matter than watches or calendars or other familiar devices that we use to mark time suggest. A moment of reflection is all that is needed to notice that there are different senses in which we use the word: clock time differs from biological time, and both differ from historical time, recreational time, working time and so on. In the theoretical realm of adolescence studies, distinctions between three senses of time have been important in advancing our understanding of adolescent phenomena. They are life time or biological time, social time, and historical time. The first of these refers to the timetable given by the individual biological nature that is controlled in the main by the specific or individual genetic pattern we each express as we live and grow. We can think with ease about this since we are used to associating chronological ages with the events and developments that have meaning in our lives. However, such indicators are only rough indicators of a person's position along a number of developmental dimensions. Not everyone is terrible at two or sweet when sixteen; some are terrible only later, and sweetness can come sooner too.

So age is not a very refined indicator of what we can expect to see because some people grow faster or bloom earlier or spurt ahead more abruptly than others. Socio-cultural factors, diet and so forth also affect what can be seen for people of the same age across time and space. Social time refers to social determinants or cultural rhythms of status change and institutional participation. Thus, we see that groups and societies differ with regard to conventional age expectations and their institutions reflect the prevailing norms. So while some groups may expect their fifteen year old females to marry and have children, the pattern for other social groups is to discourage this for five or ten or more years. In sum, while biological time refers to a person's life time, or an individual's rhythms as ordered by his or her biological program, social time refers to socially determined patterns of age-graded experience and status change, as organised by society. Historical time differs from both of these notions in that it denotes the timing of major events or the duration of conditions which shape people's lives. Wars, depressions, catastrophes like we have seen in Somalia and Bosnia illustrate these phenomena. Significant historical developments can affect levels of education, fertility, neurological development, even outlook on life and all it entails (Elder, 1980). In other words, the various time perspectives focus on and give emphasis to different matters.

This realization has underscored the importance of each adolescent's sense of his or her situation and the importance of studying that sense of situation to discern its phenomenological structure (see chapter 3). No doubt individual differences in cognitive complexity, social awareness, temperament and other personal factors can have a bearing on the extent to which the effective sense of situation at a given time is nested in, and is affected by, a larger scheme of situations that affect a person's feeling tone, mood, sense of situational significance, and striving.

Such complex considerations are a challenge for theorists. And, in the past, the principle of parsimony has driven us away from a consideration of such daunting concatenations. But there is another risk, the risk that the theory may be too simple for its subject. This tendency has been so much adhered to that a call for correction has been sounded: Said Bannister,

> As a ... test of the value of a psychological theory, I ... suggest ... if it implies that man is much less than we know him to be or ... that you are much less than you know yourself to be, then such a framework should be discarded. (Bannister, 1970, p.10)

While this may be a good direction for correcting the all too common sterility in theory, the criterion is, if taken literally, too stern; it could drive a great amount of theory into the realm of the unconscious and the unexamined. This, of course, would be unfortunate, since thereby, inadequate theory would gain protection – not elimination.

Adolescents and the Concept of Adolescence Redux

Since all adults have first-hand experience with the transition from childhood to adulthood, they have a personal basis for interest in adolescent phenomena. Accordingly, there is no shortage of stories, illustrative confessions, analyses and lore that attend to such matters. Indeed, as Keill (1967) shows well, interest in the experience between childhood and adulthood is documented throughout history, from ancient Greece to the present. Fox (1993) also shows why adolescence should not be taken as an American invention[2] of the late 19th century, (or early 20th) as do some writers. (e.g., see Santrock, 1990, pp. 16-18)

Since adults also often become parents, they frequently have an additional involvement with, and a further basis for interest in, this subject. Parents of teenagers are seldom short of reasons for having an interest in the troubles of, and troubles with, adolescents. The personal experience and current concerns of parents then, provide one impetus for the development of theory about adolescence and adolescent phenomena.

Although there is impressive evidence of widespread repression of the affective particulars from memories of adolescent experience (e.g., Douvan & Adelson, 1966) parents (and those, like teachers, in *loco parentis*) not infrequently anticipate moodiness, tempestuous urges, wild enthusiasms, intense infatuations, and all the emotions and excesses that the concept of adolescence conventionally denotes for many (especially laymen and non-specialists). In spite of the fact that over the course of more than three decades, researchers and texts have described evidence that they claim is a sound basis for criticizing and dismissing the "time of turmoil" conception of adolescence (Bandura, 1964; Elkind & Westley, 1955, 1957; Jahoda & Warren, 1965; Musgrove, 1964; Offer et al. 1988, 1989, 1992), that concept is insistently retained in the popular mind. We need to ask why this is so, and try explain the disjunction. The phenomenon of "the adolescent amnesia" (Douvan & Adelson, 1966, p.3) may be one of the elements that can help us make sense of this matter. Another factor seems more obvious. This is the character of the information environment and the domination of it by business.

Adolescence and the Cash Nexus

As indicated at the outset, a number of groups who have regular and recurrent business with young people have their reasons for interest in thought about life between the margins of childhood and adulthood too. Of these, perhaps the importance of business interest and the doings of the business world have been too little appreciated in the past. Serving this interest are those who know (in the words of a marketing expert), that

> the adolescent market is of particular importance to marketers of consumer goods for several reasons: the numbers of teens, their purchasing power, their influence on family spending patterns, and their formation of attitudes and interests that influence their consumption behavior in later life. (Moschis, 1982, p. 206)

Motivation and market researchers know that the status and other social anxieties of adolescents, along with their strivings, make them vulnerable, suggestible, and so, subject to manipulation. At every turn, mass media remind each member of their young audience that he or she can become a victim of social ostracism and cruelty. They remind each mass media user of his or her real or imaginary blemishes, flaws, and imperfections. Children see these shortcomings represented as barriers to the realization of adolescent wishes, hopes and dreams, and as the causes of defeat, humiliation and misery. Of course the other standard element of the typical commercial propaganda is a message of deliverance: that the dreaded blemish can be disguised, the flaw hidden, the weakness overcome, with the purchase of whatever product is being promoted.

While nobody has been able to assess the psychological impact of innumerable instances of these conventional commercial meddlings with our feelings, one would expect that they might increase adolescents' discontents and their disposition to be vigilant for and sensitive to holes, shortfalls or lacunae in their experience (see chapter three). This matter calls for the attention of researchers. Meanwhile, there is no shortage of signs that adolescent discontents, anxieties and intense negative urges exist in abundance; they exist not just in clinical populations. Crowds or assembled groups (like classes or gangs) are one source of evidence, since they often provide the extra-psychic (as opposed to the intra-psychic) defenses of diffused responsibility in group identity and personal submersion or denial through assumed anonymity. Over many years, one discerns a consistency between what one sees in clinical work and what one observes in teaching non-clinical youngsters. In both teaching and clinical experience with adolescents, this vigilance for shortfalls and deficiencies – for flaws, holes or lacunae – of all sorts, in all quarters, is commonplace. It is a standard feature of what is seen, and it is particularly prominent if or when anything youngsters take for granted or expect is threatened, disturbed, or when they are perturbed by new circumstances. For example, among teachers in Canada, there is lore about pupils in grade seven (and in grade eight in some provinces) that underscores a "difficult" time that is the assumed lot of those who teach these pupils (who have moved from the position of seniority and dominance as the elders of the elementary schools, to the inferior status of beginners in secondary school).

One gets the impression their alertness for and sensitivity to lacunae may naturally be more vivid and pronounced during the adolescent period than at any other period. Naturally, individual differences in this regard, due to biological givens such as variability in temperament and intelligence, as well as socio-cultural differences are evident. Indeed, with some youngsters there are telling signs of an energetic determination to deny the existence of lacunae in their lives or even in the entirety of creation (denial which suggests that acknowledgement would be too painful or menacing to bear). In any case, these matters call for study because we do not yet know (among other things) to what extent the workings of the selling machinery of mass commercial culture intensify, exacerbate or otherwise affect incipient anxieties and defences against adolescents.

Certainly, some people make great gains from these mass maulings: Each year in the USA alone, many billions of dollars come to corporate accounts as the yield from this cultivation of anxieties (Newsweek, 1990; Moschis, 1982)[2] Moreover, this enterprise that lives off "selling to the id" has more than one target market. Marketers are aware that adult anxieties arising from adult relations with adolescents are also subject to cultivation and exploitation.

The Cash Nexus and the Information Environment

There is a brisk trade in lore concerning the young which purports to distil wisdom about what adolescents are like and how to deal with them. The accompaniment is often the cant of coping packaged in "self help" ideology. This material, together with mass media content ensure that the information environment is saturated with a thick fog of swirling unreality that warms nascent impulses to action and dominates the psychological climate of many in all seasons. Advice columns in newspapers, talk shows on radio, television dramas, tabloid fantasies, TV panel palaver, and sitcoms exercise a selective and homogenizing preference for focusing on the active over the contemplative, the dramatic over the uneventful, the expressive over the taciturn, the intense and conflicted over the calm and collected. In our time, in what Postman (1986) calls "the Age of Showbusiness," public discourse and the information environment more generally, celebrate impulse expression and emotional ability. The dominant characteristic of the traffic of the information environment is immaturity, even puerility. Together, these two markets comprise a social nexus that often is, at the same time, an uneasy or nervous nexus and, hence, a cash nexus. Money can always be made from trouble – present or palpable, imagined or anticipated, natural or contrived. People can be sold whatever they can believe will preempt trouble, control threats, forestall disaster, disguise flaws, hide weakness, or otherwise protect them from the imperfections they fear will cost them safety or comfort, acceptance or love, respect or favor, happiness or opportunities, meaning or whatever when lost, will create a significant hole or lacuna in their experience (see chapter three).

Theories of Adolescence and Adolescent Phenomena

The foregoing discussion of theoretical perspectives on adolescents and adolescent phenomena underscores the complexity of this subject, and in so doing points to the difficulties that stand in the way of conceptualizing a general theory that would encompass all matters in which adolescents may be distinguished from both adults and children.

The best that is in sight as a possibility is a series of concatenation theories (Kaplan, 1964) that can guide exploration and provide frameworks for description of adolescent phenomena. As Kaplan states, the components of concatenation theories enter into a network of relations that constitute meaningful configurations or patterns which are, in effect, convergent descriptions or coherent tendency statements with reference to which facts take on their meaning (p. 298). In such a theory of psychological life, a tendency statement about thought, or feeling, or striving, would convey more meaning when considered in conjunction with tendency statements about the other two, than it would convey in isolation from them. In saying this, we recommend a study of some older works in the German tradition which have not all lost their pertinence. Included among these Remplein (1956); Spanger (1955); Lersch (1951) and even Rank (1945) whose *Will Therapy, Truth & Reality* is available in English. For this tradition kept the psyche more intact; and the full mental chorus included will which was not hidden with shallow obscurantisms (like "self-concept") that lack credible theoretical moorings, foreshorten thought, vulgarize observation, hamper insight, and impair our efforts and work (especially in the English language psychologies).

We have seen that what are taken to be the most important matters in adolescence depends on one's perspective. So, some say, the body along with its sensations and appetites, is the most important fact (a biological perspective). If something, like the centuries-old observation of adolescent surgency, lability, and vivid behavior (which was given the romantic label of *"sturm und drang"* by Hall) calls for explanation, those with a biological perspective tend to look to hormonal fluctuations or the like. Others say the social nexus and one's experience with others in it, shape the adolescent's experience and comportment (a social perspective). So the extent of *sturm und drang* might be considered as an expression of the extent of social friction or blocked social negotiation or incommensurate status assumptions held by an individual and the members of a group he wants to join. Still others say that the way the person reasons or thinks is what one looks to for the pertinent basis of explanation (a variety of psychological perspectives). So in such a case, the explanation for apparent moodiness, or for sweeping oscillations between vigorous assertiveness and the torpor of despair, might be sought in qualities of thought like egocentrism. In fact, all three of these perspectives have been, and are, favored by thoughtful theorists; and all have been found wanting on their own.

Clearly, single-aspect theories are inadequate; Lapsley (1991) shows us that Piaget's theory of logical thought does not explain adolescent egocentrism as it was supposed to, and so Piaget's (1967) turn at the *sturm und drang* question looks limp and lifeless. Offer and Schonert-Reichl (1992) tell us that the evidence is hard on the hormones explanations of adolescent turmoil too. And we have known for more than 25 years that ambitious status aspirations are a much poorer predictor of adolescent turmoil than is the possession of high status and the possession of socio- economic and cultural privileges (Travis, 1975). Indeed, the theoretical handling of this age-old mark of life between adulthood and childhood has been so poor, that some would deny the existence of the troubled waters of adolescence (Bandura, 1964). This is a reminder of a remark made some time in the early 1970s by Erikson, the author of the "identity crisis" idea. In effect, he expressed the thought that some adolescents only had an identity crisis because they thought they were supposed to have one and because they could afford to have one. In the hard times of today, we hear and see less of what, in more prosperous times, was widely thought to be the signature of adolescent experience. So much for simple signs. Identity still is a problem for youth even when times are tough. Circumstances merely force a change in surface appearances. Choices and commitments still have to be made. Similarly, *sturm und drang* may take shelter in the inner life, and current manners or disguise may go unrecognized by the casual observer. Originally the German romantics took this motif as a badge of resistance to unfreedom, as emblem for the assertion of will and of striving; as expression for indignation directed at confinement (Berlin, 1991). In modern times, choices are confined for many, the wilting of freedom represented thereby no doubt beckons indignation in youth. Theoretical blinders can prevent its detection. Traits have to be disentangled from states; temperament and other biological givens that moderate the general level of emotional lability have to be identified or conceptualized and studied in conjunction with thought content or themes and concomitant striving and choice preferences; and all this calls for appropriate (i.e. complex) multivariate designs. But this will not do by itself. Clinical studies, depth studies, and ecological studies need to be embraced as necessary too. All must inform the theoretical synthesis that is needed.

Notes

[1] The remarks on theory are necessarily general, given space, balance and other considerations. Kaplan (1964, ch. 8, pp. 294-326), Marx (1963) and Medawar (1984) are very fine works for readers who wish to consider this subject at greater length.

[2] Some Americans seem to be fond of the notion that both adolescence and adolescent psychology are American creations. This is not a view that is readily sustained. Anyone who looks into the matter will discover, with Kiell (1967) and Fox (1993), that the idea of adolescence as we know it has been around for a long time. (See also, the *Oxford English Dictionary*.) If any ethnic entity is to be credited with giving the main, original impetus to the development of adolescent psychology as a subject, the German-speaking peoples would be a more obvious nomination. Specialists in this field should know that G.S.Hall was not favorably impressed with American culture, and that he escaped to study in Germany where he became acquainted with German works and thought. An examination of Muuss (1988) leaves the reader with little room for doubt about the formative importance of German works.

[3] For a lucid analysis and an informed glimpse of the common confusions see Partington, 1987, and see Singal, 1991 for a sense of one important effect.

[4] R. Stelzer (in his 1971 Voice of America Lectures, *The Teenager's World*), estimated the direct spending of American teenagers at $21 billion; Moschis (1982) claimed that by 1979, this had grown to $30 billion; and *Newsweek*'s corresponding figure in 1990 was $56 billion. However, direct spending is only a fraction of the teen-influenced spending. Interested readers can learn much about matters such as these, from the cited sources and from periodicals such as *Journal of Marketing Research, Journal of Consumer Affairs, Advertising Age, Business Week* and the various works that

emanate from bodies like the Student Marketing Institute Inc., Youth Research Institute, and other advertising agencies that do research for and supply information and advice to businesses. Of course the organs of the fashion industries are an invaluable source too.

References

Adelson, J. (1979). Adolescence and the generalization gap. *Psychology Today.* (February) 33-37.

Adelson, J. & Doehrman, M. (1980). The psychodynamic approach to adolescence. In J. Adelson (Ed.) *Handbook of adolescent psychology.* New York: Wiley-Interscience, pp.99-116.

Auden, W.H. & Kronenberger, L. (Eds.). (1981). *The Viking book of aphorisms.* Harmondsworth, UK: Penguin.

Ausubel, D., et al. (1977). *Theory & problems of adolescent development* (2nd Edition). London: Grune & Stratton.

Bandura, A. (1964). The stormy decade: Fact or fiction? *Psychology in the Schools. 1,* 224-231.

Bannister, D. (1970). Psychology as an exercise in paradox. In D.Schultz (Ed.) *The science of psychology: critical reflections.* New York: Appleton-Century- Crofts, pp.4-10.

Barber, B. (1992) Jihad vs. McWorld. *The Atlantic Monthly,* 269, 3, 53-55, 58-63.

Beller, K. (1973) Theories of adolescent development. In J. Adams (Ed.) *Understanding adolescence: Current developments in adolescent psychology.* (2nd Edition). Boston: Allyn & Bacon, p.102-133.

Berlin, I. (1991). *The crooked timber of humanity.* New York: Alfred K. Knopf.

Bogin, B. (1993, March 6). Why must I be a teenager at all? *New Scientist.* 137, 1863, 34-38.

Buhle, P. (Ed.) (1987). *Popular culture in America.* Minneapolis, MN: University of Minnesota Press.

Coles, R. (1982). "Foreward," In M. Schwarz (Ed.) TV & teens: Experts look at the issues. Reading, Mass.: Addison-Wesley, pp. ix-x.

Csikszentmihalyi, M. & Larson, R. (1984). *Being adolescent.* New York: Basic Books.

Davis, A. (1944). Socialization and adolescent personality. In N. Henry (Ed.) *Adolescence: The forty-third yearbook of the NSSE, part i.* Chicago: The University of Chicago Press, pp.198-216.

Demos, J. & Demos, V. (1969). Adolescence in historical perspective. *Journal of Marriage & the Family, 31,* 4, 632-638.

Douvan, E. & Adelson, J. (1966). *The adolescent experience.* New York: Wiley.

Elder, J. (1980) Adolescence in historical perpective. In J. Adelson (Ed.) *Handbook of adolescent psychology.* New York: Wiley-Interscience, 3-46.

Elkin, F. & Westley, W. (1955). The myth of adolescent culture. *American Sociological Review.* 20, 680-684.

Elkin, F. & Westley, W. (1957). The protection environment and adolescent socialization. *Social Forces. 35*, 343-349.

Erikson, E. (1959). Identity and the life cycle. *Psychological Issues Monograph Series, 1*, No. 1, New York: International Universities Press.

Fishwick, M. (1985). *Seven Pillars of Popular Culture.* London: Greenwood Press.

Fox, V. (1993) Is adolescence a phenomenon of modern times? In M.Gauvin & M.Cole (Eds.) *Readings in the Development of Children.* Oxford, U.K.: Freeman.

Freud, S. (1905/1975). *Three Essays On The Theory Of Sexuality.* New York: Basic Books.

Hacker, A. (1993) Paradise lost. *The New York Review of Books 40,* 9 (13 May), 33-35.

Hall, G.S. (1904). *Adolescence.* New York: Appleton.

Harter, S. & Monsour, A. (1992) Developmental analysis of conflict caused by opposing attributes in the adolescent self-portrait. *Developmental Psychology 28,* 2, 251-260.

Huxley, A. (1980). *The human situation.* London: Triad/Chatto.

Jahoda, M & Warren, N. (1965). The myths of youth. *Sociology of Education. 38,* 2

Kaplan, A. (1964). *The conduct of inquiry.* San Francisco: SRA/Chandler.

Kiell, N. (1967). *The universal experience of adolescence.* Boston: Beacon Press.

Lakoff, G. & Johnson, M. (1980). *Metaphors we live by.* Chicago: University of Chicago Press.

Lapham, L. (1989). *Money and class in America: Notes and observations on the civil religion.* New York: Ballantine.

Lapsley, D. (1991). Egocentrism theory and the 'new look' at the imaginary audience and personal fable in adolescence. In R. Lerner, A. Petersen & J. Brooks-Gunn (Eds.) *Encyclopedia of adolescence.* New York: Garland.

Lasch, C. (1991). *The true and only heaven: progress and its critics.* New York: W.W.Norton.

Lersch, P. (1951). *Aufbau der person.* Munchen: Johann Ambrosius Barth.

Maclean's, (1993, February 22). The world of teens. 106, 8, 27-50.

Marx, M. (Ed.) (1963). *Theories in contemporary psychology.* London: Collier-Macmillan.

McQuaig, L. (1993). *The wealthy banker's wife.* Toronto: Penguin.

Medawar, P.(1984) *Plato's republic.* Oxford: Oxford University Press.

Mochis, G. (1982). Advertising to adolescents. In M.Schwarz (Ed.) *TV & teens.* Reading, MA.: Addison Wesley, pp. 206-210.

Murray, C. (1992, May 22). The reality of black America. *TLS,* no. 4651, 10.

Murray, F. (1984). The application of theories of cognitive development. In B. Gholson & T. Rosenthal (Eds) *Applications of cognitive-developmental theory*. New York: Academic Press, pp.3-18.

Musgrove, F. (1964). Youth and the social order. London: Routledge.

Muuss, R. (1988). *Theories of adolescence* (Fourth Edition). New York: Random House.

Newsweek, (1990, June). *The* new teens: What makes them different. (Special Edition, 95, 27)

Offer, D., Ostrov, E., & Howard, K. (1989). Adolescence: What is normal? *American Journal of Diseases of Children, 143*, 731-736.

Offer, D., Ostrov, E., Howard, K., & Atkinson, R. (1988). *The teenagers world: adolescents' self-image in ten countries*. New York: Plenum Medical.

Offer, D. & Schonert-Reichl, K. (1992). Debunking the myths of adolescence: Findings from recent research. *Journal Of the American Academy of Child & Adolescent Psychiatry*. 2-29.

Partington, G. (1987). The disorientation of western education. *Encounter, 68, 1*, 5-15.

Petersen, A. (1988). Adolescent development. *Annual Review Of Psychology. 39*, 583-607.

Piaget, J. (1967). *Six psychological studies*. New York: Vintage.

Postman, N. (1986). *Amusing ourselves to death: Public discourse in the age of showbusiness*. New York: Penguin.

Postman, N, (1989). Learning by story. *The Atlantic Monthly. 264, 6*, 119-124.

Rank, O. (1945). *Will therapy and truth and reality*. New York: Knopf.

Remplein, H. (1956). *Die seelische entwicklung in der kindheit und reifezeit*. Munchen: Ernst Reinhard.

Rybezynski, W. (1991). *Waiting for the weekend*. Markham, Ont.: Viking Penguin.

Sacks, O. (1984). *A leg to stand on*. New York: Harper & Row.

Santrock, J. (1990). *Adolescence* (Fourth Ed.). Dubuque, IA: Wm.C. Brown.

Scarr, S. (1993). Developmental theories for the 1990s: Development and individual differences. In M.Gauvin & M.Cole (Eds.) *Readings in the development of children*. Oxford, U.K.: Freeman, 46-62.

Schwarz, M. (Ed.) (1982). TV & teens: experts look at the issues. Reading, MA: Addison-Wesley.

Singal, D. (1991). The other crisis in American education. *The Atlantic Monthly. 268, 5*, 59-62, 65-67,

Thomae, H. & Endo, T. (Eds.) (1974). The adolescent and his environment: Contributions to an ecology of teen-age behavior. Contibutions to Human Development, Vol.1. Basel, Switz.: S.Karger.

Travis, L. & Violato, C. (1985). Experience, mass media use, and beliefs about youth: A comparative study. *The Alberta Journal of Educational Research. 31, 2*, 99-112.

Travis, L. & Violato, C. (1981). Mass media use, credulity, and beliefs about youth: A survey of Canadian education students. *The Alberta Journal of Educational Research. 27, 1,* 16-34,

Travis, L. & Violato, C. (1989). Culture, mass media, and youth. In C.Violato & A.Marini (Eds.) *Child development: readings for teachers.* Calgary, AB: Detselig, 15-34.

Twitchell, J. (1992). *Carnival culture: Trashing of taste in America.* New York: Columbia University Press.

Uhlenberg, P. & Eaggebeen, D (1986). The declining well-being of American adolescents. *The Public Interest. 82 ,* 25-38.

Wong, M. & Csikszentmihalyi, M. (1991). Motivation and academic achievement: The effects of personality traits and the quality of experience. *Journal of Personality. 59, 3,* 539-574.

World Press Review, (1993, June). Vol. 40 , 6.

3

Reconceptualizing Adolescent Experience

"Why is the measure of love, loss?" This particular question posed by the young British writer, Winterson (1992) raises a more general issue that is close to the centre of what we must understand if we are to understand the psychology of adolescents. The issue is the psychological significance of *lacunae* in the experience of adolescents.

Lacunae and the Sense of Something Missing

Not infrequently, people report that they have a sense of emptiness, mean-inglessness, or *ennui*. Such experience can move one to suppose that something is missing, that there is an important deficiency in one's experience.

Sometimes people are moved to strive, to transform the situation or fill the void, when their actions and senses detect *lacunae*, that is, gaps, holes, ruptures or other indications of absence, incompleteness or insufficiency. They make efforts to create or restore a sense of completeness, harmony, balance, or symmetry.

However, sometimes people's lives are so crowded with particular routines, preoccupations, commitments, obligations and necessary pursuits, such distractions conspire with inattention to keep their thoughts and sensibilities free from the burden of noticing what is missing in their experience.

For many adults, perhaps most, life is like that: Experience is what you get in a busy life. For people whose hands and schedules are full most of the time, little is invested in taking soundings of what is missing in experience. This contrasts with adolescent experience.

Lacunae and the Adolescent Situation

The adolescent situation and particular characteristics of the adolescent psyche in that situation, together, are likely to give *lacunae* great importance in, and infuse particular quality into, adolescent experience.

Indeed, adolescence has been likened to a moratorium. Life has been emptied of the child's world; but it has not yet been filled with adult content. Hence, there is an hiatus wherein significant experience is much desired and sought; wherein the worth of situation and experience is automatically sensed.

Thus, adolescents desire experiences of worth; they long for experience that seems authentic and meaningful; they abhor situations that are sensed to be deficient in goodness, beauty or truth. For adolescents have a marginal status and share a marginal situation.

They are regularly informed that childish ways are no longer acceptable, even as adult alternatives are new, unhoned, and frequently, not yet allowed or permitted. At the same time, they are aware that they have gained sexual maturity; and while they are relatively inexperienced in adult life, they are in possession of grown-up physical and mental powers and desires. Since it is in these circumstances that adolescents must face a series of important tasks and questions, they are likely to be sensitive to and affected by *lacunae*.

Unfortunately, teachers and others who have regular and ongoing work with adolescents, often fail to understand the nature of the adolescent situation and the particular character of adolescent experience. As a consequence, they accept the well-known lore about adolescents, and oscillate between a stance that is combative or hostile to one which idealizes youth. At best, a posture of forbearance is taken; and given the failure to realize the potential in the situation for unprecedented growth, they adopt custodial nostrums and wait for their youngsters to "get over" or "get through" adolescence.

While G. Stanley Hall (1904) did, in fact, incorporate serious errors, misinformation, and other unfortunate flaws and excesses in his famous pioneering work, he did comprehend some important features of the adolescent situation and the importance of the period for the opportunities that it affords. One can benefit from a reading of that work, even now. One gains not so much from the particulars of substance; but rather more from a glimpse of a sympathetic but not sentimental understanding, and a felicitous nobility and generosity of spirit that appreciates the opportunity of youth and the importance of adult attention to and appreciation of it.

Qualities of Adolescent Minds

Too few understand and appreciate the nature of those with the youthful energy that lights up the contours of adolescent vision with a definitiveness that betrays, as it camouflages, a spotty, skin-deep knowing; those with the adolescent enthusiasm that drowns consciousness of inexperience in a well of unpoisoned hopes; those with the teenager's will that is focused through freshly matured but untested powers of mind and character; and those with the young person's heart that is fulsomely generous because unsullied by knowledge of a world that does not care. Such is the common pattern.

The principal psychological attribute that they share, and what sets them apart from both adults and children, is a living disposition formed from that particular mix of inexperience, biological readiness, marginal status, managed experience and cultural confusion that attends the adolescent situation. That disposition is a condition of alert readiness to detect, in the experience of any situation, what will serve them well or ill in their primary project: to make something of themselves that is good, beautiful and true as seen in the light of their own (personal) understanding. Accordingly, they are especially sensitive to *lacunae*.

If teachers better understood the adolescent situation; and if they grasped better how it tends to amplify the youngsters' keenness for detecting something of truth, or beauty, or goodness in the mundane stream of situations that are arranged for their benefit; the experience of adolescents might be enhanced as teachers better anticipate *lacunae* and help youngsters discover what fills them. However, even with such change, keenness for the detection of *lacunae* will still be the principal concern of youngsters.

Mind in Situation

Consider how sensitivity to, and alertness for, detection of *lacunae* might be maximized if one is required to forsake familiar ways and, at the same time, have recourse to adult options restricted as one is urged to deal with the following questions and tasks: How does one

- cope with what the mature body suggests to others – and to oneself;
- choose among compelling alternatives;
- decide on what matters most in life;
- deal with the tension between the ideal of a balanced life and the requirements of serious commitment;
- prepare for life apart from one's family of origin;
- ensure that the person one was, is, and will be, is the same person that others see and can respect?

What commitments must one make to ensure that one can live with confidence, energy, integrity, and contentment? When one has to face such questions, one is inclined to look out for slippery slopes and be sensitive to *lacunae*.

We need to remember that in the adolescent situation a series of tasks are faced which challenge the young person for a fairly protracted period. Preparations have to be undertaken for an independent economic existence. Choices, plans and commitments have to be made for a vocation. A world view as well as scientific understanding has to be developed and adjusted. Risks have to be taken and efforts have to be made to invest oneself in reliable relations and intimacy with people beyond the family of origin.

While not all adolescents can articulate the questions posed; and while some seem oblivious to some of the tasks their lives entail, some sense of these matters is generally felt by adolescents. And a keen appreciation of and watchfulness for offenses against whatever is taken by them to be good, beautiful, and true, seems more noteworthy among adolescents, on the whole, than among children or adults.[1] However, differences between adolescents and their parents with regard to values and ideals do not explain the expected large magnitude differences between them regarding sensitivity to and vigilance for *lacunae*. Within family differences in values and ideals are usually unimpressive.

Earlier Perspectives on the Power of Shortages

Scholars have long recognized that sensed shortages can be powerful forces in human experience. Ancients, like Plato (Cornford, 1945) recognized that all men have appetites and that some men are dominated by them. Appetites for sensual pleasures and concomitant feelings have been given a central place in various psychological theories ever since.

Theories of motivation by appetite or sensation, drive reduction, needs, tissue tension and the like are common, and for some time, were the prevailing psychological orthodoxy. However, these theories have tended to be too simple to be serviceable in normal human affairs.

Several factors give rise to this inadequacy. One is the tendency of appetite theorists to take guidance and over-generalize from laboratory studies of non-human subjects. A related factor is more directly addressed in the present chapter is that deficiency theories have tended to be monophonous. That is, they tend to confer on one class of phenomena an over-riding power in the shaping of whatever is of interest.

A singular voice cannot express the entire richness and variety of human experience: human variability is a chorus that overwhelms the monophonous voice. Yet theories about adolescent phenomena tend to have a monophonous character. That is, they tend to emphasize one or another of the human psyche's aspects or provinces as pivotal in the explanation of problems or issues. Thus, the body (our sensual, appetitive or affective province) is stressed by some (like Hall, 1904; Kiell, 1967); and so emotion or affect – sensations, tensions and somatic pleasures – are given primacy. Similarly, others (like Piaget, 1972) single out our tendency to thematize experience or reason about things that matter to us; and so thought or cognition is placed at the centre.

Still others, like those who follow Skinner (Travis, 1983), give performance or behavior, pride of place; and so wilful action, or striving (conation) is at the hub of interest (Santrock, 1993).

Monophonous Theory and the Polyphony in Experience

Such monophonous theories are inadequate because the minds of humans are polyphonous. Human experience necessarily reflects an interaction of appetite, spirit and thought as together they lend their presence to imagination. Appetite (sensation, feeling, affection) with spirit (will, striving conation) and thought (contemplation, knowing, cognition) register the polyphony of experience. In each of life's situations there are feeling tones and sensations; but there are also energy demands and choices; and things to be thought about and assessed.

So memory and hopes wish and fear; signal and sign; tone and temper; figure and ground – and more, are all present in the chorus that gives voice to experience. As James (1958, p. 85) said (before specialization helped us forget) mental workings are the joint expression of "all ... faculties" or provinces of the psyche. Accordingly, for humans, desire is not a simple matter to be satisfied by just any member of a class of necessities such as food or shelter.

The Polyphonous Psyche, Human Desire, and Imagination

In adolescent psychology, the fine work of Elder (1980) has shown how, during the Great Depression of the 1930s, the widespread deprivation and dread of the same during the adolescent years invaded personalities of youngsters and persisted so that many years later, so-called cohort effects are discernible. However, one must doubt that this is the mark of such objective factors as insufficiencies of diet (as one sees in malnutrition where famine conditions prevail). Rather, there seems to have been a "Depression psychology" that calls for an explanation quite different from the contingencies of drive reduction or the like.

In his discussion of the relations between human desire, imagination, and culture, Northrop Frye (in Denham, 1980; also his *Anatomy Of Criticism*) provides a clear view of these matters. Humans, says Frye, are not content with mere food and shelter; and because roots and caves are not sufficiently satisfying (imagination calls for more than a minimum) we create "human forms of nature" as in farming and building. This process of transformation is directed by a peculiarly human species of desire. According to Frye, this human desire

> is ... not a simple response to need, for an animal may need food without planting a garden to get it, nor is it a simple response to want, or desire for something in particular. It is neither limited to or satisfied by objects, but is the energy that leads human society to develop its own form. Desire in this sense is the social aspect of what we met on the literal level as emotion, an impulse toward expression which would have remained amorphous if the poem had not liberated it by providing the form for its expression. The form of [human] desire, similarly, is liberated and made apparent by civilization. The efficient cause of civilization is work, and [verbal culture] in its social aspect has the social function of expressing ... vision[s] of the goal of work and the forms of desire. (in Denham, 1980, p. 29)

We humans are a complicated lot – even though at times it seems we are not. When we think of our biological nature we are likely to see ourselves as creatures of appetite, as creatures of sensations, as animalistic beings whose appetites and sensations feed the feelings and emotions that constitute a body's tones of pleasure, satisfaction, tension, and irritation. This is clear and simple; and, some insist that this vision of our creaturehood as somatic or sensual beings overrides all else that can be said about humans. So the old saw: each human life is the same – we are born, we suffer, and we die. When sensation and appetite disappear, so does life; that is our biological nature.

Complication sets in when we realize that we not only feel and sense; we think about feeling and sensing. Our appetites and sensations; our emotions and feelings, are all among the myriad of objects upon which our thoughts focus. We explore our feelings in thought – in retrospect, in anticipation, in contemplation. We focus our thought on our emotions and appetites to make them objects of knowledge, objects of our understanding. At times we even think that we can subject our sensational nature to reason.

Some people seem to think that here is the simple truth about our nature: we humans are essentially thinking creatures. But, of course, there is little that is simple about that. For this wishful image overlooks much – including the fact that thought, knowledge, understanding and reason (features of our cognitive life) can be, and frequently are, objects of our feelings, emotions and appetites. Indeed, one could say that the exaggeration that is discernible in the high degree of reasonableness that has been, from time to time, accorded to human nature, sensationalizes reason and the cognitive feature of our psyche.

Moreover, complication does not end there. For not only do cognitive functions focus on our affections, feelings, and sensations; and not only does particular knowledge, reason and other features of cognition become objects of our affection; we explore, augment, simplify and diminish our sensations or affections as well as our cognitions wilfully.

In the past, this capacity for striving, for spirit in performance or action has been called conation, in contrast to the two dimensions of the human psyche discussed so far: cognition on the one side, affection on the other (Allport, 1968). Insofar as action or performance can be internalized (as in thought) so too can spirit, striving or strength of will. That is, volitional control can be exercised on covert as well as overt action or performance.

The idea of concentration refers to this phenomenon. So James (1950, p. 126) observed that "attention and effort are but two names for the same psychic fact." Obviously, this complicates matters. Indeed, we are challenged to imagine any graphic means that might convey the order of complexity that the mind presents.[2]

As humans, adolescents share this complexity. They are at once, and at all times, emotional beings, thinking beings and wilful beings. The fact that they are these things simultaneously makes them, like humans of all ages, imaginative beings too.

The Everyday Work of Imagination

For present purposes, let us take imagination to be an automatic life process, like breathing. As Frye (in Denham, 1980, p. 116) says, reality is of two orders "the world that nature presents to us and the world that [humans construct] out of it, the world of art, science, religion, culture and civilization." The second world or order of reality is created by the work of imagination. As beings who are predisposed to see the look of one thing in another, humans impose impressions on whatever they encounter in nature. Features of nature are perceived on various levels as humans differ in the ways they apprehend the relationships between subjects and objects. So imagination is both receptive and constructive,[3] its work is both that of synthesis and separation. Imagination, said Frye,

> is the constructive power of the mind, the power of building unities out of units ... The material world provides a universal language of images and ... each man's imagination speaks that language with his own accent. (Frye, in Denham, 1980, pp. 20-21)

That is, imagination is at work whenever humans make likeness and contrasts; whenever one with language or other means of representation, makes some personal sense of actions, feelings, thoughts, sensations – of any and all manner of objects, conditions, and events – by means of comparison, by ordering likeness and contrast, by ratiocination. Obviously, thought of in this way, imagination is dependent on attention and memory; on sensation and affect; and on spirit and energy – as well as on cultural context subjectivized as "situation."

Accordingly, humans who are not comatose or asleep, locate themselves within and relate themselves to situations.[4] We feel, represent, makes sense of, and strive within situations (which can be "nexted" as when the present situation entails retrospection on or anticipation of other situations). Simultaneous engagement of a human's affective, conative and cognitive powers, then, is deemed to be automatic in constructing, assessing and registering his or her own order of experience. That order is the work of imagination. That order has an affective tone; some energy demands; and some magnitude of meaning.

The Joint Issue of Feeling, Thought and Striving: Imagination

Adolescents as humans, then, are complicated beings. That is, beings that know and imagine. They share the complexities of being at once, creatures of appetite, sensation, emotion, or affection; creatures of spirit, action, will, or conation; creatures of reason, reflection, thought or cognition; and creatures of imagination that think, feel and strive within situations that are automatically assessed for their novelty, significance or meaning, and energy demands. They are beings that, often without awareness, automatically sense each situation for the presence or absence of beauty, goodness, truth or meaning.

Affect and the Sense of Beauty

As creatures of affect or feeling, humans have temperaments with aesthetic potential that develops, in degree. Our aesthetic sensibilities are linked to our appraisals of form, patterns and relations in visual, auditory, intellectual[5] and social experience. Our sense of harmony in what we see and hear is pleasurable and is sensed as beautiful – just as we sense or experience beauty in social relations that are harmonious. When social experience gives rise to a sense of fellowship, a sense of concordance, or a sense of intimacy or love, we feel or have the sensation of beauty.

When there is discord, when there is monotony, when there is loneliness, there is no sensed beauty; and we sense that something is missing. We feel that there is a hole in our experience; our experience lacks something. As Read (1972) said over sixty years ago, our sense of beauty is satisfied when we are able to discern unity or harmony in our experience of relations, patterns and forms. "The sense of pleasurable relations is the sense of beauty" (p. 18). When we sense the absence of harmonious patterns, pleasurable relations, good form, our experience is felt to be lacking something. These shortfalls in aesthetic pleasure comprise one of three classes of *lacunae* that can repel us from given situations or substance or move us to transform the situations or substance in question.

Striving, Spirit or Will and the Sense of Missing Goodness

Just as the mental province of affection provides a basis for appreciation of beauty and sensitivity to its absence, so the province of conation energizes and sensitizes or predisposes humans to appraise situations or states of affairs for a sense of goodness. When we sense that our efforts will be fruitful, we have a sense of control, a sense of optimism, a sense of viability. When we sense that our experiences are good, it is because we judge them to be so. The sensed goodness arises from a tacit assessment of performance against standards or ideals – and the judgements are positive. They also buoy our spirits; they evoke a sense of potency or sergeancy; they give a sense of balance that seems right and good. We sense that we have strength and can choose, strive, act, etc. So strength of will or volition seems to be linked to our appraisal of situations for their goodness. That is, conation is to the sense of goodness as affection is to the sense of beauty in a situation.

When we sense that we have acted badly; or that we have chosen carelessly; or when we sense that our striving has been perfunctory or that we have been weak-willed or lazy, we have experience of the second class of *lacunae* that are of much importance in adolescence.

Someone has said that there are no judgments so harsh as those rendered by the young. This rings true whenever one comes within earshot of earnest adolescents trading impressions of adults that are significant, or are taken to be significant figures, in their lives.

When adolescents observe such adults fall short of their ideals or expectations, all risks and costs of self-righteous expression, extravagant vanity and exaggerated posturing are commonly and boldly ignored by the sensitive and offended youngster. Actions deemed to be less than good evoke the sense of *lacunae* that is particularly powerful during adolescence. This sensed shortfall of goodness in a situation exemplifies the second class of *lacunae* that pervade adolescent experience.

Thought and the Sense of Deficient Truth

The third class of important *lacunae* in the experience of adolescents encompasses the sensed inadequacy of truth[6] or meaning in situations.

The third aspect or province of the human psyche, cognition, informs our sense of truth and meaning in situations. Perhaps this linkage or connection is the clearest and most obvious.

We recognize this engagement of cognition in our appraisals of meaning or truth when we have the experience of sensed paradox or contradiction in a situation. Our thoughts alert us to the incompatibility of given propositions. Our attachment of meaning and a sense of truth to reason, alerts us to the presence of a *non sequitur* or other offenses to logical conventions.

So, too, in matters of fact we look for correspondence between our hunch or belief about what is the case and our observations; and when there is an absence of correspondence we sense the absence of truth in our belief or hunch. Similarly, *lacunae* of meaning are noticed when our thoughts detect a lack of coherence in argument, in narrative, or in exposition. Descriptions are also deemed deficient in meaningfulness or truth when say, a witness to a crime provides an account that is so bereft of crucial elements or details that the unity or integrity of the account is thought to be insufficient to be taken as truthful or meaningful. If elements in an account don't "hang together," if coherence or unity is not discerned, the lack of integrity is judged to be tantamount to insufficiency of meaning: the whole truth has not been told. So the cognitive province of the psyche enables us to sense the absence or presence (or degrees) of meaning or truth in situations.[7]

Moreover, in all these matters, there is something that is basic and is forgotten with cost. It is this: just as affection is prominent in our analysis of the experience of beauty; just as the province of conation is at the centre of our discussion of sensed goodness; and just as cognition is linked to the assessment of truth, we have seen that all provinces are implicated in all experiences through the work of imagination. That is to say that although, through reason, an adolescent may detect truth (or its absence) in a situation, she does so only if the situation's particulars or contents engage her affect and will so that thought about them is energized. We do not think about things that fail to engage our feelings; and we do not come to know things without choosing to attend to them and willingly contemplate them.

On Differences Within Sameness

All teachers of adolescents need to understand that thought lives with will and feeling in the human imagination; and that it will live nowhere else. As Shakespeare's[8] Hotspur put it, "But thought's the slave of life, and life time's fool . . . " (in Collins, 1961, p. 703). Accordingly, teachers who would address the lives of their adolescent students, will not confine their cares and concerns to just one or another of their mental provinces: they will speak to their imaginations; to their sense of beauty, truth and goodness.

This does not mean that they can overlook other facts: that those they teach will vary in the degree of their refinements; that some youngsters (like some adults) have ideals and standards of beauty, truth, and goodness that are unimpressive; and that *lacunae* other than those of beauty, truth and goodness, at a given time, can be more powerful and compelling than anything else.

Adolescents, like all humans, have a life in the world as well as a private, inner life. That is, they are political beings and can feel powerless. As social beings, they can be lonely. As economic beings in a pecuniary society, they can suffer a shortage of money. As family beings, they might feel unconnected. As sexual beings, they may suffer from unfulfilled desire. Any one or more of these *lacunae* can dominate the centre of an adolescent's experience at a given time.

On the Educator's Care of Adolescent Imagination

Those who would care for the life of the human imagination know and respect such facts. And they are wise who know their limits with regard to what they can see to or do this side of paradise.

However, all who teach adolescents might do well to remember that human longings or desires are as old as humanity; and, we are reminded by Frye, they are and always have been the wellsprings of human imagination. This means that any given experience of a *lacuna*, any given longing or desire, is one of a class; that others have had a corresponding experience in the past; and that of these ones, some have imagined and created some things that are enduringly good, enduringly beautiful, enduringly true.[9]

Sensitive teachers who want to address the lives, the imaginations, of their adolescent students bring such objects to their charges in a manner that indicates that they know of these matters and care about them.[10] Unfortunately, for much of the 20th century (since the 1930s) a sociological order has minimized such pedagogy. As Jacoby (1987) says, public culture has become increasingly impoverished of the influence of intellectuals.

Sociological pressures can channel behavior, can demand that people behave in a certain way which, for some, will be contrary to the ways they are temperamentally predisposed to behave or act. Imposed uniformities or ortho-doxies in teaching practice (which may be summarized or labeled as "progressive education") illustrate this phenomenon. The obvious significance of these con-ditions for adolescents is that most contemporary adolescents spend much time in school.

Adolescents and the Lacunae in "Progressive Education"

Variants of "progressive education" (Partington, 1987) that increasingly became the prevailing order of schooling since the first third of the 20th century, enforced on the bulk of youngsters in the English speaking world, a uniform pattern that runs counter to the natural tendencies of introverted or intellectual temperament (Huxley, 1980, p. 144).

But that is just the global schooling situation. The matter is more serious during adolescence. For adolescence has, for good reason, been called the metaphysical age *par excellence* (Inhelder & Piaget, 1958, p. 340). Adolescence is a period wherein even those in whom extroversion predominates are attracted to metaphysical questions, speculative thought, and idealistic formulations. The limitations and shortcomings of the prevailing pattern are, therefore, even more serious for adolescents.

Accordingly, a brief digression that identifies some features of that pattern is in order.

The uniform pattern created by the variants of progressive education arises from the persistence of popular belief or faith in progress – and what Lasch (1991) calls "the ideology of progress" (p. 14). This faith, and the slogans and nostrums that are called upon to defend or promote it, centre on the "promise of steady improvement" on the "expectation of ... open-ended improvement" (p. 47). Confusions are created and multiply, due to the grand diversity of projects and enthusiasms that get attached to schooling adventures (the putative means favored by Americans for fulfilling their expectations for improvement). Curric-ular debasement and declining achievement appear to be the constant compan-ions of school-based improvement projects (e.g., Barrett, 1990; Barzun, 1981; Jones, 1988; Simpson, 1992). A major theme that runs through the history of these endeavors is that learning is regularly regarded as a means rather than an end.[11]

In practice, those who form the progressive pattern of schooling attempt to make much of general ideas or concepts (like "problem solving" and "creativ-ity") through "projects" or "activities" that (they believe) focus pupils' attention on "materials" they are required to "manipulate." Little heed is given to those who doubt that general ideas can be anything other than shortcuts from one area of ignorance to another. And evidence that supports that view (e.g., Chipman, Segal & Glaser, 1985) is ignored.

So performances or behavior on "tasks" is given more emphasis than is the orderly acquisition of significant knowledge and disciplined understanding as previously described by others. Expression appears to be more highly prized than concision; and emotional or therapeutic care takes precedence over intellectual preparation. Overriding concern with general abstractions like "self concept," tone down demands or requirements that pupils strive to meet rigorous and impersonal standards. The emphasis on "process" subordinates content; and the emblematic "child centred" ideology of "progressives" is assumed to be adequate justification. Moreover, particulars of the "process" emphasis frequently underscore not only the progressive educator's ambivalence regarding adult authority – and even automatic distrust of it; but they also makes manifest that "loss of the good authority" which Pitt-Atkins and Ellis (1989) connect with delinquency in youth.

Perhaps even more serious is the failure to recognize costs of widespread abdication of the adult duty to identify the exemplary, and to energetically sponsor the best that has been thought, sought and wrought, as such, in the presence of adolescents. This pattern of abdication has magnified the significance and power that *lacunae* have for adolescents in our time.

When the now notorious smorgasbord of cafeteria curriculum was institutionalized, the objects of genuine art and scholarship were placed on the same table as the mass fashions of the commercial, popular culture. Progressively, the smorgasbord provided more puffery – and less and less meat. Eventually, in many places, it became predominantly the cultural equivalent of junk food.[12] This state of affairs seriously undercuts the capacity of teachers to do other than serve the custodial function of schools: their more basic cultural or educational function was debased and made more difficult.

These circumstances bear directly on the experience of *lacunae* in adolescence because so much of the life of adolescents is spent in, and is organized around, school. Accordingly, the present discussion of adolescent experience will end with a brief analysis of the experience of *lacunae* in school and the relationship between such experience and the teachers' task in the cultural situation.

The Teacher's Task, The Cultural Situation, and Lacunae.

The physicist, Paul Dirac, is credited with the observation that while the quest of the physicist is to make plain and simple what is obscure and difficult, the poet's effort is to achieve the opposite: to make complex and difficult what seems simple and obvious.

Teachers, however, must do both. Sometimes, when matters obscure and difficult are the object of pupils' curiosity, the situation may call for the teacher to make the obscure and difficult become plain and simple for them. However, at other times, teachers realize that due to the students' inexperience or relatively puerile understanding, the situation obliges the teacher to make complex and difficult what seems simple and obvious to the relatively innocent mind. They must upset an established but inadequate sense of reality. In other words, sometimes teachers try to abolish or fill *lacunae*, and at other times they try to create or draw attention to *lacunae*. The delicacy of human relations (and other considerations) require that the teacher exercises tact (Muth, 1982; Travis, 1993b; van Manen, 1991) and ensures that a balance, over time, be made between her efforts at abolition, and those aimed at creation and highlighting of *lacunae*.

The cultural changes that have taken place during the 20th century (briefly described above) have made the teachers' task more difficult because they constitute radical changes in the information environment that surrounds adolescents. While the impact of popular commercial culture may not be uniform, the pervasiveness and intrusiveness of it, and the domination of mass media by it, is indisputable. The significance of these developments becomes apparent when one notices that teachers who regard their subject as a repository of some of man's serious and durable achievements cannot count on a ready receptivity to serious or durable culture in class. Consider why this is so.

First we need to recognize that the characteristics of the popular, commercial culture (what is for most, the common culture) and those of durable, serious culture (the heritage of the best that has been thought, wrought, and said) are in tension. The latter embodies or emphasizes and celebrates traditions that stress, and require of those who would know their contents, an appreciation of order and formality and disciplined knowing. The former embodies or emphasizes spontaneity and informality; and assumes or requires nothing. Table 3.1 sets forth contracts or contraries that constitute multi-dimensional bases for sensing tension between the embodied values of mass commercial culture and serious or durable culture.

The conflict between these two sets of values produces tensions that pervade the cultural situations of teaching and learning, and of adolescent experience. One effect of the pervasiveness and intrusiveness of commercial culture is that an overvaluation of *lacunae* abolition is forced on teachers and schools; and this can push serious culture to the margins or make it disappear from the cultural situation altogether.

As Postman (1986) says teaching can become just another "amusing activity." In such circumstances, culture and teachers can become casualties or victims of the Shaherazade Syndrome: "if you bore me you die"; so enduring beauty, truth and goodness are made subordinate to what is merely arresting in the short term. Over time, the experience of *lacunae* is debased and cheapened. Again, the bad drives out the good.[13] Under these circumstances, changes in emphasis occur; the teacher becomes less the willing creator of significant *lacunae* that are introduced into the experience of adolescents in anticipation of what can be gained from the experience; but rather now, the teacher is urged to become the unwitting servant or slave to *lacunae* that are (often) a by-product of the envelopment of pupils by commercial culture and serve a commercial rather than a cultural or educational agenda. The calculation of worth becomes the calculus of "fun." Since this serves very well, the custodial function of schools (which is inherently in conflict with their educational function), there are interests and forces that provide rationalizations and other ideological defenses to support such emphases. So Apostles of the commercial dogma which says that whatever is new is better, can and have elevated "trends" and "innovations" in education above all else. In these circumstances, much confusion attends the adolescent situation.

These ostensibly in charge of education, seem to suffer from a similar sort of "lassitude about fundamentals"[14] that Iris Murdoch discerned in the public life of Britain more than thirty years ago (see Appleyard, 1984, ch. 1): more and more is demanded of schooling and education just as it becomes increasingly clear that they cannot deliver the goods demanded;[15] grim and poorly thought out schemes for the reconstruction of people and/or the world are pursued through educational recipes that, typically, have "an aesthetic impulse of grinding inconsequence," and that "for the hard idea of truth . . . have substituted a facile idea of sincerity." (Appleyard, 1984, p. 12).

Throughout the history of popular education, adolescents have been treated, at school, to what can be a creative tension that arises from the infusion of elements of serious culture into the stream of popular or common culture – Between Durable and Popular, Commercial Culture into the flow of youngsters' everyday experience; into the current of commonplaces and habits that inform their sense of everyday life and make that everyday life seem natural, fertile, and interesting. This infusion of durable culture into the ephemera of popular experience, provided opportunity for maturing intelligence to discover new and unimagined realms of experience, to discern embodiments of beauty, truth and goodness that are discontinuous with what they usually see and know. Such provision has been taken to be essential to the idea of education. The commingling of cultural contraries provided opportunities for the discovery or development of new perspectives and new possibilities (Travis, 1990). This has been especially important in enhancing life chances for those of ability who are born into disadvantaged social strata (Travis, 1984).

We have known for a very long time, that such infusions of the exemplary, of the good, the beautiful and the true, are necessary if a mind is to become educated. We have also long known, that humans have a natural tendency to perceive things "schematically . . . rather than in detail," to "represent a class of diverse things by some sort of averaged 'typical instance'" (Bruner, 1979, p. 65). Accordingly, we know that "schools must provide more than a continuity with the broader community or with everyday experience" (Bruner, 1979, p. 118) if they are to make available and draw attention to the knowledge that is "essential to an educated (person)" (p. 122). And we must also assume that effort or striving

Table 3.1
Contrasting Qualities and Values in Durable
and Toss-off Culture as Tension

Serious Culture Embraces and Embodies:	Versus	**Commercial Culture** Embraces and Embodies:
Tradition, custom	vs	Freshness, newness
Order	vs	Spontaneity
Concision	vs	Expression
Formality	vs	Informality
Restraint	vs	Enthusiasm
Modesty	vs	Immodesty
Humility	vs	Pride
Doubt	vs	Confidence

on the part of students is necessary if students are to depart from "the habitual and literal ways of looking, hearing and understanding" that, while serviceable in the child's everyday life of the recent past, are insufficient because uninfluenced or uninformed by what will make adult experience fulfilling: an educated sense of what is enduringly true, beautiful and good (Bruner, 1979, p. 67).

So under these circumstances, we might well return to the beginning of this chapter and wonder, as Winterson (1992) wondered about love's measure, if the sense of loss and lack that is so acute in adolescence, is also the measure of readiness for cultural growth, for learning of enduring beauty, goodness and truth.

To those who object that this perspective focuses only on the cares of adolescents who share an intellectual orientation that is rare, we reply (with distinguished company including Thomas Hobbes, Count Tolstoy and more) that one can easily exaggerate the differences among people. While nobody should dispute the fact that people do vary in significant, even in profoundly important ways, we all share certain qualities that can be of overriding practical importance.

One of the qualities humans share is that native sensitivity to *lacunae* of truth, goodness and beauty that is especially acute during adolescence.

Individual differences in this matter are probably much less impressive than those in most other realms. Moreover, the habit or tendency to explain behavior in terms of putatively stable dispositions of the actor even though the behavior may be channeled by situational constraints has been shown to constitute a "correspondence bias" that is correctable by "secondary appraisal" (Lazarus, 1991) or when a "need for cognition" moves one to observe and think more about such cases (D'Agostino & Fincher-Fiefer, 1992). As Tolstoy (in Ginott, 1969, p. 90) said:

> One of the most widespread superstitions is that every man has his own special, definite qualities: That a man is kind, cruel, wise, stupid, energetic, apathetic, etc. Men are not like that ... men are like rivers ... every river narrows here, is more rapid there, here slower, there broader, now clear, now cold, now dull, now warm. It is the same with every human quality, and sometimes one manifests itself, sometimes another, and the man often becomes unlike himself, while still remaining the same man.

Conclusion

In the adolescent situation, adolescents live between the borders of a receding childhood and an approaching adulthood. Quite literally, they occupy a marginal position in society. With childhood abandoned and adulthood denied, they are told they must make choices, commitments, plans and actions that are to shape the nature of the rest of their lives. This imperative to re-form themselves, to make themselves ready for adult life, evokes a notable vigilance or alertness and a sensitivity to the presence or absence of whatever each takes to be true, beautiful and good. They are watchful for *lacunae* in their situation, in themselves, and in others taken to be significant in their lives.

In these circumstances, many are drawn to an apparent obsession with fashion (broadly understood): they bet on crowds. Their sensed vulnerability, supposed flaws, feared weaknesses and real shortcomings (all advertised in mass media) are hidden, disguised or forgotten in accoutrement, noise, and swarming of energetic masses – whether buying, exhibiting or consuming the mass fare aimed at that quite predictable market. Anything or anyone that interferes with these manoeuvres; anything or anyone that is perceived as threatening their ready access to the communal disguise of light weight, disposable fashions, invites dismissal or derision.[16]

For this large proportion of adolescents, what is deemed to be good, or true or beautiful is not so much an intellectual or aesthetic judgement as it is a bet on the ad man's adage: "millions can't be wrong." For such people, standards of beauty, truth and goodness are unimpressive (though in principle, not beyond upgrading with education). Indeed, the very idea of standards is mocked by fashion consciousness. Even so, this should not lead us to conclude that such youngsters are less sensitive to *lacunae* generally, or to *lacunae* of truth, beauty and goodness particularly. On the contrary: although they may be unfamiliar with "the canon," with the works and traditions that manifest and carry the highest standards of goodness, beauty and truth in the culture, they nonetheless sense that truth, goodness and beauty matter because they are human beings. As such, they imagine; and their situation as they imagine it, seems to require the embrace of what counts in life – now, and on into the future. Here is the educators' real opportunity.

Other youngsters more privileged by circumstance, upbringing, temperament, abilities and those other accidents that bear so directly on sorting out life chances, are more readily recognized as keenly interested in and vigilant for *lacunae* of truth, beauty and goodness. Given advantaged circumstances, even those without an intellectual turn of mind can talk endlessly about utopian notions, and perfect schemes they have hatched for remaking the world and humankind – or merely their niche in the universe. Such youngsters bet on intellect as a means for manoeuvre, or a disguise for sensed shortfalls in themselves and in their experience.

Still others seek beauty, truth and goodness in intimacy – in love, sex or comradeship. The perfect bond secures everything one could need or want from truth, goodness or beauty. Their bet is on "the one" rather than on "the many" – whether the many be the divisions and diversions of intellect or the multitudes that appeal to the spirited, expressive, fashion-conscious youngsters.

Perhaps affection – appetite, emotion, feeling, sensation – is the dominant or strongest voice in the imagination or some youngsters; and they seek beauty, truth and goodness in love, in intimacy, in friendship. For others, their situation is imagined to be amenable to improvement or reform through thought. Finally, the many youngsters that prize expressive, spirited, action and repeated (endless) choosing see good in action, expression, and performance. The dominant voice in the chorus of their imagination, is that of spirit, – the wilful pursuit of, or striving for repeated confirmation and reaffirmation in groups of like-minded fellows. For them, beauty is in performance or expression; goodness is in timing – and good times; truth is in action, in willing, – and in advertising. *Lacunae* of goodness, beauty, and truth, are imagined by youngsters whose spirit is the dominant province in their mentality; whenever their situation is perceived to be too quiet; whenever thought and abstraction predominate or interfere with overt activity; where singularity, or solitude or even intimacy subordinates gregariousness and action or performance.

In sum, all adolescents are, in their own ways, especially sensitive to *lacunae* as their imaginations play upon their marginal situation; and as their lives fill the gap between the familiar dependencies and habits of childhood and the unfamiliar alternative of adult life. In their dreams and fantasies; in their choices and commitments; and in their plans, actions and interactions, they reveal what they imagine is missing in their experience. Teachers who pay attention to these matters while tending to whatsoever is true, beautiful and good in their subjects and in their relations with those about them, have so much to do that is important. Indeed, they have such a huge and lovely project (showing beauty, telling truth, doing good by doing so) they have no time for anything else; and so have no truck or trade with the social amelioration agendas that properly belong in the political arena. Besides, the provision of educational care for the imagination and curiosity of adolescents is not socially insignificant.

References

Allport, G. (1968). The historical background of modern social psychology: In G. Lindzey and E. Aronson (Eds.), *The handbook of social psychology.* (Second Edition). Reading, MA.: Addison-Wesley. Vol. 1, pp. 1-80.

Appleyard, B. (1984). *The culture club: Crisis in the arts.* London: Faber & Faber.

Arnold, M. (1960). *Culture and anarchy.* London: Cambridge University Press.

Bandura, A. (1986). *Social foundations of thought and action.* Englewood Cliffs, NJ: Prentice-Hall.

Barrett, J. (1990). The case for more school days. *The Atlantic Monthly, 255,* 5, 78-108.

Barzun, J. (1991). *Begin here: The forgotten conditions of teaching & learning.* Chicago: University of Chicago Press.

Barzun, J. (1982). The professions under seige. *Harper's.*

Barzun, J. (1981). The wasteland of American education. *The New York Review of Books, 28,* 17, 34-37.

Berlin, I. (1991). *The crooked timber of humanity.* New York: Knopt.

Bloom, A. (1987). *The closing of the American mind.* New York: Simon and Schuster.

Bruner, J. (1979). *On knowing: Essays for the left hand* (Expanded Edition). Cambridge, Mass.: Belknap of Harvard University Press.

Chandrasekhar, S. (1987). *Truth and beauty: Aesthetics and motivation in science.* Chicago: University of Chicago Press.

Chipman, S., Segal, J., & Glaser, R. (Eds.) (1985). *Thinking & learning skills, Vol. 2: Research and open questions.* Hillsdale, NJ: Erlbaum.

Collins, H. (Ed.) (1961). *The complete works of Shakespeare.* Chicago: Scott, Foresman.

Cornford, F. (Ed. & Tr.) (1945). *The republic of Plato.* Oxford: Oxford University Press.

Cumming, R. (Ed.) (1965). *The philosophy of Jean-Paul Sartre.* New York: Random House.

D'Agostino, P. & Fincher-Feifer, R. (1992). Need for cognition and the correspondence bias. *Social Cognition, 10,* 2, 151-163.

D'Souza, D. (1991). *Illiberal education.* New York: Vintage,

Denham, R. (Ed.) (1980). *Northrop Frye on culture & literature: A collection of review essays.* Chicago: The University of Chicago Press.

Elder, J. (1980). Adolescence in historical perspective. In J. Adelson (Ed.), *The handbook of adolescence.* New York: Wiley, pp. 3-46.

Eliot, T. (1962). *Notes toward the definition of culture.* London: Faber & Faber.

Frye, N. (1957). *The anatomy of criticism.* Princeton, NJ: Princeton University Press.

Frye, N. (1963). *The educated imagination.* Toronto: CBC.

Fulford, R. (1992, August 3-9). Why we shouldn't feel good about our obsession with self-esteem. *The Financial Times,* p. 23.

Ginott, G. (1969). *Between parent and teenager.* New York: Avon.

Hall, G.S. (1904). *Adolescence.* Englewood Cliffs, NJ: Prentice-Hall.

Huxley, A. (1980). *The human situation.* London: Triad/Chatto.

Jacoby, R. (1987). *The last intellectuals: American culture in the age of academe.* New York: Basic Books.

James, W. (1950). *The principles of psychology.* New York: Dover, Vol. 1 (of 2).

James, W. (1958). *Talk to teachers on psychology.* New York: Norton.

Jones, L. (1988). School achievement trends in mathematics and science, and what can be done to improve them. In E. Rothkopf (Ed.), *Review of Research in Education, 15,* (1988-89). Washington, DC: AERA.

Kaplan, A. (1964). *The conduct of inquiry.* San Francisco: Chandler/SRA.

Kiell, N. (1967). Introduction – The universal experience of adolescence. In N. Kiell (Ed.), *The universal experience of adolescence.* Boston: Beacon Press, pp. 11-21.

Lasch, C. (1991). *The true and only heaven: Progress and its critics.* New York: Norton.

Lazarus, R. (1991). *Emotion & adaptation.* New York: Oxford University Press.

MacKie, R. (1993, 18 January). Ontario schools to be overhauled. *The Globe & Mail,* p. A4.

Malcolm, J. (1981). *Psychoanalysis: The impossible profession.* New York: Knopf.

Marcuse, H. (1978). *The aesthetic dimension.* Boston: Beacon.

Muth, J. (1982). *Padagogisher takt.* Essen, Germany: Verlagesellschaft.

Paglia, C. (1992). *Sex, art, and the American culture.* New York: Random House/Vintage.

Partington, G. (1987). The disorientation of western education. *Encounter, 68,* 1, 5-15.

Piaget, J. (1972). Intellectual evolution from adolescence to adulthood. *Human Development, 15,* 1-12.

Pitt-Atkin, T., & Ellis, A. (1989). *Loss of the good authority: The cause of delinquency.* London: Viking.

Postman, N. (1986). *Amusing ourselves to death: Public discourse in the age of show business.* New York: Penguin.

Read, H. (1972). *The meaning of art.* London: Faber.

Santrock, J. (1993). *Adolescence.* (Fifth Edition). Madison, WI: Brown & Benchmark.

Simpson, G. (1992, December 16). Never mind input variables – what Canada needs is a rebellion. *The Globe & Mail,* p. A20.

Sartre, J. (1956). *Being and nothingness.* (Translated by Hazel Barnes). New York: Philosophical Library.

Singal, D. (1991). The other crisis in American education. *The Atlantic Monthly, 268,* 5, 59-74.

Travis, L. (1993). "Voice Versus Message: On the Importance of B.F. Skinner." *Canadian Journal of Special Education, 14,* 106-119.

Travis, L. (1993b, in press). The tact of teaching. *Queen's Quarterly, 100*.

Travis, L. (1990). Noisey communication and imagination in education. In R. Fiordo (Ed.), *Communication in education*. Calgary, AB: Detselig, pp. 385-396.

Travis, L. (1984). Scots proverbs & reconstruction in education. *Queen's Quarterly, 91*, 4, 825-831.

van Manen, M. (1991). *The tact of teaching: The meaning of pedagogical thoughtfulness*. London, ON: The Althouse Press.

Watson, J. (1968). *The double helix: A personal account of the discovery of the structure of DNA*. New York: Atheneum.

Wertsch, J. (Ed.) (1986). *Culture, communication, & cognition: Vygotskian perspectives*. Cambridge, UK: Cambridge University Press.

Winterson, J. (1992). *Written on the body*. Toronto: Knopf.

Zinchenko, V. (1986). Vygotsky's ideas about units for the analysis of mind. In J. Wertsch (Ed.), *Culture, communication, & cognition: Vygotskian perspectives*. Cambridge, UK: Cambridge University Press, pp. 94-118.

Notes

[1]This is an impressionistic claim and requires research. Of course, this paper is a conceptual work that is intended to chart a perspective for thought and research.

[2]Perhaps this serves as a good reminder about the limitations of pictures and images generally. However, the discovery of the structure of DNA by Crick & Watson serves as a reminder of how a well-stocked imagination can recognize and exploit the heuristic value of apposite imagery. (Watson, 1968)

[3]Berlin (1991, p. 191) says "reason units, but will . . . divides."

[4]The concept "situation" is problematical and deserves a treatise of its own. As Frye (in Denhham, 1980, p. 31) said "The choice of metaphors used to describe the relations of one subject to another is a fateful choice." Even so, for now, a situation will be considered to be phenomenological "reality." We assume (with William James) that a person's experience is what that person chooses to attend to. This may or may not entail some features of material reality that is proximate to the person. Moreover, two or more persons may sense that their experience at a given time is equivalent (that there is intersubjective accord). For more on this, see Sartre (edited by Cumming, 1965; or his *Being and Nothingness*, translated by Hazel Barnes, 1956).

[5]The importance of the sense of beauty in intellectual work cannot be overestimated (Arnold, 1960; Chandrasekhar, 1987); but, oddly, it is almost always ignored in educational psychology. [However, see Chapter 16, "Disposition and Achievement" in the present volume.] From the present perspective, it should be emphasized. Educators can demonstrate their care and understanding by showing that they care about what is beautiful, true, and good in their subjects and in their human relations. The fact that people have a personal sense of what is or is not beautiful in a situation is no excuse for neglecting

the teachers' duty to bring forth "the best" that has been thought, sought and wrought so that a shared culture can develop on other than the throw-away effusions of pop culture fashions – so it can be developed on the basis of all that is enduringly beautiful, good and true. (Also, see Marcuse, 1976).

[6]"Truth" is a singular noun, but should be understood as the name of a class (like mammals) or a family of distinct personalities because there are various types of truth: legal, logical, psychoanalytical, mathematical, religious, historical, scientific and so forth (Malcolm, 1981). However, in this context, deficiencies of correspondence between idea or belief or expectation and observation; or deficiency in coherence in matters that are expected to live together in unity seem most pertinent.

[7]Of course, all observations are ultimately subjective (Kaplan, 1964); so situations are to be understood as "phenomenological" rather than either merely objective or subjective realities. For background, see Sartre's discussion on these matters (Cumming, 1965; Sartree, 1956).

[8]William Shakespeare, *Henry IV*, Part I, Act V, Scene iv, Line 81. See Collins, H. (Ed.) (1961), *The Complete Works of Shakespeare*. Chicago: Scott, Foresman, p. 703.

[9]Here, one is tempted to address the recent controversies over the privileged status of objects or works that are part of the so-called "canon" (those creations or works of human imagination that have timeless value as opposed to those objects and subjects that are of more ephemeral value, and that are of restricted or parochial concern only). Space limitations do not permit a digression on this pertinent issue. Accordingly, the interested reader is directed to writers whose thoughts on this question have impressed: First, Mathew Arnold (1960) who, along with thinkers such as T.H. Huxley, expressed lucid thought about content issues that are at the centre of the controversy, in the 1860s and in the later decades of the 19th century. While Bloom (1987) and D'Souza (1992) are worth reading now, their thoughts are best appreciated when the mind has a perspective prepared by the likes of Arnold, T.H. Huxley (*A Liberal Education*), Barzun (1981, 1991) and A.N. Whitehead's *Science and the Modern World*. Pertinent, too, are T.S. Eliot (1962), Frye (1963) and Gramsci (see H. Entwistle's *Gramsci*).

[10]Of course, a caring *manner* is not enough; care in selection of *content* counts too. For too long the (very American) concern with "process" and behavior or performance has deflected attention away from content – with sad results (e.g., Bloom, 1987; D'Souza, 1992; Partington, 1987; Singal, 1991). As Paglia (1992) says "literature and art are the best way into the psychology of mankind because of the ambiguity and mystery. Because that is where you feel the flux, the flux of our sexual desire, the way our spirit is flowing. Fantasy and imagination . . . always flowing" (p. 270). Of course, one agrees with Zinchenko (1986, pp. 101-102) when he says that ". . . experience is richer than the system of verbal categories that one masters"; but at the same time, one accepts Huxleys' (1980, pp. 12-13) point: "one cannot overstress the necessity for words" and their role in the "abolition of the celibacy of the intellect." This resonates with Frye, who says "verbal culture expresses the work of imagination. Even the verbal structures of psychology, . . . history, . . . everything else built out of words have been informed by . . . the same kinds of myths and metaphors we find . . . in literature" (in Denham, 1980, p. 29). Unfortunately,

educators often fail to make plain the fact that educational success depends upon a good command of language.

[11]Few seem to believe that society should provide its members with the opportunity, and encourage the growth of a sense of duty or obligation, to improve or fulfill themselves through learning *just because they are humans*. Instead, the emphasis is placed on secondary gains (like a better job, higher income, or loftier status) and the credentials that are assumed to serve as tickets to ride as advertised.

[12]The evolution of the popcorn curriculum was channeled by a number of conditions and forces, including (1) the crisis of authority in society generally and in the professions particularly (Barzun, 1991, 1982; Bloom, 1987); (2) the decline in the impact of the universities on cultural life (Jacoby, 1987); (3) the emergence of the oracular status of television in the "age of show business" wherein amusement value became a superordinate value in public discourse and cultural generally (Postman, 1986); (4) the acceleration of economic decline which increased pressures on schools to retain adolescents in custody for as long as possible (Fulford, 1992).

[13]Somebody, perhaps it was T.S. Eliot (1962), said that while much of the greatest art and learning has survived centuries of neglect, one must wonder if those same noble creations can long survive popular or "entertaining" treatment.

[14]Teachers are as much to blame for the absurd range of projects with which schools have become enmeshed as is any group. For they steadfastly refuse to admit their marginal importance as a force for mending the world. A cynic might suppose that if they admitted they and the schools constitute, to use Eliot's (1962) words, a "remedy (that) is manifestly and ludicrously inadequate" (p. 106) they would lose bargaining power to get a decent living from their employment. However, like Eliot, we can adopt the view that ". . . if we combat the delusion that the . . . world can be put right by a system of instruction" (p. 107) quite useful work can be done in schools to combat ignorance and barbarity – which work, if done with care, will seem worthy enough.

[15]In Canada, provincial governments generally follow a plan that a cynic might say, confuses by design: They appoint a Royal Commission, a political instrument, that collects diverse opinions and other material that may have a patina of scholarship, and, if the Commission's report is politically correct and agreeable to the government that receives it, a propaganda exercise prepares public opinion for "reforms" that are presumed to improve all manner of things. The platitudinous language that is the trademark of both the reports and the ensuing propaganda allows everyone to read his or her cultural longings into the project and educators pretend that scholarship has produced a preponderance of evidence that gives warrant to the adventure in "improvement." This latter exercise in self deception helps hide the fact that these political exercises are *ad hoc* and non-rational adventures in governing; and are more connected with manipulation than with scholarship, understanding, culture or learning. For a current case see MacKie (1993, p. A4). Other obvious examples that come to mind are the reports of Hall-Dennis (Ontario); Worth (Alberta); and most recently, Sullivan (British Columbia). None of these exercises seems to reckon with the reasoning and observations that led T.S. Eliot (1962) to warn against "the danger that education . . . will take upon itself the reformation

and direction of culture ... (For) the more education arrogates to itself the responsibility, the more systematically it will betray culture ... (p. 107) (The) one thing to avoid is a *universalized* planning; one thing to ascertain is the limits of the plannable." (p. 109).

[16]Not all fashions are market commodities. Affectations of all sorts that one sees reproduced in monotonous rhythms include such matters as argot, gestures, speech mannerisms, "looks," recreations, standard opinions on "the issues of the day" and of course any number of products, places and people that are "in." Of course we should remember that adults are not immune to this "lifestyle." Perhaps some are not educated to transcend such lowing.

4

History of Adolescence

Adolescence is as much a social phenomenon as it is a psychological one. As societies change over time, therefore, so does the conceptualization of adolescence. The modern scientific concept of adolescence began with now famous two-volume work of G. Stanley Hall, *Adolescence* first published in 1904. Hall has since been accorded the status of the father of the psychology of adolescence. The concept of adolescence – though the term "adolescence" didn't appear until the 15th century – has its roots in antiquity, especially in the works of the early Greeks. Both Plato and Aristotle attached special significance to the transitional period between childhood and adulthood. Like many modern day psychologists, these early thinkers regarded adolescence as a time of turbulence and passion when young people begin to face the responsibilities of adulthood. This view has remained remarkably stable over time. In this chapter we shall trace the history of adolescence from its ancient roots, to Medieval views, through the Renaissance, to modern conceptions in the 18th and 19th centuries, and finally to the present day view in the 20th century.

Ancient Views

While Plato (427-347 B.C.) did not specifically develop a theory of development or adolescence, accounts of youth appear in various of his works, particularly in his dialogues, *Laws* and *The Republic*. He did, however, develop a rather extensive theory of human nature with a dualist assumption as the cornerstone of the theory. His famous dictum, *soma sema* (the body is the seat of the soul) sums up the division of body and soul. Only the soul can develop to the highest rational level but it is fettered by the body. For Plato, rational and critical thought is absent in children and appears mainly in adolescence as it is at this time that the soul is beginning to achieve it's highest plane. Moreover, innate ideas – another of Plato's pivotal concepts – are brought out fully in adolescence when reason develops. Passion and excitability were central themes in the affective aspect of adolescence for Plato, as they have been since throughout the millennia. Finally, in the third part of Plato's tripartite system of human nature (Reason, Appetite and Spirit), young people developed such headstrong will (spirit) they argue merely for argument's sake. Indeed, adolescents are so excitable according to Plato, they should not be allowed to drink wine before eighteen years of age because "fire must not be poured upon fire."

Aristotle (384-322 B.C.), one of Plato's most successful students, diverged from his teacher on the point of dualism or mind-body separation. Rather, he began with a doctrine of the unity of the physical and mental worlds. Like modern materialist psychologists such as Freud, Aristotle saw the soul as the function of the body which provides the structure. The soul then, cannot exist without the body just as the mind cannot exist without the brain.

Like Plato, Aristotle accepted the view that human development is a process whereby the soul evolves to progressively higher states culminating in Young Manhood (14-21 years of age) where the highest plane is achieved. Aristotle's description appears in *Rhetorica* and foreshadows G. Stanley Hall's descriptions of adolescence as a time of *sturm und drang* (storm and stress). The adolescent in Aristotle's description, shows strong passions, especially sexual, which are indiscriminately gratified if possible. These impulses are intense and can be violent but are of short duration and extinguish quickly. These youths can be gullible, optimistic and future oriented but at the same time, they can be obstinate and complain constantly of not being understood and of unfair treatment at home and by society generally.

Medieval Views

During the Medieval period or Dark Ages as it is also referred to, a moratorium existed on independent thinking, and the discovery of new knowledge. Remarkably, for nearly one thousand years from the total collapse of the Roman Empire in the 5th century to the 15th century and the Renaissance, the view of the world was based strictly on Christian theology and religious dogma.

During this period, children and adolescents were not accorded separate status but were regarded as miniature adults. Moreover, humanity was considered to be essentially depraved and each person entered the world tainted with original sin. Indeed, it was the original transgressions of Adam and Eve that caused the downfall of humanity into sin and introduced death: "Sin came into the world through one man and death through sin" (Genesis 3: 6-7). Plato's dualism was thus revived as the soul had a separate existence from the body. While corporeal death was inevitable, the soul would live on for eternity either happily (in heaven) or in perpetual misery and torture (in hell) if redemption had not be achieved.

This doctrine of depravity underscores innate tendencies towards badness and ungodliness. During these Dark Ages, development was seen as a process whereby the person becomes progressively worse and removed from God. The path to redemption lies in stern discipline of the child and repression of childish (sinful) impulses. The child had to be civilized. These were particularly strong views in Catholic theology before the Reformation and were subsequently revived in Calvinism in Europe and Puritanism in the United States.

Renaissance Views

The Renaissance or rebirth after the Middle Ages marked a sharp break with medieval ideals and practices, particularly in the arts, in literature, in science and in the concept of human nature. These changes began in Italy primarily during the 15th and 16th centuries and later spread throughout the world. The most pertinent views on human nature and human development are those of three philosophers: Comenius, Locke, and Rousseau.

The major break of Renaissance thought with medieval doctrine was over the doctrine of preformationism. Both Comenius (1592-1670) and Locke (1632-1704) rejected the concept of innate ideas and evil in humans and focused instead on experience and individual development. John Locke in his 1753 work, *An Essay Concerning Human Understanding*, developed the theme that all knowledge is obtained directly through the senses since the mind of the neonate was a *tabula rasa* (blank slate). For Locke, development was a gradual process from initial mental passivity to increased cognition during adolescence and not the emergence of innate depravity. Locke's view clearly foreshadowed the work of behavioral psychologist J.B. Watson who extended this idea of the *tabula rasa* in his 1924 book *Behaviorism* when he declared: "Give me a dozen healthy infants, well-formed, and my own specific world to bring them up in and I'll guarantee to take any one at random and train him to become any kind of specialist I might select." (p. 104). For both Comenius and Locke, adolescence was the final stage of human development where the individual acquires abstract thought, rationality, becomes self-directed and achieves an identity. These are themes of development which are also central to the 20th century theories of Jean Piaget and Erik Erikson.

Probably the most influential thinker of the Renaissance vis a vis human development was Jean Jacques Rousseau (1712-1778). In contrast to Comenius and Locke, Rousseau focused on affect rather than cognition. Like many of his contemporaries, Rousseau adhered to the dominant themes of his day of romanticism and primitivism as the Romantic Era prevailed in a spirit of revolt against the dogma of "reason" inherent in Medieval Scholasticism. Ultimately the static mechanistic universe of the dark ages was discarded for one dynamic evolutionary one.

Primitivism encompassed the belief that the natural or earliest conditions of humanity are glorious and ideal and are reflected in children and childhood. It was in this context that Rousseau wrote his famous book *Emile* (1780) about the development of a fictitious boy, wherein he expounded his view of children, adolescents and development. The child was close to nature, primitive and thus intrinsically good. As a noble savage, the child was naturally endowed with a sense of right and wrong. Four stages of development were proposed by Rousseau which culminated during the period of adolescence (15-20 years) when the person shifts from selfish motivations to social concerns and develops an identity. Conscience is acquired so that morality and virtuous behavior become possible; this leads into maturity which is dominated by spiritualism. Rousseau considered adolescence to be a "second birth," an idea that has been elaborated by contemporary psychoanalytic psychologists such as Peter Blos who sees adolescence as the "second individuation" (the first is completed by the end of the third year of life with the child's ability to distinguish between self and mother). As the Romantic Era gave way to the Modern Period and the revolutionary ideas embodied in the work of Charles Darwin, Rousseau and other Renaissance thinkers had firmly established the concept of childhood and adolescence.

Modern Views I: The 18th and 19th Centuries

In both Europe and the United States, industrialization radically transformed life during the 18th and 19th centuries. As society shifted from an agrian mode of production to an industrial one, people moved to cities with the resulting urbanization of society. Work now occurred outside the home (in the factories) but women and children remained at home doing "homework" while men did real work. Thus home became separated from work and children became feminized as much as women became childish. This period also was characterized by the introduction of mass education, child labor laws and mass communications, first through print, and finally through electronic media.

Such was the setting then, when Darwin (1809-1882) published his book, *The Origin of Species*, in 1859. While a number of revolutionary ideas are contained in that work, two of the most pertinent for current purposes are that: (1) species change (evolve) over time from simple to complex forms, and (2) that humans are part of the natural order with direct ancestry to infrahumans. As a result, the idea was finally accepted – grudgingly by many – that humans are part of the natural organic world rather than apart from nature and above it as had been held by Aristotle and many others since. Darwin's ideas influenced many 20th century psychologists including Sigmund Freud, Jean Piaget and Arnold Gessel, but probably had the most direct impact on the work of G. Stanley Hall (1844-1924).

Hall expanded Darwin's concept of biological evolution into a psychological theory of recapitulation. He adhered to the dictum that ontogeny recapitulates phylogeny, that the development of the individual (ontogeny) replays the entire biological history of humanity (phylogeny). Accordingly, each individual must pass through the entire development of humanity as a whole, from animal like primitivism (infancy), then to savagery (childhood), into early social forms (late childhood), and finally into more recent civilized ways of life that characterize modern times (adolescence and beyond). For Hall, "bad" behavior (during infancy and childhood) was natural, normal and inevitable, but one could take consolation in the fact that it would disappear as development progressed. This has been borrowed and expanded in modern popular culture when adults reassure each other that badly behaved children and adolescents are "just going through a phase."

The most lasting contribution that Hall has made to the study of adolescence is the idea that it is a time of *sturm und drang* or storm and stress. Hall borrowed this theme from 18th and 19th century German literature, especially the works of Goethe and Schiller who depicted youth as full of idealism, commitments to goals, and riddled with passion and suffering. In this genre, adolescents were depicted as moody, given to outbursts of deep personal feelings and as revolting against the established and old. While this theme of storm and stress was not original with Hall and can be traced at least as far back as the works of Plato and Aristotle, and has been a common theme throughout the millennia, he formalized this idea and legitimized it as "scientific." It has been a dominant theme governing adolescent research and therapy throughout the 20th century even though the bulk of empirical evidence now indicates that adolescence is a relatively tranquil period of smooth transition: most adolescents do not experience undue trauma and turbulence (Offer, Ostrov, Howard & Atkinson, 1988; Violato & Holden, 1988).

Modern Views II: The 20th Century

In addition to the main theme of *sturm und drang* and youth as a time of renewal and struggle against injustice, a number of dominant images and stereotypes of adolescence have dominated the 20th century. These stereotypes of youth coincide roughly with each decade of this century beginning in the 1920's.

Modern day depictions of the 1920s youth characterize those adolescents as fun loving, carefree, and self-indulgent. The depictions of youthful gaiety in the 1920s reflects the magnanimous mood of the period buttressed by economic expansion.

Conditions changed drastically in the 1930s. Life under conditions of the "dirty thirties" was bleak. Young people are depicted during this period not as fun loving and carefree, but rather as having a social conscience and heightened awareness of others. Nevertheless, the young of the 1930s did not actively protest or rebel against the social system – that would be left to a later generation.

The end of the 1930s was marked by the cataclysm of World War II. The previously dislocated youth now had a clear goal: young men went to war and young women assisted the war effort at home. The depiction of adolescents during the 1940s were that they were serious, committed to a purpose, patriotic and heroic.

The United States emerged from World War II triumphant. It was the most powerful nation on Earth with a vibrant economy and a hopeful outlook to the future. In the expansive mood of the times, the image of the youth paralleled that of the 1920s: adolescents were seen as silly, flighty, fun-loving and foolish. By the end of the 1950s, the images began to change. The adolescent as portrayed by James Dean in *Rebel Without A Cause* began to dominate. As the title of the film indicates, the young were becoming rebellious without understanding the underlying reason. The storm and stress theme was emphasized; adolescents were portrayed as emotionally turbulent, ready to strike out, frequently for no apparent reason.

By the 1960s the dominant image of youth characterized young people as visionaries. The visionary was distinguished by a purity of moral vision, a saint-like creature battling heroically against the immense forces of evil that surround him as embodied in "The Establishment." Popular theories of adolescence such as Erik Erikson's, as well as influential books such as *The Vanishing Adolescent* (1959) by Edgar Z. Friedenberg and Theodore Roszak's, *The Making of a Counterculture* (1969), together with films, television depictions, adolescent psychology textbooks, novels and magazines descriptions, helped to create, legitimize and sustain the stereotype of the young as engaged in a gallant, if hopeless struggle against the corruption of the adult world.

Protest, dissent and rebellion began to wane by the early 1970s and a new stereotype of youth arose: the me generation. In marked contrast to the visionary victim, the youth of the me generation did not care about social causes, their fellow humans or justice. Moreover, they endorsed "The Establishment" and certainly did not want to overthrow it. The main goal was to fully exploit its potential and to get for oneself as much out of it as possible.

The 1980s again produced a new stereotype of adolescence. This image of young people as "serious but troubled" shows adolescents as committed to school and work but troubled by economic uncertainty, the possibility of nuclear war, world famine and the break-up of the family. Unlike the visionary, however, the serious but troubled young are not willing to protest or rebel as they see these problems fatalistically and hopelessly. Many of the elements of this stereotype appeared in an article "Growing Pains" in a popular magazine: "If a generalization had to be made, I would say most of us are scared ... our attitudes are colored by hints of pessimism that arise from other issues that confront us ... Part of that pessimism may reflect the fact that we do not seem to be as idealistic as past generations," wrote a 17 year old high school graduate (*Macleans*, 1987, September 7, p.45). These serious but troubled youth are realistic rather than idealistic.

The Future of Adolescence

This is the social, cultural and historical milieu, then, in which we currently study adolescence. It is now a specialty unto its own in medicine, psychology and education. There are numerous learned and scientific journals such as *Adolescence, Journal of Youth and Adolescence*, and the *Journal of Adolescence*, that publish research findings in the area. There have been two handbooks of adolescence published in the last decade, *Handbook of Adolescent Psychology* (1987) edited by Vincent Van Hasslet and Michel Hersen, and another by the same title edited by Joseph Adelson (1980). Adolescence as a scientific, medical and educational specialty is here to stay.

As we approach the end of the 20th century, two main and contradictory themes govern theory and research in adolescence (Coleman, 1978). The first is the classical or storm and stress view, and the second is the empirical view which holds that adolescence is relatively peaceful and harmonious. Psychiatrists, clinical psychologists and social workers who study abnormal adolescents tend to adhere to the classical view while those who study normal adolescents espouse the latter view. The main task for researchers and theoreticians in the next several decades is to integrate and synthesize these apparently contradictory points of view into a more satisfactory explanation and understanding of adolescence.

References

Coleman, J.C. (1978). Current contradictions in adolescent theory. *Journal of Youth and Adolescence, 7*, 1-11.

Offer, D., Ostrov, E., Howard, K.I., Atkinson, R. (1988). *The Teenage World*. New York: Plenum Press.

Violato, C., Holden, W. (1988). A confirmatory factor analysis of a four-factor model of adolescent concerns. *Journal of Youth and Adolescence, 17*, 101-113.

5

Skinner, Behaviorism and Adolescence

B.F. Skinner was an impressive methodological innovator, a gifted inventor, a resourceful debater, and an untiring polemicist whose name became synonymous with the most durable and the most empirically tidy and clear variety of behavioral psychology. His voice became the poetic expression of the vision, hopes and wishes of romantic but apolitical materialists who haven't come to terms with the fact and implications of their subjectivity.

In 1917, Yeats, Nobel prize-winning poet, observed that "we make out of the quarrel with others, rhetoric, but of the quarrel with ourselves, poetry" (in Gross, 1987, p. 68). This insight helps us identify sources of creative tension in Skinner. For Skinner was a critical mind whose thoughts placed him at odds with the drift of humanity in general and psychologists in particular. At the same time, while he lived by dint of his thoughts and was convinced that the issue of those thoughts was critical to human survival, he dismissed thought (and the inner life generally) as being of no consequence to the conduct and fate of humanity. In sum his quarrels with himself and others made for rhetoric and poetry.

Skinner seemed to suppose that he and his kind are the hope of humanity's future. He thought we are doomed unless we give up the notion that human life differs from the other stuff of the universe: our attachment to the idea that we are free to choose the course of our behavior, he supposed, is misguided. Humanity, he said, must embrace his physics of behavior (that left out indeterminacy) or we will perish (e.g., Skinner, 1971).

In America, where scholarship and intellectual distinction are well below the mark that separates the lesser from more important things in public consciousness, Skinner was a notable and therefore, an anomaly. Why did he achieve that stature of notable in the public's consciousness? How did he cross that threshold of indifference and even hostility to intellectuals that is so obvious in the public culture of America? How did he become a notable beyond the world of pigeon talk and rat work – which is the world wherein he spent his best years?

The Master's Voice

What was said of the poet Pope can be said of Skinner: In his best writings "is the voice of the Master which the dog is devoted to, rather than the Master's message." (Porter, 1991, p. 4).[1] Skinner's voice was most audible in what is arguably his best book: *Science and Human Behavior* (1953). Many apparently assumed that the critical matter was Message; they failed to appreciate the subtlety of interplay between voice and message that exists in both poetry and prose.

We might think: here is a real scientist, a master of his subject; a thinker who cares about The Big Questions; an intellect that sees the relations between his subject and those Big Questions; a sharp mind that can cut to the quick; a magisterial voice that pronounces on the future; a cultivated humanist worthy of a following; a realist with a moral vision.

The fact of hunger in the world has profound significance. As the poet Auden said (in Williams, 1952)

> Hunger allows no choice
> To the citizen or the police . . . (p. 460).
> And I knew that Those to whom evil is done
> Do evil in return. (ibid, p. 458)

Skinner appears to not only have understood these things, but to have the means to address them with effect. He had read widely and was familiar with Marx and the latter's injunction to all: that we must not stop at mere description of the world – the pressing task is to change it. Skinner, like Auden, seemed to grasp the plight of humanity:

> Defenceless under the night
> Our world in stupor lies . . . (ibid, p. 460)

And Auden's words reveal the affirmative spirit that both he and Skinner expressed:

> Yet, dotted everywhere,
> Ironic points of light
> Flash out wherever the Just
> Exchange their messages;
> May I, composed like them
> Of Eros and of dust
> Beleaguered by the same
> Negation and despair,
> Show an affirming flame. (ibid, p. 460)

Confident about the meaning of what he observed, Skinner left behind concerns about meaning: in the modern battle between Voice and Meaning, he took the side of Voice.[2] The authoritative and moral tone would be his instrument for good – even though poets like Auden warn us

> . . . poetry makes nothing happen; it survives
> In the valley of its saying where executives
> Would never want to tamper . . .
> (in Williams, 1952, p. 456)

Perhaps like Auden, Skinner realized that, given the state of the world, he had few real options. (He said often enough that freedom is an illusion). So Auden, the poet who said "poetry makes nothing happen," confessed

> All I have is a voice
> To undo the folded lie
> The romantic lie in the brain
> Of the sensual man-in-the-street
> And the lie of Authority
> (in Williams, 1952, p. 456)

With Science as his sceptre, Skinner would command the muse to reveal how humanity could predict and control human behavior; and perhaps that muse did obey with whispers of a few minor secrets. But like Auden, Skinner wanted to "undo" a "romantic lie"; and he too resorted to the Voice of a poet with which he attempted to enchant the orb and transform base unruliness to precious order.

In effect, his own behavior mocked the truth of his claims (e.g., Skinner, 1971) to have discovered laws of human behavior that require the would-be reformer to abandon the pen and soapbox and manipulate cues for and consequences to behavior. Skinner's position was awkward since the particulars of his "science" require much: (1) more proximal contact between the behavioral engineer and individual humans; and (2) a more evenly distributed understanding of that science (as well as of its most critical resource "reinforcers"[3] than Skinner (or the world) affords.

Meanwhile, outside the lab, the counterparts to his starved pigeons persist in their hunger, powerlessness and unfreedom; while the counterparts to himself, who have resources to distribute or withhold according to the patterns that interest them, continue to enjoy the freedom to act as they will.

Skinner would have had us all turn our gaze on behavior and its consequences. He would have all join his celebration of a putative "science of behavior" from which, he assumed, a technology of teaching had been developed that could help actualize his vision of the new scientific man living in a society of just desserts.

The Visionary Moralist As Scientist

Skinner seemed to regard himself as a man with the future in his bones. He had the sensibilities of a scientist and, what in 1914, D.H. Lawrence called a "futurist" (see Ellman & Feldelson, 1965, pp. 431-36). That is, he had what is usually called a vision of the new man; and his envisioned new man was to be technical man – a prototype for all humanity. That hoped-for technological humanity of the future, would share a moral scheme: a moral scheme of just desserts.[4]

Now as Lawrence saw them, "futurists are stupid" (ibid, p. 436). He said: because they "look for the phenomena of the science of physics to be found in human beings . . . they are crassly stupid." (ibid). We might well consider why Lawrence would say this. In doing so the guidance of another eminence, Northrop Frye, can be helpful.

Frye was perhaps the most important literary scholar from the English-speaking world in the twentieth century. Although he was at least the intellectual equal of Skinner, very few of the people who could identify Skinner and some scent of his work could do the same with regard to Frye. Still Frye, had something to say about the cultivation of powers that are important to the realization of Skinner's moral vision.

In 1953, (the year *Science and Human Beahvior* appeared) Frye said:

> All the arts show us . . . that there are two orders of reality: The world that nature presents to us, and the world that human society constructs out of it, the world of art, science, . . . culture . . . civilization. (in Denham, 1980, p. 116)

The first order – the world that nature presents to us – is what Skinner said was his order. The second order – what human society constructs out of the first – is Frye's world of human imagination – the issue of the inner world Skinner would exclude from his science of behavior.

As a man who understood good science to be a material concern, Skinner regarded the subjective or inner life to be epiphenomenal and immaterial – hence beside the point. Material reality, which encased or encompassed it, subordinated it, controlled it. The material reality given by nature contained subjectivity. Objective reality (the container) was bigger than the inner life (the contained) and forced the inner world to be subject to its laws. He did not seem to recognize that even in thinking in this way, he demonstrated that the imagination can force a change in the order of things: that natural, material reality can be subordinated to thought so that the container becomes a thing contained – a thing subjected.

Although this capacity is both a curse and a blessing, subjectivity can transcend the limitations of the objective (given material reality). By going beyond the given, imagination can envision both an end state and a means by which the imagined end can be actualized. Hence, Frye can simply say, that the imagination takes the natural order of reality and makes something more of it: ". . . art, science, . . . culture, civilization." So seeds, soil, and water are organized into agriculture; so pattern, needle and threads are organized into cloth. The obduracies of nature, in general, and man in particular, require subjective involvement if these good ideas are to become sufficiently contagious to survive (Bandura, 1986). Still, Skinner refused this view and stuck with his nostrums that favor contingencies of consequences as the carrier of culture and intelligence. Unlike Frye, Skinner had no time for imagination. Frye, says Denham (1980) took imagination to be

> . . . a universal perceptive faculty (that) varies among men according to the degree they can create the forms of culture from their perceptions. [And while]

not all men are artists . . . all men . . . can at least educate their imaginations into a constructive awareness. (pp. 22-3).

Imagination is the power we have to reconcile contraries or opposites (Travis, 1990). We can treat apparently conflicting forces, entities or qualities as inseparable features of an encompassing or greater unity. "The imaginative vision can transform nature from a container to a thing contained. Imagination is our constructive power to build 'unities out of units'" (Denham, 1980, p. 20).

Frye supposed that all humans have some idea or concept of a world that they want to live in – "some mental model of an imagined possible experience" (ibid, p. 22). We "desire" to live in this imagined world; and the desire moves us to try to realize the imagined experience. This desire "is unlimited" . . . because it "is part of imagination" (ibid). But only those who have an energetic and strong imagination (i.e., an educated imagination) "train themselves to see clearly, to pass through sight into vision, to possess imagination as a structural power" (ibid).

Skinner would, in banning things mental, have us abandon imagination, and have us commit ourselves to his putative "science of behavior" and derivative technologies he supposed, would enable us to make manifest his vision of the future.

Many were influenced in that direction. Many accepted his misleadingly simple claims on behalf of the power of consequences. Certainly this seems so in American education – and in the schooling practices found in other countries too.

Again, we note that Skinner's moral vision is a vision of a society of just desserts. The word just is to be understood in two ways: in the sense of "what is fitting or appropriate"; and in the sense of "nothing but" or "exclusively."

Again, recall that Skinner supposed that the course of objects, conditions and events that immediately follow a course or train of behavior is, potentially, the most important influence on the future career of that species of behavior. He called all such subsequences "consequences" (whether or not they were, in fact, consequences).[5]

Moreover, we recall Skinner disliked punishment and would have aversive subsequences eliminated from the resources of behavior managers in his utopia. A moral scruple is given the gloss of science. So there was to be just dessert – no cabbage or turnips – after a course of action.[6] With his principles of consequences Skinner wanted to attach man to principles of the universe (e.g., Skinner, 1981). But in this quest there are serious risks. As James said, people sometimes have a tendency to seek

the universe's principle . . . some illuminating or power-bringing word or name. That word names the universe's principle, and to possess it is, after a fashion, to possess the universe itself. 'God,' 'Matter,' 'Reason,' 'the Absolute,' 'Energy,' are so many solving names. You can rest when you have them. You are at the end of your metaphysical quest. (in Ellman & Freidelson, 1965, p. 438).

Skinner's attachment to "consequences" as the primary principle of explanation is kin to this class of phenomena that James described. For in that multi-colored blend of yarns which together comprise the fabric we call human psychology, Skinner would make his thread, his "science of behavior," the whole cloth. And with his cloth most of mental life is wrapped up and tossed out as so much rubbish.

Lord Halifax once said that "the mind like the body, is subject to be hurt by everything it taketh for a remedy" (Auden & Kronenberger, 1981). Skinner, of course, never tired of telling us that his behaviorism was a remedy for the mind.

Perhaps to the extent a behavioral orientation informed the work of educators, a concern for enriching the mental powers of youngsters with knowledge (and such other mental furnishings as sensibilities, understanding and taste) may not have been cultivated as assiduously as it might otherwise have been. Such may be a consequence of the touting of Skinner's science of consequences – certainly it seems to have been a subsequence. William James is persuasive on such matters. Said James,

> Mans' chief difference from the brutes lies in the exuberant excess of his subjective propensities. Prune his extravagance, sober him, and you undo him. (in Auden & Kronenberger, p. 4)

From time to time, Skinner (e.g., 1984, 1989) himself, was moved to express the widely felt sense of dismay at the evidence (e.g., Barrett, 1990; Hirsch, 1989; Jones, 1988) of poor learning and apparently inadequate teaching in American schools. Still, he persisted in believing that his science could deliver the goods if only people would embrace it and give up on their beliefs in the importance of mental phenomena. He did not seem to realize the full extent to which he and his followers had succeeded in persuading educators that they should focus on and place relatively greater emphasis on behavior and consequences than on mental contents like discursive or declarative knowledge, aesthetic sensibilities, refinements of taste, tact and so forth. He did not seem to realize the extent to which schools had become devoted to that one aspect of the human psyche or soul which he championed: performance.

The Voice of Performance: Skinner as an Aspect Psychologist

This "aspect" emphasis is not peculiar (Travis & Coté, 1989). Most psychological work in this century has been focused on one or another aspect (i.e., one or another of the provinces) of the soul or human life. Modern psychologists seem to be inclined or predisposed to aspect psychology – to make more of one province than of the others.

On reflection, all will be able to identify prominent champions of cognition, famous apologists for affection, and celebrated advocates of conation. Perhaps this tendency to favor one or another aspect or province of the psyche is so widespread, we need to be reminded that the human condition and the terms of life force a traffic and trade between the provinces. The voice or expression of any one province is inevitably affected by that traffic and trade since the terms of life are a confederation that forces all provinces to be present in experience. In other words the voice of sensation, like the voice of reflection or that of action, always emanates from a crowd.

However, at a given time and circumstance, at the level of both society and that of an individual person, one voice or another may be heard above the assembly. Nowadays, in the American society of psychologists, the voice of Cognition is loudest and most insistent. (At the level of the individual this is not as obvious). The apostles of the so-called "cognitive revolution" appointed thinking, reasoning, knowing and calculation as their favored songs for our time.

In the first decades of this century Affection seemed to be the favored sound. Freud made appetite, sensation, feeling, emotion and instinct the dominant chord upon which all else rested. The manifest weight of the overburden that was alleged to both reveal and obscure the sensational but latent themes of appetite's experience was much more than behaviorists like Skinner were willing to bear. However, this did not mean that appetite, sensation, instinct (or Affection) was to be denied. In Skinner's science, appetite gets little acknowledgement. Even so, it is a silent partner: the pigeons and rats are starved.

So affection (especially as given expression through appetite) would be an ally or supporter as Skinner made the voice of Conation the dominant sound in American psychology in the decades that intervened between the era of Affection (the early decades of this century) and the era of Cognition (that followed shortly after mid-century). This voice of Conation spoke for the province of performance, of action, of will and spirit.

Accordingly, Skinner fixed his attention on an ongoing exchange between that province of life the ancients, like Plato (Travis & Coté, 1989) called appetite (or sensation) and what they called spirit. He noticed the symmetry of the exchanges. He noticed that living beings have spirit, that is, they behave; and that behavior or spirit perpetuates itself by adapting to the exigencies of life. Sensation informs spirit about those exigencies; and this enables spirit (activity or behavior) to further perpetuate the functioning of appetite. Skinner's scientific work (as opposed to his poetry or polemics) is all about that.

Essentially, he charted the rhythms of performance as confined by appetite and limited options. In this, he saw no need and made no room for thought. So in Skinner's thinking, thought is dismissed as a matter of no consequence. Questions of meaning do not arise. For Skinner, all humans, like the mythical figure Sisyphus, are condemned to perform; and our performances are independent of thought and feeling. He failed to appreciate the point of Camus (1942; see Ellman & Freidelson, 1965) who shows how the imagination of Sisyphus can make him heroic; that the futile and hopeless labor to which humankind is subjected can be transcended or surmounted; that with the imagination we get freedom; that "crushing truths perish from being acknowledged" (p. 852). So we can imagine that Sisyphus takes joy in the struggle.

Like Sisyphus, we all find our burdens again after a break. But how much more bearable these burdens are when we can imagine that "the struggle towards the heights is enough to fill a man's heart. One must imagine Sisyphus happy" (p. 852).

This is what is sad about Skinner's impact on education. For to the extent educators took (and take) a behavioral orientation to their work, they fail to give meaning its central place: so we get Machiavelli rather than Castiglione – will rather than contemplation – as the institutionalized focus for schooling.

His writings clearly show that Skinner, himself, read widely; and that he read not for food pellets, praise or prestige. He read for reasons of no simple sort. Among the most obvious of his motives is the desire to understand. Skinner read Ibsen and concluded that "the desire for order led him . . . to defining, to delimiting, an aspect of life into a word and hence to deal with the word . . . " (Skinner, 1976, p. 267). Fortunately, he did not attempt to disclose the details of any "complex schedule" of "consequences" that directed his reading of Proust's formidable *A la Recherche du temps perdu;* Reymont's (four volume work) *The Peasants*; Dostoyevsky's *The Brother's Karamazov;* and the impressive list of other works he mentions or describes – from Chekov, Frost, Bergson, Moliere, Racine, and Russell to the likes of Shaw, Wells, Joyce, Pound and Oscar Wilde.[7] Nor does he try identify the "discriminative stimuli" that cued the following verbal behavior: Said Skinner, (1976, p. 266) while Chekov claimed to be objective and produced "little more than short stories"; and Flaubert's indulgence in interpretive prose forced him to be subjective; Dostoyevsky might constitute the "near perfect compromise of sub- and objectivity." Clearly, some of the time, Skinner read to learn, to know and to understand; to discover, to feel, and to imagine.

Skinner was an intellectual, a man of ideas. The curious thing is that he supposed that the inner life could mean so little in a reckoning of what counted in human behavior; that this central fact of his life suggested so little to him about the place of thought, meaning, feeling and knowledge in the lives of others.

Through reading, Skinner partook of what Frye (Denham, 1980, p. 30; Frye, 1971) called mythos (verbal imitation of action), ethos (verbal imitation of feeling) and dianoia (verbal imitation of thought). Yet his interest in these furnishings of the inner life would not be obvious (or even readily suspected) from a reading of his publications (save his autobiographical works). Frye's contents of experience are notably absent from Skinner's conceptualization of human experience and its relation to human behavior.[8]

Assessing Skinner: The Importance of Perspective

These observations might lead some to wonder about the man's sincerity. An unkind or ungenerous person might be inclined to say that B.F. stood for Bad Faith. The blunt reasoning for this view would resemble the following: First, Skinner (e.g., 1981) claimed that on the basis of what he observed, one should conclude that the course of human behavior is selected by the train of consequences that follow any given species of such behavior. Second, if one looks at Skinner's own behavior, say his work, one notices that there are two distinct streams. That is, he had two aspects: scientist/inventor and polemicist/poet. The first stream is the descriptive and technical steam that had to do with what he supposed justified his beliefs. The other stream is the polemical work through which he tried to persuade sceptics and others of the merits of his convictions.

In both streams of work he appeals not to the irrational flow of subsequences or consequences to select the shape of reality that follows each of his contributions. Rather, he appeals to that which he repeatedly and persistently consigns to the heap of putative inconsequentials: mentalistic or inner life phenomena – reason, thought, the mental effusions and effulgences by which many of us make a living. In fact, if he had been suspected of having only small mental coins to invest in his audience, he wouldn't have made so much money or held his post at Harvard for so long.

So those who would say B.F. stood for Bad Faith would argue that he appealed to mental powers as a way to gain more influence for his (mental/imaginative) vision rather than on the power of selective consequences which, had he worked in consistency with his claims, he would arrange by other means. These same cynics might also say that, as a trained observer, Skinner noticed that regular pattern wherein human behavior nearly always seems unaffected by admonitions – of the sort Skinner resorted to quite frequently and regularly. (His exhortations did sell well – and may have in other ways, influenced the ways people behaved, but not necessarily for the better).

While the foregoing characterization (a bad faith interpretation) does not do justice to the man or to the importance of his work it cannot be dismissed entirely either. For Skinner was a worldly man. He knew that his polemics appealed to those who need to believe and have little they can look to. He understood that his books sold well because of the appeal of the author's moral vision of the new man and the accompanying vision of a society of just desserts. He may have eventually realized (to repeat Auden's thought) that he had only his voice, the power of poetry – the rhythm of repetition, in the absence of an adequate political culture.

The end state that Skinner imagined (his society of just desserts) and the means through which the end state he imagined, was to be realized (his science of behavior and his technology of consequences) have no connection and probably cannot have any connection. His mistake was a common mistake of his time and culture: He imagined that technique can be a substitute for politics.

It not clear that Skinner understood the limitations of his psychology qua science of behavior. While his view that in effect took "cognitive science" to be something akin to an oxymoron (e.g., see Skinner, 1990) is compelling, he undoubtedly would be unfriendly toward the view that his science traded significance for empirical respectability. Any science depends upon imagination; and if any science deserves or is worthy of the name science, it will have produced and will denote some reliable knowledge – both conceptual (facts or declarative knowledge – and valid propositions about them) and procedural (know how or reliable ways of making sense of the subject substance). Knowledge is, like the processes upon which it depends, a psychological fact. Any science that takes human behavior as its subject must come to grips with knowledge and imagination – not rule them out of court. The only situations where they don't matter are desperate situations – and even then, as Bettleheim (1980) has shown, imagination can be vital to survival in some such situations (such as concentration or "death" camps).

Although this is not an usual or peculiar situation with men, Skinner's reach seems to have exceeded his grasp. And while Arthur Koestler's characterization of behaviorism as a "monumental triviality" (Bower & Hilgard, 1981, p. 207) may entail a little hyperbole, we have reason to notice the shortcomings of behaviorism at its best (Skinner's brand) – particularly with regard to those realms (such as teaching) where Skinner made some of his more flamboyant claims for it (e.g., Skinner, 1968; 1984; 1989).

Quite clearly, there is more to teaching than the mere organization of consequences. Yet, Skinner said otherwise. Evans (1976) quoted him: "That's all teaching is, arranging contingencies which bring about changes in behavior" (p. 90).

Skinner himself, inadvertently supplies some of the reasons why one should be sceptical about the adequacy of his position. For instance, he says "the teacher doesn't have too many reinforcers at her disposal. That is one of the tragedies of education" (in Evans, 1976, p. 90). Moreover, he says, the social situation in schools (and elsewhere) requires the "conformity" that arises from such mental possessions as "manners, customs . . . " consideration for and deference to other people (ibid, p. 91).

In addition, there are reasons to suppose that, as Hilgard (in Evans, 1976) says, "Skinner's theory is performance theory, not learning theory" (p. 74); that reinforcement "affects mainly performance . . . rather than learning" (Bower & Hilgard, 1981, p. 206).[9] To the extent that this is the case, educators should be wary of Skinner's putative "technology of teaching" (Skinner, 1989; 1984; 1968). Certainly, nobody should suppose that Skinner's basic "principles and procedures" are readily "applied" or that they will, when so employed, invariably yield advantage. As Hilgard (in Evans, 1976) says

> You don't just pin the theory on the practical situation . . . The ingenuity that
> is actually involved . . . goes beyond . . . theory . . . You (must) show ingenuity
> and inventiveness . . . . (p. 74)[10]

Furthermore, important evidence suggests that the school achievement and motivation of some (able) pupils can actually be impeded by attempts to organize pupils' classroom experience according to scheme of consequence contingencies (Bower & Hilgard, 1981, pp. 204-205). So, what is to be made of Skinner's claims for his psychology?

To borrow a phrase from Kurt Vonnegut (1976, p. 176) who was thinking of anthropology at the time, Skinner wrote "poetry which pretends to be scientific." He used argument; he made use of observation; he displayed erudition; but he dwelled on the evocation of moods – just as Yeats (1961, p. 195) says the poet does: He used "explanatory and scientific writing . . . to make us partakers at the banquet of moods." Simone Weil said:

> the poet produces the beautiful by fixing his attention on something real . . .
> The authentic and true values – truth, beauty and goodness – in the activity of
> a human being are the result of one and the same act, a certain application of
> the full attention to the object. (in Miles, 1986, p. 234)

This is what Skinner did. He was fixed in his attentiveness; and the light of the poetry of consequences dawned.[11] He shed light on the way the spirit (behavior) of hungry animals can be shaped by manipulation of appetite and concomitants thereof (through feeding). The rhythms of the refrain were measured and sung well in the main – although researchers showed that factors like expectancy (e.g., Bolles, 1972), symbolic processes, efficacy expectations, foresight (Bandura, 1986) and species memory (e.g., Seligman & Hager, 1972) complicate matters far more seriously than Skinner anticipated.

According to Gioia (1991) the poet Wallace Stevens said that "the purpose of poetry is to contribute to man's happiness" (p. 105). Skinner seems to have put his considerable expressive resources in the service of this end. The appeal his writings had for public consciousness was a poetic appeal (if we grant the Platonic insight that poetry is the exploitation of our yearning to see ourselves as victims). For his polemics claim that humanity is victimized by the stickiness of mentalistic notions. A public that is impatient with the messiness of thought, of ideas, of emotional and cognitive complication is understandably, attracted (paradoxically) to ideas which say that such matters don't matter: All that does matter is performance, plain and simple. These ideas, blessed by a distinguished scientist, are bound to be attractive to many.

Although Skinner would not want to live thoughtlessly or among thoughtless people, he nonetheless, may have gained an impressive following including many for whom thought is painful or aversive (as it often is when its' object is important). Such victims of thought might want to be recognized as victims, and might also find in Skinner's writings the poetry that speaks to their yearnings.

Among scholars in psychology who yearn for signs of regularities in our subject, Skinner's refusal to hide the slack and flux in aggregations and statistical manipulations of observations that are merely assumed or declared to be equivalent had a sterling appeal because that refusal was heroic: Skinner faced the demands of materialist science squarely, boldly and beautifully. However, his most ardent followers seem to refuse recognition of the fact that to take that stance, Skinner had to find very special ground. That ground was the ground upon which life is notably confined, its degrees of freedom severely reduced by inflated appetite, simplified sensation, and restricted options. In sum, Skinner staked his general claims on the particulars that attend desperate situations. His extrapolations from the lab, if accepted require a generous grant of poetic license.

Poetic licence was an account upon which Skinner drew heavily when he extrapolated beyond the lab; and it sustained his polemical work which was, in the poetic tradition, an exercise in repetition:

... Wonderful for those who keep away from meaning, living somewhere better
...

The Longer-Term Meaning of Meaningless Psychology

In the main, where some good sense of the nature of humans is important, people who do practical work cannot afford to be sectarian in their attachments to ideas. No single aspect of the soul can become sovereign or elevated over the other aspects of the psyche without inflating the costs of hubris. Practical workers, like educators, insofar as they do their work better from having knowledge of psychology, are wise if they avoid offending the gods of any province of life or experience. The realms of reflection, affection and action all command respect and attention.

While generally, people might expect scientists to know and think; artists to feel and create; and professionals to know and act; the unpractised or unfeeling scientist, like the thoughtless or unworldly artist or the uncaring or immodest professional can turn knowledge, emotion and action into forces that demean and diminish humanity. At all levels of society, and in all people, the same provinces of the soul assemble to take stock of experience as life is lived. In some groups and individuals, and in different times or situations, the voice of one or another province may be stronger and rise above the others.

Where striving, or performance is of interest to an observer, Skinner's thought and work may provide a route to insight. Certainly this seems to be widely recognized in the fields of behavior therapy and in applied behavior analysis generally (where, at a given time, the therapist or analyst must focus on a very small number of people). But if the reflections of the strivers are deemed to be important for some reason; or if the affect of the performers matters, some other conceptual framework is required to complement the observations that derive from the Skinnerian perspective. Generally, those who work with people and do so with even the minimal care and sensitivity that decency requires, have to take account of their fellow humans' cognition and their affect as well as conation.

However, researchers have been known only rarely, to incorporate design features that allow for a reading of not only the contents and processes of all the major provinces of the psyche, but their interplay as well. In the absence of observations from such frameworks, one is left with a patchwork of bewildering diversity that has no coherence or unifying qualities or themes on which a practitioner may draw.

In these circumstances, a coordinating strategy might be helpful. Accordingly, something like Niels Bohr's principle of complementary description[12] seems to be needed in psychology – at least in any psychology that purports to speak to the macro-world of extra-laboratory experience. That is, we need complementary concepts and descriptions.

As Barrow (1988) says, Bohr's legacy entails the view (1) that all things in nature, observer and observed, are irrevocably linked; (2) that the limitations of naive realism must be faced; (3) that elements of some traditional philosophical conflicts (e.g., free will versus determinism) are candidates for complementary treatment in the sense that the adoption of one of these viewpoints renders the other meaningless; (4) that some epistemic values are complementary (e.g., clarity and accuracy are in some circumstances, mutually exclusive – hence the need to treat them as complementary).

This strategy of adopting complementary descriptions has some prospect of breaking out of the crisis of sterility and stagnation, the impasse in psychology, the aspect focus has wrought; and it may lead as well, to a higher, more fruitful, level of theorizing. In the event of such progress, one might well expect the full potential of Skinner's work to emerge; for nobody has done a better job of conceptualizing the means for making objective and material the conative or performances aspect of psychological life.

Meanwhile, at this time, we are unable to reject the conclusion that Skinner's attempt at bringing conceptual unity to psychology by reducing all its contents to matter-in-motion was bold and noble but mistaken. For all that matters does not always become material; and all things material do not always matter. Said the poet Yeats (1961) "Our thoughts and emotions are often but spray flung up from the hidden tides that follow a moon no eye can see" (p. 189). However, in our thoughts, symbols evoke with such power one nods automatic agreement when one reads that "symbolism . . . is the substance of all style" (ibid, p. 155). We notice that sometimes words "take light from mutual reflection, like the actual trail of fire over precious stones" (ibid, p. 193). And, more often, they don't. Nothing in Skinner's work enables us to predict or control when the spray of emotion, the dawning of light or the tide of thought will or will not occur. Yet without the tide, the spray and the dawn noted in coincidence and thematized "in the exuberance of our subjective propensities" (as James put it) we are mere brutes. And while brutal we too often are, we have the capacity and taste for pretending otherwise.

So, "man has wooed and won the world and has fallen weary" of things seen without illusion (Yeats, 1961, p. 192-3). Skinner's natural poetry is not spellbinding or even convincing. We are not moved by mere qualities inherent in objects, conditions or events (which a more naive realist than was Skinner might suppose. Skinner tried to escape this problem by adopting a circular definition of reinforcers – see Note 3). Accordingly, we cling to our mentalistic notions, the signs of an inner life that makes life beyond the skin more tolerable, and at times even meaningful. So said Yeats (1953),

> Our modern poetry is imaginative. It is the poetry of the young. The poetry of the greatest periods is a sustained expression of the appetites and habits. Hence we select where they exhausted. (p. 281).

Skinner sang the same song for a long time – over fifty years he rendered his own standard on the theme of habits. He was apparently not unlike other poets and musicians who, according to the poet Yeats (1961, p. 171), "see the whole work in the first impulse": Skinner found his theme early (in the late 1930s) and sang it until the end. And it was a worthy tune with which we all may learn to harmonize one day.

References

Auden, W.H. & L. Kronenberg. (Eds.) (1981). *The viking book of aphorisms.* Markham, ON: Penguin.

Bandura, A. (1986). Social foundations of thought and action. Englewood Cliffs, NJ: Prentice-Hall.

Barrett, M. (1990). The case for more school days. *The Atlantic Monthly, 266,* 5 (November), 78-81, 84, 86-87, 90-91, 94, 96-98, 100, 104-106.

Barrow, J. (1988). Complementary concepts. *TLS.* No. 4438 (April 22-28), 457.

Bettleheim, B. (1980). Ssurviving and other essays. New York: Vintage.

Bolles, R. (1972). Reinforcement, expectancy and learning. *Psychological Review, 79,* 394-409.

Bower, G. & E. Hilgard. (1981). *Theories of learning* (Fifth Edition). Englewood Cliffs, NJ: Prentice-Hall.

Camus, A. (1942). Absurd freedom. (From the Myth of Sisyphus). In R. Ellman & C. Freidelson (Eds.), *The modern tradition.* New York: Oxford University Press, pp. 844-852.

Castiglione, B. (1528/1928). *The book of the courtier.* (Translated by T. Hoby in 1561). London: Everyman Library.

Denham, R. (Ed.) (1980). *Northrop Frye on culture and literature.* Chicago: University of Chicago Press.

Ellman, R. & C. Freidelson (Eds.) (1965). *The modern tradition.* New York: Oxford University Press.

Evans, R. (1976). *The making of psychology.* New York: Knopf.

Frye, N. (1963). *The educated imagination.* Toronto: C.B.C.

Frye, N. (1988). *On education.* Toronto: Fitzhenry & Whiteside.

Gioia, D. (1991). Can poetry matter? *The Atlantic Monthly, 267,* 5 (May), 94-98, 100, 102-106.

Gross, J. (Ed.) (1987). *The Oxford book of aphorisms.* Oxford, UK: Oxford University Press.

Hobbes, T. (1651/1958). The Levianthan. Indianapolis, IN: Bobbs-Merrill.

Hirsch, E. (1989, 2 March). The primal scene of education. *The New York Review of Books, 36,* 3, 29-35.

James, W. (1909). Pluralism, pragmatism and instrumental truth (From A Pluralistic Universe). In R. Ellmann & C. Feidelson (Eds.), *The modern tradition.* New York: Oxford University Press, pp. 437-440.

James, W. (1958). *Talks to teachers.* New York: Norton.

Jones, L. (1988). School achievement trends in mathematics and science, and what can be done to improve them. In E. Rothkopf (Ed.), *Review of Research in Education,* Vol. 15, 1988-1989. Washington, DC: A.E.R.A.

Lawrence, D.H. (1914). The physics of human character. In R. Ellman & C. Feidelson (Eds.), *The modern tradition.* New York: Oxford, pp. 435-436.

Machiavelli, N. (1513/1908). *The prince.* (Translated by W. Marriott). London: Everyman Library.

Miles, S. (Ed.) (1986). *Simone Weil: An anthology.* London: Virago Press.

Porter, P. (1991). The recording angels. *TSL.* No. 4589, (15 March), 3-4.

Reich, W. (1942/1971). *The function of the orgasm.* New York: Farrar, Straus, & Giroux.

Reich, W. (1945/1969). *The sexual revolution* (Fourth Edition). New York: Farrar, Straus, & Giroux.

Seligman, M. & J. Hager (Eds.). (1972). *Biological boundaries to learning.* New York: Appleton-Century-Crofts.

Shakespeare, W. (circa 1608/1966). *The tragedy of Coriolanus.* New York: Signet.

Skinner, B.F. (1953). Science and human behavior. New York: Free Press.

Skinner, B.F. (1968). *The technology of teaching.* New York: Appleton-Century-Crofts.

Skinner, B.F. (1971). *Beyond freedom and dignity.* New York: Knopf.

Skinner, B.F. (1976). *Particulars of my life.* New York: Knopf.

Skinner, B.F. (1981). Selection by consequences. *Science, 213,* No. 4507, 501-504.

Skinner, B.F. (1984). The shame of American education. *American Psychologist, 39,* 9, 947-954.

Skinner, B.F. (1985). Cognitive science and behaviourism. *British Journal of Psychology, 76*, 3, 291-301.

Skinner, B.F. (1989). Teaching machines. *Science,* Vol. 243, No. 4898,. 1535.

Skinner, B.F. (1990). Can psychology be a science of mind? *American Psychologist, 45*, 1206-1210.

Travis, L.D. (1990). Disposition and achievement. University of British Columbia. Unpublished manuscript.

Travis, L.D. & A. Côté (1989). Plato, Piaget and Pedagogy. In C. Violato & A. Marini (Eds.), *Child development.* Calgary: Detselig, pp. 97-112.

Uvarov, E., D. Chapman & A. Isaacs (1979). *The penguin dictionary of science* (5th Edition). Harmondsworth, Middlesex, UK: Penguin Books.

Vonnegut, K. (1976). *Wampeters foma & granfalloons (opinions).* New York: Dell.

Wann, T. (Ed.) (1965). *Behaviorism and phenomenology.* Chicago: University of Chicago Press.

Williams, O. (Ed.) (1952). *A little treasury of modern poetry* (Revised Edition). New York: Charles Scribner's Sons.

Yeats, W.B. (1953). *The autobiography of William Butler Yeats.* New York: Macmillan.

Yeats, W.B. (1961). *Essays & introductions.* New York: Macmillan.

Notes

[1]Porter, P. (1991, March 15). The recording angels. *The Times Literary Supplement.* No. 4589, 3-4.

[2]In his autobiography, Skinner (1976) tells us that he gave up the ambition to become a writer when he realized that he had nothing to say (p. 264). But because he believed "science is the art of the twentieth century" (p. 291) he was still the artist who, like Samuel Butler (in Auden & Kronenberger, 1981, p. 328) might believe "we are not won by arguments but by tone ... temper ... the manner which is the man ... " So Skinner wrote – whether or not he would be a writer.

[3]Reinforcers are objects, conditions or events which strengthen given behavior (i.e., increase its duration or recurrence rate) when instances of said behavior are followed by either the removal of the object or event ("negative reinforcement") or encounters with (as from presentation of) the object, condition or event that reinforces the behavior of interest ("positive reinforcement").

[4]It is this poetic or visionary element in his work – that vision of a better man and a better world – that had such great appeal to the public consciousness. This visionary element, helped Skinner become the anomalous intellectual (in America – the notable intellectual) in public consciousness. As Yeats (1961) says poetic writing differs from scientific writing in that the former, unlike the latter, is ". . . wrought about a mood or a community of moods . . . and if it uses argument, theory, erudition . . . and seems to grow

hot in assertion or denial, it does so merely to make us partakers of the banquet of moods." (p. 195). A better description of Skinner's more popular works would be hard to find.

[5]The facts of Skinner's career may have disproved Samuel Johnson's wry claim that nobody benefits more than do physicians, from the public's incomprehension of the difference between subsequence and consequence. Skinner made much from that confusion.

[6]We are reminded of that revival and burgeoning of interest in the ideas and works of Wilhelm Reich (1942; 1945) in the decade between 1965 and 1975. The literate young became intrigued when they discovered that Reich advocated the elimination of restrictions on adolescent sex. Skinner's advocacy of just desserts has a similar basis for appeal.

[7]Frye's (1988, p. 141) discussion of the "education of will" entails a contrast of Renaissance writers – particularly Machiavelli (1513), Castiglione (1528) and Shakespeare (circa 1608): Machiavelli's *Prince* is seen as a treatise that speaks to the education of the will. The pattern for the education of the prince is the pattern for the education of the will. Emphasis is placed on action as opposed to contemplation. Both Nietzsche and Dewey are seen to be carriers of this line of thought. Castiglione's *Courtier* in contrast, is a pattern for the education of the would be advisor to the prince. Such person would be immersed in the arts, in leisure class virtues, in things that enhance the inner life, the contemplative life. Shakespeare's fable of the belly and the members, in *Coriolanus,* is also treated as pertinent by Frye. The belly, being accused of doing nothing by the members, is rebelled against; but the members soon learn that they cannot get by without the belly (even though it just sits there and absorbs food). The point is that a digestive (a contemplative) presence is necessary.

[8]Frye's mental provinces are clearly derivatives from Aristotle's POETICS. In literature, the elements of Ethos corresponds to those dimensions of life we call feeling, affection, emotion, sensation, appetite, and instinct. In the same context, Mythos connotes conation, spirit, and will; and it denotes action and performance. Dianoia, the last but not least domain in Frye's triadic scheme, is the cognitive province, the realm of thought, reason, reflection, calculation and contemplation. Implicitly, Frye supposes, (most sensibly) that all three are implicated in the work of imagination and intuition. Accordingly, we might make the following primary connections; but we would be wise to remember that spirit, appetite and thought are only conceptually separable:

mythos	ethos	dianoia
spirit	appetite	thought
will	emotion	reason
conation	affection	cognition
action	sensation	reflection
goodness	beauty	truth

I MAGINATION

INTUITION

[9]Of course Skinner (e.g., 1953, p. 111) denied there is a difference between competence and performance.

[10]This echoes William James who recognized in 1899, that the limitations of psychological theory will always be such that mental and personal strengths on the part of the teacher will be required to transcend them. (James, 1958, p. 24).

[11]To be sure, this was not an original theme: Thomas Hobbes, for example, wrote of "the science of consequences" in the middle of the 17th century; and his famous *Leviathan* (1651) incorporates some of his thinking on this subject in the first part. Of course the subject matter of poetry is ancient; and besides, Hobbes was not especially poetic on that subject.

[12]While Bohr was specifically concerned with the phenomena of quantum theory in physics, Barrow (1988) says he regarded this doctrine as having far wider applicability than in the quantum measurement problem (p. 457). Barrow renders Bohr's definition of complementarity as follows: "Our position as observers in a domain or experience where unambiguous application of concepts depends essentially on conditions of observation demands the use of complementary descriptions if . . . description is to be exhaustive" (p. 457). Put another way (by Uvarov, Chapman & Isaacs, 1979, p. 88) ". . . Evidence relating to atomic systems that has been obtained under different experimental conditions cannot necessarily be comprehended by one single model. Thus, for example, the wave model of the electron is complementary to the particle model." So we suggest that evidence relating to psychological systems that is obtained from different conditions of observation require complementary models. The challenge of coordinating and transcending the divided particulars and grasping the nature of the interactions between the divisions or provinces parallels the challenge in physics, of developing a unified field theory.

Introduction
Section Two: The Context of Adolescence

This second section of *Advances in Adolescent Psychology* consists of five chapters. Each of them focuses attention on particular features of the context of adolescence.

The concept of context is somewhat vague, even though it likely strikes most people as something familiar enough, as a notion that has the sense of the plain and simple. This vagueness becomes apparent and problematical when we consider the dilemma or twin hazards that are built into *Webster's* pertinent definition of context: "the whole situation, background or environment [that is] relevant." . . . One can opt for an interpretation that is all too-illusive to convey or denote precise meaning; or one can choose to indulge in theory-begging.

The standard academic response to this situation is to make use of modifiers (as in "historical context," "economic context," "social context," "cultural context," "home context," "school context," "work context," and so forth). This illusive solution does seem to reduce the inclusiveness problem somewhat; but it doesn't eliminate it; nor does it rid us of theory-begging. Even so, since our options are all flawed, and we are not totalistic adolescents who will have nothing to do with anything that is short of pure goodness, perfect beauty, or unadulterated truth, we will opt for the academic solution. Accordingly, while there can be, and are, many contexts of adolescence, in this section, we are thinking of the "cultural" context of adolescence. Even then, we confess that the word "culture" is used in an inclusive sense in this context!

The first chapter is primarily concerned with the schooling context of adolescent experience. But the reader will notice how porous that schooling context is. For features of the larger, more encompassing or surrounding culture come pouring into the school context as psychology in the schools, and culture in the schools are scrutinized in "Truths, Concerns and Consequences." In this chapter, the living or operative educational psychology of schooling is, as it is apprehended, subjected to critical analysis.

In the course of this analysis, what is taken for "truth" in schooling, is placed under scrutiny, just as we might do with "truth in advertising." The importance or value of scepticism is underscored in the course of this analysis, because credulous people, who apparently are numerous, fail to notice the shaky claims that are made on behalf of (1) a putative progress in psychological research which in turn is touted as a sound basis for educational programs that substitute processes for content as curricula, (2) ill-founded educational "innovations," (3) programs whose ostensible primary purpose is social amelioration.

An argument is mounted to the effect that, more than the rational apprehension of "truth" or preponderant evidence, what Northrop Frye (1963) called "myths of concern" are the more usual inspiration for that stream of misadventures in schooling that get cloaked in such ideological honorifics as"innovation," "trend," "reform" and the like. This mythology is discussed and illustrated; and consequences that follow from the acceptance of these myths of concern are described.

Agencies and entities that have a stake in plentiful stupidity and ignorance are identified and compared with those who might cherish the goal of minimizing these human qualities. Emphasis on people as opposed to "processes" "mechanisms" and things or commodities, is put forward as a corrective to the excesses of faith that has heretofore been evident when human factors and durable cultural content are subordinated to the mechanics and apparatus of would-be production. The teacher's personality, as opposed to his or her "technique" or "method" is embraced as the most plausible agent or factor that can infuse schooling with that cultural and personal meaningfulness that adolescents, so frequently, sense is absent.

This first chapter, "Truths, Concerns and Consequences," sets a tone, suggests an outlook, and provides some background for consideration of the other chapters that follow in this "Context" section. The tone for this section is, in the main, critical of the cultural context of adolescence as we know it, in the more prosperous modern countries with liberal traditions, institutions and economies. For the mass commercial culture that enriches the few at the expense of the many (e.g. Galbraith, 1992; Heilbroner, 1992; Hughes, 1993; Lapham, 1989; McQuaig, 1993; Smythe, 1981) sells human possibility short; and it does so as it enmeshes adolescents in its tasteless web of junk – from foods to fashions, from fads to the "life-style" fettishes of a deathly consumerism. Its apologists even add insult to injury by misattributing authorship and ownership of this "culture" to adolescents when they speak of it as "youth culture."

For nobody who looks into the industries of popular music, clothing, or any of the other products that get associated with the notions of "teen taste," "teen talk" or "youth culture," will come away with the idea that such fare is contrived by youth for youth and with the profits of the enterprises pocketed primarily by youth. On the contrary; one comes away from such snooping with the conviction that so-called youth culture is an adult-sponsored notion that disguises and mystifies the doings of adults of notable cunning and avarice (Buhle, 1987; Smythe, 1981; Travis, 1975; and chapter 7 of this volume). Youth culture is just one sub-division or part of mass commercial culture – that accumulation of commercially promoted contrivances that have shoved aside and replaced the traditional folk cultures that evolved according to the dynamics of conditions and events that generally, were not commercially contrived by a "consciousness industry" or infused into the information environment by design.

Nowadays, the mass commercial culture is everywhere: it is pervasive and intrusive; and it dominates the information environment of even the most isolated individual. For the technological apparatus of the electronic communication revolution is now everywhere; and its domination by commercial interests and values virtually makes the ideology of business, a total system of envelopment. Thus, the information environment can pervade and dominate the less encompassing contexts of household or family; neighborhood or community; school or educational system; and even government or nation state.

This situation has to be understood if we are to understand adolescent experience. A variety of analytic frameworks that encompass the parts and the whole, as well as the relations between, and dynamics within them, have been conceptualized. For example, Bronfenbrenner's (1979) ecological framework is one such system that can be helpful – although it is a rather general framework of micro, meso and macro systems. This framework is in the tradition of Kurt Lewin, Roger Barker and of course, Thomae.

George Gerbner's (1972) works and those of Albert Bandura are also helpful in providing ways of thinking about social-psychological contagion phenomena. Similarly, Buhle (1987) who provided recent descriptions of popular culture contents that are widely disseminated and consumed add to the tradition of earlier works by Dwight McDonald, Clement Greenberg, Raymond Williams, Denys Thomson, Dallas Smythe (1981) and others that have helped define a sense of the situation.

To repeat, the context of adolescent experience today, in much of the world, is primarily a commercial culture context which incessantly implores people to "buy something." Were the latter just a tiresome message delivered in tones of admonition, it would not be so powerful, pervasive, invasive and subversive to intelligence, cultivation and the higher human possibilities. Unfortunately, those who have the wherewithal to give it its character, have far more money, talent, technique, and psychological subtlety (employed in pursuit of their own economic ends) than all the agencies that care for serious culture and those elements of the schooling apparatus combined. They sow seeds of self-doubt, irrational fears, social anxiety, and acquisitive desires. And they reap bumper-crops by fertilizing imaginations with the mass dissemination of images that portend pain and possible troubles; and images of relief or deliverance, on the faces of those whose blemishes, weaknesses, flaws, and fears have been hidden, abolished, or disguised in the parables of advertising and in the formulae programs of television. The message of deliverance from a close call with disgrace, humiliation, or other form of failure or disaster, through purchase and use of some commodity, or adoption of a current "look," or "lifestyle," is the common coin (or is it "con"?) of the realm. Herein may be the source of what Hughes (1993) calls "the twin fetishes of victimhood and redemption" (p.11) that hobble our public institutions today.

While the social ecology and information flow lines are now quite well known, more attention needs to be directed to going beyond stereotypes studies and maps of type or case contagion. We need studies of the extent and particulars of correspondences between recurrent or semi-permanent features of the macro-culture's information environment and the recurrent, semi-permanent features of the inner-life of the adolescent populations that are surrounded by that macro-culture's information environment. The "seven pillars" of Fishwick's (1985) *Seven Pillars of Popular Culture* can comprise a promising structure for the analysis and description of these information features. These seven pillars, says Fishwick (p.15) signify what the ancient Greeks denoted with seven crucial words or categories: demos, ethnos, heros, theos, logos, eikons, and mythos . In the following space, these expressions are listed beside a brief description of their respective referents:

A Framework for the Analysis of the Information Environment and the Phenomenological Structure of Adolescent Thoughts*

DEMOS : the people as a whole (as opposed to the elites); the unity or communality of the people; common folk

ETHNOS : the divisions, sub-groups of the people; them and us

HEROS : uncommon, superior persons; paragons who bear grace,grit, courage, and the possibilities of life

THEOS : popular faith; popular sense of the sacred; things divine; and rites and ceremonies attached thereto

LOGOS : the right words, potent words that convey thought and form and portend consequence

EIKONS : pictures, images, representations that are lastingexpressions of uneducated convictions about everyday matters; cheery reassurances to be applauded (not debated – not for the learned)

MYTHOS : brave and bold stories that explain how things are and how they came to be so; models of heroism, courage, enigmas; dreams and concerns of a culture

---

*Adapted from M. Fishwick (1985) The seven pillars of popular culture. London: Greenwood Press.

Analyses of what the apparatus of popular commercial culture transmits, will yield the common cliched sense of Fishwick's categories, since, as he says, "popular culture is a haven for cliches [as] are some modern societies [where] human beings become a cliche, a stereotype . . ." (p. 29) and because, as Sutherland (1992) said, television and radio have been surrendered to commerce (p. 16).

The counterpart to these features of commercial culture and the information environment that is saturated with them, can also be derived from what is transmitted in schools. With such divergences as might be detected between the mass mediated "pillars" and the schools' versions, observations of the sense adolescents have of such things can be compared with both. Analyses of this sort can advance us beyond the sub-context by sub-context plodding which to date, has given us the conventional fare we have seen.

Humans tend to turn to stories as a means of divining or creating meaning in all sorts of information. Accordingly, Northrop Frye's "archetypes of story-telling" or Fishwick's "seven pillars" may give us insight and enhance our understanding of the typical modes of apprehension which adolescents share.

In this second section on the context of adolescence, the second chapter approaches a macro analysis of the popular cultural context of adolescence. This paper which was originally a chapter in a doctoral thesis (Travis'), has been revised for this volume. This type of analysis continues to be basic and necessary; but we are now in a position to go beyond this as we've seen.

The next two chapters (three and four) are written this same tradition of information environment analysis; but they focus on specific media and certain images found therein. The final chapter adds to our sense of what cultural context means in the shaping of adolescent experience, by making cross-cultural comparisons of the concerns of adolescents in Hong Kong and those expressed by Canadian adolescents. The difficulties that are peculiar to cross-cultural research that embraces samples from different language communities are met in this study. These last three chapters illustrate the types of studies that have, up to the present, informed our sense of contextual impacts on adolescents.

References

Bronfenbrenner, U. (1979). *The ecology of human development.* Cambridge, MA: Harvard University Press.

Buhle, P. (Ed.) (1987). *Popular culture in America.* Minneapolis: University of Minnesota Press.

Fishwick, M. (1985). *The seven pillars of popular culture.* London: Greenwood Press.

Galbraith, J.K. (1992). *The culture of contentment.* Boston: Houghton-Mifflin.

Heilbroner, R. (1992). *Twenty-first century capitalism.* (The 1992 Massey Lectures). Toronto: C.B.C/Anansi.

Hughes, R. (1993). *Culture of complaint: The fraying of America.* Oxford: Oxford University Press.

Lapham, L. (1989). *Money and class in America.* New York: Ballantine.

McQuaig, L. (1993). *The wealthy banker's wife: The assault on equality in Canada.* Toronto : Penguin.

Smythe, D. (1981). *Dependency road: Communications, capitalism, consciousness, and Canada.* Norwood, NJ: Ablex.

Sutherland, J. (1992, July 31). Engulfed by trash? *TLS.*, 16.

Travis, L.D. (1975). Political economy, social learning & activism. Edmonton: Unpublished doctoral dissertation, The University of Alberta.

6

Truths, Concerns and Consequences

"Boredom with established truths is a great enemy of free men." With this sly and penetrating observation, Bernard Crick began his celebrated work *In Defense of Politics* (Crick, 1964, p. 15). As we reflect on psychology and its place in education, we may realize that many have been imprisoned by convictions and how boredom with established truths in psychology and education threatens nobody – free or otherwise. Indeed, boredom with these modest truths, together with criticism, may help free us from the burdens which continue to accumulate from commitments and promises which we cannot keep. For captives of faith show that truth can imprison too – especially when the faith is unwarranted.

Our purpose in this chapter is to consider psychology's orientation to education, schooling and teacher preparation since these are such important elements in the context of adolescence. This requires that we pay attention to truth so that our reflections are informed by the light of truth's beacon. Psychology in education has a past which has been sufficiently dark and unenlightened to warrant this attempt. Let us then look first at our relations with truth before we see how it has been treated by educational psychology in the past and then consider what psychology's place in education might be.

Is Truth in Education and Psychology Like Truth in Advertising?

According to one authority on advertising "truth is a feeling, not a fact" (Martineau, 1971, p. 119). Studies of education make one wonder if this is the case in education too (e.g., MacKinnon, 1960; Scheirer & Kraut, 1979). One would think that truth would be of special interest and concern to educators. In reckoning all matters in education, truth (of the secular sort) seems pertinent; and if truth is called for, then one might expect educators to call on secular truth's relatives which represent it best: evidence and reason. Such expectations are based on a consistent pattern of self-advertisement. Over recent centuries, educated persons have set themselves apart from others, and they have, by tradition, been distinguished on the basis of their loyalty to a secular or profane trinity: truth, beauty and goodness (Adler, 1981). Secular truth, like truth decreed by authority or truth taken on faith, does not stand alone. This trinity, like the religious counterparts, is united by relationships among the three parts of the triumvirate. However, instead of metaphorical or metaphysical kinship which describes the relations of religion, goodness and beauty are tied to one another and to secular truth by principles of reason and evidence (Magee, 1973; Russell, 1965). Since the fifteenth century recourse to evidence as a principal source of unity has increased as reason was observed to be insufficient on its own much of the time (Russell, 1965). Reliable truth, in secular matters then, is not revealed by faith or reason alone, but through evidence, which, if reliable, is good and if good is beautiful. Adequate truth for the educated person derives, then, not from mere knowledge of beauty or goodness (inspired or revealed without recourse to the profane world or even decreed within it); rather truth, to be adequate, depends upon knowledge of profane evidence within the limits of the grasp of reason (which is beautiful) (Magee, 1973; Popper, 1979). Truth for educated persons in the modern era is attached by evidence and reason to beauty and goodness; and the secular mind calls on evidence and reason to help it find or construct and convey whatsoever is true (Adler, 1981). All of this is what one is led to expect from advertisements for the educated mind (e.g., Barzun, 1961).

However, when one looks to discover the extent to which psychologists and educators, as a rule, place such truth and evidence and reason at the centre of their deliberations, work and decisions (as suggested by the foregoing consideration) one finds something else rather too frequently (e.g. see Anderson & Travis, 1983; Barzun, 1981; Herrnstein, 1982; MacKinnon, 1960; Scheirer & Kraut, 1979; Shore, 1979, p. 2).

Truth and Consequences: Hell as the Truth Seen Too Late

Throughout the ages, poets and wisemen have tried to persuade us that we would do well to pay close attention to our relationships with truth. But poets and wisemen are resented or ignored by the vast majority of humankind (which is, of course, neither poetic or wise). Moreover, truth is usually represented as a singular entity (whether particular or general) not as a family whose members are frequently antagonistic to one another and whose members change appearance to a moving observer, as if programmed to suspect one another as well as any interested observer (Malcolm, 1983). Represented as an isolate – simple, stable and uniform – apparently truth can be safely treated with indifference or worse. Not surprisingly then, people as a rule have tended to be ambivalent about truth in general (and even hostile to particular truths). Perhaps this is why we are regularly enjoined to seek truth, revere it, tell it, and be liberated by it. Even so, seers and seekers show us and tell us that we take truth badly; that we will take only a little of it at a time – and that even then we prefer to disguise it (Travis, 1979). One of the durable themes of psychoanalysis is that human kind has a tendency to deny, disguise or distort unpleasant truth, and hence, individuals and groups are seen, regularly, to be unprepared for danger. Bettleheim (1980), for example, follows Freud in tradition if not in style, by drawing upon ample historical and cultural material to illustrate this important insight. Apparently, we close our eyes to unpleasant truths just as we do when faced with a sandstorm. While this may reduce some immediate grief, it can be dangerous in the longer term. Although one might expect psychologists to be aware of this and hence, be able to take measures to ensure they are not victimized by this tendency, this expectation is not always warranted (Travis, 1979; 1980). Although there are additional reasons for the fact that whole segments of a putative nomothetic mosaic in psychology remain a faded dream as separate pebbles are thrown before our gaze, truth in psychology consists of small non-cumulative fragments (Koch, 1981) which irritate and frustrate us because we know not where they fit in life's puzzles. Even so some deny and others disguise this unsettling state of affairs: it seems it is difficult to admit that the family of truth is no more but no less fractious and fractionated than is the family of man.

Human beings then, (at least in this time – sometimes called "The Age of Trash") seem to receive or encounter truth in all its variety, as small particles. While these granules of truth can be irritating as is frequently the case with the fine grains which are slowly ground in the mills of so-called justice (Martineau, 1971, p. 119), they can evoke a range of (defensive) reactions – from boredom to obsession with or conversion to a faith.

The characteristic tendency of people (at least in our time and place) to be exaggerated in rejecting the past and whatever is old (Plumb, 1971; Wills, 1977) guarantees a regular and ample supply of trouble. This is so for at least two reasons: first, as Gary Wills (1977, p. 22) says "what is true is old"; and second, we forsake old insights which provided the basis for deciding what is or is not pleasing in what is new (e.g., Plumb, 1971). With regard to the latter, we can invoke memory of Descartes' (seventeenth century) insight that truth is most readily cornered if one pursues it with doubt (rather than faith) as one's chief ally.

Doubt, Faith and Truth

Although Jacoby's (1975) "social amnesia" is plausible, it may not constitute an adequate explanation of the tendency in question. In any event, the wish to believe seems to have won faith the place of pride in our so-called secular society[1] and Cartesian doubt is cherished only among members of that minority of the officially educated population who are genuinely educated. As credentials have gained currency, their supply has been inflated; and the hard understanding that backs them (for many who trade in them) has been debased and devalued just as is the case for the backing for other inflated currencies (Armbruster, 1977; Astin, 1979; Atkin, 1981; Collins, 1979; Elias, 1983; Eurich & Kraetsch, 1982; Jones, 1981; Mitchell, 1978; Thurow, 1975; Travis, 1983). In these circumstances, it is understandable but ironic that faith in technique or technology has soared even as those (like teachers) who have little technical culture (Lortie, 1975) advertise their possession and use of it (Greer, 1983) while their numbers increase and their technical prowess may actually decline (at times) (Atkin, 1981; Coker et al., 1980; Howsom, 1981; Lyons, 1980; Watts, 1980).

Belief or faith are invoked because the extent of reliable, empirical truth in psychology which could be called upon to develop a technology for education did not warrant the role and place accorded psychology in education or the promises and expectations associated therewith during the past quarter century or so (Anderson & Travis, 1983). While psychology warrants a place in education for such understanding as it might lend (Travis, 1983), psychology warrants no tribute for technological advantage or gains (Cole, 1979; Hilgard, 1977; Spence, 1959).

An Historical Perspective

Even though everyone was given fair warning about the limits of what could be expected of psychology by Wundt (Bronfenbrenner, 1979, p. vii) and James (1962), the two most prominent founders of the "modern" version of this enterprise, the clamor of promoters and believers in what Northrop Frye (Denham, 1980; Frye, 1967, 1973, 1982a, 1982b; McKillop, 1979) would call a "myth of concern" (discussed below) has smothered the sound of those clear, cautionary notes. The bases for Wundt's scepticism about the capacity of psychology to say anything of consequence about socio-cultural questions; and the obvious implications of James' argument that psychology's technological usefulness in education is restricted by the extent or degree of each teacher's inventiveness or originality, have been ignored in the rush to deal with concerns. Although reason and evidence favored the scepticism of Wundt and James, belief or faith in the constructive and ameliorative powers of psychology (as technology in and through education) has grown so surely and steadily for so long, few can remember that school was once thought of as a limited thing (not a continuous and continuing matter); that learning once signified the possession of knowledge and understanding (not a content-free process); that when learning was considered as a process it was considered to be a serious, focused and significant undertaking (not amusing, whimsical or arbitrary). At one time, some people understood that while material circumstances governed everyday life, and while these circumstances and that life could be very rude indeed, the life of the mind sometimes could subordinate such circumstances since the heart of thought and culture (particularly truth, goodness and beauty) was as close as the nearest reading lamp. Unfortunately, when American psychology abandoned the mind in the early decades of the twentieth century and attached itself to concerns with processes of learning, it abandoned interest in the condition of learning: the condition of one having knowledge, understanding and meaning. The pursuit of processes of learning was a pursuit of processes of acquisition which in turn were given social sanction and were enmeshed with the pursuit of happiness and the mythology of "possessive individualism" (Macpherson, 1964). The pursuit of psychology which lent itself to understanding was rejected in favor of what Bettleheim (Brown, 1970, p. 280) called a "phallic psychology" characterized by aggressive manipulations, technological interventions or intrusions designed to alter nature, society or existing conditions, objects or events. The modesty that marks the receptive, contemplative posture was ignored as the pride of presumed wisdom and fertility was thrust up at each display of socio-cultural weakness.

Of course, teachers could not make direct assaults on any, leave aside all, socio-cultural weaknesses. They might try to educate or lead their charges to understanding of particular matters; but they could have no more practical aim (Huthins, 1968, p. vii). While they might be attracted to contentless processes and skills (e.g., Sternberg, 1983) as curricular pursuits, what Russell (1965, p.

454) called a form of madness, they would be singularly ill-equipped to engender and ineffectual to bring about advancement of many of them through the employment of what Hilgard (1977) calls "medicine cabinet treatments" favored so much by psychologists. Consequently, we should not be surprised to see distressing indications of poor returns on educational investment when impossible objectives are pursued and attainable ones are neglected (e.g., Armbruster, 1977; Astin, 1979; Hutchins, 1969; Jones, 1981).

The achievement evidence is not encouraging (e.g., Kasouf, 1984; Lerner, 1983), and the socio-cultural complaints remain and grow long with disappointment, rancor and enmity among the publics (e.g. Skinner, 1984). The bases for concern are thus exacerbated by misdirected emphases in psychology and education. Instead of pursuing gains of greater understanding which might one day allow for a mitigation of the rudeness of life (sometimes in some limited circumstances), we seem to lose ground as misplaced effort and inadequate understanding are invested in futile attempts to ameliorate political and socio-cultural defects by would-be technical means of altering contentless processes (Anderson & Travis, 1983; Travis, 1983).

Myths of Concern and the Establishment of Truth

The rudeness of life, exacerbated by socio-cultural weaknesses, has provided people with bases for concerns – especially concern about bringing and holding together the social conditions which protect oneself and the objects of one's care. Hence, the basis for the development of the myth of concern which Frye describes:

> As a culture develops, its mythology tends to become encyclopaedic, expanding into a total myth covering a society's view of its past, present and future, its relations to its gods and its neighbors, its traditions, its social and religious duties and its ultimate destiny . . . *The myth of concern, a closed myth – intolerant of dissent and anxious for continuity – exists to hold society together,* so far as words can help to do this. *For it, truth and reality are not directly connected with reasoning or evidence, but are socially established.* What is true for concern is what society does and believes *in response to authority,* and a belief, so far as a belief is verbalized, is a statement of willingness to participate in a myth of concern (Frye, 1973, pp. 36-37).[2]

The character of the dominant myths of concern may help explain how the contours of psychology in this part of the world have been formed, and why education, particularly schooling, has become so saturated with psychological condensates which are assumed to confer technical advantages in spite of the warnings of Wundt and James and accumulated evidence (e.g., Anderson & Travis, 1983; Stephens, 1967). For in this part of the world, psychology, education and social mythology are so entwined with one another (e.g., Stanley, 1981), we have to reckon with myth as well as truth if we want to locate psychology's place in education.

Two examples come to mind immediately; and while available space precludes more than passing mention of them, their notoriety should compensate for brevity of treatment. First, Butterfield's (1965) celebrated exploration of the psychology of historians which showed the futility of appointing ideas as agents (e.g., pp. 40-47) and the absurdity of entrusting historical truth to textbooks and the manufacturers of commercial literature (e.g., pp. 100-106) has not been effective in diminishing either practice since this work appeared in 1931, although this may not always be recognized (Plumb, 1971). The force of Whig myths of progress for instance cannot, apparently, be checked by mere evidence and reason; and commerce, careers and other concerns served by the textbook industry are not to be denied by the bagatelles of scholarly integrity, competence and truth.[3] Similarly, the myth, the wish, the cultural longing, expressed in the mistaken belief that self-conceptions are related to educational achievement (Scheirer & Kraut, 1979) also seems to persist undiminished in spite of "the overwhelming negative evidence" (p. 145) which an interested amateur observer would have noticed long ago: there has been a "persistent failure" (p. 140) in serious studies "to find the expected links between self-concept and academic achievement" (p. 144).

While there is insufficient space here for a dissection of our shared vision of society or mythology, as Frye (e.g., 1967, p. 105) calls it, or for a description of the units of that mythology (myths) which express our concerns about ourselves (p. 106), we may notice, following Frye (1967), that our modern mythology includes a social mythology which reaches us at two main levels. The first of these "is based fundamentally on cliche and stock response" acquired in contacts with family, mass media and neighbors. Moreover, especially in the U.S.A. before Sputnik (and perhaps after) "elementary education . . . consisted very largely of acquiring a stock response mythology known as the American way of life" (Frye, 1967, pp. 110-111). The second "emerges in general education and liberal arts courses, where we become aware of the thinkers who have helped shape our mythology" (p. 112). The latter focuses on alienation, anxiety, hopes, fears, and such other psychological states as arise from our social condition (pp. 112-113).

Ours is an ego-centred mythology at both levels. At both levels "the structure of ideas, images, beliefs, assumptions, anxieties and hopes which express a generally held view of man's situation and destiny" (Frye, 1967, p. 105) – the mythology – is infused with and turns on the secular concepts of psychology (which have replaced the less profane counterparts of the mythology that was superseded by our modern mythology) (pp. 104-115). So themes in our curriculum – in history, sociology, criminology, political economy, literature, education, and other subjects in addition to psychology – treat anxiety, fear, alienation, the pursuit of happiness or another psychological state as origins, agents or causes (Butterfield, 1965; Magee, 1973; Russell, 1965) – "explanatory fictions" as Skinner (1953) called such things.

Perhaps, as Shur (1977) suggests, and Skinner (1971) seems to concur, self-absorption of this sort may not be only a substitute for but a buttress against social change. In any case, the popularity of psychology has made psychology immensely successful (in conventional terms); but such popularity and success does not derive from the intrinsic merit of what psychology has to offer now (in technological terms) (Brophy, 1983; Glaser, 1982; Hilgard, 1977; Koch, 1979, 1978, 1981; Scriven, 1969; Spence, 1959; Travis, 1979, 1980). Nor is it likely to gain such technical leverage as would be required to overcome education's inherent difficulties which arise from the dynamic complexities of the character of judgement and decision demands; and the indeterminacies of aesthetic and affective interplay that inevitably accompany the human interactions of education. As Stanley (1981) and Stent (1975) have argued and Scriven (1969) has shown, some difficulties will not submit to technical solution because of the nature of what is involved. One need search no further than the mischief self-regulation (both conscious and unconscious sorts) creates for prediction of human behavior.

Presumably, there are limits to everything – including science (from which technology is derivative).[4] Euler's three-body problem, for example, has stymied mathematicians and physicists for centuries (Rensberger, 1973; Scriven, 1969); but this has not discouraged many psychologists and educators from believing that they can solve teachers' many-body problems in classrooms which entail many more (and more dynamic) variables than are considered in Euler's problem. In effect, such people seem to believe that technical solutions of a psychopedagogical sort are possible even when an understanding of what is involved is lacking.

Accordingly, we are faced with a situation which Michael Cole describes well. He says of psychology:

We are faced with the paradox of a successful science that tells us precious little about the concerns that beckon us to it (Cole, 1979, p. viii).

Myths of Concern and Consequences

Contemporary culture in general and schooling in particular have become so infused with the modern mythology of concern for the psychological condition of the self that other content has been crowded out (Gross, 1978; Lash, 1979). Education and learning are now too much thought of as processes (just as psychology as a subject itself has made little room for content other than processes). This has become noticed by others (e.g., Barzun, 1961, 1981; Wiener, 1967) who warned us about this too over twenty-five years ago when measured school achievement began its steady decline to the present low state (Astin, 1979; Ehrenreich, 1985; Eurich & Kraetsch, 1982; Jones, 1981). Like Barzun (1981), the father of cybernetics, Norbert Wiener, said in the mid-1950's:

We are in a period in which forms have largely superseded educational content and one which is moving toward an ever-increasing thinness of educational content (Wiener, 1967, p. 182).

Although psychology pays little heed to what actually takes place in schooling (Hilgard, 1977; Hyman, 1979; Spence, 1959), the schools have increasingly emphasized what Cole (1979, p. ix) calls the "contentless processes" of psychology. Concern with the object and advantage of knowing subject matter or what-to-think--about-when has frequently given way to concern with the pupil's

subjectivity *per se* and especially with self-conception, self-esteem, self-pro-
cesses – and teaching pupils "how to think" (as if an all purpose algorithm has
been formulated). Perhaps this is the educators' way of supporting a commercial
culture which thrives on ignorance (e.g. Ewen, 1977; Gordon, 1975; Hapgood,
1975; Laxer & Martin, 1976; Shur, 1977).

Certainly, there is no difficulty in seeing notable limits to the extent of our
society's commitment to the minimization of ignorance and stupidity (e.g.
Lorimer, 1979; Martin & Macdonell, 1982; Ostry, 1978). Of course, the existence and character of such limits is sometimes denied in, and frequently
obscured by the ceremonial bombast which inevitably accompanies graduation
rituals, fund-raising drives, election campaigns and other forms of light entertainment. However, the slightest lapse of credulity allows one to penetrate
beyond the surface reality which suggests that in this society, learning and
intelligence are valued, cherished and cultivated with much cash and more
commitment – for and from everyone.

Consider the proposition that the formal provisions for education (e.g. taxes,
statements of official purposes, infrastructures, rituals, rhetoric, and so forth)
comprise, sustain and reproduce a surface reality which hides the existence of
stakeholders, of vested interests, with at least as much commitment to and far
more cash invested in the cultivation of ignorance and stupidity than is the case
with learning and intelligence (Cannel & Macklin, 1974; Gorz, 1968; Hall &
Whannel, 1964; Hodgson, 1976; Hutchins, 1969; Lapham, 1981; Mander, 1978;
Monaco, 1978; Rosenberg & White, 1964, 1971; Travis, 1975, pp. 156-227;
Tuchman, 1974; Williams, 1968). Several considerations, when taken together,
provoke that thought. First, the supply of ignorance and stupidity never seems
to falter: This made P.T. Barnum a minor prophet and many more great profits.
Second, apparent realities – surface appearances (to repeat) – suggest that serious
and elaborate efforts are invested in developing informed intelligence: This
makes a fair living for quite a large number of folks and a poor set of prospects
for a larger number who count on the promise of such appearances. Third, these
appearances mislead however, since those in whose custody the culture and
learning and pupils are placed need not be noticeably learned or cultivated or
intelligent or even interested in such matters: This makes disappointment common and squabbling over education a mass participation sport for all seasons.
Indeed, great numbers – large proportions – of the teaching force (because they
do not love learning; because they don't know it; and because they seem to
believe, wrongly, that the locution "love of learning" refers not to the learned
condition or the outcome – as it does – but to the process) inadvertently teach
pupils to have a mixture of hostility, disrespect and indifference for learning by
their example and by replacing learning with bogus substitutes (knowing not
what they do). Society demonstrates its complicity, carelessness and disregard
by giving license to such persons and practices. So frequently, pupils are kept
busy looking for objects of whimsical and transitory wishes as they are enmeshed
in processes which have been substituted for content. Surely this common sham
which probably preempts learning and the cultivation of intelligence to some
(probably unknowable) degree also serves interests and agendas external to

schools and education as the uninformed pursuit of illusory notions about what comprises self-interest at any moment recreates bases for concern (e.g. Stanley, 1981). Disregard for truth has consequences to be sure. Some members of that particularistic and fractious family called Truth suffer our boredom or neglect better than do others. And some bear the burden of believers (or the faith full) much better than others.

A Return to Persons from a Reassessment of the Past

If psychology's prominent place in education is to be sustained, it will require a switch from reliance on the truths of faith or concern to reliance on those truths created from evidence cornered and interrogated by sceptical reason which forces such truths to stand up to doubt. Without the benefit of searching and researching doubt, even reasonable evidentiary (profane) truths eventually lose their reasonableness, beauty and goodness (Popper, 1979). As Popper says, only through criticism can knowledge advance (Magee, 1973, p. 14). This is to say, we have to abandon and forsake some comforting or reassuring hags of faith, and settle for the charms and transitory embraces of provisional truths. However, mere exhortations will not bring about the proposed change of course.

The superiority of sceptical reason over credulity in its adroitness in handling evidence must be demonstrated regularly and repeatedly. This requires a reassessment of some past work as well as the critical appraisal of present and future work. With regard to the former, we need to consider how evidence bearing on the place and significance of person factors in education has been handled. For this issue seems to have been crucial in the determination of the orientation psychology has taken to educational matters and the directions that have been taken in education too. In particular, we need to reassess the matters which led to the de-emphasis of content which consists of subject matters – matters that are made subjects of persons, and persons who subjectify matters – both object and subject, teacher and taught. We need to understand how we decided to ignore, downplay or overlook the significance of the person who teaches as content and the person who teaches as representor and mediator of other content. As the poet Yeats asked, "how can we know the dancer from the dance?"[5] These considerations require that we re-examine some work from the early 1960's.

What was new in 1962 as Getzels and Jackson (1963) prepared to announce the death of the notion that so-called "presage" variables mattered, was the claim of discovery, that there was no evidence of consequential relationships between teacher characteristics and teacher effectiveness. Only after work which focused on teacher characteristics was abandoned in the wake of the Getzels and Jackson (1963) assessment did another significant realization which should affect the manner in which one assesses the Getzels/Jackson conclusion gain in audience.

Only in 1968 did a restricted (interested) public consisting of those who study personality *per se* learn that personality assessment devices generally lack reliability and validity (Mischel, 1968). Since the teacher characteristics data assessed by Getzels and Jackson were yielded by such conventional devices and procedures which Mischel (1968) found wanting, the conclusion which Getzels and Jackson, as well as others, drew (that teacher characteristics and teacher effectiveness are unrelated) is questionable. Unfortunately, the custom of ignoring old evidence and the procedures which are indissociable from such evidence (since they affect the character of it) and the pack-wisdom of educational researchers seem to have been so widely followed, that a mere five years (1963-1968) was a sufficiently long period that the significance of Mischel's (1968) analysis for assessing the merits of the Getzels and Jackson conclusion was missed.

Besides this, of course, the concerns of the time ran against the notion that one could properly discriminate between people in matters that then seemed to be more obviously associated with doing good than with being good at showing and telling particular things. Teaching and education were not then linked so closely to cultivation and learning (as a condition) as they were to dreams of emergent opportunity and liberation: learning as putatively emancipating processes. It is not easy to think about denying anyone the chance to do good. So why be choosy?

Moreover, teacher shortages were common in those days; and there was little evidence that many were (properly) sceptical about the (doubtful) power of curriculum to run counter to extra-school cultural currents or its capacity to be teacher-proofed. Accordingly, curricular tinkering (i.e., process concerns) rose and attention to teacher characteristics fell as concerns swelled the granular bits which would not gain much notice on their own (Herrnstein, 1982). Few seemed to realize that the people present in class are content too; and that perhaps the facts of their social-psychological existence are constants or continuities of content. Few acknowledged that teachers are a continuing presence in the dynamic interactions or flux of interpersonal relations, objects, subjects, activities, wishes, hopes, fears, regrets – the panoply of life in school (and life out of school in school) – and that such living persons are at least as important as are the facts of the processes they formally set in motion, encourage or discourage or the other nonprocess particulars of subject matter which they choose to neglect or select and emphasize as matters of significance.

Perhaps the real hidden curriculum has been the most widely and regularly-taught lesson which societies that are careless about who represents learning and cultivation every day at school teach: learning and cultivation aren't very important. No investment, no planning are required to teach this if learning and culture are represented by those who are not learned or cultivated or by people who care little for such things. Moreover, inertia is a very considerable ally in this regard.

Those of us who discern the limitations and shortcomings of what has passed for psychological wisdom, have to show the more credulous and faithful what doubt has won us. In addition, when we discern a possible means by which truth can be compounded with reason and evidence (rather than confounded by belief and faith), we may secure a place of illumination for psychology in education. In this regard, some useful comments have been made in recent years.

Sanders' (1981) ideas about the limits of past and extant psychological explanations of teaching-learning connections are generally consonant with the present perspective. Like him (p. 74), we may urge that serious consideration be given to the structure (and substance) of social relationships as we pursue gains in understanding of teaching-learning phenomena. The inescapable social character of education (whether it be of the sort where a single soul informs his or her socially-fitted psyche through observation or assimilates the thoughts of an absent other in reading; or whether it be that which can arise in face-to-face or recorder-to-mass audience encounters), the social content of education should persuade even the most self-centred psychologist that when we have educational concerns, we must have social awareness – if we are to gain more than mere specks of psycho-pedagogical or psycho-educational truth. This social awareness entails an awareness of the desirability of restoring the consideration of persons as of first rank significance in our thought and deliberations. Accordingly, our problems are not merely technical, or methodological or even conceptual: psychological truth can gain educational significance insofar as it is compounded or alloyed with social truth (which should not in any event be seen as beyond educational psychology). In addition, the conceptualization and study of educationally-relevant personal qualities, defined and described in social (i.e., relational) terms (Travis, Violato & White, 1983) might yield a marked increased in our understanding of teaching and learning too. Oscar Wilde's (Addington, 1977, p. 658) general observation seems pertinent where teaching, learning and education are considered: "It is personalities, not principles, that move the age." Indeed, psychology's contribution to the understanding of education may turn on and stem from what it can reveal about persons – teachers and learners – in the social contexts of education. So we notice Handley's (1973, p. 5) admonition (which is conventionally ignored):

> The teaching process and the learning process cannot be looked at [fruitfully] in isolation from personality. Neither can the personality of the teacher and that of the learner be looked at in isolation from each other.

Since, as the redoubtable Paul Meehl (1978) says of our unsuccessful hunt in which fecund processes and efficient techniques have been the elusive quarry, our "so-called theories" are "scientifically unimpressive and technologically worthless" (p. 806), we have little to lose in reorienting ourselves. Wundt and James knew long ago and some, like MacKinnon (1960) knew nearly three decades ago that psychology's significance in education depends upon the grasp of a basic fact: the person called teacher controls the quality of education in that nothing can be done to transcend the teacher's limitations (and this, of course, includes the case of autodidacts).

In 1960 some like MacKinnon (1960) knew that (1) the quality of schools and learning in them depended then, as now, upon the quality of teachers; and (2) the quality of teachers depended then, as now, upon their knowledge and level of cultivation – which in turn is assured most reliably through selection (Wilson, Mitchell, Barclay, Jenkins, MacKay, Turner & Young, 1984).

Conclusion

The foregoing considerations suggest the desirability of an alternative, contrasting perspective or orientation. The outlines of such an orientation arise from several themes of criticism which focus on the way we construe what is involved in our endeavors and the relation of this manifest content to the forces that organize our lives.

Since the mid 1950s Bruno Bettelheim has recurrently drawn attention to contrasting psychological orientations which, ordered as they are by the language of depth psychology, turn on sexual distinctions. In *Symbolic Wounds* (1954) he described an orientation of phallic aggressiveness which betrayed an "overvaluation of the penis" prototype (with accompaniment of anxiety about losing the same). Phallic psychology, he said, is signified by the aggressive manipulation of nature by technological means (p. 136). The inner world of fantasy and dreams informs the phallic tendency to intrude, to isolate, to possess or break down objects and force them to conform to the visions which preserve self-consciousness (see also Brown, 1970, pp. 175, 200). This Apollonian psychology contrasts with the more feminine Dionysian tendency to give (rather than take) to unify (rather than break down); to encompass the whole body in ego organization (as opposed to genital organization of ego). While the masculine orientation is instrumental and treats objects as means, the feminine tendency orients to objects for themselves. Bettelheim says that the intrusive, phallic orientation is absorbed by "feats" that must be performed "to prove oneself" (a man, a scientist, a professional and so forth). By "overasserting masculinity" in these terms, a denial of what are socially considered to be feminine impulses or qualities (sans penis) is expressed (1954, p. 108). The self-defeating and mischievous consequences of this "tool thinking" in education are described by Bettelheim in a later essay "The decision to fail" (*Surviving*, 1980, pp. 142-168). He argues that "concentration on efficiency in developing a skill at the expense of emphasis on its deeper purpose makes the skill seem unimportant" (p. 150). If we think of and treat reading and learning as tools (as means) we create barriers to scholarship and the unity of subject and object: process obsession precludes content absorption; action emphasis preempts contemplative syntheses. Powell (1985, p. 10) calls this "use" orientation (to education) "barbarism."

The fact of the pervasiveness in education of the masculine psychology with its "tool thinking" is nicely demonstrated by Dobson, Dobson and Koetting (1982). They show that the dominant language of educational discourse derives from the adoption of military, industrial, technical and medical treatment metaphors; and that technical control (rather than say, love and growth) is the most salient value. They say "behind our manifest language is a metaphor which carries latent meanings to events," and techniques, skills, management and treatments subordinate or diminish humanity and its associated connotations and values in teachers and taught alike (p. 25). Learning is treated as a product, a commodity, or increasingly, as processes which are putatively technical and mechanized (Menosky & Moss, 1984; Skinner, 1984). Papagiannis, Klees and Bickel (1982) show us that there is plenty of reason to conclude that a self-legitimizing technological ideology has provided the illusion of change even as promised benefits from educational "innovations" have "failed to materialize" and while expenditures on "products" or commodities have increased steadily (Lamb, 1985).

A reorientation which gives more emphasis to the object (a feminine emphasis) and less to the (phallic) action seems warranted. Contemplation of wholes or unities is needed to balance the action on isolated constituents or elements which manipulative intrusions take as a focus (in presuming subordinate capabilities, for example, in complex learning). A de-emphasis of aggressiveness and concomitant estrangement between competitors for skill commodities, and an increase in discouragement of the commodity fetish (through emphasis on people as makers of meaning and understanding) might help reduce cultural decay and alienation from learning and truth. Technical truth in psychology and education is very limited and oversold; and faith in it is exaggerated and grotesque (Stanley, 1981).

In accordance with the foregoing considerations, a more feminine and less phallic orientation to education might be adopted by educational psychologists. We have reason to be more contemplative and less intrusive; more social and less commodity oriented; more person and less methods centred; and more content and less process absorbed.

This will require that we recognize the shortcomings of the conventional faith and its vestments and metaphors. In particular, criticism suggests that the treatment metaphor might be replaced with one like "teacher as autocatalyst" or "teacher as plenipotentiary of the cultural crown of mature understanding"[6] which force us to recognize the ancient truth which people like James (1962) expressed so clearly.

However, the well established (but old and generally bypassed) truth that "teachers make the difference" is, for too many, awkward – even unpleasant. The implications of widespread acceptance of this proposition are costly and otherwise inconvenient for gadget sellers, methods peddlers, "innovators" of all kinds (Lamb, 1985; Menosky & Moss, 1984). Moreover, faith in the illusion of technique is cheaper than the costs (of several sorts) which would attend emphasis on persons and their selection; and is more in tune with the *zeitgeist* which favors commodity over human, action over contemplative, phallic over feminine orientations. Accordingly, as we are imprisoned by the conviction that teaching is instructional "treatment," we lose sight of the fact that such a belief requires that we deny or forget that in education, "treatment" is just a metaphor – certainly not a full blown theory much less a technological fact. Simple questions make this clear. For instance, when does instructional treatment begin? Of what does it consist? Does it begin when the teacher "acts"; or does it begin when she appears; or when her appearance or some feature or quality of that appearance is noticed? How much of it is dancer and how much dance; how much enchantress and how much is chant - or is it chance? Indeed, which features of a teacher's demeanor, attributes and actions would or could be excluded? Moreover, does a limited set of conditions in which one teacher is embedded have "treatment" equivalence with the same set of conditions excepting for a different teacher or different (larger) context? These are only some of the questions which are awkward for those who would develop "prescriptive theory" (read treatment) such as those who like to call themselves "instructional psychologists" (Glaser, 1982). We know that "external validity is more than skin deep" (Berkowitz & Donnerstein, 1982, p. 245); that the mundane realism which dominates teachers' thought and action (Hilgard, 1977) is at war with the experimental realism that the instructional psychologists must champion (Glaser, 1982); that the indeterminate and uncontrollable interpretations of situations (for both those who would be treated and those would treat) create Orne's notorious "two experiment problem" (Adair, 1982, p. 1406) and the "behavior identity problem" (Secord, 1982, p. 1408) which we have known about for a very long time (Melton, 1959; Spence, 1959) but have not faced as squarely and non-defensively as some psychologists like Neisser (Bevan, 1982, p. 1313) and Koch (1969; 1978; 1981) who are not educational psychologists. Accordingly, our troubles evoke concerns which in turn evoke leaps of faith or belief in "treatments" as more trustworthy than people as sources of relief, deliverance, repair, enlightenment or whatever value is regarded as curative, restorative, or educative. Many careers, much expense and an astonishingly large number of man-years have been invested in this cheap-in-the-short-run but expensive-in-the-long-run course (Lamb, 1985; Lerner, 1983; Menosky & Ross, 1984).

Perhaps we, like our corporate organizers, should take the current confusion as a cue to reorient ourselves. However, we, unlike those who would exchange people for chips, and pain (ours) for profit (theirs), can turn from technology to people as a focus for study, and a source of possible educational gain. In doing so, we would be wise if we forsake the mistaken assessment practices, the misleading treatment conceptions, the malappropriate process emphasis and the absurd power pretensions which have brought us so little and cost us so much. Psychology's orientation to education, if it is to bring advantage is more promising as a people orientation; and its place is with people more than process.

Notes

[1.]Credulity, its care and feeding, has become so rife (Lapham, 1981; Finaly, 1979; Travis & Violato, 1981, 1985) that groups of concerned people have organized to help the publics detect intellectual rubbish and other trash so common in our age (e.g., Fisher, 1982, p. 1).

[2.]Emphasis added.

[3.]See Walter Karp's essay (Textbook America. *Harper's*, 1980, *260*, 1560, 80-88) for a discussion which illustrates this point in some detail. Here we see where concerns for "industrial cooperation," a "cooperative disposition," and a Dewey-eyed view of history, society and "democracy" were apparently present for the burial of history under the burden of "social studies." The dismal procession that formed there and after (e.g., see Atkin, 1981; and *Social Education*, 1981, 45, 6) has evoked recurrent expressions of acute distress in the U.S. (e.g. see *The Progressive*, 1982, March; *Newsweek*, 1983, May

9). In Canada we might wonder what is signified by the practice, widespread in British Columbia, wherein teachers and pupils alike, now talk unselfconsciously of "socials" and omit "studies" without any sign of embarrassment. Apparently, the "socialized disposition" can be carefree – perhaps because it is not taxed – even when the climate of the times is nasty and prospects are dark. But then since little reading is done (Travis & Violato, 1981, 1985) few will think of the pertinence of the admonition:

Do not go gentle into that good night.

Rage, Rage, against the dying light" (Dylan Thomas).

[4.]Stent (1975) is one of many who have described "the limits to the scientific understanding of man." Perhaps the existence of such limits is no reason for despair: after all, science has never been nor is it now, the sole source of know-how, or of truths or of wisdom.

[5.]Yeats (1967, p. 245) completes this poem "Among school children" with the couplet:

O body swayed to music, O brightening glance

How can we know the dancer from the dance?

[6.]These examples are taken from an invited paper which was read to the European Association for Research and Development in Higher Education (EARDHE) by L.D. Travis in Frankfurt (F.R.G.) in September, 1983. Its title is "Teacher as content and the metaphor problem: Teacher selection and preparation revisited."

References

Adair, J.G. (1982). Meaning of the situation to subjects. *American Psychologist, 37,* 12, 1406-1408.

Addington, R. (Ed.) (1977). *The Portable Oscar Wilde.* Harmondsworth, UK: Penguin.

Adler, Mortimer (1981). *Six Great Ideas.* New York: Collier.

Anderson, C.C., & Travis, L.D. (1983). *Psychology and the Liberal Consensus.* Waterloo, Ont: Wilfred Laurier University Press.

Armbruster, F.E. (1977). The more we spend the less children learn. *The New York Times Magazine* (August 28), Section 6, Part I, 9-11, 43-54, 56, 60.

Astin, A. (1979). *Four Critical Years.* San Francisco: Jossey Bass.

Atkin, J.M. (1981). Who will teach in high school? *Daedalus, 110,* 3, 91-103.

Barzun, J. (1961). *The House of Intellect.* New York: Harper.

Barzun, J. (1981). The wasteland of American education. *The New York Review of Books, 28,* 17 (November 5), 34-37.

Berkowitz, L., & Donnerstein, E. (1982). External validity is more than skin deep: Some answers to criticisms of laboratory experiments. *American Psychologist, 37,* 3, 245-257.

Bettelheim, B. (1954). *Symbolic Wounds.* Glencoe, IL: Free Press.

Bettelheim, B. (1980). *Surviving (and other Essays).* New York: Vintage.

Bevan, W. (1982). A sermon of sorts in three plus parts. *American Psychologist, 37,* 12, 1303-1322.

Bronfenbrenner, U. (1979). *The Ecology of Human Development: Experiments by Nature and Design.* Cambridge, Mass.: Harvard University Press, 1979.

Brophy, J.E. (1983). Only if it were true: A response to Greer. *Educational Researcher, 12,* 1, 10-13.

Brown, Norman O. (1970). *Life Against Death: The Psychoanalytic Meaning of History.* Middletown, Conn: Weslayan University Press.

Butterfield, H. (1965). *The Whig Interpretation of History.* New York: Norton.

Cannel, W., & Macklin, J. (1974). *The Human Nature Industry.* Garden City, N.Y.: Anchor/Doubleday.

Coker, H., Medley, D., & Soar, R. (1980). How valid are expert opinions about effective teaching. *Phi Delta Kappan, 62,* 2, 131-134, 149.

Cole, Michael (1979). Foreword. In U. Bronfenbrenner (Ed.), *The Ecology of Human Development.* Cambridge, Mass: Harvard University Press.

Collins, R. (1979). *The Credential Society.* New York: Academic Press.

Crick, B. (1964). *In Defense of Politics.* Harmondsworth: Penguin.

Denham, R.D. (Ed.) (1980). *Northrop Frye on Culture and Literature: A Collection of Review Essays.* Chicago: University of Chicago Press.

Dobson, R., Dobson, J., & Koetting, J. (1982). The language of teaching-effectiveness and teacher-competency research. *Viewpoints in Teaching and Learning, 58,* 2, 23-33.

Ehrenreich, B. (1985). America's illiteracy program. *Mother Jones, 10,* 111, 54.

Elias, T. (1983). Calif. teachers put to test. *The Province* (January 13), p. A11.

Eurich, A.C., & Kraetsch, G.A. (1982). A 50-year comparison of University of Minnesota freshman's reading performance. *Journal of Educational Psychology, 74,* 5, 660-665.

Ewen, S. (1977). *Captains of Consciousness: Advertising and the Social Roots of the Consumer Culture.* New York: McGraw-Hill.

Finlay, R. (1979). The strange sceptical mood on campus. *Saturday Night* (October), 35-40.

Fisher, K. (1982). The spreading stain of fraud. *APA Monitor, 13,* 11, 1, 7-9.

Frye, Northrop (1963). *The Educated Imagination.* Toronto: CBC Publication.

Frye, Northrop (1967). *The Modern Century.* Toronto: Oxford University Press.

Frye, Northrop (1973). *The Critical Path.* Bloomington: Indiana University Press.

Frye, Northrop (1982a). *The Great Code.* New York: Academic Press.

Frye, Northrop (1982b). *Divisions on a Ground: Essays on Canadian Culture.* Toronto: Anansi.

Getzels, J.W., & Jackson, P.W. (1963). The teacher's personality and characteristics. In N.L. Gage (Ed.), *Handbook on Research on Teaching.* Chicago: AERA/Rand McNally, pp. 506-582.

Glaser, Robert (1982). Instructional psychology: Past, present future. *American Psychologist, 37*, 3, 292-305.

Gordon, L. (1975). *The Consumers' Handbook: 99 Commercial Rip-Offs and How to Spot Them.* Toronto: McClelland & Stewart.

Gorz, André (1968). *Strategy for Labor.* Boston: Beacon Press.

Greer, R.D. (1983). Contingencies of the science and technology of teaching and pre-behavioristic research practices in education. *Educational Researcher, 12*, 1, 3-9.

Gross, M.L. (1978). *The Psychological Society.* New York: Random House.

Hall, S., & Whannel, P. (1964). *The Popular Arts.* Toronto: Hutchinson.

Handley, G.D. (1973). *Personality, Learning and Teaching.* London: Routledge and Kegan Paul.

Hapgood, D. (1975). *The Screwing of the Average Man.* New York: Bantam.

Herrnstein, R.J. (1982). IQ testing and the media. *The Atlantic, 250*, 2, 68-74.

Hilgard, E. (1977). Psychology's influence on educational practices: A puzzling history. *Education, 97*, 3, 203-219.

Hodgson, G. (1976). *America in Our Times.* Garden City, N.Y.: Doubleday.

Howsam, R.B. (1980). The workplace: Does it hamper professionalization of pedagogy? *Phi Delta Kappan, 62*, 2, 93-96.

Howsam, R.B. (1981). The trouble with teacher preparation. *Educational Leadership.* (November) 144-147.

Hutchins, R.M. (1968). *The Learning Society.* New York: Mentor.

Hyman, I. (1979). Psychology, education, and schooling: Social policy implications in the lives of children and youth. *American Psychologist, 34*, 10, 1024-1029.

Jacoby, Russell (1975). *Social Amnesia.* Boston: Beacon.

James, William (1962). *Talks to Teachers on Psychology (and to Students on Some of Life's Ideals)* [Originally Henry Holt, 1899]. New York: Dover.

Jones, L.V. (1981). Achievement test scores in mathematics and science. *Science, 213* (July 24) 412-416.

Kasouf, D. (1984). U.S. report blames failure to motivate! *Times Higher Education Supplement* (November 2), p. 8.

Koch, S. (1969). Psychology cannot be a coherent science. *Psychology Today, 3*, 4, 14, 64, 66-67.

Koch, S. et al. (1978). Psychology and the future. *American Psychologist, 33*, 7, 631-647.

Koch, S. (1981). The nature and limits of psychological knowledge: Lessons of a century qua "science." *American Psychologist, 36*, 257-269.

Lamb, J. (1985). Programming the first generation. *New Scientist.* 25 March, 34-37.

Lapham, L.H. (1981). Gilding the news. *Harper's 263*, 1574, 31-39.

Lasch, C. (1979). *Culture of Narcissism.* New York: Warner/Norton.

Laxer, J., & Martin, A. (Eds.) (1976). *The Big Tough Expensive Job: Imperial Oil and The Canadian Economy.* Don Mills, Ont.: Press Porcépic.

Lerner, B. (1983). Facing the unpleasant facts about achievement. *The Public Interest, 72,* 129-132.

Lorimer, J. (1979). The political economy of Canadian publishing. In D. Drache (ed.), *Debates and Controversies.* Toronto: McClelland and Stewart, pp. 141-159.

Lortie, B. (1975). *Schoolteacher.* Chicago: University of Chicago Press.

Lyons, G. (1980). Why teachers can't teach. *Phi Delta Kappan, 62,* 2, 108-112.

MacKinnon, F. (1960). *The Politics of Education.* Toronto: University of Toronto Press.

MacPherson, C.B. (1964). *Possessive Individualism.* Toronto: Oxford University Press.

Magee, B. (1973). *Popper.* London: Fontana/Collins.

Malcolm, J. (1983). Six roses ou cirrhose? *The New Yorker* (January 24), 96-100, 103-106.

Mander, J. (1978). *Four Arguments for the Elimination of Television.* New York: Morrow Quill.

Martin, W.B., & Macdonnel, A.J. (1982). *Canadian Education (Second Edition).* Scarborough, Ont.: Prentice-Hall.

Martineau, P. (1971). *Motivation in Advertising.* New York: McGraw-Hill.

McKillop, A.B. (1979). *A Disciplined Intelligence.* Montreal: McGill – Queen's University Press.

McNett, I. (1980). Psychologist influence on human development rapped. *APA Monitor, 11,* 1, 6, 15.

Meehl, P. (1978). Theoretical risks and tabular asterisks: Sir Karl, Sir Ronald and the slow progress of soft psychology. *Journal of Consulting and Clinical Psychology,*

Melton, A.W. (1959). The science of learning and the technology of educational methods. *Harvard Educational Review, 29,* 2, 96-106.

Menosky, J., & Moss, G. (1984). Computer worship. *Science 84, 5,* 4, 40-46.

Mischel, W. (1968). *Personality and Assessment.* New York: Wiley and Sons.

Mitchell, R. (1978). Testing the teachers. *The Atlantic Monthly, 242,* 6, 66-70.

Monaco, J. (1978). *Media Culture.* New York: Delta/Dell.

Ostry, B. (1978). *The Cultural Connection.* Toronto: McClelland and Stewart.

Papagiannis, G., Klees, S., & Bickel, R. (1982). Toward a political economy of educational innovation. *Review of Educational Research, 52,* 2, 245-290.

Plumb, J.H. (1971). *The Death of the Past.* Boston: Houghton Mifflin.

Popper, K. (1979). Creative self-criticism in science and in art. *Encounter, 53,* 5, 10-14.

Powell, E. (1985). The heresy that education must be useful. *Manchester Guardian Weekly, 132,* 2, (January 13) p. 10.

Rensberger, B. (1983). On becoming human. *Science 83, 4,* 3, 38-46.

Rosenberg, B., & White, D. (Eds.) (1964). *Mass Culture: The Popular Arts in America.* Toronto: Collier-Macmillan (Free Press).

Rosenberg, B., & White, D. (Eds.) (1971). *Mass Culture Revisited.* Toronto: Van Nostrand Reinhold.

Russell, B. (1965). *A History of Western Philosophy*. New York: Simon & Schuster.

Sanders, J.T. (1981). Teacher effectiveness and the limits of psychological explanation. *McGill Journal of Education, 16,* 1, 67-75.

Scheirer, M.A., & Kraut, R.E. (1979). Increasing educational achievement via self-concept change. *Review of Education Research, 49,* 1, 131-149.

Schrank, J. (1977). *Snap Crackle and Popular Taste*. New York: Delta/Dell.

Schur, E. (1977). *The Awareness Trap: Self-Absorption Instead of Social Change*. New York: McGraw-Hill.

Scriven, M. (1969). Psychology without a paradigm. In L. Breger (Ed.), *Clinical-Cognitive Psychology: Models and Integration*. Englewood Cliffs, N.J.: Prentice-Hall, pp. 9-24.

Secord, P.F. (1982). The behavior identity problem in generalizing from experiments. *American Psychologist, 37,* 12, 1408-1409.

Shore, R. (1979). Servants of power. *APA Monitor, 10,* 11, p. 2.

Skinner, B.F. (1953). *Science and Human Behavior*. New York: Free Press.

Skinner, B.F. (1971). *Beyond Freedom and Dignity*. New York: Knopf.

Skinner, B.I. (1984). The shame of American education. *American Psychologist, 39,* 9, 947-954.

Spence, Kenneth (1959). Relation of learning theory to the technology of education. *Harvard Educational Review, 29,* 2, 84-95.

Stanley, Manfred (1981). *The Technological Conscience: Survival and Dignity in an Age of Expertise*. Chicago: The University of Chicago Press/Phoenix.

Stent, G.S. (1975). Limits to the scientific understanding of man. *Science 187,* (21 March), 1052-1057.

Sternberg, R.J. (1983). Criteria for intellectual skills training. *Educational Researcher, 12,* 2, 6-12, 26.

Stephens, J. (1967). *The Process of Schooling*. Toronto: Holt, Rinehart and Winston.

Thurow, L. (1975). Education and economic equality. In D. Levine and M. Bane (Eds.), *The Inequality Controversy*. New York: Basic Books.

Travis, LeRoy D. (1975). Political economy, social learning and activism: Toward a theory of educational turmoil. Unpublished thesis, University of Alberta.

Travis, LeRoy, D. (1979). Hinterland schooling and branch-plant psychology: Educational psychology in Canada today. *Canadian Journal of Education, 4,* 40, 24-42.

Travis, LeRoy, D. (1980). On our defenses and underdevelopment. *Canadian Journal of Education, 5,* 2, 103-110.

Travis, LeRoy, D. (1983). Some reflections on the place of psychology in education and schooling (with some special attention given to teacher education). *Alberta Psychologist, 12,* 2, 3-6.

Travis, LeRoy D., & Violato, C. (1981). Mass media use, credulity and beliefs about youth: A survey of Canadian education students. *Alberta Journal of Educational Research, 27,* 1, 16-34.

Travis, LeRoy, D., Violato, C., & White, W.B. (1983). The transsituational consistency of behavioral persistence in children: A study of person-systems variability. Unpublished manuscript, University of British Columbia.

Travis, LeRoy D., & Violato, C. (1985). Experience, mass media use, and beliefs about youth: A comparative study. *Alberta Journal of Educational Psychology, 31,* 99-112.

Tuchman, G. (Ed.) (1974). *The TV Establishment.* Englewood Cliffs: Prentice-Hall.

Watts, D. (1980). Admissions standards for teacher preparatory programs. *Phi Delta Kappan, 62,* 2 (October), 120-122.

Wiener, Norbert (1967). *The Human Use of Human Beings: Cybernetics and Society.* New York: Avon.

Williams, R. (1968). *May Day Manifesto.* Hammondsworth, U.K.: Penguin.

Wills, Garry (1977). Imprisoned in the sixties. *The New York Review of Books, 23,* 21 & 22 (January 20), 20-23.

Wilson, J., Mitchell, L., Barclay, A., Jenkins, D., MacKay, B., Turner, D., & Young, J. (1984). Selecting "the best": Entry to initial teacher training in the colleges of education in Scotland. *Scottish Educational Review, 16,* 2, 88-103.

Yeats, W.B. (1967). *The Collected Works of W.B. Yeats* (Second Edition). London: Macmillan, pp. 242-245.

7

Culture, Mass Media and Youth

Youth or adolescence is as much a cultural phenomenon as it is a psychological one. Thus in order to fully understand the experience of youth and the behavior of young people within society, we must understand the culture that forms the background of behavior (Broughten, 1983; Enright, Levy, Harris & Lapsley, 1987). In modern society, popular or mass culture is increasingly dominated by mass media, particularly television (Fiske, 1987). In this chapter we will examine some important aspects of culture, values, mass media, and youth.

Values and Culture

Hannah Arendt has suggested that culture or any elements within it begins to be called a value[1] when it becomes a social commodity which can be cashed in on. Cultural phenomenon, contended Arendt, "are transformed into values when the cultural philistine [seizes] upon them as a currency by which he [can buy] a higher position in society" (Arendt, 1971). As a result, the basis for profitable business arises. Cultural phenomenon which are called values or valuable can be marketed as commodities. They are then, as Arendt pointed out, what values have always been, exchange values; and, in the exchange process, they are transformed "worn down like an old coin." So, for growth benefits and profits, the cultural value becomes popularized by the instruments of the market economy's entertainment and other industries. Unfortunately, in the process, the culture is debased; serious matters are trivialized and made vulgar. "Entertainment industry's mass media," wrote Arendt "ransack the entire range of past and present culture for material which is transformed so as to become entertaining . . . the transformations include the re-written, condensed, digested . . . kitsch" (Arendt, 1971, p. 98).

In these circumstances, the durable art and learning which embody serious culture is threatened. For the exchange market of consumer society is anti-cultural. Everything is fair game for commercial exploitation. Works of high quality and standards of excellence are placed in jeopardy. Standards, distinctions, discriminations, discipline, and intellectual functions fall helplessly before the formidable apparatus assembled and utilized in contemporary commercial processes. Scientific technology (mass communication media), philanthropy (the seller's flattering attribution of freedom, equality, perfectibility and limitless potential to all people), combine with the trappings of art (layout, style, and so on) to vulgarize everything for commercial ends.

A pertinent example of the ransacking of culture by the exchange market of consumer society for commercial ends was the Tutankhamen exhibitions that opened in the summer of 1978 in Seattle Washington. For months before the opening in July, the mass media (i.e., scientific technology) had saturated the environment with propaganda and advertisements in an effort to promote the "happening." A recurrent emphasis was put on the monetary value of the art objects, their age and the "mystique and unparalleled beauty" of ancient Egyptian art (i.e., the trappings of art). Books, pamphlets, newspaper advertisements and articles and television commercials and programs on the Tutankhamen "treasures" (i.e., values), as well as other promotional paraphernalia (towels, shirts, posters) had appeared before the opening and continued throughout the show.

By the time of the opening then, virtually everyone in the Pacific Northwest and elsewhere, has heard about the "event." When the display had been open for only several weeks and already throngs of people had flocked to the "cultural event," surprise was expressed.

The "unanticipated" reaction, one reporter hypothesized[2] was merely a manifestation of the American people's unquenchable thirst for knowledge and culture (i.e., philanthropy: the seller's flattering attributions).

However, the enthusiastic response by the public is probably more readily accounted for by the factors which one woman who was interviewed, admitted drew her there: "I've read and heard so much about it," she said, "that I thought I'd come and see for myself."

One government official summed up the purpose of the whole affair: "It brings in tourist dollars," he said. Another example of the exploitation of culture for commercial ends, was the exhibition "The Spirit Sings" at the Glenbow Museum in Calgary during the 1988 Winter Olympics. The exhibition was given massive world-wide visibility which was, ironically, enhanced by Native groups protesting the exploitation of their culture. Even the protests of the exploitation became an advertising phenomenon.

Values and Fashion

In consumer society, cultural criticism is subjected to and made impotent by an economy of values based on fashion. "Even the avant-garde," wrote Renato Poggioli in his book, *The Theory of Avante-Garde,*

> . . . has to live and work in the present, accept compromises and adjustments, reconcile itself with the official culture of the time and collaborate with at least some part of the public. These adjustments . . . compromises, reconciliations and collaboration, are also reciprocal and are rendered necessary by the intervention of a powerful factor, fashion . . . Fashion's task, in brief, is to maintain a continual process of standardization. (Poggioli, 1971, p. 79)

When a culture is industrialized, avant-garde activity is marketed for the entertainment of mass audiences. And since marketing transforms avant-garde activity into popular spectator or participatory sport, avant-garde effort becomes irrelevant and impotent. No criticism, whether it be embodied in art of politics or the disciplined revision of a body of knowledge, is strong enough to withstand vulgarization. In commercial culture, everything that is not easily understood or remediable must be transformed so that it is effortlessly understood or remediated. Condensations, digests, stereotypes and devices such as those Jacques Barzun called "thought cliche's" are utilized for these purposes. "The thought cliche," wrote Barzun,

> is an idea or a phrase contrary to fact which is clung to because it sounds familiar and feeds a half-attentive wish for thought. The thought cliche' does more than misinform; it weakens attention, curiosity and critical sense. (Barzun, 1961, p. 51).

We can compile a long list of terms and phrases which are currently used with great frequency as thought cliche's. Self-realization, self-concept, terrorist, women's movement, parenting, computer literacy, individuality, gifted, creativity, learning disabilities, inclusive education and information and knowledge explosion, are just a few examples that are common.

The debased ideas the thought cliche' represents are used for marketing as in the "knowledge industry" which might more properly be called the information or explanations industry. So, sociology has emerged as a part of popular (mass) culture (e.g., Alvin Toffler's *Future Shock* (1971) and *The Third Wave* (1980)). And so has psychology. The mass circulation of periodicals like *Psychology Today* indicates that pop soc has company in the form of pop psych. The likes of Thomas Harris' *I'm OK You're OK* (1973), Joyce Brother's *The Successful Woman* (1989), and Gloria Steinem's *Revolution From Within* (1992) and *Moving Beyond Words* (1994), are but four examples of explanation or how-to-formula books, of which the mass person is fed a steady diet. Nationally syndicated radio psychologists, Dr. Joy Browne and Dr. Ruth Wertheiner and television psychologist Dr. Don Dutton "Secret Lives," are electronic media versions of the pop psych books.

The press and electronic media treatments of politics, economics and education, have created a pop pol, pop ec, and a pop ed crit.[3] Radio talk-show hosts, journalists, television news commentators and a claque of assorted other philistines and propagandists, discuss the meaning of this or that political issue, prescribe cures for a moribund economy and pass judgment on what education can or should be. And the simple-mindedness and frivolous nature of the resulting discourse, bedevil those who are affected by serious and other sorts of contributions to the fields in question. This process has popularized and degraded the idea of cultural change. A dramatic example of the force of mass media, employing cultural degradation, is the role they played in spreading rebellion and turmoil in recent times.

The Marketing of Rebellion and Revolution

In the decade of the 1960s "revolution and rebellion" were marketed in the form of mass culture. Fragments and phrases from McLuhan and Marcuse, from Mills and Marx, were picked up, stripped of meaning and bandied around with regularity. Slogans from newsworthy and otherwise exploitable but serious and erudite activists, were appropriated, isolated, juxtaposed with trivia and otherwise exhausted of their remnants of meaning through their use in commercial apparatus. In Hollywood for example, a series of movies called the "now" movies, was produced in an attempt to cash in on "the revolution." Among the now movies that were produced, Nora Sayre, in her book *Sixties Going on Seventies*, listed "The Activists," "Getting Straight," "The Strawberry Statement," "RPM" and "Woodstock." The spectacle reminded Sayre that Graham Greene had said in 1935 that "there's always money to be picked up in a revolution" (Sayre, 1974, p. 73). To call what had happened, and what was happening revolution though, is to pervert language. What was being touted as revolution and revolutionary, were merely fads and fashions. Nevertheless, it served the entertainment industry well to pass mass culture off as revolution.

As the turmoil became commonplace, the fashionable phrases that had been manufactured by the entertainment industry served in lieu of analysis for both the mass media and many of the more recently activated pupils. An increasing incidence of activism and the coincident debasement of its ideology made radicalism attractive for the susceptible to mass media exploitations. And the exploitation was thorough. "Mind blowing" became a major industry. Rock music became connected with rebellion and, it was assumed, was an attack on all the despised values of the – "Establishment" – competition, commercialism, elitism and capitalism. However, it was obvious to even the most devout disciples of "the revolution" that no more than a tiny elite of rock musicians ever had any political content and those that did were soon corrupted by the allure of fame and fortune. Two of the great pontiffs of rock-'n-roll, John Lennon and Janis Joplin, wanted no misunderstanding.

"You say you want a revolution," sang John Lennon, "well

you can count me out."

Janis Joplin wanted no mistake made either, "My music isn't

supposed to make you riot," she said. (Hodgson, 1976, p. 341)

More recent rock stars who have rejected the ascription of social and political criticism to their music are Bruce Springsteen and Bruce Cockburn.

By 1971, the more perceptive members of the alternate press had come to realize what was happening. Craig Pyes for example, wrote an article under the title "The Rolling Stone Gathers Moss . . . [and] Money." And an article in *The Los Angeles Free Press* warned that some publications profited from promoting rock as rebellion – "the economism of the guitar" (the belief that music can solve the problems of the world). Despite these criticisms, this form of profiteering has continued to the present with "We Are The World," "Band Aid" and the rock benefits in England for the victims of soccer violence constituting three examples.

Nevertheless, in the late 1960s, many seemed to believe that rock music could cure the ills of the world (many still believe it). The exploitation by the mass media and its associated entertainment industry spread a set of debased ideas about social change. The faddish belief that changes in hair-styles, in dress, in argot, in sexual behavior, drug usage and schooling constitutes a rejection of the social order, and a preparation and instrument for revolution, became widespread. The mass media could readily associate honorific and attractive images and loaded but empty words with the fashions sold as the indispensable values of a revolutionary life style. Companies hired house hippies to sell their wares. Hip enterprise paid off. Thus, Alan Trachtenburg could describe the irony of the supposedly new style which was advertised as being more authentic:

> The fact that it is also fashionable does not seem to occur to its defenders . . . Revolution has come to mean something dangerously close to sheer impulse . . . Is the 'American Way' really in danger from such gestures? This has become a pleasant fantasy and . . . a piece of vicarious entertainment for the middle-class itself. (Trachtenburgh, 1971, p. 128-129)

And so that the middle-class could be vicariously entertained and transformed into docile but appeased consumers, simple isolated slogans and catchwords like participation, freedom, individuality, creativity, revolution and innovation filled the air. While the masses were entertained and congratulated by this vapid flow, mass media people and other entrepreneurs, collected the profits.

Making Change: Politics and Education

All along of course, liberal capital has placed a high premium on scientific and technological creativity, innovation and reform. Since criticism is a *sine qua non* of innovation and reform, its value to the liberal economy and state has been readily apparent to at least some members of the owning class. For reform and innovation in both state and industry was regarded by elements of the owning class, from at least the early nineteenth century, as a means of retaining and enhancing the value of their possessions and reducing the power of the radical critics. As a consequence, an expert on motivation in advertising could eventually write: "we have institutionalized change and innovation as part of our American way of life" (Martineau, 1971, p. 162). Similarly, Joseph Featherstone, a thoughtful educator, could observe that "what Americans call education innovation turns out with uncanny frequency to be 'reform entrepreneurship' or saleable, marketable, profitable but usually ineffectual techniques to forestall ethnic and class warfare" (Featherstone, 1972, p. 29). So for example, computer based instruction, teaching machines, micro-computers and assorted other gadgetry which were touted as great educational innovations, turned out to be little more than profiteering by manufacturers and sellers of these products.

As the nineteenth century reached its close and industrialization continued to proceed, adjustments had to be made to both assist the process and accommodate its economic, political and social effects. Intellectual labor then, gained value. Criticism and reform were formalized, professionalized and isolated in professional enclaves (e.g., legislatures). By these means, the criticisms of the dissidents could be anticipated and the dissidents themselves along with their ideas could be put to use in the service of the liberals' interests as professional critics and academics. And if the critical work could be made attractive, criticism could be purchased and dissidents co-opted and trouble spots and weaknesses within the system could be identified and treated through reforms. In the bargain, the hegemony of property could be preserved.

When the advantages and benefits of membership were seen as an improvement on the conditions of life and work that were endured by most people in the USA, the ranks of the learned professions swelled. Education it was assumed -- mistakenly as it turns out – was the Great Equalizer. One of the reasons that education was believed to be the Great Equalizer, stems from the peculiar meaning that Americans typically attach to the term "equality." The liberal ideology of the American state, emphasizes equality of opportunity rather than equality of conditions. Most Europeans on the other hand, are more concerned with equality of condition since the American definition equates equality with freedom to grasp opportunity which ensures a sizeable population of tramps as well as millionaires. The idea of equality of opportunity as the expression is habitually used by Americans, presupposes inequality since "opportunity" means opportunity to rise above others in a class society. It simultaneously presupposes equality, since it implies that the inequalities embedded in class society have to be counteracted. "Equality of opportunity could only become a reality in a society without classes" observed T.B. Bottomore in his *Elites and Society,* "the notion itself would then be otiose" (Bottomore, 1966, p. 148). In any case, the notion of equality of opportunity is both conservative and self-contradictory. Nevertheless, the liberal consensus held that widespread education would ensure equality of opportunity. And in the post-war abundance of liberal America, this assumption seemed to be borne out. Some people could and did acquire a lot which was more comfortable that of their parents and the modal condition of people generally. The success stories (often used as such in the mass media) seemingly demonstrated the validity of the Great American Myth that if you only worked hard enough, acquired enough education and grasped opportunity when it presented itself, success was inevitable. And so it came to be accepted as a general rule that success, defined as joining the ranks of the learned professions (e.g. physicians, lawyers, and so forth), was possible for everyone. The high visibility which was given to exemplary success stories in the mass media, seemed to fortify this rule. The rule, is of course, that only a tiny minority can ever achieve success and it is only those from truly exceptional circumstances that rise above abject mediocrity. The behavior of the mass electronic and printed media however, serves the liberal ideology well in blurring the reality of inequality that is inherent in a system dominated by monopoly capital.

But, those who "arrive" (achieve success) can sell their critical services to maintain their gains and reinforce the myth that all are equal and everyone can win in a competitive system. Thus, professional ranks serve as a buffer between owners and less privileged workers. The latter work to acquire the benefits and status of the more privileged servants – the professionals whose advantages and functions are often related to the control of the many, less privileged servants. It is out of this context that some of the more sophisticated social critics and activists of the late 1960s regarded university professors and other professionals as modern equivalents of Plato's guardians in that their selection, preparation and management of students, allegedly made students into ideal servants for the owners or rulers – in the manner of Plato's artisans.

By the time innovation in industrial processes made new mass media available, the industrial system had created conditions which required a literate mass. The necessity for propaganda had been created:[4] the state needed propaganda to govern; the owners needed it to manage labor and market; the individual needed it to face his condition because, to quote T.S. Eliot, human kind cannot bear very much reality.

Jacques Ellul (1973) has argued that modern man is in the position of needing outside help since the complexity of life presents him with the necessity for making decisions on matters about which he is ignorant. Ellul felt that events and developments are beyond most people's intellectual scope and that the world's economic and political problems cannot be grasped. Thus propaganda offers a remedy by providing the illusion of explanation and understanding.

Mass Media and Popular Opinion

Matthew Arnold, some one hundred years ago, expressed concern about the necessary degradation and simplification that values and ideas must undergo when they are prepared for mass consumption. Those who control mass communications and structure the propaganda, he feared, will exercise control and influence by "trying to give the masses, as they call them, an intellectual food prepared and adapted in the way they think proper for the actual condition of the masses. The ordinary popular literature is an example of this way of working on the masses" (Brown, 1963, p. 133).

The power that the mass media has in forming popular opinion and values though, has superseded by a noticeable margin, even Arnold's greatest fears. The mass media provides both the explanations and some of the subject matter that needs to be explained. News, daily created, selected and presented according to formulae, creates a need for explanations and analysis. Serious commentary, advice columns, public affairs programs, pop psych and the like furnish the explanations and answers which give a semblance of order and coherence to the myriad of detail. So when Walter Cronkite ended his broadcasts with "And that's the way it is . . . " what he really meant was that's the way it has been made to look like by selection and fabrication into a saleable product. For the news as we know it, is not merely information, or even merely processed information, but is a balanced combination of both "show" and "business" a kind of corporate vaudeville. N.B.C. official Reuven Frank, in reference to the production of the news, said that television journalism's main purpose is to provide joy, sorrow, shock and fear. The transmission of information is not a particularly important element (Epstein, 1973, p. 39).

At the same time that we are frightened, shocked, made happy or sad, self-images, self-justifications are donated; social, political, and moral standards are codified; ideas are standardized; categories, thought patterns and opinions are supplied; collective beliefs are formed; stereotypes and prejudices are hardened; fashions are created and values are sold. Among the values peddled are popular opinions and criticisms which are also used to sell other values from soap to entertainment. In short, ubiquitous mass media creates a common sense of what comprises "common sense." It also reinforces what Ortega Y. Gasset suggested was the fantastic assumption that uncommon sense is necessarily inferior to the common variety (Ortega, 1961).

Those who flatter the ignorant, together with athletes, beauty queens, and assorted other celebrities or heroes, comprise a vicarious aristocracy with whom bonds of community are reinforced in the mass' fantasies by simplification and homogenization.

Ancient man's idols – animals, trees, stars, statues – have been replaced by modern man's idols – politicians, actors and actresses, sports heroes, *Playboy* bunnies and even prostitutes and pornographic stars.[5] Armed with the capital, labor motivation research, market analysis, mass media and other devices and skills, the commercial apparatus can condition and exploit appetitive habits or predispositions for fashions which glitter with values. Opinions are sold alongside soap, values with pantyhose, ethics with deodorant, and ideas with toilet paper.

The commercial apparatus is assisted and advised by a sophisticated and highly developed body of motivational research. The work in this area has emphasized the following values as being particularly useful and effective programs designed to modify the behavior of those who encounter mass media: individuation (self-indulgence, self-expression, self-congratulation); adventure (romance, fun, thrills, excitement); newness (modernity, being up to date, having the latest, being in style); and youth (sex, action, health, virtue as well as the other values listed and more). Indeed, the value of youth has been associated so frequently with other values that a cult of youth and a youth industry exists where selling to the id is the norm.[6]

The Cult of Youth

Studies of the popular culture also provide a rich documentation of how and for what ends the cult of youth is cultivated (Burgess & Gold, 1985; Fiske, 1987). What is commonly called a youth culture is in fact, really a provided culture wittingly and cleverly manufactured and sold to exploit the purchasing power of the affluent young. This provided culture is also aimed at the youths' more elderly counterparts who frequently reflect a sense of nostalgia for their lost youth and a fear of death in ways they imitate in dress, language and behavior generally, the attractive young. The creation of artificial wants, the objects of which are what Arendt called values, is facilitated by saturating the environment with a thicket of unreality: illusions, synthetic novelty, and happenings –

planned, planted or incited pseudo-events.[7] And, considering the ubiquity of the mass media, this thicket of unreality finds its way into the awareness of all but the most discerning people. As millions of people spend millions of hours attached to millions of television sets by a kind of psychological umbilical cord, the illusions and myths that dance inside the mysterious screen, are bound to diffuse into the collective psyche.

Within the provided culture of commercial music, dance, dress, argot, comportment and so forth, certain themes are repeated emphatically. Along with the associations of youth with vivacity, action, sex, modernity, adventure, and health, there is an emphasis recurrently placed on physical appearance and a disdain and hostility toward adult institutions and conventional social and moral customs.

A subtle message, intended to inspire mass audiences to greater heights of consumerism, accompanies the incessant repetition of the provided culture's themes. If certain artificially and arbitrarily created standards of dress, behavior, physical appearance, speech patterns, sexual mores and body cleanliness are not met, people are repeatedly told, they are somehow deficient, defective, out of style, morally compromised, and stuffed shirts. Unsightly hair and body odor offend; bad breath can cause the loss of loved ones or worse; incorrect toothpaste usage can ruin one's sex life; odors in the home can upset the bridge game; spotty glasses can destroy a party and show the hostess up for what she really is – incompetent – and graying hair may cause a marriage breakup at the very least. Thus, the very instrument that emphasizes individuality, creativity and spontaneity, ensures that the masses are made homogeneous in their opinions, beliefs, consumption of material goods, comportment, appearance, values, ideas and moral standards.

Pseudo-events designed to market the fashionable values, carefully contrived to constitute the image of the celebrity, are prototypical. For example, the latest, glamorous hero (e.g. Mick Jagger), or anti-hero (Michael Jackson is a recent example especially in view of the child molestation charges), with his retinue of managers, flunkies, promoters and groupies (young girls who offer sex to the star), is to appear. He is besieged by a youthful crowd who have broken police cordons (arranged before hand by the promoter of the contrived but seemingly spontaneous happening). The action is video and audio taped; broadcast and televised live; and filmed for a soon to be released documentary. The audience of the documentary will be mainly other young people who have come to find out about what the young think, or value, or feel, or want, or believe in, or object to, or are concerned about. Or perhaps the film may be about what the young are trying to tell their supposedly out-of-touch, morally compromised but authoritarian and repressive elders. The celebrity meanwhile, has dropped an apparently spontaneous phrase which is quickly reproduced on decals, posters, shirts and other paraphernalia which might include the latest hit record (also soon to be released) or ghost written book. As one pop-culture impresario confided to Stuart Hall and Paddy Whannel, the authors of a study of popular culture: teenagers have their tastes changed for them. What is valued depends upon what is supplied. Entrepreneurs attempt to "pre-empt and manipulate tastes directly . . . always in the direction of some [lucrative, commercial] formula" (Hall & Whannel, 1964, p. 282). Hall and Whannel concluded that the sociology of teenage tastes can be studied as an aspect of the sociology of the entertainment business.

Youth Culture

A great amount of effort has been expended by the commercial apparatus in the last twenty or so years, in the selling of trivial differences by marketing a counter culture of youth. The youth culture is generally represented as a self-sufficient, youth-generated, peer-dominated, spontaneous expression of a set of teenage values and precocious activity. The deceptive appearance of this youth culture, however, can be readily traced to the activities of the commercial apparatus. The youth culture can be readily created and maintained because of the emotionally charged content, the de-emphasis of verbalization, the simple-mindedness of the subject matter and the limited emotions that are dealt with in this commercially prepared (synthetic) life style. The easy maintenance of this life style of course, is not hindered by the vanity, ignorance and limited experience of the young which, in proportions, may be faithful reproductions of those qualities in all people. The promoters of pop culture flatter adolescents and exploit their ignorance by incessantly praising them for being more sophisticated, progressive, and creative than their allegedly pathetic elders. Moreover, it is widely asserted that adolescents have created a new and better culture. Many social and behavior science people write books and articles and speak in serious tones of the youth culture, the great influence of peers, and the decline of adult influence. M. Munns' "The Values of Adolescents Compared with Parents and Peers" (Munns, 1972), Theodore Roszak's *The Making of a Counter Culture* (Roszak, 1969), and David Elkind's *All Grown Up with Nowhere to Go* (Elkind, 1984), are three examples of works of this kind.

Nevertheless, we may have witnessed a decline of sorts, though it is not a decline of adult influence *per se* as some people are wont to purport. Perhaps what has occurred is the decline of the influence of adults who have in the past, exercised power without rivals, as the influence of other adults has increased. So when once such adults as parents and teachers and other traditional adult models may have exercised considerable influence, this power may have been recently shifted to sports heroes, entertainers and other entrepreneurs. This development unfortunately, has been mystified by people who mistakenly take the effects to be the cause: Peer influence (the effects of the increased influence of businessmen whose instruments include the mass media) is supposedly diminishing adult influence. Peer influence, thanks to the mass media accounts, is mistaken as the cause rather than the result of the common factors which informs teenage actions.

Although some characteristics of a small minority group may set a trend when, for example, it is publicized as news or human interest, the commercial collosus can readily co-opt and transform the object of interest (creeping ordinariness) for its own purposes through the use of simplification, stereotype, and its other wealth of capital, devices and techniques.

Christopher Lasch observed how people deceive themselves by believing they, on their own, transform themselves and their surroundings when they adopt (unconsciously) the rhetoric and debased ideas which saturate their experience. "Revolution" wrote Lasch, "became the emptiest of cliche's and was used indiscriminately by radicals, liberals, conservative, advertising men, and the media, usually to describe changes that were non-existent" (Lasch, 1971).

So, through the debasement of ideas and the commercially prepared life style, eventually, anyone could for example, become a week-end hippie. All that was necessary was the appropriate accouterments to effect the appearance formula, the modification of drug usage and the appropriate conventions of speech. Then, of course, it is only a small step to adopt this comportment during the entire week. The modern young executive could substitute drugs at rock concerts, for alcohol at the cocktail party.

Similarly, promoters could increase their gate receipts by paying fees to Yippie celebrities (who had books to promote) to appear at rock concerts. Or, television producers could take advantage of the novelty: the aura of verisimilitude and contemporaneity; the action and adventure; the romance, sex and youth, associated with student activism and protest, by featuring such material in not only the news, documentaries and drama; but real living activists could be exploited (and co-opted) on talk shows. The producer of one such series called "Head-Master," gave as the description of the "now" subject matter: student militancy, marijuana, sex, education. Indeed, the mutual exploitation of mass media and activists, was an important phenomenon in both the spreading of turmoil and its subsequent elimination. The transformation of serious attempts to produce the dramatic changes in the economic, political and social arrangements (which were implicit in the profound criticism) into various sorts of fashions and fads, effectively neutralized any force that could have caused change, because, since it was transformed into fashion, could not endure for long. This is not to argue of course, that factors like a down turn in the economy, repression, co-optation, extinction of behavior for lack of instrumental effects, fatigue, self-indulgence and replacement of one youth population by another as time passed, were unconnected to the decline of turmoil. Clearly, such a complex phenomenon as student activism does not readily lend itself to a single-factor explanation. Nevertheless, transformation of activism into mass culture was a key factor in its subsequent elimination.

However, just as the seriousness of political activists' program, content, and goals was compromised and reduced when their words and actions were sandwiched between "sit-com" and commercials; and just as their criticisms were reduced to hackneyed pap by the commercial blending machine's commentators and imitators, the association of youth with activism and turmoil through the same events, could become a nearly universal habit of mind.

As the commercial blending machines were reducing serious criticisms to mindless patter, they were at the same time building up stereotypes of youth. The build-up of a stereotype or image of youth could be expected because, as we have seen, mass media content is governed primarily by profit seeking and format. The ambiguities and complexities of events and phenomena are eliminated through simplification procedures based on selective principles, style, tone, and design to build-up stereotypes that are offered for dealing with reality. Both large audiences, which are demanded for profit maximization, and format which must be designed to minimize costs and maximize sales, require simplification and repetition.

Youth Stereotypes in Mass Media

In this manner, several stereotypes and images of youth have been given massive and sustained visibility in the mass media. One of the effects of the high visibility that these stereotypes have been given may well be that of making the mythical image come true. For not only are the adults who have commerce with adolescents part of the audiences; adolescents themselves are also bombarded with the definitions inherent in the image. All the ingredients of the self-fulfilling prophecy are present.

The stereotypes of youth that have been presented in mass media roughly coincide with each decade of this century beginning in the 1920s. As is currently and have been depicted in mass media, eight distinct stereotypes of adolescence have received massive and sustained visibility. These will be described in turn.

Modern day depictions of the 1920s youth characterize those adolescents as fun loving, carefree, and self-indulgent. This period in history was one of general prosperity and economic expansion and perceptions of children and youth are influenced by economic and political ideologies (Brighten, 1983; Reigel, 1972). Enright et al (1987) have also shown that descriptions of adolescents have varied over time in consonance with particular economic conditions. The depictions of youthful gaiety in the 1920s then, reflects what is now generally believed to have been the magnanimous mood of the period.

Conditions changed drastically in the 1930s. A world wide recession had taken hold with resultant poverty, misery, unemployment and a general dislocation. Accordingly, mass media depictions of youth portray adolescents as quite different than the previous stereotypes. No longer full of youthful gaiety, the adolescent of the period is depicted as troubled and socially aware. Life under the conditions of the "dirty thirties" is portrayed as bleak and young people are shown to have questioned their social system as something that had clearly gone wrong. Some Americans were still enthusiastic about the Russian Revolution that had occurred in 1917, and young people are shown as considering the Soviet experiment as a viable possibility. Despite heightened awareness and a social conscience, however, the young of the 1930s did not actively protest or rebel against the social system – that would be left to a later generation.

The end of the 1930s was marked by the cataclysm of World War II in which both Canada and the United States were active participants. The previously dislocated youth now had a clear goal: young men went to war and young women assisted the war effort from home. From these changes arose the next youth stereotype: the 1940s heroic and patriotic adolescent. If the young of the previous decade were confused and purposeless, and young men of the 1940s are depicted as committed, full of purpose, reliable, patriotic and even heroic. Meanwhile, the young women are depicted as loyal, trusting and committed to the national effort in whatever way they could (usually in some domestic capacity). Both men and woman, however, are portrayed as serious and heroic.

As the war ended and the 1940s gave way to the 1950s, the image of youth underwent a change as well. The United States emerged from World War II triumphant. It was the most powerful nation on Earth with a vibrant economy and a hopeful outlook to the future (Hodgson, 1976). Contrasted to Europe and Japan, Canada and the US promised the good life. The image of youth under these conditions paralleled that of the stereotype in the 1920s. Both were periods of economic expansion and young people were promised full participation in these prosperous conditions. The good life was defined by material possessions and full-fledged consumerism. As the highly successful American war industry turned to produce peace time materials, everyone was promised participation including the young with their growing affluence. Adolescence for that period was depicted as a time of silliness and flightiness, a time which adults had to suffer through as their teenagers would pass through this stage. Thus the dominant image is one of adolescents as fools. By the end of the 1950s, however, the images began to change. The adolescent as portrayed by James Dean in "Rebel Without a Cause" began to dominate. As the title of the film indicates, the young were becoming rebellious without understanding the underlying reason. The storm and stress theme was emphasized and adolescents were portrayed as emotionally turbulent, ready to strike out, frequently for no apparent reason.

By the 1960s one image or stereotype of youth which was given high visibility, characterized the young person as a visionary. The visionary was distinguished by a purity of moral vision. In the way of the prophets, he was also a victim: he was betrayed, exploited, coerced, neglected and otherwise mal-treated by a venal adult world which perpetuated corruption through insidious manipulations of the perceptive, insightful, knowledgeable, morally precocious but powerless young. Yet, this embodiment of wisdom and virtue, in the face of victimization by adult corruption, could be a man of action. Faithfully repro-duced in the stereotype, was the simple but time-honored dramatic formula (for thrilling and instructing the unsophisticated) consisting of a saint-like creature battling heroically against the immense forces of evil that surround him.

The counterpart of the active visionary or hero, is the anti-hero – a kind of passive visionary victim. A popular song by Kris Kristofferson which recounted the trials and tribulations of a youth described as "a hairy headed hippie" for example, contains all the elements of the passive visionary victim. Kristofferson juxtaposed the suffering of the precociously moral youth who is finally held down by "three strapping brave policemen" that cut his hair, with the circum-stances that resulted in the nailing of "the Savior to the cross."

The elements shared by both the passive and active visionaries however, were youth, moral superiority, precociousness, powerlessness and victimization. And both these stereotypes were given sustained visibility on television, in movies, and in popular literature. Edgar Z. Friedenberg's popular book *The Vanishing Adolescent*, was probably implicated in the creation and popularization of what its author later admitted, was an unfortunate portrayal. The book, said Friedenberg "pictures the young as engaged in a gallant, if hopeless struggle with the timidity and corruption of the adult world, usually in the person of school officials. It would have been more accurate to picture the American youth rather as already deeply implicated in the deeds and values of their culture. Mostly they go along with it and sincerely believe that in doing so they are putting down trouble makers and serving the best interests of their community" (Schrag, 1967).

By the early 1970s, protest, dissent and rebellion began to wane and once again, a new stereotype of youth arose in mass media: the me generation. Young people, in this stereotype, are depicted as turning away from "causes" and becoming concerned with self and gaining an advantage. In marked contrast to the visionary victim, the youth of the me generation did not care about social causes, their fellow humans or justice. Moreover, they endorsed "the establishment" and certainly did not want to overthrow it or challenge it. The main goal was to fully exploit its potential and to get for oneself as much out of it as possible. A popular song of the 1970s "Looking Out for Number One" by Bachman-Turner Overdrive succinctly summed up the stereotype.

The 1980s again produced a new stereotype of adolescence. This image of young people as "serious but troubled" shows adolescents as committed to school and work but troubled by economic uncertainty, the possibility of nuclear war, world famine and sexual behavior. Unlike the visionary, however, the serious but troubled young are not willing to protest or rebel as they see these problems fatalistically and hopelessly. Many of the elements of this youth stereotype appeared in an article "Growing Pains," in *Macleans* (1987). In it many young people report uneasiness and pessimism about the future. With reference to young people, a 17-year-old high school graduate wrote, "If a generalization had to be made, I would say most of us are scared . . . our attitudes are colored by hints of pessimism that arise from other issues that confront us . . . Part of that pessimism may reflect the fact that we do not seem to be as idealistic as some past generations. (*Macleans*, 1987, Sept. 7, p. 45). Rather than idealism, these youth are depicted as pursuing (vigorously and competitively) an education, career and work. In contrast to the visionary victim, the serious but troubled adolescent is realistic rather than idealistic.

A new stereotype of adolescence has emerged for the 1990s. This image of young people as "young fogies" shows adolescents as world weary, living with broken families, AIDS, a drug abuse epidemic, environmental degradation, economic uncertainty, a collapsing world order and a bleak future generally. In this stereotype, these weighty problems of adult society are cast upon young people before they are prepared to deal with them. The image of the world weary "young fogy" is depicted in television shows such as "Blossom," "Fresh Prince of Belaire," and "Beverly Hills 90210." This image also abounds in the print media and was captured aptly in a cover story in *Maclean's* (Feb. 22, 1993). Robertson Davies' statement that "One of the really notable achievements of the 20th century has been to make the young old before their time," is cited favorably in this cover story as capturing the essence of today's youth. So like the 1980s "serious but troubled" youth, this new image of young people characterizes them as troubled and pessimistic. Beyond that, they are also depicted as jaded, world weary and hopeless, forced into the concerns and problems of middle age before their time.

Stereotypes and the Self-Fulfilling Prophecy

The high visibility of these mythical stereotypes, in the way of the self-fulfilling prophecy, may make the stereotype come true since the very object of the stereotyped perception accept this image. One study of the visionary victim stereotype (Meisels & Canter, 1971) uncovered evidence which indicates that some young people indeed had been affected by the flattering stereotype. In this study, when students were asked to indicate the extent to which they, their parents, and their peers agreed with the statements about contemporary issues, it was found that on political issues like the Vietnam war, students were in agreement with what they perceived their parent's values to be, but differed with what they perceived to be peer values. The data from this study further shows that students consistently overestimated in a progressive direction, the attitudes of their peers. The students though, were far less progressive than they or others imagined. Finally, a striking feature of the data is that these students placed their own positions between those of their parents on one side and their peers on the other, with remarkable consistency. Obviously, these students themselves were influenced by the propaganda about a generation gap which didn't exist.

In studies by Travis and Violato (1981, 1985) it was found that both undergraduate university students and veteran teachers adhered to stereotypes of youth as depicted in mass media. Moreover, those subjects who watched more television and read more magazines where the stereotypes were prominent than subjects who used less of this media fare, tended to place the most credence in the stereotype. A second factor which influenced adherence to the stereotype was credulity; the more credulous subjects were of television depictions, the more they adhered to the stereotypes. Subjects who were sceptical of mass media generally, placed little credence in the youth stereotypes. Clearly, mass media depictions do influence the perceptions of at least some viewers.

Summary and Conclusion

Business, to recapitulate, with its array of advertisers and mass media resources, develop and cultivate the worship of youth by unremittingly conditioning an association of its wares with youth, virtue, wisdom and all things valuable. The effects of this are not merely commercial. All distinctions are obliterated under the general categories which are used. When the visionary stereotype was prominent, for example, even the most ignorant adolescents were instructed by *Time* to "educate your parents." That cover story entitled "When the Young Teach the Old Learn" which appeared in the August 17, 1970 edition of that magazine, includes testimony from millionaire businessmen and prominent politicians about how "my children wakened me." One parent proclaimed that "my sons put me on the right track." "My children," another confessed "transformed me from a clod into a citizen." Of the serious, but troubled adolescents of the 1980s, one psychologist wrote, "today's children are growing up scared" (Gerber, 1987, p. 37). A teacher reported that today's youth are concerned about "getting their careers organized. They want to earn money." Such items, in combination with other manifestations of youth worship, may well convince some young that they feel, think and behave in consonance with the stereotype. And, some adults may come to believe this as well.

By way of summary then, a stereotype of youth based on some characteristics of a small elite typically is given high visibility. A "generation gap," for example, which did not exist was repeatedly and unrelentingly advertised as being real. Pessimism and concern about nuclear war with its resultant holocaust, is constantly advertised as a real and dominant aspect of today's youth. These stereotypes and the attendant propaganda produce in some adults and adolescents a tendency to perceive youth as a homogeneous mass, the defining attributes of which are inappropriate. Distinctions are obliterated by the thought cliche' when the global category youth is used in such familiar generalizations as "today's youth are alienated" or "today's youth are troubled about their future." This process and its consequences is aptly described by Ezra Pound's observation that "when the application of a word to things goes rotten, i.e. becomes slushy and inexact, or excessive or bloated, the whole machinery of social and individual thought goes to pot."

When images of the sort we have discussed are repetitiously placed before the various publics (which include the young), we should not be surprised if many come to believe the popular images. Youth exists within a culture and, as we have seen, there are many reasons why the cult of youth and subsequent stereotypes should be manufactured by mass media. A full understanding of adolescence, however, requires a critical analysis of the host culture including the political economy, educational ideology, values and mass media function of that culture.

Notes

[1]Values are frequently taken to be abstractions: categories of thought which are, as Charles Anderson of the University of Alberta puts it, "conceptions of the desirable." For our purposes, this definition is useful and we can take as referents for the abstractions, those sorts "of objects, conditions or events which are reinforcing to man, either immediately or in the long run" (Anderson, 1965).

[2]This reporter appeared on the sensationalistic American public affairs program, 20/20.

[3]i.e., popular politics, popular economics and popular educational criticism.

[4]Jacques Ellul has defined propaganda as "a set of methods employed by an organized group that wants to bring about the active or passive participation in its actions of a mass of individuals, psychologically unified through psychological manipulations incorporated in an organization." Ellul insists that the popular assumption that propaganda necessarily involves lying is not only inaccurate, but misleading as well: "For a long time propagandists have recognized that lying must be avoided. In propaganda truth pays off . . . " Obviously, truth or facts can be used in many different ways.

[5]e.g., Xaviera Hollander, the author of *The Happy Hooker,* and Linda Lovelace, the leading actress in the pornographic film "Deep Throat."

[6]Selling to the id refers to the sales tactics that associate products with love, sex, success and so on such that the products are in effect, promised to bring pleasure in addition to their prescribed function. So for example, adolescents are frequently told, via the mass media apparatus, that their sexual or interpersonal problems and difficulties can be wiped away as easily as they can wipe away their pimples, with a dab of Clearasil. Other examples of selling to the id are only too common and can be found in abundance in advertisements peddling toothpaste, hair shampoo, clothing of various sorts, cars, cosmetics, soap, stereo equipment, furniture as well as in many others.

[7]Pseudo-events possess the following characteristics: they are staged primarily for the purpose of being reported and reproduced on a massive scale; they are arranged for the convenience of the mass media; time and other relations are distorted so that the resulting ambiguity can arrest interest or attention (and thereby be newsworthy); they are generally intended to be self-fulfilling prophecies (Boorstin, 1964, p. 12).

References

Anderson, C.C. (1965). Psychological contributions to education: The origin and modification of values. *Alberta Journal of Educational Research, XI,* 4.

Arendt, H. (1971). Society and Culture. In B. Rosenberg & and White, D. (eds) *Mass culture revisited.* Toronto: Van Nostrand Reinholt.

Bandura, A. (1971). *Social learning theory.* Morristown, N.J.: General Learning Press.

Barzun, J. (1961). *The house of intellect.* New York: Torchbooks.

Blair, G.M., & Pendelton, C. (1971). Attitudes of youth toward current issues as perceived by teachers and adolescents. *Adolescence, VI,* 24, 424-428.

Boorstin, D. (1964). *The image. A guide to pseudo-events in America.* New York: Harper.

Bottomore, T.B. (1966). *Elites and society.* Middlesex: Penguin.

Brown, J.A.C. (1963). *Techniques of persuasion: From propaganda to brainwashing.* Middlesex: Penguin.

Brighten, J. (1983). The cognitive developmental theory of adolescent self and identity. In B. Lee and G. Noam (eds.). *Developmental approaches to the self.* New York: Plenum.

Burgess, J.A. & Gold, J.R. (eds). (1985). *Geography, the media and popular culture.* New York: St. Martin Press.

Busby, L. (1988). *Mass communications in a new age.* Glenview: Scott, Foresman.

Ellul, J. (1973). *Propaganda. The formation of men's attitudes.* Toronto: Vintage.

Elkind, D. (1984). *All grown up and nowhere to go.* Boston: Addison Wesley.

Enright, D.R., Levy, V.M., Harris, D., & Lapsley, D.K. (1987). Do economic conditions influence how theorists view adolescence? *Journal of Youth and Adolescence, 16,* 541-559.

Epstein, E.J. (1973). *News from nowhere.* New York: Random House.

Featherstone, J. (1972). Reconsideration: John Dewey. *The New Republic.* July 8, 27-32.

Fiske, J. (1987). *Television culture.* London: Methuen.

Gerber, GT. (1987). Growing pains. *Macleans.*

Gorz, A. (1968). *Strategy for labor.* Boston: Beacon.

Hall, S., & Whannel, P. (1964). *The popular arts.* Toronto: Hutchinson.

Hodgson, G. (1976). *America in our time.* New York: Doubleday.

Jahoda, M., & Warren, N. (1965). The myths of youth. *Sociology of Education.*

Kopkind, A. (1974). T.V. Guide. *The New York Review of Books.*

Lasch, C. (1971). Can the left rise again? *New York Review of Books.*

Martineau, P. (1971). *Motivation in advertising.* Toronto: McGraw-Hill.

Meisels, M., & Canter, F. (1971). A note on the generation gap. *Adolescence.*

Munns, M. (1972). The value of adolescents compared with parents and peers. *Adolescence.*

Ortega, Y. Gasset, J. (1961). *The revolt of the masses.* London: Unwin.

Poggioli, R. (1971). *The theory of the avante-garde.* New York: Harper and Row.

Reigel, K. (1972). Influence of economic and political ideologies on the development of the self. *Psychological Bulletin, 78,* 129-141.

Roszak, T. (1969). *The making of a counter culture.* Garden City: Doubleday.

Sayre, N. (1974). *Sixties going on seventies.* New York: Doubleday.

Schrag, P. (1967). Education's romantic critics. *Saturday Review.*

Stelzer, R. (1971). Keeping up with the Jone's teenagers. In Voice of America Forum Lectures. *The Teenagers' World.*

Trachtengurgh, A. (1971) Culture in rebellion: Dilemmas of radical teachers. In B. Rosenberg and White, D. (eds) op. cit.

Travis, L.D. & Violato, C. (1985). Experience, mass media use and beliefs about youth: A comparative study. *The Alberta Journal of Educational Research, 31,* 99-112.

Travis, L.D. & Violato, C. (1981). Mass media use, credulity and beliefs about youth: A survey of Canadian education students. *The Alberta Journal of Educational Research, 27,* 16-34.

8

Images of Adolescence in English Literature

Images of youth abound in the electronic and print media and a number of studies have now been conducted to analyze how youth and adolescents are depicted in these media. Ewen (1977), for example, has suggested that a concept or symbol of youth has become crystallized in modern society. Youth has become a "broad cultural symbol of renewal, of honesty, and criticism against injustice" (Ewen, 1977, p. 139). In addition to this broad cultural symbol, youth has also been depicted in varying ways in both the print and electronic mass media.

In the mid sixties, Adelson (1964) observed that mass media stereotypes of youth had undergone change. The prevailing stereotype had been one of the "adolescent as fool": "callow, flighty, silly and given to infatuations, wild enthusiasms and transient moodiness" (Adelson, 1964, p. 1). By the mid sixties and into the 1970s, the stereotype of youth depicted adolescents as "visionaries" who were distinguished by a purity of moral vision (Adelson, 1964: Travis & Violato, 1981). Other studies reported by Bandura (1964), Jahoda and Warren (1965), and Musgrove (1964) have also drawn attention to the stereotypes or images of youth which have been given massive and sustained visibility in the mass media. More recent studies (Travis & Violato, 1985) have focussed on the effects that these images have on the perceptions of youth by teachers, and the depiction of youth in British newspapers (Falchikov, 1986; Porteous & Colston, 1980). The main and most stable characteristic of adolescence throughout these depictions is that it is a time of turbulence or "storm and stress." While many current studies of adolescence indicate that this developmental period is relatively peaceful and smooth for most people, this notion of "storm and stress" has its roots in antiquity (Coleman, 1978) but was formalized by G.S. Hall (1904) in his description of adolescence as a period of *sturm und drang*.

While the debate as to whether or not adolescence is a period of storm and stress has not yet been concluded, this has been a persistent and durable image of youth. It is our aim in this paper to examine the extent to which "youth" in English literature has been portrayed in consonance with the above images. To this end, we shall analyze some selected works of major authors from medieval times to the modern era. Works of the following authors will be analyzed: Chaucer, More, Locke, Shakespeare, Bayly, Milton, Prior, Wordsworth, Coleridge, Hazlitt, and Dickens.

The medieval writer Geoffrey Chaucer (1340-1400) is generally acknowledged as one of the first great poets who wrote in English. In his *Prologue to Canterbury Tales,* he characterized youth in the person of the squire. Chaucer's description of the squire contains at least three dimensions of youth stereotypes. First, the squire is depicted as frivolous and devoted to love and silly pleasures. The youthful squire, twenty years old, was ornately dressed in spring symbols (Throughout the millennia Spring has been used as a symbol of rejuvenation and has been associated with love, sex and joy). Chaucer described the squire's apparel in the lines, "Embroidered was he like a medow/all full of fresh flows, white and red." (Chaucer, 1963, p. 6-7). The allusion to spring is continued as the squire "was as fresh as is the month of May." (p. 7, L. 92). Not only was he adorned in spring attire, but his personality matched the season. Like spring he was joyful not sombre. This joyful demeanor is described in the lines, "singing he was, or fluting all the day." (p. 7, L. 97-98). The second stereotyped attribute of adolescence which the squire possessed was lust and turbulent sensuality: "so hot he loved, that at night time He slept no more than does a nightingale." (P.7, L96). The third cliched characteristic of the squire was his adventuriousness and activity. Chaucer's squire was a warrior who could joust and "well could he sit on a horse, and fairly ride." (p. 7, L. 94). He was also "wonderfully agile, and great of strength." In the cavalry the squire had been engaged in several campaigns where, as Chaucer explained, "He bore himself well." (p. 7, L. 84). Finally, Chaucer provided us with insight into the medieval ideal for the education of a son of the nobleman. Upon completion of his education, the squire "could songs make and well composed, joust and also dance, as well draw and write." (p. 7, L. 99). This was a liberal education in medieval times: studies in music, art, literature, skills in warfare, and an initiation into courtly behavior.

While Chaucer described aspects of society as they were, Thomas More (1478-1535) who wrote *Utopia* in 1516, projected a vision of a perfect society, of things as they might be, not necessarily as they were. More envisioned universal education, euthenasia and divorce by mutual consent, as well as many things we are still striving for, such as the abolition of a materialistic society. In his spirit of farsighted reform, More gave humane explanations for personal and social problems. He attributed the motivation for crime to poverty, he suggested that incompatability led to divorce (not just wanderlust or a mean spirit), and he suggested that the lack of an ability to love is due to lack of security.

More's Utopian youths were distinguished from children (who were defined as five years old or less) and adults (by marriage). A Utopian maid was permitted to marry at age eighteen and a male at age twenty-two. More does not contrast the emotional or psychological nature of youth to adults and children suggesting that he did not believe that youths were fundamentally different. This implies a smooth transition from childhood to youth to adulthood.

More's main concern for youth was education. He believed that primary education should be universal and that the responsibility for the education of children should fall to the priests. More placed emphasis on moral training as well as on academic learning. Pre-dating modern psychologists, More felt that education should be based on an understanding of the human mind and how children learn. More anticipated Locke's *tabula rasa* ("clean slate") view of the human mind (1790) by almost two hundred years and thereby prescribed early indoctrination "while children are still at an impressionable age" and that they be "given the right ideas about things ... and if thoroughly absorbed in childhood, these ideas will persist through adult life" (More, 1965, p. 83).

As well as predecessing Locke, More's view was in consonance with Bandura's (1977) social learning theory that one learns by observing others. Incorporating social learning principles such as modelling (Bandura, 1977), More suggested utilizing meal times as a formal learning experience. Youths and adults were to be seated together but staggered such that they would necessarily have to interact. More prescribed this on the following basis: "The theory being that the respect for the older generation tends to discourage bad behavior among the younger ones" (1965, p. 83). The older people should not "monopolize the conversation about serious matters, but draw out the younger ones" (p. 84). While More underscored the malleability of the human mind, he also incorporated a hereditary component into his "learning theory." When the young are to select a job, for example, More suggested that most children should be brought up to do the same work as their parents "since they tend to have a natural feel for it" (p. 75).

More did not portray adolescents as self centered and flighty; at least he did not consider this a necessary aspect of adolescence. Unlike Chaucer's youth, More's were to eschew mood swings and rapid emotional change. Adults were to impose strict discipline on the young and any deviance from acceptable codes of behavior would result in public disgrace for the responsible adult. Disgrace was not the only punishment to be imposed for deviance, however. Succumbing to sensual pleasures such as pre-marital sexual intercourse, for example, could disqualify the offender from marriage. This harsh punishment does not mean that More believed that youth did not have excessive passion, rather it suggests that he believed that it could be and should be controlled.

William Shakespeare's (1564-1616) depiction of youth has greater similarities to Chaucer's rendition than to More's. For Shakespeare, youth was the transition between childhood and adulthood and was characterized by excess, passion and sensuality. This is in marked contrast to More's view of youth as rather unremarkable and inconspicuous. In the play, *The Merchant of Venice,* for example, two women, Portia and Nerissa are to be disguised as young men. They discuss the transition in roles to which they must adapt to be convincing. Portia explains that she must,

> ... speak of frays like a fine bragging youth, and tell Quaint lies, How honorable ladies sought my love, which I denying they fell sick and died.
> ... And twenty of these puny lies I'll tell .... (Shakespeare, 1974, L.68-75)

A similar depiction of youth as a stage of exuberance and excess is again given in *Henry IV, Part I.* King Henry admonishes his son and chastises him for bad behavior. In exasperation, the King asks the adolescent how he could engage in such behavior. The prince replies

> Myself as many I am charg'd withal; yet such extenuation let me beg. I may for somethings true, wherein my youth hath faulty wand'red and irregular ....
> (L. 20-28)

The extenuating circumstances that the Prince invoked were, in short, that he was going through the stage of adolescence of which he is confident that he can eventually purge himself.

In the play, *Romeo and Juliet,* Shakespeare makes little direct reference to youth. We do know that Juliet is not yet fourteen as her father explains that "she hath not seen the change of fourteen years." (L. 9). A prospective suitor, Paris, however, does not consider this as too tender an age for marriage as he replies that "younger than she are mothers made" (L. 12). We are not directly told much about Romeo either. We know that he was a "virtuous and well governed youth" with a prediliction for falling in love. Romeo was just getting over the loss of another when he fell hopelessly in love with Juliet.

In *Romeo and Juliet,* Shakespeare's view of youth is best understood by an examination of the actions of young people in the play. Adolescents engage in irresponsible sword play which leads to the unexpected and tragic death of Mercutio and Tybalt at the hands of the impassioned Romeo. This irresponsible and impassioned behavior is also seen in the relationship between the two protagonists. Romeo and Juliet fall in love and become "betrothed in one night." This hasty, hot-blooded behavior is again displayed when Romeo, believing Juliet dead, kills himself. Foolishly, he has committed suicide on a mistaken belief which could easily have been corrected with less impulsivity. When Juliet finds Romeo dead, she too kills herself without any hesitation. Such then, is Shakespeare's depiction of youth as irresponsible, impulsive, quick to passion, and hot headed. These qualities frequently lead to disaster and self destructive behavior.

This depiction of youth in the plays of the latter 16th century underwent considerable change in the didactic prose of the early 17th century. Though Lewis Bayly (1565-1631) was a contemporary of Shakespeare, his world view was markedly different. Bayly, an Anglican divine, titled his major work which he dedicated to the Prince of Wales, *The Practice of Piety* (1602). According to one expert, this work "was so much venerated by the Puritans, that certain envious clergymen asserted that its authority, was for its admirers, equal to the Bible" (Baker, 1975, p.515). In this treatise, Bayly characterized youth as a distinct stage. He saw adolescence as a time when people lacked character and were governed by indiscretion. While this description is not in opposition to Shakespeare's view, the latter was amused by youth and even sympathetic to it. Bayly, however, was not amused by the coarseness of youth, Indeed, he was intolerant of it and characterized youth in the following way:

> What is youth but an untamed beast all whose actions are rash and rude, not capable of good council when it is given and ape like delighting in nothing but toys like babies? (Bayly, 1975, p. 517)

Moreover, youth was a "burden" to "be rid of," "a servile state of . . . bondage," "not worthy of description." While this stance may appear harsh, Bayly was even less sympathetic to the infant who was ". . . a brute having the shape of man . . . conceived in the heat of lust, the secret of shame and stain of original sin . . . all imbued in the blood of filthiness" (Bayly, 1975, p. 516).

These descriptions of adolescence and infancy are in consonance with elements of psychodynamic theory as formulated by Freud in the early 20th century. Freud similarly characterized the human infant as instinct driven and id dominated, reveling in its own excrement and infantile sexual urges. Later, in adolescence, the person was depicted as a slave to powerful, indomitable sexual urges which can only be "disguised as civilized behavior" (Freud, 1930). Contemporary psychoanalytic views of adolescence and youth continue to emphasize the "dark" nature of humans as did Bayly (Blos, 1979).

Though John Milton (1608-1674) was a Puritan, he was more benign in his views about adolescence than was Bayly. Like many other commentators, Milton saw youth as a stage in development and felt that education should be the primary focus at this time. He proposed a program for educating boys from twelve to twenty one. Milton's suggested curriculum began with simple books and proceeded to more difficult reading as the youth's became more intellectually sophisticated. The core of Milton's curriculum included mathematics, logic, and literature. To round things off, Milton also suggested including the study of music, wrestling, and military manoeuvre in the young man's curriculum (Baker, 1975, p.775).

Milton not only saw youth as a time for intellectual development, but like Chaucer, he saw youth as a time of joy. In his poem *L'Allegro* (The Happy Man) (Baker, 1975), Milton utilizes the symbols of youth to describe the carefree, pleasure-seeking man. Associated with spring the happy man invokes "jest and youthfull jollity." (L.26). The young man disdains insightful contemplation but prefers the pleasures of daydreaming:

> There let Hymen oft appear in saffron robe, with taper clear, and pomp, and feast, and revelry, With mask and antique pagentry: Such sights as youthful poets dream on summer eves by haunted streams. (L.125-130)

Although Milton accepts these pleasures as appropriate for a youth, the same does not apply for an adult. He degrades the simple pleasures by comparing them with the ecstasies of the contemplative life in the companion poem to *L'Allegro, IL Penseroso* (The Contemplative Man). In these lines he expands on his feelings towards the contemplative life:

> But let my due feet never fail
> To walk the studious cloisters pale,
> And love the high embowed roof . . .
> And bring all heav'n before mine eyes.
> (L.155-165)

By the end of the 17th century Puritanism had become a word of contempt, and Locke had published his *Essay Concerning Human Understanding*. There is little in the literature of the period, however, to suggest a change in the way adolescence was viewed. For the poet Mathew Prior (1664-1721) youth was still viewed as a stage where pleasure, passion and love were of prime concern. This concern is alluded to in Prior's poem *Ode*. In the first stanza there is a sense of urgency as Prior invokes love to come while he is in the proper stage for accepting its benefits, without the caution of reason, which interferes with love's course in latter years. He wrote:

While blooming Youth, and Gay Delight
Sit on thy rosey cheeks confest,
Thou hast, my Dear, undoubted Right
To triumph o'er the destin'd Breast.
My reason bends to what thy Eyes ordain.
For I was born to Love, and Thou to Reign.
(Noyes, 1956, p.223)

For Prior time not only decays the body, "soon must those glories of thy face/the fate of vulgar beauty find," (L. 15-16) but dulls the mind as well, "A talking dull Platonic I shall turn;/Learn to be civil, when I cease to burn" (L. 29-30). Because of this impending decay he urges love to "Haste Celia, haste, while Youth invites" (L. 37).

Following Prior, the Romantic Era began and prevailed in a spirit of revolt against the dogma of "reason." This reason consisted of a narrow rationalism and posited a mechanized universe that was to be explored by a mechanized philosophy. The intellectuals rejected the reductionism and static view that inhered in this philosophy. Ultimately the concept of a mechanistic universe was discarded for an evolutionary perspective (Noyes, 1956).

A dominant idea of the Romantic period was primitivism – the belief that the natural or earliest conditions of humanity are glorious and ideal and are reflected in children and childhood. Both Wordsworth and Coleridge expressed confidence in the intuitive wisdom of the child, and Byron's ideal sexual love called for a removal of the barrier of a civilized society, which is where he placed his youth Don Juan with the maid Haidee. Modern day views similarly reflect this primitivism in a "sentimental" view of the child (Kessen, 1979) who is depicted as natural, intuitive and uncorrupt.

William Hazlitt (1778-1830) wrote of how feelings in youth identify us with nature, where we have strong feelings and little experience (Noyes, 1956, p. 676). He says that in youth "we are like people intoxicated or in a fever, who are hurried away by the violence of their own sensations . . . " (Noyes, 1956, p. 676).

William Wordsworth (1770-1850) was a poet who, like Piaget (1980), saw adolescence as a unique stage of cognitive development. He believed the thoughts of youth were different in quality from the child's, not only because of experience, but because of a change in the internal workings of the mind, irrespective of external influences. On the other hand, he saw childhood as a stage of innocence aptly portrayed in the poem *We are Seven*. Wordsworth tried to explain to a child of eight years that her brother and sister are dead, so that only five children remain, but the child's reply was "Nay, we are seven" (Noyes, 1956, p. 251).

For Wordsworth, a child is innocent and close to God. The naivete of a child is again shown in the poem *Ode*. Here he explained how age and experience shut us off from nature: "shades of the prison house begin to close upon the growing boy" (L. 67-68). The youth, however, is not fully divorced from nature; he is just farther removed from it than the child because "The Youth, who daily farther from the east/must travel, still is nature's priest" (L. 71-72). But by manhood the separation from nature, God and the vision of heaven is completed. Thus,

Wordsworth wrote "At length the man perceives it die away/and fade into the light of common Day" (L. 75-76). Though youth is a stage and the cognition of youth may differ from that of adults, there is the implication in the ode that experience contributes to this separation. Wordsworth explained how the innocence of the child is lost: "Full soon thy soul shall have her earthly freight,/and custom lie upon thee with a weight."

Whatever the reason, Wordsworth wrote about a change in thought processes for youth as explained in *The Prelude*:

> ... My seventeenth year was come;
> And, whether from this habit rooted now
> My own enjoyments; or the power of truth
> Coming in revelation, did converse.
> (L.385-393).

Wordsworth reiterated the difference in kind between the thoughts of a youth and of a grown man in *Lines Composed a Few Miles Above Tintern Abby*. As a youth his perceptions of nature were "Their color, and their forms, were then to me/an appetite; a feeling and a love/that had no need of a remoter charm." As, that time passed and Wordsworth became a man, his view changed: ". . .For I have learned/to look on nature, not as in the hour/of thoughtless youth; but hearing often times/the still, sad music of humanity" (L. 79-81). It can be concluded from Wordsworth's use of the word "nature," that he meant that which is valuable in life. Therefore, if appreciation of nature changes as one ages, it can be assumed that one's world view has likewise changed. The process of development is thus the process of moving away from nature.

It was in the nineteenth century when the sentimental view of children and childhood gained impetus and became conventional wisdom (Teeter, 1988). Industrialization, child labor laws, urbanization, mass education, and mass communications, were some factors that created a fertile ground for writers like Charles Dickens to enhance and popularize the sentimental view of children during the early Victorian Era. Dickens depicted children as helpless and abused pawns who struggled for survival against a predominantly uncaring adult population. The institutions and the social economic framework of industrial England were depicted as adversaries to the welfare of children.

Two of the most popular child characters of Dicken's stories are *Oliver Twist* and *David Copperfield*. Oliver Twist was orphaned while his mother, husbandless, died giving him birth. Oliver was relegated to the parish system where life for children was horrific:

> Oliver should be "farmed," or in other words, that he should be despatched to a branch-workhouse, some three miles off, where twenty or thirty other juvenile offenders against the poor laws, rolled about the floor all day, without the inconvenience of too much food or too much clothing. (Dickens, 1959, p.4)

Dicken's primary intention, however, was not to expose the harsh realities of a cruel system. His self declared purpose was to show that good can be found amidst the vilest evil. Dickens shared the modern day trait theorists belief (e.g. Allport, 1966) that stable dimensions of the person can transcend the demands of situational exigencies (Violato, 1988). Thus young Oliver was subjected to all sorts of adversity but the young man's strength of character allowed him to rise above many unfavorable circumstances. Dickens, in the third edition of *Oliver Twist*, wrote in the preface: "In this spirit . . . I wish to show in little Oliver, the principle of Good surviving through every adverse circumstance." Thus Dickens established the belief in the inherent goodness of children in the domain of popular culture. This belief was logically extended into adolescence by the 1960s, when the image of the young person as a "visionary victim" became popular (Adelson, 1964). Like Oliver, the latter day visionary was morally precocious but was exploited and maltreated by a venal adult world. Both in the stereotype created by Dickens and in that created by mass media in the 1960s (Travis & Violato, 1981), was the simple but time-honored formula consisting of a saint-like creature battling against the immense forces of evil which surround him.

David Copperfield did not suffer the deprivations that Oliver Twist did. Although his father died when he was young, David had a caring and protective mother to watch over him until he was eight. When his mother remarried, however, David came to know the adversities of life. His step-father arranged for David to attend a school where intimidation and humiliation were the main pedagogical strategies employed. David's formal education ended abruptly when his mother died and at ten years old he became a laborer "in the service of Murdstone and Grinby." (Dickens, 1921, p. 116). Even at eleven, David began to show adolescent impetuosity spending all his money on sweets, thus depriving himself of a proper meal (p. 121). Later on, at the age of seventeen, and in stereotyped adolescent fashion, David fell hopelessly in love (p. 203). Throughout the novel Dickens uses David to depict the "storm and stress" of adolescence and the transcendent nature of the "Goodness" of youth. For both David Copperfield and Oliver Twist, life was full of turbulence, excess, and passion.

In the foregoing discussion, it is evident that there is little variance in the perceptions and depictions of youth over the generations. With the possible exception of More, all of the authors reviewed in the present chapter from Chaucer to Dickens, depicted youth as a stage in development in which sensuality, excess, and turbulence prevail in one form or another. More's concept of youth as a time of smooth transition from childhood to adulthood is noteable in that it is the exception and in agreement with modern day empirical views (Coleman, 1978).

Theories about human development and about the nature of humans are imbedded in the broader sociocultural milieux in which they are conceived and thrive (Kessen, 1979; Reigel, 1972). Thus in addition to mass media stereotypes (Adelson, 1979; Falchikov, 1986. Travis & Violato, 1981), perceptions of children, adolescents and their development are influenced by economic and political ideologies as well (Broughton, 1983; Buck Morss, 1975; Ewen, 1977; Reigel, 1972). In a recent empirical study by Enright, Levy, Harris and Lapsley (1987), for example, it was shown that descriptions of adolescents have varied over time in consonance with particular economic conditions in the twentieth century. In times of economic depression, psychological theories have emphasized adolescent immaturity and emotional instability while in more prosperous times, youths have been depicted as mature and stable (Enright, et al, 1987). It is clear then, that sociocultural, political, economic, and ideological factors influence perceptions of youth as do particular mass media stereotypes.

In the present chapter we have tried to show that youth has been depicted in remarkably similar ways in major literary works from Chaucer to Dickens. The main themes of youth in these works is that it is a time of turbulence, excess, and passion. This characterization of adolescence as a time of storm and stress is in consonance with G.S. Hall's (1904) depictions.

If adolescence is indeed a cultural artifact (Adelson, 1979. Bandura, 1964; Kessen, 1979) whose nature is influenced by a number of factors, then it is likely that it is also an expression of the literary voices which have preceded us for hundreds of years. For a fuller understanding of how adolescence is conceived, it is necessary to examine the sociocultural milieux in which it is embedded. Since the literary tradition of a culture forms an important part of the sociocultural environment, the way that we conceive of adolescence in modern times is reflected in English literary tradition.

References

Adelson, J. (1979). Adolescence and the generalization gap. *Psychology Today, 12,* February 1, 33-37.

Adelson, J. (1964). The mystique of adolescence. *Psychiatry, 27,* 1-5.

Allport, G.W. (1966). Traits revisited. *American Psychologist, 21,* 1-10.

Baker, H. (1975). *The later renaissance in England.* London: Houghton Mifflin.

Bandura, A. (1977). *Social learning theory.* Englewood Cliffs, NJ. Prentice-Hall.

Bandura, A. (1964). The stormy decade: Fact or fiction? *Psychology in the Schools, 1,* 224-231.

Bayly, L. (1975). *The practice of piety* In H. Baker, *The later renaissance in England,* London: Houghton Mifflin.

Blos, P. (1979). *The adolescent passage: Developmental issues.* New York: International Universities Press.

Broughton, J. (1983). The cognitive developmental theory of adolescent self and identity. In B. Lee and G. Noam (Eds.)., *Developmental approaches to the self.* New York: Plenum.

Buck Morss, S. (1975). Socio economic bias in Piaget's theory, and its implications for cross-cultural studies. *Human development, 18,* 38-49.

Chaucer, G. (1963). *Canterbury Tales.* New York: Barron's Great Neck (Translated by Vincent Hopper).

Coleman, J.C. (1978). Current contradictions in adolescent theory. *Journal of Youth and Adolescence, 7,* 1-11.

Dickens, C. (1959). *Oliver Twist* London: Collins Publishers.

Dickens, C. (1921). *David Copperfield* London: Sotheran Publishers.

Enright, D.R., Levy, V.M., Harris, D, & Lapsley, D.K. (1987). Do economic conditions influence how theorists view adolescents? *Journal of Youth and Adolescence, 16,* 541-559.

Ewen, S. (1977). *Captains of consciousness: Advertising and the social roots of consumer culture.* Toronto: McGraw-Hill.

Falchikov, N. (1986). Images of adolescence: An investigation into the accuracy of the image of adolescence constructed by British newspapers *Journal of Adolescence, 9,* 167-180.

Freud, S. (1930). *Civilization and its discontents.* London: Hogarth Press.

Hall, G.S. (1904). *Adolescence* (Vols. I and II). New York: Appleton.

Jahoda, M. & Warren, N. (1965). The myths of youth. *Sociology of Education, 38,* 2.

Kessen, W. (1979). The American child and other cultural inventions. *American Psychologist, 34,* 815-820.

More, T. (1965). *Utopia.* Markham, Ontario: Penguin (Translated by Paul Turner).

Musgrove, E. (1964). *Youth and social order.* London: Routledge.

Noyes, P.R. (1956). *English romantic poetry and prose.* London: Oxford University Press.

Piaget, J. (1980). Intellectual evolution from adolescence to adulthood. In R.E. Muuss (Ed.)., *Adolescent behavior and society.* (3rd ed.). New York: Random House.

Porteus, M.A. & Colston, N.J. (1980). How adolescents are reported in the British press. *Journal of Adolescence, 3,* 197-207.

Reigel, K. (1972). Influence of economic and political ideologies on the development of developmental psychology. *Psychological Bulletin, 78,* 129-141.

Shakespeare, W. (1974). *Plays. The riverside Shakespeare.* Boston: Houghton Mifflin. The Middle Ages to the Modern Period.

Teeter, R. (1988). The travails of 19th century urban youth as a precondition to the invention of modern adolescence. *Adolescence, 28,* 15-18.

Travis, L.D., & Violato, C. (1985). Experience, mass media use and beliefs about youth: A comparative study. *The Alberta Journal of Educational Research, 31,* 99-112.

Travis, L.D, & Violato, C. (1981). Mass media use, credulity and beliefs about youth: A survey of Canadian education students. *The Alberta Journal of Educational Research, 27,* 16-34.

Violato, C. (1988). Interactionism in psychology and education: A new paradigm or a source of confusion? *Journal of Educational Thought, 22,* 4-20.

9

Stereotyped Television Portrayals of Adolescents

While a great deal has been written about the image of youth depicted on television, very few of these analyses are based on empirical work (Peterson & Peters, 1983; Travis & Violato, 1989). Many writers (e.g., Ewen, 1977; Murray, 1980) have indicated that several stereotypes dominate television portrayals of youth, but these have been identified through non-empirical content analysis methods. Current research and theory indicate that television generally influences the world view of its audience to some degree by conveying elaborate images of everyday life (Peterson & Peters, 1983). Television may also be a major vehicle for spreading a "language and culture of youth" throughout society with a focus on issues such as sexuality, heterosexual relationships, music preferences, clothing tastes, friendship ties, peer acceptance, and the use of drugs and alcohol (Peterson & Peters, 1983; Roe, 1983; Travis & Violato, 1989). Given that the nature of adolescent stereotypes as depicted on television are not well understood and that these stereotypes may influence audience belief and behavior, the present study aimed to employ an empirical technique (factor analysis) to identify the main elements of adolescent images as depicted on television.

It is thought that television provides representations of adolescents who behave in more deviant ways than other age groups and may encourage the belief that heightened turmoil is part of the teenage role (Roe, 1983; Signorelli, 1987; Seltzer, 1982; Travis & Violato, 1985). Although current scholarship has challenged descriptions of adolescents as being in conflict with the adult world (e.g., Coleman, 1980; Offer, Ostrov, Howard & Atkinson, 1988; Violato & Holden, 1988), very different images of youth culture are commonly depicted on television. Adolescents are commonly represented as confused, rebellious, and preoccupied with sex, alcohol, and drugs (Peterson & Peters, 1983; Travis & Violato, 1989). These themes in the televised portrayal of adolescents are given widespread and repeated visibility. Youth is frequently associated with vivacity, action, sex, and modernity, with an emphasis on physical appearance and a disdain and hostility toward adult institutions and conventional social and moral customs (Travis & Violato, 1989).

The foregoing formed the general basis of the present study. The main purpose of this study was to empirically examine the nature of adolescent stereotypical portrayals in current television programming. Specifically, factor analysis was employed to empirically derive the main stereotype elements of adolescence as portrayed on television.

Method

Observational recordings were made from 60 episodes of 13 different television programs amounting to approximately 30 hours of content, including advertisements (which were not included in the analysis). Two raters were used to independently rate 39 episodes (65% of the data); the inter-rater reliability was r = .96. All of the episodes were broadcast on television during March and April of 1991.

The shows observed included Degrassi High, Northwood, Wonder Years, Doogie Howser M.D., Fresh Prince of Bel Air, Blossom, Growing Pains, A Different World, Married With Children, Family Ties, Family Matters, Roseanne, and The Cosby Show. These particular shows were selected because of their main focus on adolescent characters and themes. This sample of programs, although not exhaustive, was considered to be a representative sample of prime-time and popular programming appealing to both adult and adolescent audiences.

A checklist of 13 stereotypes variables, identified as main elements of adolescent stereotypes by Travis and Violato (1985, 1989) and Peterson and Peters (1983), was used to rate adolescent behavior presented in the observed television episodes and included rebellion, criticism of adults, conflict with adults, manipulation of adults, storm and stress, egocentrism, peer pressure and acceptance, fashion and materialism, values and modernity, sexuality and dating, social awareness, and adult-like maturity.

An adolescent using drugs or breaking laws would be instances of rebellion. Adolescent criticism of adults would be exemplified by youths laughing at, mocking, or insulting an adult, whereas an argument or disagreement would constitute conflict with adults. An adolescent lying to an adult to get out of a situation or avoid punishment would be considered a manipulation of adults. Storm and stress would be exemplified by exaggerated turmoil relative to the actual problem severity. An example of egocentrism would be an adolescent focusing on the implications for self when another individual is having problems. Peer pressure and acceptance would be constituted by acceptance or rejection of an adolescent by a peer group or peer group pressure to conform.

Fashion and materialism, values and modernity, and physical appearance are variables that relate to the "culture of youth." Fashion and materialism would be depicted by a focus on money, clothes, hair and material goods and by "being cool." Values and modernity would be reflected by referents to teen idols or examples of adolescent preferences, such as rap music. Any references, positive or negative, to body or face would be examples of physical appearance. Sexuality and dating, also related to the youth culture, would be typified by adolescent instances of physical contact, such as kissing, discussions of the opposite sex, or sexual commentary, both connotative and denotative.

Adolescent social awareness would be constituted by examples of environmental consciousness or references to issues such as racism. Adult-like maturity would be typified by examples of adolescent behavior that is very moral, wise, or sensitive, not necessarily in keeping with the character, and typically occurs at the end of a program once an adolescent has "learned their lesson." All of these were coded for their frequency of occurrence in the televised episodes.

Results

The stereotype variables rated on the checklist were totalled and rank-ordered according to the highest frequency of occurrences which was also expressed as a percentage of the total number of occurrences (see Table 9.1). Sexuality appeared as a stereotypical theme by a high degree, with appearance themes falling in the middle of the hierarchy and rebellion (rank = 11) falling low in the hierarchy.

The frequency of occurrence of the themes were intercorrelated (Pearson product-movement) and the resulting matrix is reported in Table 9.2.

This matrix was then factor analyzed (principal component extraction) and based on a Scree Test and the amount of variance accounted for, it was decided to extract four principal factors. This solution provided the most parsimonious model and the four factors (eigenvalues = 5.58, 2.06, 1.63, 1.37) accounted for 81% of the total variance in the data. These four factors were then rotated to the normalized varimax criterion and the resulting matrix is reported in Table 9.3.

Factor 1, labelled Rebellion and Peer Orientation accounted for 53.0% of the common variance while Factor 2 (Culture and Values) accounted for 19.6%, Factor 3 (Anti-Adult) 15.4%, and Factor 4 (Precocious and Serious) accounted for 12.0% of the common variance. As can be seen from Table 9.3, five variables (rebellion, conflict with adults, storm and stress, peer pressure, social awareness) load heavily on Factor 1, while five variables (manipulation of adults, egocentrism, values and modernity, physical appearance, sexuality and dating) load on Factor 2. Three variables load on Factor 3 (criticism of adults, conflict with adults, fashion and materialism) and two factors load on Factor 4 (social awareness, adult maturity.

Discussion

The results of the present study indicate that the stereotypical themes of adolescence as identified by several writers (Jahoda & Warren, 1965; Ewen, 1977; Peterson & Peters, 1983; Travis & Violato, 1985, 1989) are clearly present and widespread in popular or prime-time televised programs focused on adolescent characters. The main strength of the present study was the use of empirical methodology to identify the main elements of adolescent stereotypes. Four main factors were identified through factor analysis: (1) Rebellion and Peer Orientation, (2) Adolescent Values, (3) Anti-Adult, and (4) Precocious and Serious.

Table 9.1
Rank Order of Stereotyped Themes
Based on the Frequency of Occurrence

Rank	Theme/Stereotype	F(n)	F(%)	F(n)Hour
1	Sexuality/Dating	272	20.4	9.1
2	Criticism of Adults	163	12.2	5.4
3	Egocentrism	142	10.7	4.7
4	Fashion/Materialism	116	08.7	3.9
5	Values and Modernity	106	08.0	3.5
6	Physical Appearance	94	07.1	3.1
7	Manipulation – Adults	93	07.0	3.1
8	Conflict with Adults	86	06.4	2.9
9	Storm and Stress	79	05.9	2.6
10	Peer Pressure/Accept	77	05.8	2.6
11	Rebellion	41	03.1	1.4
12	Social Awareness	33	02.4	1.1
13	Adult-like Maturity	31	02.3	1.0
	Total	1333	100%	
	Average/Episode	22.2		

The theme found to occur most frequently in the present study was sexuality and dating. In a study by the National Federation for Decency (1977), it was found that there were 2.8 sexual references per hour on general prime-time television programming over a 15 week period. The rate of sexual references on general prime-time programming during the 1980s has remained constant or increased somewhat (Liebert & Sprafkin, 1988). By contrast, in the present study it was found that were 9.1 references to sexuality and dating per hour of programming with a focus on adolescent characters, approximately 3 times as frequent as in general prime-time programming. Clearly sexual references are frequent on television generally and especially prominent in shows with adolescence as content. Less frequent, but still nevertheless prominent, are themes of adult criticism, egocentrism, fashion, modernity, and physical appearance.

Table 9.2
Pearson Product-Moment Intercorrelations
of the Adolescent Themes

Variable	1	2	3	4	5	6	7	8	9	10	11	12	13
1 Rebellion	-												
2 Adults-Criticism	12*	-											
3 Adults-Conflict	67	35	-										
4 Adults-Manip.	45	11	50	-									
5 Storm and Stress	69	-03	63	25	-								
6 Egocentrism	15	-06	24	46	14	-							
7 Peer Pressure	83	-14	56	30	76	23	-						
8 Materialism	46	51	59	40	11	30	48	-					
9 Modernity	38	-10	44	61	21	74	23	34	-				
10 Appearance	38	07	44	37	18	74	35	58	87	-			
11 Sex/Dating	59	13	36	41	46	62	57	51	52	66	-		
12 Social Aware	62	-08	41	03	53	22	75	30	21	42	54	-	
13 Adult Maturity	-14	31	14	04	07	-06	-10	-14	01	02	01	41	-

*All coefficients have been rounded to two decimal places and the decimal point has been dropped.

Factor 1 – Rebellion and Peer Orientation – was the most prominent in the data accounting for 53% of the common variance. This is consistent with depictions of adolescents in other popular media such as newspapers (Falchikov, 1986; Porteous & Colston, 1980), as well as in serious English literature (Violato & Wiley, 1990), and influential theories of adolescence (e.g. Blos, 1979; Erikson, 1968). The second factor – Adolescent Values – based on a youth or adolescent culture accounted for approximately 20% of the common variance. As with Factor 1, adolescents have been widely depicted as having a youth culture or a counter culture (Friedenberg, 1959; Lasch, 1978, 1984; Roszak, 1969) which is spontaneously generated by adolescents. The Anti-Adult factor – the third to emerge – is separate from the rebellion and peer orientation in that it is specifically focused on criticism of adults in authority (parents, teachers) and directed towards adolescent fashions. This is a modern day depiction of the fictitious generation gap (Adelson, 1979). Finally, factor 4 – Precocious and Serious – reflects a particularly prominent stereotype of the 1980s of the adolescent as serious and concerned about social issues, war and peace, and other global concerns (Travis & Violato, 1989; Violato, 1991).

Table 9.3
Factor Matrix Orthogonally Rotated
to the Normalized Varimax Criterion

Variable	Rebellion & Peer Orientation Factor 1	Adolescent Values Factor 2	Anti-Adult Factor 3	Precocious and Serious Factor 4
Rebellion	.88	.23	.15	-.19
Criticism of Adults	-.17	-.08	.89	.28
Conflict with Adults	.59	.26	.58	.05
Manipulation of Adults	.20	.55	.36	-.17
Storm and Stress	.85	.06	.03	.07
Egocentrism	.04	.91	-.04	-.00
Peer Pressure/Accept.	.94	.17	.06	-.09
Fashion/Materialism	.29	.37	.75	-.18
Values and Modernity	.13	.92	.05	-.02
Physical Appearance	.20	.88	.17	.08
Sexuality and Dating	.49	.63	.16	.07
Social Awareness	.76	.21	-.07	.51
Adult-like Maturity	-.00	-.02	.11	.95
Eigenvalue	5.58	2.06	1.63	1.37
% Common Variance	53.0	19.6	15.4	12.0

The widespread visibility of youth stereotypes in mass media (particularly adolescent television shows) and other sources (e.g. textbooks, literary works) may operate through the "cultivation effect" to shape viewers' beliefs, attitudes and behavior (Comstock, 1977; Liebert & Sprafkin, 1988; Tan, 1979). Liebert and Sprafkin (1988) argued that television generally portrays the most commonly held cultural stereotypes or "mainstream views." They suggested that those people who hold such views will not be influenced much by television (except to have their beliefs confirmed), but those who do not hold the mainstream view but watch a great deal of television will be influenced over time in the direction of the mainstream. Travis and Violato (1981, 1985) and Meisels and Chanter (1971), for example, found that adolescents, education undergraduates, and veteran teachers adhered to stereotype depictions of adolescents as a function of the amount of mass media (particularly television) use and the subjects' credulity vis a vis mass media. Accordingly, the greater the use of mass media and the more confidence placed in it as an accurate portrayal of social, economic and political reality, the greater was the adherence to youth stereotypes.

There is also substantial evidence to indicate that television depictions of sexuality has a cultivation effect on youthful observers. Baran (1976), for example, found that high school students who attribute a high realism to televised sexual portrayals (which are generally glamorous and glorious), were least satisfied with their own sexual practices, regardless of whether they were virgins or had already had coital experience. Moreover, a large proportion of adolescents (more than 50%) believe that televised depictions of sexuality are realistic (Louis Harris & Associates, 1986). Given that the most frequently occurring references in adolescent shows are to sexuality and dating, it is likely that some viewers' perceptions, beliefs and even behavior are influenced or "cultivated" by the stereotyped depictions.

Notwithstanding the stereotyped depictions on television, most current research and scholarship indicates that most adolescents are not particularly rebellious or peer oriented, do not orient particularly to an adolescent culture, are in harmony with most significant adults in their lives, and are not particularly precocious or seriously concerned about global issues and problems (Bibby & Posterski, 1985; Jahoda & Warren, 1965; Nurmi, 1991; Offer et al., 1988; Peterson & Peters, 1983; Roe, 1983; Travis & Violato, 1989; Violato & Holden, 1988; Violato & Kwok, 1991). By and large adolescents maintain close and open relationships with their parents, share similar values of the home, do not suffer undue storm and stress, and are as ignorant (or knowledgable) and unconcerned (or concerned) about global issues as most significant adults in their lives. The general picture is one of continuity of development from adolescence to adulthood rather than discontinuity as depicted in the stereotypes.

Conclusions

Quite clearly, televised portrayals of adolescents, whether in comedic depictions (e.g. Growing Pains), or alleged serious drama (e.g. Degrassi High), have little connection with reality but reflect widespread stereotypes of adolescents present in the culture generally, in English literature (Violato & Wiley, 1990), in newspapers (Falchikov, 1986), as well as in film and television. Further research of the present sort (i.e. factor analysis) could be applied to newspaper depictions of adolescents, to literary depictions (e.g. in the modern novel) and to film depictions. Moreover, the present study should be replicated employing another (and larger) sampling of televised episodes of adolescent shows. Meanwhile, there appears to be four main factors underlying televised depictions of adolescents.

References

Adelson, J. (1979). Adolescence and the generalization gap. *Psychology Today, 12,* 33-37.

Baran, S. (1976). Sex on TV and adolescent sexual self-image. *Journal of Broadcasting, 20,* 61-68.

Bibby, R., & Posterski, D. (1985). *The emerging generation: An inside look at Canada's teenagers.* Toronto, Canada: Irwin Publishing.

Blos, P. (1979). *The adolescent passage.* New York: International Universities Press.

Coleman, J.C. (1980). *The nature of adolescence.* New York: Methuen.

Comstock, G. (1975). The effects of television on children and adolescents: The evidence so far. *Journal of Communication, 25,* 25-34.

Erikson, E. (1969). *Identity: Youth and crisis.* New York: Norton.

Ewen, S. (1977). *Captains of consciousness.* McGraw Hill: Toronto.

Falchikov, N. (1986). Images of adolescence: An investigation into the accuracy of the image of adolescence constructed by British newspapers. *Journal of Adolescence, 9,* 167-180.

Friedenberg, E.Z. (1959). *The vanishing adolescent.* Beacon Press: Boston.

Jahoda, M., & Warren, N. (1965). The myths of youth. *Sociology of Education, 38,* 139-149.

Lasch, C. (1984). *The minimal self.* Norton: New York.

Lasch, C. (1978). *The culture of narcissism.* Warner Books: New York.

Liebert, R. & Sprafkin, J. (1988). *The early window: Effects of television on children and youth.* (3rd ed.). New York: Pergamon Press.

Louis Harris and Associates (1986). *American teens speak: Sex, myths, TV, and birth control.* New York: Planned Parenthood Federation of America.

Meisels, M., & Canter, F. (1971). A note on the generation gap. *Adolescence.*

Murray, J.P. (1980). *Television and youth.* Boys' Town N.E.: Centre for the Study of Youth Development.

National Federation for Decency. (1977). *Sex on Television.* Tupelo, MS.

Nurmi, J-E. (1991). How do adolescents see their future? A review of the development of future orientation and planning. *Developmental Review, 11,* 1-59.

Offer, D., Ostrov, E., Howard, K., & Atkinson, R. (1988). *The teenage world: Adolescents' self-image in ten countries.* New York: Plenum Publishing.

Peterson, G., & Peters, D. (1983). Adolescents' construction of social reality: The impact of television and peers. *Youth and Society, 15,* 67-84.

Porteous, M., & Colston, N. (1980). How adolescents are reported in the British Press. *Journal of Adolescence, 3,* 197-207.

Roe, K. (1983). *Mass media and adolescent schooling.* Almquist & Wiksell: Stockholm.

Roszak, T. (1969). *The making of a counterculture.* Doubleday: Garden City.

Seltzer, V. C. (1982). *Adolescent social development.* D.C. Heath: Lexington.

Signorelli, N. (1987). Children and adolescents on television. *Journal of Early Adolescence, 1,* 255-268.

Tan, A. S. (1979). TV beauty ads and role expectations of adolescent female viewers. *Journalism Quarterly, 56,* 283-287.

Travis, L., & Violato, C. (1981). Mass media use, credulity and beliefs about youth: A survey of Canadian education students. *The Alberta Journal of Educational Research, 26,* 16-34.

Travis, L., & Violato, C. (1985). Experience, mass media use and beliefs about youth: A comparative study. *The Alberta Journal of Educational Research, 31,* 99-112.

Travis, L., & Violato, C. (1989). Culture, mass media and youth. In C. Violato & A. Marini (Eds.), *Child development: Readings for teachers* (pp. 15-34). Calgary, Alberta: Detselig Enterprises.

Violato, C. (1991). History of adolescence. In S. Friedman, M. Fisher and S. Schonberg (Eds.), *Comprehensive adolescent health care,* Quality Medical Publishing: St. Louis.

Violato, C. & Kwok, D. (1991). A cross-cultural study of adolescent concerns: A comparison of Chinese Hong Kong and Canadian adolescents. Paper presented to the Canadian Psychological Annual Convention, Calgary, Alberta, June.

Violato, C., & Holden, W. (1988). A confirmatory factor analysis of a four-factor model of adolescent concerns. *Journal of Youth and Adolescence, 17,* 101-112.

Violato, C., & Wiley, A. (1990). Images of adolescence in English literature: The middle ages to the modern period. *Adolescence, 25,* 253-264.

10

A Cross-Cultural Validation of a Four-Factor Model of Adolescent Concerns

In a recent comprehensive review, Nurmi (1991) concluded that the content and timing of adolescent's interests, goals and concerns reflect expected life-span development characterized as developmental tasks, normative life-tasks, or milestone events (cf, Larson & Ham, 1993). As adolescents grow older, they first become interested in the developmental tasks of late adolescence (education) and then in tasks of early adulthood (future occupation and family). Irrespective of their age, however, young people are interested and concerned about life events they expect to manifest themselves at the end of the second and the beginning of the third decade of life. While these anticipations account for adolescents hopes, concerns and worries generally, there are substantial sex, socioeconomic status and cultural differences that affect these as well (Dodds & Chong-de, 1992; Nurmi, 1987; Solantus, 1987). Thus, more research is required to explore further and clarify sex, socioeconomic and cultural differences in the hopes, interests, worries and goals of adolescents. The main purpose of the present study was to validate cross-culturally a four-factor model of adolescent concerns with a sample of Hong Kong Chinese adolescents. A secondary purpose was to explore sex and age-related differences on these concerns.

In a recent factor-analytic study, Violato and Holden (1988) developed a four-factor model of adolescent concerns: (1) Future and Career, (2) Health and Drugs, (3) Personal self, and (4) Social self. The Future and Career factor included concerns about school grades, future schooling, career planning, etc., while the Health and Drug factor underlay concerns about sexual behavior, smoking, and substance use. Concerns about identity, relationships to parents, family and friends, and existential concerns (e.g. "Who Am I?") formed the Personal self factor. The fourth factor, the Social self, was composed of concerns about the appearance, extracurricular activities (e.g. sports, clubs), part-time work and relations to friends. This was proposed as a general model of adolescent concerns since it was derived from various data based on American, British, Australian and Canadian adolescents (Violato & Holden, 1988).

One of the most consistent findings in the study of adolescent concerns is that concern about future schooling and career and school and educational adjustment ranks most highly (Abel & Gingels, 1968; Collins & Harper, 1974; Offer, Ostrov, Howard & Atkinson, 1988; Nicholson & Antill, 1981; Nurmi, 1991; Payne, 1988; Solantus, 1987). These worries and concerns are clearly related to normative life-tasks such as getting an education and getting a job. These concerns, however, have been found to vary somewhat according to a number of factors such as age, culture and research methods (Bennett, Klein & Derevenski, 1992; Nurmi, 1988, 1991; Solantus, 1987; Sundberg, Poole & Tyler, 1983). Barton (1985) comparing British and Finnish adolescents, for example, found that the British young people had more worries about future occupation while Finnish youths were more concerned about issues of peace and war. Bentley (1983) found that Zwazi girls were less concerned about their occupation then Scottish girls who tended to express more concern about personal happiness. American adolescents have been found to differ in their concern about future career from Taiwan Chinese (Kuo & Spees, 1983), Indian (Mehata, Rohila, Sundberg & Tyler, 1972) and Dutch youths (Sundberg & Tyler, 1970). Poole and Cooney (1987) found that Singaporean adolescents were more interested in their future education and work than Australians, while Seginer (1988) found Israeli Jewish youth to have fewer concerns than Israeli Arabs about future education, work and career as did Seginer and Halagi (1991). Austrian adolescents have been found to be less concerned about future work than British youth (Solantus, 1987), while Sundberg, Poole and Tyler (1983) found no such differences between American, Indian and Australian adolescents. Overall, these cross-cultural differences seem to reflect the differences in typical developmental tasks of each culture as well as current societal features (e.g. threat of war, level of unemployment) (Bennett et al., 1992; Nurmi, 1991).

Offer and Offer (1975), Offer et al. (1988), Bibby and Posterski (1985), Nicholson and Antill (1981), Eme, Maisiak and Goodale, (1979), Sundberg et al., (1983), and Violato and Holden (1988) all found that concern about physical development, health, and drug use was fairly widespread. These researchers have all found that adolescents are concerned about their height, weight, general health, physical appearance as well as smoking and alcohol use. In addition to these concerns, themes of concern about the development of the "self" have been consistently uncovered (Bibby & Posterski, 1985; Craig-Bray & Adams, 1986; Erikson, 1959; Cantor, Norem, Niedenthal, Langston & Browery, 1987; Eme et al., 1979; Nurmi, 1991; Violato & Holden, 1988). Adolescents express concern surrounding this development of the self in two sorts of themes: (1) a personal or private self, and (2) a social or public self. The personal self does involve personal relations, but concerns here focus more on "existential" matters such as "Who am I?" and "what is the purpose of life?." A related but separate theme is the social self, which is a focus on more overt observable characteristics and relationships. This involves such factors as personal appearance, relations to friends, sexual behavior and orientation, current jobs, and social and athletic activities. Violato and Holden (1988) found that the personal self and private self factors were identifiable empirically but they were correlated. A similar pattern of findings were reported by Adwere-Boamah and Curtis (1993) in a test of the Violato and Holden (1988) four-factor model with a large sample (n = 1 543) of predominantly African-American (76%) and Hispanic (12%) lower socioeconomic adolescents form a Northern California urban school district.

Cross-cultural sex differences in adolescents' concern are also frequently uncovered. The pattern of differences indicates that sex-differences are greater in traditional societies compared with more urbanized ones. Typically, in more traditional cultures, female concerns are more in keeping with stereotyped females roles than in urbanized cultures (Bently, 1983; Nurmi, 1989; Solantus, 1987). While the foregoing indicates the general concerns expressed by adolescents, the pattern and importance of concerns vary to a great extent according to a number of variables such as age, gender and culture. Accordingly, the co-variation of the extent of concern with these variables still requires substantial investigation. The present study, therefore, was undertaken in an attempt to further validate cross-culturally, with a sample of Hong Kong Chinese adolescents, the four factor model of adolescent concerns proposed by Violato and Holden (1988). The full model consists of four basic factors on which adolescent concerns are thought to be organized: (1) Future and Career, (2) Health and Drugs, (3) Personal self, and (4) Social self. The Personal self and Social self are thought to be correlated as is the Social self with the Future and Career factor. The problem was conceptualized as a confirmatory factor analysis. The schematic for this is depicted in Figure 10.1. A secondary purpose of the study was to establish a hierarchy of adolescent concerns, and to explore sex and age differences in these concerns.

Method

Subjects

A sample of 585 (317 males = 54%; 268 females = 46%) adolescents of Chinese ethnic origin from Hong Kong (mean age = 16.1 years, SD = 9.3) participated in the present study. The subjects came from 5 junior and high schools that agreed to participate in the present study. The number and percentage of subjects on each age category were as follows: 12, n = 27 (4.6%); 13, n = 106 (18.1%); 14, n = 114 (19.5%); 15, n = 116 (19.8%); 16, n = 103 (17.6%); 17, n = 42 (7.2%); 18, n = 35 (6.0%). Based on father's occupation, the number and percentage of subjects classified into each of the following socioeconomic categories were as follows: (1) professional/managerial (e.g., physicians, executives) = 85 (14.5%); (2) entrepreneurial (e.g. self-employed businessmen) = 45 (7.7%); (3) skilled labor (e.g., licensed workers such as plumbers) =330 (56.4%); and (4) unskilled labor (e.g., clerks, laborers) = 125 (21.4%). All subjects were Asian.

Procedures

Subjects completed a questionnaire in their regular class. In addition to questions about age, grade, sex, ethnicity, and father's employment, the questionnaire contained 14 items measuring concerns. The present questionnaire was an adaptation of the questionnaire used by Violato and Holden (1988). In the present study, respondents indicated their degree of concern on a 4-point Likert Scale (1 = never concerned; 2 = sometimes concerned; 3 = frequently concerned; 4 = constantly concerned). The Chinese version of the questionnaire is in Appendix A.

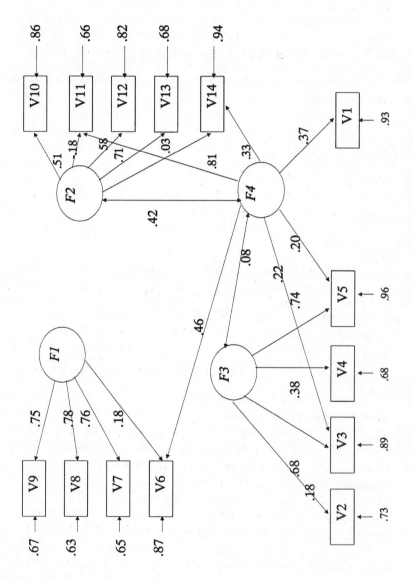

Figure 10.1. A Four-factor Structural Model of Adolescent Concerns

Results

The results are presented in two basic sections: (1) Fitting the four-factor model to the data employing Structural Equation Modeling (SEM) techniques, and (2) Descriptive results for the whole sample as well as an analysis of sex and age differences.

Table 10.1

Matrix of Pearson Product Moment Correlation Coefficients of 14 Variables

Variable	1	2	3	4	5	6	7	8	9	10	11	12	13	14
1 Grades	–													
2 Parents	16*	–												
3 Appearance	10	05	–											
4 Smoking	-02	09	01	–										
5 Identity	14	14	12	15	–									
6 Friends	19	27	20	02	25	–								
7 Alcohol	03	10	06	58	17	05	–							
8 Career	27	16	12	03	23	23	11	–						
9 Drugs	-02	09	04	59	16	03	57	13	–					
10 Sex	03	07	09	21	13	11	15	15	21	–				
11 Part-time job	04	09	12	15	08	07	19	18	17	24	–			
12 Future School	39	21	14	-02	22	21	07	42	04	08	09	–		
13 Activities	10	04	28	12	13	14	11	14	09	40	24	10	–	
14 Family	20	51	08	05	15	31	13	13	07	12	02	28	09	–

*All coefficients have been rounded to two decimal places and the decimal point has been dropped.

Fitting the Model to the Data

Using SEM techniques with EQS computer program (Bentler, 1992), the data were fit to the four-factor model specified above. First, Pearson product-moment correlation coefficients were computed for all pairs of items on the concerns scale. The resulting 14 x 14 correlation matrix (Table 10.1) was fit to the four-factor using maximum likelihood estimation. The schematic for the model, together with the factor loadings, residuals (unique variance), and inter-correlations between the factors or endogenous variables are depicted in Figure 10.1.

As can be seen from the path diagram (Figure 10.1), sexual concerns (V6), drug use (V7), smoking (V8), and alcohol use (V9) all load on the first factor (F1), Health and Drugs, although V6 loads more substantially (loading = .46) on F4 (Social self) than on F1. Concerns about grades (V10), career (V12), and future schooling (V13) load heavily on F2 (Future and career), while concerns about outside activities (V11) loads lightly (loading = -.18), and part-time job (V14) loading is negligible (.02) on F2. These latter two variables (V11, V14), load most heavily on F4 as do V1 (concerns about appearance), V3 (concerns about friends), and V5 (concerns about identity). These latter two variables (V3, V5) also load on F3 (Personal self) as do concerns about parents (V2) and family (V4). Two latent variables (F2 and F4) were correlated as expected (r = .42) although the correlation between F3 and F4 is near zero and nonsignificant (r = .08) contrary to the model specifications. Nevertheless, the overall pattern of loadings and pattern of correlations between the factors clearly follow the proposed model and result in interpretable and theoretically meaningful factors.

The Health and Drug factor (F1) accounts for the greatest proportion of common variance (45.1%) and has loadings from items which tap concerns about health and substance use as was expected. The Future and Career factor (F2) has all theoretically meaningful loadings and accounts for 28.7% of the common variance. The remaining two factors – Social Self (F4) and Personal Self (F3) – account for 15.5% and 10.8% of the common variance. Both have items that identify them in a theoretically meaningful way. The Comparative Fit Index (CFI) of the data to the model was 0.864 with a Residual Mean Square (RMS) of 0.056. Nearly 80% (79.05%) of the standardized residuals (83 of 105) had values 0.0 ± 0.1. The CFI can be interpreted to indicate the amount of "explained variance" in the data (Bentler, 1992). Accordingly in the present study, 86% of the variance in the data is accounted for by the four-factor model (CFI = 0.864). This can be considered a satisfactory fit of the data to the model.

Descriptive Results and Sex and Age Differences

The mean ratings of each of the fourteen variables for the whole sample as well as for males and females and each age category are summarized in Table 10.2.

Based on the size of the mean for each variable, each item was assigned a rank from 1 to 14. From Table 10.2 it can be seen that concerns about grades, friends and future schooling rank first, second and third respectively. Concerns about smoking, drugs and alcohol are at the bottom of the hierarchy, ranking 12th, 13th and 14th respectively. Concerns about appearance, activities and identity are in the middle of the hierarchy (7th, 8th and 9th respectively). This hierarchy of concerns for the Chinese Hong Kong sample was compared to the hierarchy for the original Canadian sample in the Violato and Holden (1988) study. The rank order correlation coefficient, is r_s = .68. This is a strong correlation although several items were rated differently. Particularly, the concerns about friends was given a much higher rating (2) by the Hong Kong sample than by the Canadian sample (9). Moreover, the means on each of the items tended to be comparatively higher for the Hong Kong sample indicating more general concern overall by the Chinese subjects vis a vis the Canadian adolescents (see Violato & Holden, 1988). So while there is some obvious similarity in the rank-order of concerns between the two samples, there are some notable differences as well.

Sex Differences

In order to test for sex-differences, multivariate analysis of variance (MANOVA) procedures were employed with the fourteen variables as dependent measures and sex as an independent variable. Thus a one-way MANOVA with 2 – levels of the independent variable (sex) was conducted. The results indicated an overall sex-difference (Wilk's lambda = 0.36; Approximate F = 43.21; $p < .01$). For a more fine-grained analysis, each of the fourteen variables were subsequently analyzed by analysis of variance (ANOVA). From an inspection of the mean ratings by males and females (Table 10.2), it is evident that there are a number of sex-differences. Females, compared to males, rated grades, future schooling, appearance (all $p < .01$), friends and family (both $p < .05$) as sources of greater concern. Conversely, compared to females, males rated outside activities (e.g., dating), sexual feelings (both $p < .01$) and identity ($p < .05$) more highly as sources of concern. Females, then, showed generally greater concern for interpersonal relationships, appearance and schooling issues, while males were more self-focused (e.g. on sexual feelings and identity).

Age Differences

To test for age or developmental differences, MANOVA procedures were employed as before. Thus a one-way MANOVA with 7 – levels of the independent variable (age) was conducted. The results indicated an overall age-difference (Wilk's lambda = 0.41; Approximate F = 4.44; $p < .01$). For a more fine-grained analysis, each of the fourteen variables were analyzed by ANOVAs. The results in Table 10.2 indicate age or developmental differences on four variables: grades, family, appearance, alcohol use. To determine the developmental trends in each of the variables, a post hoc multiple range test (Tukey's HSD) was employed. For concern about grades, there is a clear trend for concern to diminish as age increases; it was the 12-year-olds who showed the greatest concern ($p < .05$). For getting along with family, the 12-year-olds were more concerned than the other age groups who don't differ from each other except that the 18-year-olds are the least concerned ($p < .05$; see Table 10.2). The 18-year-olds are also less concerned about appearance than the other age groups ($p < .01$) who don't differ from one another. Finally, this same pattern of concern (Table 10.2) obtains for alcohol use ($p < .05$) with 18-year-olds indicating the least concern. The general pattern of these developmental differences indicate that the youngest subjects are generally more concerned while the oldest subjects are the least concerned. On all four variables, it was the two most extreme age groups (either 12 or 18) who differed significantly from the others.

Discussion

The major results of the present study may be summarized as follows: (1) The fit of the concerns data to the four-factor model was satisfactory, (2) The

Table 10.2

Mean Ratings of Seriousness of Variables of Concern Age (Years)

Variable	Rank	Total Sample (n=585)	Male (n=317)	Female (n=268)	12 (n=27)	13 (n=106)	14 (n=114)	15 (n=116)	16 (n=108)	17 (n=42)	18 (n=35)
Grades	1	3.31 (.78[1])	3.19	3.44**	3.63	3.46	3.25	3.41	3.18	3.21	3.06**
Friends	2	3.29 (.69)	3.23	3.35*	3.44	3.39	3.28	3.34	3.12	3.38	3.26
Future School	3	3.21 (.87)	3.10	3.34**	3.37	3.31	3.02	3.20	3.16	3.26	3.23
Family	4	3.16 (.89)	3.08	3.26*	3.44	3.27	3.07	3.24	3.12	3.12	2.83*
Career	5	3.11 (1.01)	3.04	3.20	3.41	3.03	3.04	3.15	3.11	3.38	3.06
Parents	6	3.10 (.89)	3.10	3.13	3.41	3.18	2.99	3.18	3.07	3.10	2.94
Appearance	7	2.90 (.82)	2.76	3.06**	3.00	2.99	2.93	3.02	2.83	2.91	2.46**
Activities	8	2.42 (1.01)	2.51	2.31*	2.56	2.32	2.45	2.37	2.38	2.48	2.31
Identity	9	2.34 (1.09)	2.24	2.45*	2.52	2.49	2.28	2.17	2.47	2.21	2.34
Part-time Job	10	2.07 (1.09)	2.07	2.06	2.15	2.30	2.04	2.00	1.97	1.74	1.91
Sex	11	2.19 (1.04)	2.38	1.97**	2.07	2.15	2.17	2.16	2.15	2.14	2.31
Smoking	12	1.93 (1.15)	1.93	1.93	2.04	2.09	1.85	1.96	1.87	1.81	1.91
Drugs	13	1.92 (1.19)	1.87	2.00	2.07	2.21	1.74	1.78	2.02	2.17	1.63
Alcohol	14	1.80 (1.06)	1.77	1.84	2.26	1.82	1.63	1.93	1.81	1.69	1.51*

*$p < .05$; **$p < .01$; [1]Standard Deviation

hierarchy of concerns of the present sample was similar to that of the original Canadian sample but there were some notable differences, and (3) There were some noteworthy sex and age differences on the ratings of some concerns.

The fit of the present data to the four-factor model was satisfactory with approximately 86% of the variance in the data explained by the proposed model. Nevertheless, there were some elements of the model which did not result in a good fit. Specifically, several loadings had somewhat smaller loadings (or negligible ones) than expected. The variable about identity concerns (V5), for example, failed to load highly on either Social self (F4) or Personal self (F3) but resulted in a large residual (.96). The difference in this pattern of loadings compared to the original Canadian sample (Violato & Holden, 1988) undoubtedly reflects differences in socialization and child-rearing patterns and practices between Western and Hong Kong Chinese adolescents (Berndt, Cheung, Lau, Hau & Lew, 1993; Cheung & Lau, 1985; Dodds & Chong-de, 1992; Feldman, Rosenthal, Mont-Reynaud, Leung & Lau, 1991). Western adolescents, especially American and Canadian ones, tend to have a much greater focus on the self compared to Chinese young people (Stigler, Smith & Mao, 1985) who are reared in a culture that emphasizes parental control, filial piety, respect for elders and family obligations (Bond, 1991; King & Bond, 1985; Kwok & Violato, 1993). Accordingly, the unclear pattern of loadings from V5 ("Who am I?") and the resulting large error variance of this variable may be due to the subsidiary cultural relevance of this concern in the present sample.

Further supporting evidence for this interpretation is the negligible correlation (r = .08) between F3 (Personal self) and F4 (Social self). This correlation was substantial (r = .53) in the original Canadian sample and is expected theoretically. The present results indicate that the Personal self and Social self are orthogonal in the Hong Kong Chinese sample. Moreover, concerns about the self (V5) ranked relatively low in the hierarchy of concerns (9th) compared to the original Canadian sample (it was 5th), while concern about friends (V3) ranked much more highly (2nd) in the present sample than the Canadian one (9th). The overall rank-ordering of the present sample varied somewhat from the original Canadian sample. These discrepancies in emphasis on concerns and their interrelationships probably reflect the greater focus on the Hong Kong Chinese adolescents cultural influence of filial piety, parental control, respect for elders and family obligations compared to Western adolescents (Bond, 1991; Stigler et al., 1985).

The sex and age differences in the present study are consistent with previous findings (Bennett et al., 1992; Nurmi, 1991). Adolescent boys tend to be more self-focused while girls tend to be more concerned about the future and interpersonal relationships. In the present sample, girls were more concerned about appearance than boys as is consistently the case in other research (Nurmi, 1991; Violato & Holden, 1988), perhaps because social norms continue to emphasize appearance more for females than for males (Jacklin, 1989). Similarly, the greater concern for interpersonal relationships and schooling issues for the girls compared to the boys again probably because of differential social norms for boys and girls.

The general pattern of differences across age suggested that the youngest subjects had heightened concern on some variables (grades, future schooling, appearance, alcohol use) compared to older subjects. There were no other developmental differences. These heightened concerns of the younger subjects probably reflect the comparative "newness" of these normative life-tasks (i.e. future and schooling issues, appearance, and alcohol use) compared to older subjects who may have had time to adapt to these demands (Nurmi, 1991). This is consistent with the findings of Larson and Ham (1993) who concluded that early adolescents experience greater "distressed affect" in response to negative life events compared to preadolescents. The results from the present study indicates that this greater distress probably diminishes over time into middle and late adolescence.

In conclusion, the results from the present study provide support for the cross-cultural generality and validity of the four-factor model of adolescent concerns. The original four-factor model (Violato & Holden, 1988) was developed and validated primarily with Western adolescents. Accordingly, a test of the model with data from adolescents who have fundamentally different life experiences, are reared with different parenting styles and have different aspirations and goals (Berndt et al., 1993; Bond, 1991; Stigler et al., 1985) should be robust. As well, the pattern of sex and age differences were the same for the Hong Kong Chinese sample and the original Canadian one. The main differences found in the present sample was the orthogonality of the social and personal self compared to Western adolescents. This difference was explained as resulting from the cultural and child-rearing differences between Western and Hong Kong Chinese adolescents. Nevertheless, further research is required to identify more precisely the psychological mechanisms underlying this difference. The four-factor model also requires further validation with other cultures as recent other work indicates that it is applicable to other cultural groups (Adwere-Boamah & Curtis, 1993). Meanwhile, the present results suggest that the four-factor model has substantial cross-cultural generality and validity.

References

Abels, H., Gingles, R. (1968). Identifying problems of adolescent girls. *Journal of Educational Research, 58,* 389-391.

Adwere-Boamah, J., & Curtis, D.A. (1993). A confirmatory factor analysis of a four-factor model of adolescent concerns revisited. *Journal of Youth and Adolescence, 22,* 297-312.

Barton, E. (1985). Threat of war in the minds of children. *Lancet,* 8422, 226.

Bennett, A., Klein, C., & Deverensky, J.L. (1992). A developmental examination of adolescent fears. *Canadian Journal of School Psychology, 8,* 69-79.

Bentler, P.M. (1992). *EQS structural equations program manual.* Los Angeles: BMDP Statistical Software.

Bentley, A.M. (1983). Personal and global futurity in Scottish and Swazi students. *Journal of Social Psychology, 12,* 223-229.

Berndt, T., Cheung, P., Lau, S., Hau, K., & Lew, W. (1993). Perception of parenting in mainland China, Taiwan, and Hong Kong: Sex differences and societal differences. *Developmental Psychology, 29,* 156-164.

Bibby, R.W., & Posterski, D.C. (1985). *The emerging generation.* Irwin Publishing: Toronto.

Bond, M.H. (1991). *Beyond the Chinese face: Insights from psychology.* Hong Kong: Oxford University Press.

Cantor, N., Norem, J., Niedenthal, P., Langston, C., & Brower, A. (1987). Life-tasks, self-concept ideals and cognitive strategies in a life transition. *Journal of Personality and Social Psychology, 53,* 1178-1191.

Cheung, T.S. (1986). Sex differences in the effect of academic achievement on self-esteem: A Hong Kong case. *Social Behaviour and Personality, 14,* 161-165.

Cheung, P.C., & Lau, S. (1985). Self-esteem: Its relationship to the family and school social environment among Chinese adolescents. *Youth and Society, 16,* 438-456.

Craig-Bray, L., & Adams, G.R. (1986). Different methodologies in the assessment of identity: Congruence between self-report and interview techniques? *Journal of Youth and Adolescence, 15,* 191-204.

Collins, J., & Harper, J. (1974). Problems of adolescents in Sydney, Australia. *Journal of Genetic Psychology, 125,* 189-194.

Dodds, J., & Chong-de, L. (1992). Chinese teenagers' concerns about the future: A cross-cultural comparison. *Adolescence, 27,* 481-486.

Eme, R., Maisiak, R., & Goodale, W. (1979). Seriousness of adolescent problems. *Adolescence, 14,* 93-98.

Erikson, E. (1959). *Identity and the life cycle.* New York: Norton.

Falchikov, N. (1986). Images of adolescence: An investigation into the accuracy of the image of adolescence constructed by British newspapers. *Journal of Adolescence, 9,* 167-180.

Feldman, S.S., Rosenthal, D.A., Mont-Reynaud, R., Leung, K., & Lau, S. (1991). Ain't misbehavin': Adolescent values and family environments as correlates of misconduct in Australia, Hong Kong, and the United States. *Journal of Research on Adolescence, 1,* 109-134.

Havinghurst, R.J. (1948). *Developmental tasks and education.* New York: McKay.

Jacklin, J. (1989). Female and male: Issues of gender. *American Psychologist, 44,* 127-133.

King, A.Y., & Bond, M.H. (1985). The Confucian paradigm of man: A sociological view. In W. Tseng, & D.Y. Wu (Eds), *Chinese culture and mental health* (pp 29-45). New York: Academic Press.

Kuo, S., & Spees, E.R. (1983). Chinese American student life-style: A comparative study. *Journal of College Student Personnel, 24,* 111-117.

Kwok, D., & Violato, C. (1993). Gender and concerns: Similarities and differecnes between Canadian and Hong Kong Chinese adolescents. *Psychologia, 36,* 1-10.

Larson, R., & Ham, M. (1993). Stress and "storm and stress" in early adolescence: The relationship of negative events with dysphoric affect. *Developmental Psychology, 29,* 130-140.

Marcia, J.E. (1966). Development and validation of ego identity status. *Journal of Personality and Social Psychology, 3,* 551-558.

Marcia, J.E. (1980). Identity in adolescence. In J. Adelson (ed.), *Handbook of adolescent psychology.* New York: John Wiley & Sons.

Mehata, P.H., Rohila, P.K., Sundberg, N.D., & Tyler, L.E. (1972). Future time perspectives of adolescents in India and the United States. *Journal of Cross-Cultural Psychology, 3,* 292-302.

Nicholson, S.I., & Antill, J.K. (1981). Personal problems of adolescents and their relationship to peer acceptance and sex-role identity. *Journal of Youth and Adolescence, 10,* 309-325.

Nurmi, J.E. (1991). How do adolescents see their future? A review of the development of future orientation and planning. *Developmental Review, 11,* 1-59.

Nurmi, J.E. (1989). Development of orientation to the future during early adolescence: A four-year longitudinal study and two cross-sectional comparisons. *International Journal of Psychology, 24,* 195-214.

Nurmi, J.E. (1988). Experience of the threat of war among Finnish adolescents: Effects of thinking about the future, and comparison of methods. *Medicine and War, 4,* 199-210.

Nurmi, J.E. (1987). Age, sex, social class, and quality of family interaction as determinants of adolescents future orientation: A developmental task interpretation. *Adolescence, 22,* 977-991.

Offer, D., Ostrov, E., Howard, K., & Atkinson, R. (1988). *The teenage world: Adolescents' self-image in ten countries.* New York: Plenum.

Offer, D., & Offer, J.B. (1975). *From teenage to young manhood.* New York: Basic Books.

Payne, M.A. (1988). Adolescent fears: Some Caribbean findings. *Journal of Youth and Adolescence, 17,* 255-266.

Poole, M.E., & Cooney, G.H. (1987). Orientations to the future: A comparison of adolescents in Australia and Singapore. *Journal of Youth and Adolescence, 16,* 129-151.

Seginer, R. (1988). Adolescents facing the future: Cultural and sociopolitical perspectives. *Youth and Society, 19,* 314-333.

Seginer, R., & Halagi, H. (1991). Cross-cultural variations of adolescents' future orientation: The case of Israeli Druze versus Israeli Arab and Jewish Males. *Journal of Cross-Cultural Psychology, 22,* 224-237.

Solantus, T. (1987). Hopes and worries of young people in three European countries. *Health Promotion, 2,* 19-27.

Stigler, J.W., Smith, S., Mao, L. (1985). The self-perception of competence by Chinese children. *Child Development, 56,* 1259-1270.

Sundberg, N.D., Poole, M.E., & Tyler, L.E. (1983). Adolescents' expectations of future events – A cross-cultural study of Australians, Americans and Indians. 415-427.

Sundberg, N.D., & Tyler, L.E. (1970). Awareness of action possibilities of Indian, Dutch, and American adolescents. *Journal of Cross-Cultural Psychology, 1,* 153-157.

Travis, L.D., & Violato, C. (1989). Culture, mass media and youth. In C. Violato and A. Marini (eds), *Child Development: Readings for teachers.* Calgary: Detselig.

Violato, C., & Holden, W.B. (1988). A confirmatory factor analysis of a four-factor model of adolescent concerns. *Journal of Youth and Adolescence, 17,* 101-113.

Appendix A

關注程度量表

你對下列各事項的關注程度是怎樣？
請在此表上評估每一項。

1. 永不關注
2. 有時關注
3. 時常關注
4. 非常關注

1. 我的考試成績	1 2 3 4
2. 與父母相處	1 2 3 4
3. 我的個人外表	1 2 3 4
4. 吸煙	1 2 3 4
5. 關於 " 我是誰？ " 的問題	1 2 3 4
6. 與朋友相處	1 2 3 4
7. 飲酒	1 2 3 4
8. 決定職業	1 2 3 4
9. 吸毒	1 2 3 4
10. 我對性的感受	1 2 3 4
11. 在學時有兼職	1 2 3 4
12. 我的就學前景	1 2 3 4
13. 結交異性	1 2 3 4
14. 與家人相處	1 2 3 4

請填寫下列各項：

15. 性別：＿＿＿＿＿＿＿

16. 級別：＿＿＿＿＿＿＿

17. 年齡：＿＿＿＿＿＿＿

18. 父親職業：＿＿＿＿＿＿＿

19. 母親職業（如有工作者）：＿＿＿＿＿＿＿

Introduction
Section Three: Nature of Adolescence

This section on the nature of adolescence consists of six chapters. While on the surface they appear to cover a disparate range of material, at a deeper level all six chapters contain either empirical evidence or theoretical implications for the understanding of the nature of adolescence. Given the complexity, ambiguity, contradictions and paradoxes inherent in the concept and study of adolescence, various theoretical, methodological and ideological underpinnings are evident in the chapters that comprise this section. We have invited two former students and current colleagues, Mark Atkinson and Mark Genuis, to contribute chapters to this section because of their recent work in these areas that explore aspects of the nature of adolescence. Atkinson explores some aspects of the ecology of emotional experience in late adolescents, while Genuis discusses the implications on development of childhood attachments.

In Chapter 11, "Adolescent Concerns," we present the results of an empirical study that involves testing a four-factor model of adolescent concerns. This is presented as a general model of adolescent concerns as derived from various data based on American, British, Australian and Canadian adolescents. Four factors are proposed: (1) Future and Career, (2) Health and Drugs, (3) Personal self, and (4) Social self. The Future and Career factor includes concerns about school grades, future schooling, career, etc., while Health and Drug factor underlies concerns about sexuality, smoking, and substance use. Concerns about identity, relationships to parents, family and friends, and existential concerns (e.g., "Who Am I?") forms the personal self factor. The fourth factor, the Social self, is composed of concerns about appearance, extracurricular activities (e.g. sports, clubs), part-time work and relations to friends. The model fits the data very well and it is thus proposed as a general model around which adolescent concerns are organized.

Chapter 12, "The Long Term Implications of Childhood Attachment," focuses on attachment theory. The original relevant model was articulated by Bowlby (1969). The basic idea is that human infants, like the *neonates* of other species, form affectional bonds with their caregivers (i.e. mother). The nature of the bond that is formed is thought to be the prototype of all later love relationships. If the original attachment bond is "insecure" (because the mother was either a poor caregiver, was absent or was abusive), this will affect the emotional development and organization in negative ways. The child and adolescent will become psychologically maladapted and emotionally labile. Conversely, if the mother was attentive, responsive, and provided love and tenderness during the first few years of life, a "secure" bond or attachment ensues. Such a child is likely to become well adjusted, happy and emotionally stable. Substantial research efforts have documented the development of secure and insecure attachment patterns. Isabella (1993), for example, has identified empirically the origins of attachment patterns in the first year of life. While there is substantial speculation and theorizing about the long-term effects of varying patterns of attachment on the developing individual, there is a paucity of either clinical or empirical evidence on this. Genuis' chapter focuses on this problem.

"Anger and Sadness Experiences in Late Adolescence" by Mark Atkinson constitutes the thirteenth chapter in this collection. In this chapter, Atkinson summarizes the results of some research which assessed the types of situations and thoughts occurring during adolescent's experience of anger and sadness. The data for the study was based on the information provided by 149 university students about the emotional events in their daily life. Atkinson employed a modified Experience Sampling Methodology (EMS) initially developed by Larson and Csikszentmihalyi (1983). This allowed Atkinson to study the social ecology of anger and sadness so as to explore both the causes of these emotions as well as their intensity and duration.

In chapter 14, "Beliefs About Youth," we report the results of a national survey of education students and their beliefs about youth. While we conducted this work some time ago (1975 - 1980), the results are still timely and compelling. They show that our sample of students adhered rather strongly to dimensions of adolescent stereotypes that were pervasive at that time. Moreover, intensity of the subjects adherence with the stereotype covaried with their use of mass media. The heavy users of television, newspapers and magazines were the stereotypes were given massive and sustained exposure, tended to have stronger adherence to the stereotypes than did subjects who used more serious fare (e.g., literary magazines). While we were unable to conclude that this media use and the belief in the stereotypes were causally related because this was a correlational study, we nevertheless favored this as an explanation. It is possible that those who adhere to the stereotypes already are attracted to mass information and entertainment which confirms their biases. Nevertheless, further exposure will then solidify and consolidate these beliefs.

In the foregoing study, we utilized university students who were enrolled in teacher education programmes across Canada. Since they were undergraduate students with little formal exposure with young people in the classroom, we wondered if their beliefs were in accordance with mass media because they had little exposure to real young people. It followed therefore, that experienced teachers who have had substantial experience with young people would have beliefs more in accordance with reality and less so with mass media stereotypes. Accordingly, we conducted an empirical study of experienced teachers. Surprisingly, we found that the experienced teachers had an even more distorted view of youth in accordance with the stereotypes than did the undergraduates. These results are reported in chapter 15, "Teacher Beliefs About Youth." This natural follow-up to the study reported in chapter 14, led us to the conclusion that actual exposure to young people is not only no guarantee that this will result in more realistic beliefs, but that pervasive stereotypes may override reality. Given the heterogeneity and variability of young people, it is, perhaps, not surprising that teachers can impose any their stereotypes on adolescents.

The last paper in this section, chapter 16, "Disposition and Achievement," focuses on the inherent conflict between learning and devotion to erudition and the curtailing of base impulses which this requires. In brief, the argument hinges on the following: there are irreconcilable facts and forces in education that set the tone of what can occur. Bernfeld (1973) aptly characterized this condition of education as the situation faced by Sisyphus, the mythical figure who was condemned to eternally roll a rock up a hill whereupon it would promptly roll down again. For the teacher as well as the student there is a clash of wills. The desires and will of the teacher are not those of the pupils. As one group of pupils become somewhat civilized by the teacher's effort, they are promptly replaced by the incoming group who are ignorant. Like Sisyphus, the teacher must start the process anew, only to be condemned to repeat it eternally.

Learning and teaching, is then intrinsically laden with conflict. As Freud (1961) had observed some decades ago, conflict arises from the opposition of culture and instinct. Education, learning and erudition are then, naturally in conflict with impulse, hedonism and desire. These must be quelled for sustained effort in learning to occur. This is the main theme that is elaborated in the first half of chapter 16. The second part of the chapter is a report of the results of empirical studies which have probed the relationship between disposition and achievement.

Taken together then, these six chapters of section three while representing disparate topics, methods and theories, nonetheless probe important elements of the adolescent experience. These various approaches reflect the complexity, nuances and heterogeneity of adolescence itself.

References

Bowlby, J. (1969). *Attachment and loss: Vol. 1: Attachment.* New York: Basic Books

Bernfeld, S. (1973). *Sisyphus and the limits of education.* Berkeley, CA: University of California Press.

Freud, S. (1963). *General psychological theory: Papers on metapsychology.* New York: Collier/Macmillan.

Isabella, R.A. (1993). Origins of attachment: Maternal interactive behavior across the first year. *Child Development, 64,* 605-621.

Larson, R., & Csikszentmihalyi, M. (1983). The experience sampling method. In H. Reis (ed), *New directions in naturalistic methods in the behavioral sciences.* San Francisco: Jossey-Bass.

11

Adolescent Concerns

Some theorists continue to argue that adolescence is inherently a period of "storm and stress" (e.g. Westwood, 1986). Many others (e.g., Adelson, 1979; Offer & Offer, 1975; Siddique & D'Arcy, 1984), however, regard adolescence as a period of relatively smooth transition for most people. Coleman (1978) has analyzed these two apparently contradictory points of view in some detail. The storm and stress or classical view as Coleman (1978) called it, has its roots in antiquity but was formalized and augmented by G.S. Hall (1904) in his description of adolescence as a period of *sturm und drang*. The opposing point of view called the "empirical" perspective, is characterized by the assertion that the teenage years are much more stable and peaceful than the storm and stress theorists would have us believe (Coleman, 1978). Both Coleman (1978) as well as Siddique and D'Arcy (1984) have suggested that the classical and empirical points of view may not be contradictory at all; it depends on one's focus. For some people, adolescence indeed is characterized by storm and stress, while for others, it is relatively peaceful. In any case, while the debate has not yet been concluded, most theorists would agree that adolescents do face a number of problems of adjustment. Considerable research has now been conducted into the type and seriousness of adolescent problems as reported by adolescents themselves. The major purpose of the present study was to propose a four-factor model of adolescent concerns based on the available empirical evidence and to test the "goodness of fit" of this model based on an empirical study of adolescent concerns. A secondary purpose of the present study was to explore the relative seriousness of adolescent concerns and to study any sex and age differences which may emerge.

Adolescent Concerns

One of the most consistent findings in the study of adolescent concerns, is that school and educational adjustment problems and concerns about future schooling and career, rank most highly with adolescents. In their study of adolescent females, for example, Abel and Gingles (1968) found that school and educational problems ranked most highly with problems related to family and home ranking last. Morgan (1969) found that concern about future educational and vocational plans were prevalent in both male and female adolescents. In their study of 164 Australian high school students, Nicholson and Antill (1981) also found that concerns about grades, future schooling and career were dominant in their sample. Collin's and Harper's (1974) study turned up similar findings as did Offer's and Offer's (1975) work with American adolescents. Bibby's and

Posterski's (1985) major study involving a national sample of 3 530 Canadian adolescents, produced corroborative findings. They found that 68% of their sample indicated that their future school and career plans concerned them "a great deal" or "quite a bit" (p. 60). Rutter (1980) and Rutter et al. (1979) have also confirmed that school and career concerns dominate the concerns of adolescents. Quite clearly, the first theme or factor that underlies adolescent's concerns is school and future career considerations.

A second factor or theme which seems to underlie adolescent concerns involves health, physical development and drug abuse. Offer and Offer (1975) found that concern about physical development, health and drug use was fairly widespread. Bibby and Posterski (1985) reported that general health including height and weight concerned 44% of their sample "a great deal" or "quite a bit." Nicholson and Antill (1981) also found that health and physical development was a major concern as did Collins and Harper (1974). In their study of 240 American adolescents, Eme et al. (1979) also found that concerns about drug use, alcohol, and smoking were present. A second theme or factor of concern, therefore, involves health and drug use worries.

The third and fourth themes or factors underlying adolescent concerns have to do with aspects of the development of the "self." Erikson (1959) has proposed that the major task of adolescence is the crystallizing of a self-definition and a feeling of self-integrity called "identity." This idea has proved to be of immense heuristic value in the study of adolescence and continues to inspire empirical work (e.g. Craig-Bray & Adams, 1986). Adolescents themselves express concerns surrounding this development of the self in two sorts of themes: (1) a personal or private self, and (2) a social or public self. The personal self does involve personal relations but concerns here focus more on "existential" matters such as "Who am I?" and "What is the purpose of life?" Nearly half (44%) of the adolescents studied by Bibby and Posterski (1985) for example, indicated that questions about the purpose of life and one's identity troubled them a "great deal" or "quite a bit." Similarly, Nicholson and Antill (1981) found that "personal psychological relations" figured heavily as an area of concern as did Eme et al. (1979). A related but separate theme underlying adolescent concerns is the social self which is a focus on more overt observable characteristics and relationships. This involves such factors as personal appearance, relations to friends, sexual behavior and orientation, current jobs and social and athletic activities. Eme et al. (1979) found that personal appearance ranked as the greatest concern for adolescents. Bibby and Posterski (1985) found that 44% of their sample were worried "a great deal" or "quite a bit" by their "looks" and 35% had similar concerns about loneliness and relations to friends. Nicholson and Antill (1981) found that social-psychological relations involving friends, co-workers and others was a major theme of concern. Moreover, 73% of Bibby's and Posterski's (1985) subjects felt that friends had influenced their life "a great deal" or "quite a bit" while 85% said that the way their parent's brought them up had the same influence.

From the foregoing discussion, therefore, it seems clear that four main themes or factors underlie the majority of adolescent concerns. By way of summary, these are: (1) Future and Career, (2) Health and Drugs, (3) Personal Self, and (4) Social Self. It is suggested that the latter two factors (Personal and Social Self) are separate but related since many concerns are both of a personal and social nature in self-definition. Moreover, it is suggested that the Social Self also derives input from Future and Career concerns and plans so that this factor is also related to the Social Self. Based on the foregoing considerations, the following empirical model was proposed.

A Four-Factor Model

It is proposed that adolescent concerns emanate from four basic factors which can be empirically derived. To reiterate, these are: (1) Future and Career, (2) Health and Drugs, (3) Personal Self, and (4) Social Self. It is predicted that concerns about school grades, future schooling, career planning, part-time jobs, etc. will load on the Future and Career factor. Concerns about sexual behavior, smoking, drug and alcohol use are predicted to load on the Health and Drug factor while concerns about identity, relations to parents, family and friends, and existential concerns will load on the Personal Self factor. Concerns about appearance, extra-curricular activities (sports, clubs, groups, etc.), part-time work and relations to friends will load on the Social Self factor as will concerns over sexual impulses and identity. Finally, it is predicted that the Social Self factor will be correlated to the Personal Self factor and the Future and Career factor. The major purpose of the present study was to explore the validity of this model using confirmatory factor analysis with a large group of adolescents. The secondary purposes of the study was to establish a hierarchy of adolescent concerns and to explore sex and age differences in these concerns.

Method

Subjects

Subjects were 439 students (263 males - 60%; 176 females - 40%) from 10 junior high and high schools in a large prairie city (population = 600 000).The subjects ranged in age from 12 to 19 years with a mean of 15.2 years and a standard deviation of 1.72. The number and percentage of subjects in each grade were as follows: Grade 8, n = 97 (22.1%); grade 9, n = 56 (12.8%); grade 10, n =135 (30.8%); grade 11, n = 58 (13.3%); grade 12, n = 93 (12.2%).

The majority of subjects were Caucasian (n = 383; 87.2%) while the rest were Oriental (n = 15. 3.4%), Black (n = 23; 5.3%), Asian (n = 12; 2.7%), and Native Indian (n = 6; 1.4%). Based on father's occupation, the number and percentage of subjects that are classified into each of the following categories were as follows: (1) Professional/managerial (e.g, physicians, executives) = 110 (25.1%); (2) entrepreneurial (e.g. self-employed businessmen) = 98 (22.3%); (3) skilled labor (e.g. licensed workers such as plumbers) = 127 (28.9%); and (4) unskilled labor (e.g. clerks, laborers) = 104 (23.7%). The present sample is very close to representing these socioeconomic categories in the general Canadian population (Statistics Canada, 1981, p. 271).

Procedures

Subjects completed a questionnaire in their regular class. In addition to questions about age, grade, sex, ethnicity, and father's employment, the questionnaire contained 14 items measuring concerns. The present questionnaire was an adaptation of the questionnaire used by Eme et al. (1979, p. 97-98). In this study, respondents were required to rate each of 14 items from 0 ("I never worry about it") to 3 ("This is a constant worry to me"). In the present study, respondents indicated their degree of concern for each item on a 4 point Likert scale (1 = never concerned; 2 = sometimes concerned; 3 = frequently concerned; 4= constantly concerned). The 14 items dealt with the following concerns: (1) personal appearance, (2) interaction with parents, (3) interaction with friends, (4) general family interactions, (5) identity ("Who Am I?"), (6) sexual impulses, (7) drug use, (8) smoking, (9) alcohol use, (10) grades, (11) extra-\curricular activities (e.g. sports), (12) career, (13) future schooling, and (14) part-time job while in school. Completion of the questionnaire required approximately 20-30 minutes.

Results

The analyses of the present data were done in three basic steps: (1) means for each item for the total sample and for two subgroups (sex and grade) were computed and analyzed, (2) the items were intercorrelated and factor analyzed, and (3) the "goodness of fit" of the data to the proposed four-factor model was computed using linear structural relationship (LISREL) techniques (Joreskog & Sorbom, 1984) employing maximum likelihood estimates.

Mean Ratings of Items

The mean rating for each item for the total sample, for males and females, and for grade were computed. Differences in mean ratings for sex and grade were analyzed by analysis of variance. These results are summarized in Table 11.1.

For the whole sample, grades were rated as having the highest degree of concern ($\overline{X}$ = 3.01), with career ($\overline{X}$ = 3.00) and appearance ($\overline{X}$ = 2.92) ranking second and third respectively (see Table 11.1). Concerns about alcohol use ($\overline{X}$ = 1.65), drug abuse ($\overline{X}$ = 1.49), and smoking ($\overline{X}$ = 1.47) ranked 12th, 13th and 14th respectively. These findings are remarkably similar to those of Eme et al (1979) who found that physical appearance, career, and grades ranked first, second and third respectively. Smoking and drug use concerns ranked second last and last respectively. In both the present study and the Eme et al. (1979) study, social relational concerns (interactions with friends, parents and family) ranked in the middle zone of the hierarchy. These same general patterns have been found with Australian adolescents (Collins & Harper, 1974; Nicholson & Antill, 1981), other American samples (Offer & Offer, 1975; Morgan, 1969), and with Canadian adolescents (Bibby & Posterski, 1985).

In the present study, there were notable sex differences in grades and appearance items with females expressing greater concern about them than did males (see Table 11.1). These findings are in consonance with those of Eme et al. (1979) and Nicholson and Antill (1981). In both these studies and the present one, it is generally adolescent girls who are most concerned about appearance and grades but there are no systematic sex differences on other concern items.

Table 11.1

Mean Rating of Seriousness of Variable of Concern

Variable	Total Sample[a]	Male[b]	Female[c]	8[d]	9[e]	10[f]	11[g]	12[h]
1. Grades	3.01	2.92	3.13*	3.23	2.79	2.93	3.09	2.96*
2. Career	3.01	2.92	3.13*	3.23	2.79	2.93	3.09	2.96*
3. Appearance	2.92	2.78	3.14**	3.07	3.00	2.87	3.18	2.62**
4. Future Schooling	2.83	2.81	2.87	2.91	2.38	2.92	2.96	2.84**
5. Identity	2.36	2.34	2.39	2.25	2.25	2.39	2.75	2.26**
6. Job	2.28	2.30	2.26	2.30	2.11	2.33	2.46	2.14
7. Activities	2.20	2.18	2.22	2.37	2.13	2.14	2.23	2.12
8. Family	2.10	2.08	2.13	2.18	2.05	2.16	2.13	1.99
9. Friends	2.08	2.02	2.18	2.23	2.02	2.06	2.32	1.87*
10. Parents	2.00	1.99	2.02	1.98	1.91	2.07	2.05	1.97
11. Sex	1.94	1.98	1.86	2.10	1.79	1.94	2.09	1.78
12. Alcohol	1.65	1.66	1.63	1.67	1.44	1.67	1.59	1.72
13. Drugs	1.49	1.49	1.48	1.62	1.32	1.53	1.21	1.50*
14. Smoking	1.47	1.44	1.51	1.71	1.29	1.50	1.25	1.34**

[a]$n = 439$; [b]$n = 263$; [c]$n = 176$; [d]$n = 97$; [e]$n = 56$; [f]$n = 135$; [g]$n = 58$; [h]$n = 93$;
*$p < .05$; **$p < .001$

From Table 11.1, it can be clearly seen that there are grade differences on several items of concern. It is the older pupils (grade 11 and 12) who are more concerned about grades, career, and future schooling than are the younger pupils (grades 8 and 9). This is probably due to the fact that these matters are of more in immediate concern to the older pupils than the younger ones. By contrast, the younger pupils are more concerned about their appearance, friends, drug abuse and smoking than are the older pupils. Interestingly, it is the middle groups (grades 10 and 1 1) who are more concerned about identity issues than either the younger or older pupils. This is likely due to the fact that it is these age groups (15 and 16 year olds) who have the highest probability of being in the transition phase between psychological moratorium and identity achieved (Erikson, 1959). Thus, identity issues would be of heightened concern. These age related findings are consistent with the findings of Collins and Harper(1974) and Nicholson and Antill (1981). The general findings of the present study that career and grades are of primary concern together with sex and age differences, are entirely consistent with findings from many other studies (Abel& Gingles, 1968; Bibby & Posterski, 1985. Collins & Harper, 1974; Offer & Offer,1975; Morgan, 1969; Nicholson & Antill, 1981).

Factor Analysis

Pearson product-moment correlation coefficients were computed for all pairs of items from the questionnaire. The resulting correlation matrix is shown in Table 11.2.

Table 11.2
Matrix of Pearson Product Moment Correlation
Coefficients of Fourteen Variables

Variable	1	2	3	4	5	6	7	8	9	10	11	12	13	14
1. Appearance	–													
2. Parents	13*	–												
3. Friends	27	34	–											
4. Family	19	46	47	–										
5. Identity	34	23	48	45	–									
6. Sex	17	19	29	23	29	–								
7. Drugs	00	-01	08	07	12	22	–							
8. Smoking	-03	-01	08	07	06	22	75	–						
9. Alcohol	04	07	15	16	18	20	55	54	–					
10. Grades	21	12	13	21	15	16	02	04	09	–				
11. Activities	22	11	25	17	22	24	03	03	07	24	–			
12. Career	10	16	07	18	17	19	03	01	08	41	22	–		
13. Future School	11	12	09	15	13	11	02	03	007	40	18	51	–	
14. Part-time Job	16	11	12	16	15	15	12	07	07	16	17	33	25	–

*All coefficients have been rounded to two decimal places and the decimal point has been dropped.

As indicated in the model of adolescent concerns, it was expected that there should be four underlying factors in the data. The correlation matrix, therefore, was factored into four principal components. The communalities were estimated by iterating the factoring routine until convergence at the .001 level was achieved. Convergence required 18 iterations, There were four eigen-values greater than one: 3.39, 2.15, 1.61, and 1.03. Of the total variance, 58.4% was accounted for by the four factors. The four factors were orthogonally rotated to the normalized Varimax criterion. The resulting rotated factor matrix is shown in Table 11.3.

The first factor with loadings from drugs, smoking, and alcohol, was the predicted Health and Drug factor. Sex concerns, with a health component, also has a minor loading on this factor. The second factor, Future and Career, has predictably heavy loadings from grades, career, and future schooling. Minor loading from extra-curricular activities and part-time job concerns are also consistent with expectations. The third factor, the Personal Self, has loadings from parents, friends, family and identity which also load on the fourth factor, Social Self. Since these two factors both deal with aspects for the self (Personal and Social), it follows that identity should load on both as does friends with approximately equal loadings on both factors. Appearance, sex and extra-curricular activities also load on the fourth factor with a minor loading from family. The overall pattern of loadings clearly follow the proposed model and result in interpretable and theoretically meaningful factors.

Table 11.3
Factor Matrix Orthogonally Rotated to the Normalized Varimax Criterion

Variable	Factor I Health and Drugs	Factor II Future and Career	Factor III Personal Self	Factor IV Social Self
1. Appearance	-.03	.13	.09	.49
2. Parents	-.01	.12	.56	.10
3. Friends	.08	.01	.49	.51
4. Family	.08	.14	.74	.23
5. Identity	.10	.09	.37	.55
6. Sex	.24	.16	.18	.34
7. Drugs	.87	.02	-.02	.04
8. Smoking	.87	.02	-.01	.00
9. Alcohol	.63	.07	.11	.09
10. Grades	.02	.52	.08	.20
11. Activities	.02	.25	.06	.39
12. Career	.01	.78	.10	.06
13. Future School	.01	.66	.07	.06
14. Part-time Job	.08	.35	.08	.16
Percent of Common Variance	46.5%	29.3%	17.8%	6.5%
Eigen Values	3.39	2.15	1.61	1.03

Fitting the Data to the Model

Using the linear structural relationships analysis (LISREL VI) (Joreskog & Sorbom, 1984), the data were fit to the four-factor model specified above. The schematic for the model, together with the factor loadings, theta-delta coefficients (unique variance) and intercorrelations between the factors or endogenous variables (Joreskog & Sorbom, 1984), are depicted in Figure 11.1.

The Goodness of Fit Index (adjusted for degrees of freedom) was 0.958 (X^2=84.58; df = 66; $p > .06$). The root mean square residual was 0.04. As can be seen from the Factor matrix (Table 11.3), and the path model (Figure 11.1), variables 1, 3, 5, 6, 11 and 14, load on the Social Self factor. Variables 2, 3, 4 and 5 load on the Personal Self factor. The Social Self factor and Personal Self factor are correlated at $r = .53$ (Figure 11.1). Variables 6, 7, 8 and 9 load on the Health and Drug factor, while variables 10, 11, 12, 13 and 14 load on the Future and Career factor. As predicted, the Future and Career factor is correlated with the Social Self factor ($r = .36$; see Figure 11.1). Not predicted, but intercorrelated, were factors F_2 (Future and Career) and F_3 (Personal Self) at $r = .32$. Nevertheless, as can be seen from the Goodness of Fit Index above and the Chi-Square results, the data fit the model remarkably well.

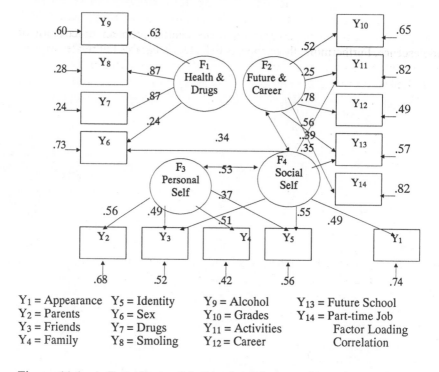

Y1 = Appearance Y5 = Identity Y9 = Alcohol Y13 = Future School
Y2 = Parents Y6 = Sex Y10 = Grades Y14 = Part-time Job
Y3 = Friends Y7 = Drugs Y11 = Activities Factor Loading
Y4 = Family Y8 = Smoling Y12 = Career Correlation

Figure 11.1: A Four Factor Model of Adolescent Concerns and Parameter Estimates Using LISREL VI with Maximum Likelihood Estimates.

Discussion

The main purpose of the present study was to propose and empirically test a four-factor model of adolescent concerns. From the accumulated research on adolescent concerns from adolescents from Canada, the U.S. and Australia, it appears that adolescent worries or concerns have four basic themes: (1) future schooling and career, (2) health, appearance and drug use (including alcohol and smoking), (3) personal or private self, and (4) social self. A four-factor model was proposed and empirically tested using factor analysis and LISREL procedures. The data based on 439 adolescents, showed a very good fit to the four-factor model. This suggests that, indeed, most adolescent concerns may emanate from these four basic underlying factors.

The hierarchy of concerns indicating the relative seriousness of these to adolescents was remarkably similar in the present study as to many previous findings (Abel & Gingles, 1968; Bibby & Posterski, 1985; Collins & Harper, 1974; Eme et al. 1979; Morgan, 1968; Nicholson & Antill, 1981). The most worrisome problems for adolescents tend to be school related (such as grades) and physical appearance. Problems of identity and other existential concerns such as questions of the "meaning of life" are secondary or tertiary. This runs against the expectations of Erikson (1959) and other "identity" or ego theorists (e.g. Craig-Dray & Adams, 1986; Marcia, 1966) who posit that identity formation and concerns surrounding this are *the* central problem or concern of adolescence. Furthermore, there appears to be two separable but related aspects of identity: a personal self and a social self. These two factors have shared elements (relations with friends, questions of "Who am I?") and unique elements (for Personal Self = relations with parents and family; for Social Self = appearance, sexual concerns and extra-curricular activities). The popular topics of adolescence which are given high visibility in the mass media (e.g., Falchikov, 1986) and are depicted as characterizing adolescents, are not of very great concern to adolescents themselves. These "pop" topics include sex, alcohol, drugs and smoking. The focus on these topics by mass media is completely out of proportion to the extent to which these pre-occupy or characterize adolescents (Falchikov, 1986).

The sex and age (grade) differences in the present study are consistent with previous findings (e.g., Nicholson & Antill, 1981). It is adolescent girls who are most concerned about their appearance perhaps because social norms continue to emphasize appearance more for women than for men (Maccoby & Jacklin, 1974). Older adolescents show greater concern over grades and career decisions than younger adolescents, while younger groups are more pre-occupied with smoking and drug abuse.

The present four-factor model is a parsimonious and powerful explanatory framework of adolescent concerns. The varied and apparently disparate concerns seem to emanate from four basic factors. The current model, however, is in need of further testing and research. Cross cultural research would be particularly relevant since the theoretical bases on which the model was derived was based onAustralian, Canadian and American adolescents in the first place. The parsimony of explanation of the model warrants further work.

References

Abel, H., & Gingles, R, (1968). Identifying problems of adolescent girls. *J.Educ. Res.* 58: 389-391.

Adelson, J. (1979). Adolescence and the generalization gap. *Psychology Today,*12:(9), 33-37.

Bibby, R.W., & Posterski, D,C. (1985). *The Emerging Generation,* Toronto: Irwin.

Coleman, J.C. (1978). Current contradictions in adolescent theory. *J. Youth Adoles.* 4:349-358.

Collins, J., & Harper, J. (1974). Problems of adolescents in Sydney, Australia. *J. Genet. Psychol.* 125:189-194.

Craig-Bray, L., & Adams, G.R. (1986). Different methodologies in the techniques? *J. Youth Adoles.* 15:191-204.

Eme, R., Maisiak, R., & Goodale, W. (1979). Seriousness of adolescent problems. *Adolescence.* 14:93-98.

Erikson, E.H. (1959). *Identity and the Life Cycle*, New York: Norton.

Falchikov, N. (1986). Images of adolescence: an investigation into the accuracyof the image of adolescence constructed by British newspapers. *J.Adoles.* 9:167-180.

Hall, G.S. (1904). *Adolescence.* Vol. I and II. Appleton, New York.

Joreskog, K.G. & Sorbom, D. (1984). *LISREL VI: Analysis of Linear Structural Relationship by the Method of Maximum Likelihood.* Mooresville, Indiana:Scientific Software, Inc.

Maccoby, E., & Jacklin, C. (1974). *The Psychology of Sex Differences.*Stanford: Stanford University Press.

Marcia, J.E. (1966). Development and validation of ego identity status. *J.Person. Soc. Psychol.* 3:551-558.

Morgan, J. (1969). Adolescent problems and the Mooney Problem Checklist. *Adolescence* 4:111-126.

Nicholson, S.I. & Antill, J.K. (1981). Personal problems of adolescents and their relationship to peer acceptance and sex role identity. *J. YouthAdoles.* 10:309-325.

Offer, D., & Offer, J.B. (1975). *From Teenage to Young Manhood.* Basic Books,New York

Rutter, M. (1980). *Changing Youth in a Changing Society.* Harvard UniversityPress, Cambridge, Mass.

Rutter, M., Maughan, B., Mortimore, P.,Ouston, J., & Smith, A. (1979).*Fifteen Thousand Hours: Secondary School and Their Effects on Children.*Open Books, London.

Siddique, C.M. & D'Arcy, C. (1984). Adolescence, stress, and psychologicalwell-being. *J. Youth Adoles.* 13:459-473.

Statistics Canada (1981). *Canada Year Book: 1980-81,* Ottawa, Minister of Supply and Services.

Westwood, M. (1986). The health of Canadian youth: A developmental perspective. *Health and Promotion,* Winter:2-5.

12

The Long Term Implications
of Childhood Attachment

Mark Genuis

The theory of attachment (Bowlby, 1969) draws on several intellectual traditions such as ethology, psychoanalysis, and cognitivism to create an integrated body of knowledge about human emotional development. Attachment theory is particularly concerned with the development of human emotions from a life span perspective (Ainsworth, 1985), hypothesizing that observable behavior is directed by people's emotions, specifically in relation to important figures within their lives. A recent and essential focus for the development of the theory of attachment is that of the long-term implications of attachment. Theorists and researchers have hypothesized that insecure attachment patterns in infancy and early childhood are strong predictors of maladaptiveness and psychopathology in adolescence and adulthood (Cicchetti & Howes, 1991). Others, however, have maintained that early childhood attachments are superseded by the effects of maturation and therefore are not related to the long-term mental health (e.g. Goldsmith, Bradshaw, & Rieser-Danner, 1986). The issue remains unresolved, however, as there are presently a dearth of studies on the long-term effects of secure and insecure attachment patterns.

The focus of this chapter is on theoretical formulations and research findings based on attachment theory. This includes a discussion of the definition of attachment based on the model originally posed by Bowlby (1969). Moreover, the issues related to the development of attachment behavior as well as identified patterns of attachment and the long-term implications for these patterns are addressed. Because the focus of this work is on the long-term effects on children due to different types of attachment, the importance of specific factors influencing the development of secure infant-caregiver attachments is underscored.

Definition of Attachment

The theory of attachment has as its key concept the behavioral system of individuals. An explanation of the enduring attachments that children and older individuals make to particular figures is made from these behaviors called attachment behaviors (Bowlby, 1982). The definition presented by Bowlby (1973) has been widely used in research in the area of attachment. Bowlby's definition of attachment behavior also formed the basis of the Strange Situation test designed by Ainsworth and Wittig (1969). The Strange Situation is an assessment procedure which has been used as the primary method of assessing infant and childhood attachments to caregivers (Sroufe, 1985). In the following discussion, the terms attachment behavior and attachment are defined.

Attachment Behavior

Attachment behavior has been defined consistently through a variety of studies by numerous researchers (Bretherton, 1991). Those deserving credit for originally making the important distinction between attachment and attachment behavior include Ainsworth (1972), Bischof (1975), Bowlby (1982), Sroufe and Waters (1977) and Bretherton (1980). Bowlby (1982) combined the work of these researchers and defined attachment behavior as referring to any of the various forms of behavior that a child commonly engages in to attain and/or maintain a desired proximity. At any one time some form of such behavior may be either present or absent and which it is, to a high degree, dependent on the condition obtaining at the time (pp. 371-372).

Attachment theorists, based on the theory of natural selection, have posited that historically such behavior has, and continues to have, survival value for the infant and/or child (Ainsworth & Bowlby, 1991). Proximity to the primary caregiver is sought by the infant who feels safe when the attachment figure is available. Infants and young children require the maintenance of such proximity because they have not yet developed the internal representational models (hereafter referred to as "working models") of their primary caregivers and therefore require frequent reminders of the caregiver's availability. Accordingly, the safety of the present surroundings are ensured (Sroufe, 1988).

As children develop secure and predictable models of the primary caregiver, themselves, and themselves in relation to the primary caregiver, they are able to sustain longer periods of time away from the attachment figure without experiencing distress (Bowlby, 1982). The children are able to trust the secure base of the models that have been constructed through numerous encounters with the primary caregiver (Weiss, 1991). An example of this is young children's exploring behavior (Bowlby, 1982).

Children are secure in exploring their surroundings as long as the primary caregiver is readily available. As children are able to trust that the caregiver will not abandon then, they explore their world further and for longer periods of time. A second example of the secure base has been demonstrated through the Strange Situation. It has been consistently observed that infants and children who are securely attached to their primary caregiver exhibit various levels of distress upon separation from the attachment figure in a strange situation, but are not immobilized with fear as are children who are anxiously attached. Securely attached infants and children also consistently welcome the return of their primary attachment figure with joy. Subjects assessed as having insecure attachments demonstrate a variety of confusion, anger and anxiety when reunited with their primary caregivers (Grossman & Grossman, 1991).

Along with attachment behavior comes the strongest of emotions, including love, fear, anxiety, anger and sadness. The specific emotions experienced by children depends on the proximity and safety attained through the attachment behavior exhibited. That is, through the availability of the primary caregiver. The emotional elements may be profitably discussed within the realm of the specific attachment.

Attachment

To say that children have an attachment to, or are attached to someone, is to say that they are strongly disposed to seek proximity to and contact with a specific figure and to do so in certain situations, notably when a child is frightened, tired or ill. The disposition to behave in this way is an attribute of the child, an attribute which changes only slowly over time and which is unaffected by the situation of the moment (Bowlby, 1982; p. 371).

For a child to be securely attached to a caregiver, that child must feel safe and secure in that caregiver's presence and therefore, be motivated to initiate attachment behavior when the child feels threatened in any way. Along with the feelings of safety and security come intense feelings of love and joy (Bowlby, 1988).

According to this theory, it is thought that between birth and approximately six months of age, an attachment to, (perhaps better stated as a preference for) the primary caregiver is developing. At approximately six months of age infants are able to further demonstrate this preference as they are now better able to direct their attention as well as to seek the proximity of a specific individual or individuals (e.g., Belsky & Nezworski, 1988). Within the time period of the first six months of life, it is posited that infants are developing an intense affectional bond to their primary caregiver and increasingly direct their emotions toward that person (Ainsworth & Bowlby, 1991). The development of the bond is furthered when children elicit attachment behavior and experience varying levels of success in maintaining proximity to the primary caregiver. Such a bond leads to infants or young children establishing internal working models of themselves, their primary caregivers, and themselves in relation to their primary caregivers (Ainsworth, 1989).

All human infants without significant biological abnormalities, however treated, form an attachment to the persons who care for them (Bowlby, 1982). It is the quality of the attachment relationship that varies depending on the quality of care experienced by the infant. If the emotional bond is positive and care is consistent, the working models will develop in a like manner, and a secure attachment will result (Main, 1991). Sroufe (1988) argued that these early experiences, and the relationship to which they lead exercise important influences on later development.

Considerable attention has been paid to the influence of infant and child temperament on the development of attachment. (e.g., Belsky & Nezworski, 1988). It has been found that although a particular temperament can be identified at birth, infants also have an impressive array of abilities in many domains and their temperament, especially within the first year of life, is labile (Dodge & Richard, 1985). Bell and Ainsworth (1972) reported evidence confirming the influential role of the caregiver on the course of development of attachment security. The findings of their comparison of 23 infants indicated that in the first three months of life caregiver behaviors did not correlate significantly with how much a baby cried. By the end of the first year of life, however, mothers who had attended promptly to their crying babies had babies who cried much less than did the babies of mothers who had left them to cry ($r = .49, p < .01$). Therefore, with consistent demonstrations of care by the primary caregiver, the behavior of the infant changed. Similar findings were reported by Moss (1967). Such findings are in direct contradiction to the theory of "spoiling" presented in traditional psychoanalysis (Freud, 1905). In fact, Ainsworth and Bowlby (1991) explicitly argued that timely and appropriate close bodily contact does not "spoil" infants and does not lead them to be fussy and clingy; evidence suggests that the opposite phenomenon occurs (e.g., Bowlby, 1982).

Development of Attachment

Attachment theory postulates that children's ties to their mothers is the product of the activity of numerous behavioral systems that have proximity to the primary caregiver as the predictable outcome (Bowlby, 1982). Although the ontogeny of attachment behavior is complex and individual differences are at their greatest in the first year of life, fairly typical attachment behavior is exhibited by almost all children in the second year of life. Aside from the developing ability of children to explore their world in new ways at this age, it has been argued by Bower (1989) and Bowlby (1980) that children develop "person permanence" by the end of the first year of life and are therefore able to maintain an image of the primary caregiver longer than an infant under one year of age would (this idea is analogous to the concept of object permanence espoused by Piaget (1972)). It is important to note, however, that before the age of 16 to 24 months, the images themselves as well as the child's ability to maintain them are still quite unstable (Greenspan & Lieberman, 1988).

In assessing the quality of attachments of infants as well as describing infant moods in various situations, Greenspan and Lieberman used general descriptive categories of affective-thematic inclinations including: (a) interest and attentiveness; (b) relaxation and/or calmness; (c) dependency (including holding or comforting-type behaviors, etc.); (d) pleasure or joy (including enthusiasm); (e) assertiveness (explorativeness and curiosity); (f) protest or other distinct forms of displeasure, including anger; (g) negativism or stubbornness; (h) self-limit setting (often not seen until children are at least 18 months of age); and (i) after the age of three, empathy and more stable feelings of love.

Patterns of Attachment

In the original work examining the child's tie to a primary caregiver, Ainsworth (1963) observed the development of the infant-caregiver relationship in a sample of 28 unweaned Uganden babies and their mothers. She was particulary impressed with the how the children used their mothers as a secure base from which to explore the world and as a haven of safety. As a result of the direct observation done on these subjects, Ainsworth divided the infants into the categories of securely attached, insecurely (anxiously) attached, and nonattached (Ainsworth, 1963). In a follow up longitudinal study conducted in Baltimore, a formal procedure called the Strange Situation Test was developed for assessing the attachment of infants to their primary caregivers (Ainsworth & Wittig, 1969). Through this project, Ainsworth realized that the infants who were initially classified as nonattached were indeed attached but in a very insecure way. These infants were subsequently assessed as having anxious attachments of the avoidant type (Ainsworth, Blehar, Waters, & Wall, 1978).

Although the inclusion of the avoidant category helped to explain the attachment of a higher percentage of the children, there was still a portion of the subjects who remained unclassifiable in the present secure, ambivalent, and avoidant categories (Main, 1991). In a recent review of the videocassettes of the Strange Situation behavior of many infants considered unclassifiable in the above categories, Main and Solomon (in press) found that these infants displayed an array of disorganized and/or disoriented behaviors. Such behaviors included the freezing of all movement, or exhibiting stereotyped movement in the parent's presence (Main, 1991).

As a result of the research conducted, two main categories of attachment type have been identified. These are secure and anxious. Anxious attachment is further subdivided in ambivalent, avoidant and disorganized/disoriented. Each category is defined by behavioral demonstrations of infants and young children. A description of these behaviors of children in the Strange Situation procedure (Ainsworth & Wittig, 1969) is found in Table 12.1.

Table 12.1
Behavioral Outcomes of Attachment Type

Secure Attachment

Children appear confident that their primary caregiver is available, responsive, and helpful should the infant or child encounter any adverse experiences or frightening situations. After a distressing or alarming event, securely attached infants also take great comfort in and are soothed by close body contact with their primary caregivers.

Anxious Attachment

Ambivalent

Children appear to be uncertain whether their primary caregiver will be available or responsive to their needs when attachment behavior is displayed. Such children oscillate between seeking proximity and contact with their primary caregiver and resisting such contact and interaction. These children are not able to use their caregivers as a secure base from which to explore unfamiliar surroundings and strange situations. These children demonstrate considerable emotional conflict

Avoidant

Children demonstrate no confidence that they will received care when it is sought. They appear to expect rejection when exhibiting attachment behavior. The emotional conflict that these children demonstrate is more hidden than in the case of ambivalently attached children. These children exhibit considerable avoidance behavior, which is often incorrectly assessed as denoting detachment.

Disorganized/Disoriented

Children act as though both the environment and the attachment figure are sources of threat to them. The dilemma results in a conflict between two incompatible behaviors: 1. to seek proximity to the attachment figure, and 2. to avoid proximity with that same figure as they pose a threat. The behaviors elicited by infants appear as a contradiction or inhibition of action as it is undertaken. Freezing as though there were no alternative solutions for the infant, or some other behavior that is indicative of the fear and confusion experienced.

Implications of Attachment Security into Adolescence

Attachment strategies developed in infancy are hypothesized to remain stable throughout childhood, adolescence and adulthood. In comparison to secure attachment strategies, insecure attachments involve alternative patterns of interaction: an avoidant, an ambivalent, or a disorganized strategy. Grossman and Grossman (1991) argued that these differences, even if relatively minor, appear to make a difference in the quality of a person's emotional life. When under pressure or stress, persons using insecure attachment strategies may turn out to be more susceptible to psychological ill-health. This vulnerability depends on an intricate interplay of the quality of the working models, the social-emotional support experienced by the individual in the present and current emotional stress. The specific type of psychopathology, if any, which results may also depend on the delicate interplay of these variables.

Numerous longitudinal findings have supported the notion that chronic problem behaviors in childhood portends future problem behavior, emotional instability, and delinquency in both adolescence and adulthood (e.g., Olweus, 1979). The underlying cause(s) of these deficits in emotional stability have not, however, been adequately addressed. Theoretically, because the attachment classifications and related behavior have been consistently found to remain stable throughout childhood (e.g., Main, 1991), it is logical to hypothesize that attachment type is a strong predictor of emotional security, delinquent behavior, and psychopathology in adolescence.

Attachment stability from childhood to adolescence

Kobak and Sceery (1988) studied university students to assess whether working models are or are not associated with differences in affect regulation. Representations of self and others were also tested. Self-report measures were used to gather data on perceptions of self and others. Result revealed that subjects having had a secure attachment to a primary caregiver in infancy and early childhood, were rated as more ego-resilient (p < .001), less anxious (p < 0.05) and less hostile by peers (p < 0.001) and reported little distress and high levels of social support (p < 0.05) in late adolescence. The group sampled by Kobak and Sceery (1988) consisted of university students and thus generalization from their work may be inappropriate.

Serbin, Peters, McAffer, and Schwartzman (1991) conducted two longitudinal studies on females assessed as aggressive, withdrawn and aggressive-withdrawn. The first study consisted of data gathered from medicare records of 853 women. The second study focused on a data set from 38 females. Serbin et al. (1991) attempted to draw a connection between childhood patterns of aggressive and/or withdrawn behavior and later gynaecological problems suggesting problematic sexual activity, adolescent pregnancy, parenting and home environment. Although no direct measures for emotional attachment to caregivers were obtained, the behavior patterns observed by Serbin et al., (1991), have been proposed as indication of attachment by many theorists (e.g., Cicchetti and Howes, 1991).

Medical records of the female subjects were examined for a six year period. The final sample for whom medical records could be obtained was 853 women. Risk ratios (RR) were calculated with each of the of six reproductive outcomes (pregnancy, birth, pregnancy termination, birth control, gynaecological problems and, sexually transmitted disease) within each of the three age groups (grade 1, 4 and, 7). Results from this first study demonstrated that women initially assessed as aggressive in grade one were significantly more likely to have gynaecological problems and to be using birth control between the ages of 11 and 17 years than were subjects in the contrast group (RR= 2.04 and 2.55 respectively, p < .05). Women assessed as aggressive in grade 4 were significantly more likely than subjects in the control group to have contracted at least one sexually transmitted disease (RR = 1.54, p. < 05) between the ages of 14 and 20 years. Subjects of the aggressive group first assessed in grade 7 had significantly higher rates of pregnancy, use of birth control, and gynaecological problems between the ages of 17 and 23 years (RR = 1.36, 1.25 and, 1.19 respectively, p < .05).

For women assessed as being aggressive-withdrawn in grade one, a review of their medical records demonstrated that between 11 and 17 years of age significantly more of these women than those in the control group were using birth control and/or had gynaecological problems (RR = 1.75 and 1.65 respectively, p < .05). In the aggressive-withdrawn sample of women assess in grade four, significantly more women presented with pregnancy and childbirth when the women were between 14 and 20 years of age (RR = 2.05 and 2.56 respectively, p < .05).

From the results of study one, Serbin et al. (1991) concluded that childhood aggression in girls is a predictor of early, problematic patterns of sexual activity. The pattern demonstrated by subjects who scored high on both aggression and withdrawal in middle childhood is quite dramatic as 48 percent of these subjects became pregnant between the ages of 14 and 20 years. The purpose of the second study presented by Serbin et al., (1991) was twofold. First they attempted to examine the home environment and parenting behavior of a sub-sample of women from the previous study who had become mothers in their teens or early 20's. Second, they investigated any connections between mothers' aggression and withdrawal scores in childhood and early developmental progress in their offspring.

From the eligible subjects in the initial sample, 38 women agreed to participate in the second study. The mean age of the women was 22 years (SD = 2.1) and the average age of the children was 24 months (SD = 18) at the time of testing. The subsample was representative of the original group on aggression and withdrawal (means were close to the 50th percentile). Serbin et al. (1991) also conducted analyses predicting the developmental delay of the offspring of this sample of women. A regression equation included aggression, withdrawal, mother's age when she became pregnant, and child's age as predictor variables. The equation predicting developmental delay was significant (R = 0.74, $F_{4,32}$ = 4.45, p < .0001), with all predictors demonstrating significance except for withdrawal. The authors concluded that mother's childhood social history has direct relevance for parenting and home environment. These results provide support for the hypothesis that childhood attachment is stable in the long-term. Attachment is primarily a social construct and thus the social environment Serbin et al., (1991) refers to, may be related in an important way to childhood attachment. The sample size in the second Serbin et al., (1991) study is small and therefore the results must be interpreted with caution. There were also no direct assessment of childhood attachments and so the connection between this study and attachment theory is, at present, tenuous.

Attachment in adolescence

Armsden and Greenberg (1987) tested two hypotheses: (1) that adolescents with qualitatively different attachments to parents and peers would differ in proximity seeking and in well-being, and (2) that the associations between negative life change and psychological symptomatologies was expected to be weaker for the group of adolescents who were more securely attached. Two attachment groups were defined according to a set of decision rules regarding the interrelationships among the subscores obtained on the attachment measure. The sample consisted of 86 students (32 male and 54 female) ranging in age from

17 to 20 years (mean age = 18.6 years). The majority (over 80 percent) of the subjects were Caucasian and approximately 15 percent were either Asian or Asian-American.

Results demonstrated that family self-concept was strongly associated with parent attachment ($r = .78$). Peer attachment was not related to the measures of family environment. Females scored significantly higher on Mother Utilization ($F_{1,84} = 13.0$, p < .001) and Parent Utilization ($F_{1,84} = 4.25$, p. < 05). Females also reported more negative life change ($F_{1,82} = 6.9$, p < .01) and were less consistent than males in their self-concept ($F_{1,84} = 21.45$, p < .0001). Nonsignificance were found across cultures.

Positive and negative life change both significantly predicted self-esteem ($F_{1,84} = 8.4$, p < .01 and $F_{1,84} = 15.7$, p < .001 respectively) and life satisfaction ($F_{1,84} = 22.6$, p < .001 and $F_{1,84} = 19.7$, p < .001 respectively). Both peer and parent attachment also predicted self-esteem ($F_{1,84} = 26.6$, p < .001 and $F_{1,84} = 33.3$, p. < .001 respectively) and life satisfaction ($F_{1,84} = 9.0$, p < .01 and $F_{1,84} = 25.6$, p < .001 respectively).

Each of positive life change, negative life change, peer and parent attachment were significantly related to the criterion measures of depression/anxiety, resentment/alienation, irritability/anger, and guilt. The only exception was that parent attachment was not found to be a significant predictor of either irritability/anger or guilt. The low security parent attachment group did report significantly more negative life change than the high security group ($t_{55} = 2.04$, p < .05). The authors concluded that the perception of family relationships continued to be linked to well-being, but called for further research to support their findings.

In a study examining the extent and function of parental attachment among college students, Kenny (1987) distributed self-report questionnaires to a sample of 173 (100 male and 73 female) first year university students. As a framework for the study, Kenny used the ethological model of attachment, noting the relevance of the secure base phenomenon and its relation to published empirical work that has documented the persistence of family ties into adulthood (e.g., Main, 1991). Assertion and dating competence were used as the dependent variables in a multiple regression analysis conducted by Kenny (1987).

Results presented a four-factor solution for the female group (quality of relationship; parental role in providing emotional support; parental fostering of autonomy; and adjustment to separation) and a three factor solution for males (General attachment, which included items describing the quality of the parental relationship, perceptions of parents as a source of support, and parental fostering of autonomy; adjustment to separation and; parental protection and interference).

In the multiple regression analyses for the female sample, factor one (quality of relationship) and factor four (adjustment to separation) both significantly predicted high levels of self-reported assertion ($F_{1,98} = 23.73$, p < .001 and $F_{2,97} = 27.00$, p < .001 respectively). Only adjustment to separation significantly predicted dating competence ($F_{1,98} = 6.74$, p < .01). For the male sample, factor 2 (adjustment to separation) was the sole factor that significantly predicted level of assertion and dating competence ($F_{1, 71} = 8.67$, p < .001 and $F_{1,71} = 8.91$, p <

.001 respectively). Kenny (1987) argued that the consistency of the influence adjustment to separation has on assertion levels and dating competence implies that students who feel lonely and lacking in confidence are not likely to feel assertive or to be experiencing feelings of success in establishing intimate relationships. In assessing the factors specifically describing the characteristics of the parent-child relationship, only the quality of the parental relationship was significantly correlated with the assertion measure. Lastly, the quality of parental relationship and the adjustment to separation factors were the best combined predictor of assertion (R = .51, $F_{2,97}$ = 17.01, p < .001).

From the results of study, Kenny (1987) argued that the ethological notion of attachment as providing a secure base of support seems to be applicable for furthering the understanding of the strength of family relationships in adolescence. The researcher noted that many of the subjects continued to turn to their parents as a source of help when needed and valued the help obtained as contributing to self-confidence. Parents were generally perceived by the subjects in this sample as being supportive of the independence of the subjects as well as being available as a source of support when needed. This is consistent both with the theoretical postulates of Bowlby (1973, 1982) and appears parallel with the attachment behavior observed in infants having secure attachments. Kenny also argued from the data collected that through close parental relationships with their children, the female subjects were able to overcome any societal pressure for women to be unassertive. The same was found for males, however they are not believed to have the same societal pressure towards unassertiveness. Interestingly, the significant relationship between parental relationship and assertiveness in subjects indicates that in both genders, the influence of parents on their children has the ability to outweigh societal pressures, at least in the area of assertiveness, in both positive and negative dimensions. The final conclusion made by Kenny (1987) was that "popular views and psychological theory regarding the need to diminish parental ties need to be revised. Despite societal emphasis on the importance of becoming autonomous, an interdependence with the family members often persists at least through late adolescence" (p. 27).

Armstrong and Roth (1989) argued that the connection between leaving home or loss of a love relationship and the onset and recurrence of eating-disorder symptomatology is well documented and that the connection can be explained clearly by attachment theory. They also argued that the recent exclusive focus in psychology on autonomy has made it difficult to get a full picture of the role of attachment and attendant separation distress across the adaptive range. The authors pointed out the dearth of research examining healthy, mature styles of intimacy to recognize the difficulty of examining attachment issues in adulthood. Accordingly, the purpose of the study was to examine the implications of Bowlby's attachment theory for eating disorders.

These researchers hypothesized that eating disorder patients would manifest anxious attachment and separation-based depression. The sample consisted of 27 women, 11 of whom had a primary diagnosis of anorexia nervosa, 12 with a diagnosis of bulimia nervosa, and the remaining four subjects with atypical eating disorders. The modal age of the sample was 20 years, and ranged from 17 to 43 years of age. Subjects were from relatively high socioeconomic status and education level (one-half were college students and another one-third were working at professional or skilled jobs). This demographic data is typical of the majority of eating-disorder studies (Armstrong & Roth, 1989).

No differences were found between varieties of eating disorder as well as between age groups. This led the Armstrong and Roth (1989) to treat the clinical sample as a single group. Large differences were found between the percentage of eating disorder subjects and control subjects who demonstrated anxious attachment (96 and 27 percent respectively). Significant differences for the control group between the mild and severe separation pictures on the Hansburg's (1986) separation anxiety test, whereas nonsignificant findings resulted for the eating disorder group. This finding indicates that the eating disorder subjects are not differentiating between mild, every day type separations and relationship ending types of separations. This lack of distinction is inappropriate from an attachment theory perspective.

The authors concluded that a typical pattern emerges showing the eating disorder group as having "severe anxious attachment and chronic separation depression characterized by overreaction to minor separations and considerable self-blame, anger, and rejection as well as denial of the painful experiences" (p. 151).

The nonsignificant finding between age groups in this study lend empirical support to the notion of stability of attachment type throughout the lifespan. The clarity of definitions stand out as a strength in the Armstrong and Roth (1989) study. The lack of statistical information provided limits the findings to some degree. Nevertheless, the information provided lends empirical support for the theoretical notion that attachment type directly affects emotional development, and that insecure attachment is significantly more related to psychopathology than secure attachment.

Ryan and Lynch (1989) examined the construct of emotional autonomy, as proposed by Steinberg and Silverberg (1986), in adolescent and young adult samples. The argument proposed by Ryan and Lynch (1989) was that the measures of emotional autonomy and independence were invalid and that researchers were instead measuring emotional detachment from parents. The definition of detachment provided by Ryan and Lynch (1989) is consistent with that proposed by Bowlby (1973). Detachment was defined as representing loss and separation, wherein a person having an attachment to a caregiver is severed from a source of guidance, affection, or nurturance. Ryan and Lynch (1989) also argued that some forms of detachment from the family are associated with an experienced lack of parental support and acceptance, which is not conducive to independence and may actually interfere with the consolidation of identity and the formation of a positive self-concept. Steinberg and Silverberg (1986) followed the definition of emotional autonomy proposed by Douvan and Adelson (1966), who conceptualized emotional autonomy as the degree to which the adolescent or young adult has been able to cast off infantile ties to the family. Ryan and Lynch (1989) reexamined this construct of emotional autonomy, particularly with regard to its distinction from the issues of detachment and independence. They conducted three studies using the Emotional Autonomy Scale (EAS) and the Inventory of Adolescent Attachments (IAA). In summary, the findings from the Ryan and Lynch (1989) studies indicated that emotional autonomy was associated with less felt security and utilization of parents in young adolescents, greater perceived parental rejection (versus acceptance) in both mid-adolescent and young adult samples, and less experienced family cohesion and parental acceptance in young adults. Evidence supporting the premise that emotional autonomy may be most meaningfully construed as emotional detachment resulting from the loss of developmentally appropriate attachments was provided.

Summary of Findings

From the foregoing discussion, a number of findings may be summarized. First, attachment was presented by Bowlby from an ethological perspective (Ainsworth & Bowlby, 1991) and has been demonstrated to be consistent across cultures. Second, attachment appears to remain consistent from childhood through adolescence and into adulthood. Third, negative or anxious attachment is related to lowered self-esteem and perceived lovability in adolescence as well as psychopathology and deviant behavior. Fourth, parents appear to be the primary focus in the development of psychopathology and delinquency, and the attachments to each parent differs but is instrumental to human development from infancy into adulthood. Fifth, there appears to be no sex differences in attachment patterns to parents. Hierarchical attachments to primary, secondary and tertiary caregivers and relations may be a more appropriate way of conceptualizing familial relations.

Methodological Issues

First, in some of the studies, attachment is not clearly defined and from the methodology and assessment instruments used, the framework from which the researchers were working is not clear (Armsden & Greenberg, 1987; Kwakman, Zuiker, Schippers, & de Wuffel, 1988). Accordingly, because there is presently a paucity of empirical literature directly assessing the stability of attachment from infancy and early childhood through to adolescence and adulthood, it is appropriate for researchers to present the definition of attachment on which their work is based.

Some of the studies that deal with special populations have not employed appropriate matched control groups (Armsrong & Roth, 1989). This is an important consideration in such research in order to provide the adequate data to make necessary comparisons, such as rates attachment styles in between as well as within groups and relationship of attachment style to pathology, behavior and so on.

The majority of studies assessing older adolescents and young adults utilize college students as subjects. There is a need for research to be conducted with subjects who represent a more diverse group than university students as this group generally represents a more privileged segment of the population (Kenny, 1987, 1990; Violato & Genuis, 1993). Representative samples are required before generalizations from the empirical findings can be made.

A variety of instruments have been used to assess attachment of adolescents to their parents. The instruments vary in their ability to assess the construct of attachment as defined in the Bowlbian sense and none are complete in the sense of encompassing the four types of attachment now recognized in the literature. Further research is required to develop an instrument that can assess adolescent attachment in full accordance with the theoretical position taken by attachment theorists. Evidence for construct validity is also urgently required. This would require the assessment of both childhood and present attachment to primary and secondary caregivers along all four recognized dimensions.

Most studies examining attachment in adolescence focus on this concept without considering the development of attachment from early childhood. Further research is required to test the hypothesis held by attachment theorists (e.g., Bretherton, 1991) that the infant's and young child's attachment is a stable construct and changes only when in life circumstance that are different in important ways for the child change (Vaughn, Egeland, Waters, & Sroufe, 1979). Vaughn et al. (1979) have demonstrated the stability of attachment into childhood, but further support for such stability beyond this period is required.

In assessing the implications for attachment, focus should be placed on attachments to parents (or parent substitutes) and information needs to be assessed differentially for each parent as well as for both parents together as a system. The reason for this is found in the theories of Bowlby (1969, 1973, 1980, 1982) and Ainsworth and Bowlby (1991), where the attachment to the primary caregiver is hypothesized to be where a child's working models are established. The behavior (internal and external) of the person is thought to be moulded according to the security of attachment in these early relationships and so the measures of attachment to peers (e.g., Armsden & Greenberg, 1987) serves as a confirmation of the belief that secure attachments affect peer relationships in a positive manner. It does not indicate that the peer relationships in adolescence replaces the importance of the attachment to the primary and secondary caregivers. Empirical evidence supporting the notion of the importance of the adolescent's relationship with his parents predicting and influencing psychological health and peer relationships is numerous (e.g., Gallagher, 1976). Reports have been more epidemiological in nature and thus have not focused on the theoretical notion of emotional attachment of the child to the primary caregiver. Further research is required to confirm or reject the preliminary findings reviewed above.

Summary

From the foregoing review, the following findings may be summarized: (1) universal definitions of attachment and attachment behavior have been arrived at, (2) infants may be predisposed to forming a secure attachment relationship with one main caregiver and other attachment relationships with subsequent figures in a hierarchical manner, (3) the actual antecedents events leading to the development of secure infant-primary caregiver attachment are numerous and have been proposed and revealed empirically, (4) four specific attachment styles have been empirically supported (secure, anxious-ambivalent, anxious-avoidant, and anxious-disorganized/disoriented), (5) the long-term effects of secure and insecure attachments to a primary caregiver have not been definitively supported in the empirical literature, (6) anxious attachment in infancy and early childhood, may provide for a significantly increased risk of the development of psychopathology in adolescence, and indeed adulthood as well, and, (7) working models developed from insecure attachment relationships in early life appear to remain stable throughout life. The sensitive periods of development, however, has been argued to remain strongest through the immature years of development (from birth through adolescence).

References

Ainsworth, M.D.S. (1963). The development of mother-infant interaction among the Ganda. In B.M. Foss (Ed.), *Determinants of infant behaviour* (Vol. 2, pp. 67-112). London: Methuen.

Ainsworth, M.D.S. (1972). Attachment and dependency: A comparison. In J.L. Gewirtz (Ed.), *Attachment and dependency* (pp. 97-137). Washington, DC: Winston.

Ainsworth, M.D.S. (1989). Attachments beyond infancy. *American Psychologist, 44,* 709-716.

Ainsworth, M.D.S. (1991). Attachments and other affectional bonds across the life cycle. In C. M. Parkes, J. Stevenson-Hinde, & P. Marris (Eds.), *Attachment across the life cycle*. London: Routledge.

Ainsworth, M.D.S., Blehar, M.C., Waters, R., & Wall, S. (1978). *Patterns of attachment: A psychological study of the strange situation.* Hillsdale, NJ: Erlbaum.

Ainsworth, M.D.S., & Bowlby, J. (1991). An ethological approach to personality development. *American Psychologist, 46,* 333-341.

Ainsworth, M.D.S., & Wittig, B.A. (1969). Attachment and exploratory behaviour of one-year-olds in a strange situation. In B. M. Foss (Ed.), *Determinants of infant behaviour* (Vol. 4, pp. 111-136). London: Methuen.

Armsden, G.C., & Greenberg, M.T. (1987). The inventory of parent and peer attachment: Individual differences and their relationship to psychlogical well-being in adolescence. *Journal of Youth and Adolescence, 16,* 427-454.

Armstrong, J.G., & Roth, D.M. (1989). Attachment and Separation difficulties in eating disorder: A preliminary investigation. *International Journal of Eating disorders, 8,* 141-155.

Bandura, A. (1977). *Social learning theory.* Englewood Cliffs, N.J.: Prentic-Hall, Inc.

Bell, S.M., & Ainsworth, M.D.S. (1972). Infant crying and maternal responsiveness. *Child Development, 43*, 1171-1190.

Belsky, J., & Nezworski, T. (1988). Clinical implications of Attachment. In Belsky, J. & Nezworski, T. (Eds.), *Clinical Implications of attachment*. Hillsdale, New Jersey: Lawrence Earlbaum Associates.

Blacher, J., & Meyers, C. (1983). A review of attachment formation and disorder of handicapped children. *American Journal of Mental Deficiency, 87*, 359-371.

Bower, T.G.R. (1989). *The rational infant: Learning in infancy*. New York: W. H. Freeman and Company.

Bowlby, J. (1969). *Attachment and loss: Vol. 1. Attachment* (1st ed.). New York: Basic Books.

Bowlby, J. (1973). *Attachment and loss: Vol. 2. Separation: Anxiety and anger*. London: Penguin Books.

Bowlby, J. (1980). *Attachment and loss: Vol. 3. Loss: Sadness and depression*. London: Penguin Books.

Bowlby, J. (1982). *Attachment and loss: Vol. 1. Attachment* (2nd ed.). London: Penguin Books.

Bowlby, J. (1988). *A secure base: Clinical applications of attachment theory*. London: Routledge.

Bretherton, I. (1980). Young Chldren in stressful situations: The supporting role of attachment figures and unfamiliar caregivers. In G. V. Coelho & P. J. Ahmen (Eds.), *Uprooting and Development*. New york: Plenum Press.

Bretherton, I. (1991). The roots and growing points of attachment theory. In C. M. Parkes, J. Stevenson-Hinde, & P. Marris (Eds.), *Attachment across the life cycle*. London: Routledge.

Christenson, R.M. & Wilson, W.P. (1985). Assessing pathology in the separation-individuation process by an inventory. *Journal of Nervous and Mental Disease, 173*, 561-565.

Cicchetti, D., & Howes, P. (1991). Developmental Psychopathology in the context of the family: Illustrations from the study of child maltreatment. *Canadian Journal of Behavioural Science, 23*, 257-281.

Dodge, K., & Richard, B. (1985). Peer perceptions, aggression, and the development of peer relations. In J. Pryor & J. Day (Eds.), *The development of social cognition*. New York: Springer-Verlag.

Douvan, E., & Adelson, J. (1966). *The adolescent experience*. New York: Wiley.

Epstein, S. (1983). *Scoring and interpretation of mother-father-peer scale*. Unpublished manuscript, University of Massachusetts.

Freud, S. (1905). Three essays on the theory of sexuality. *The complete psychological works of Sigmund Freud* (Vol. 7). London: Hogarth Press.

Gallagher, J.R. (1976). *Emotional Problems of Adolescents*. New York: Oxford University Press.

Goldsmith, H.H., Bradshaw, D.L., & Rieser-Danner, L.A. (1986). Termperament as a potential developmental influence on attachment. *New Directions for Child Development, 31*, 5-34.

Greenspan, S.I., & Lieberman, A.F. (1988). A clinical approach to attachment. In Belsky, J. & Nezworski, T. (Eds.), *Clinical Implications of attachment*. Hillsdale, New Jersey: Lawrence Earlbaum Associates.

Grossman, K.E., & Grossman, K. (1991). Attachment quality as an organizer of emotional and behavioral responses in a longitudinal perspective. In C. M. Parkes, J. Stevenson-Hinde, & P. Marris (Eds.), *Attachment across the life cycle*. London: Routledge.

Hansburg, H.G. (1986). *Adolescent separation anxiety test*. New York: Robert E. Krieger.

Kenny, M.E. (1987). The extent and function of parental attachment among first -year college students. *Journal of Youth and Adolescence, 16*, 17-29.

Kenny, M.E. (1990). College seniors' perceptions of parental attachments: The value and stability of family ties. *Journal of College Student Development, 31*, 39-46.

Kobak R.R., & Sceery, A. (1988). Attachment in late adolescence: Working models, affect regulation, and representations of self and others. *Child Development, 59*, 135-146.

Kwakman, A.M., Zuiker, F.A., Schippers, G.M., & de Wuffel, F.J. (1988). Drinking behavior, drinking attitudes, and attachment relationship of adolescents. *Journal of Youth and Adolescence, 17*, 247-253.

Main, M. (1991). Metacognitive knowledge, metacognitive monitoring, and singular (coherent) vs. multiple (incoherent) model of attachment: Findings and directions of future research. In C. M. Parkes, J. Stevenson-Hinde, & P. Marris (Eds.), *Attachment across the life cycle*. London: Routledge.

Main, M., & Solomon, J. (in press). Procedures for identifying infants as disorganized/disoriented during the Ainsworth Strange Situation. In M. Greenberg, D. Cicchetti, and M. Cummings. (Eds.), *Attachment in the preschool years: Theory, research and intervention*, Chicago: University of Chicago Press.

Moss, H.A. (1967). Sex, age and state as determinants of mother-infant interaction. *Merrill-Palmer Quarterly, 13*, 19-36.

O'Brien, E. (1981). *The self-report inventory: Construction and validation of a multidimensional measure of the self-concept and sources of self-esteem*. Unpublished manuscript, Amherst: University of Massachusetts.

Piaget, J. (1972). The stages of intellectual development of the child. In S. Harrison & J. McDermott (Eds.), *Childhood psychopathology* (pp. 157-166). New York: International Universities Press. (Originally published, 1962).

Ryan, R.M., & Lynch, J.H. (1989). Emotional autonomy versus detachment: Revisiting the vicissitudes of adolescence and young adulthood. *Child Development, 60*, 340-356.

Serbin, L.A., Peters, P.L., McAffer, V.J., and Schwartzman, A.E. (1991). Childhood aggression and withdrawal as predictors of adolescent pregnancy, early parenthood, and environmental risk for the next generation. *Canadian Journal of Behavioral Science, 23*, 318-331.

Spitz, R., Emde, R., & Metcalff, D. (1970). Further prototypes of ego formation. *Psychoanalytic Study of the Child, 25*, 417-444.

Sroufe, L.A. (1985). Attachment classification from the perspective of infant-caregiver relationships and infant temperament. *Child Development, 56*, 1-14.

Sroufe, L.A. (1988). The role of infant-caregiver attachment in development. In Belsky, J. & Nezworski, T. (Eds.), *Clinical Implications of attachment.* Hillsdale, New Jersey: Lawrence Earlbaum Associates.

Sroufe, L.A., and Waters, E. (1977) Attachment as an organizational construct. *Child Development, 48*, 1184-1199.

Steinberg, L., & Silverberg, S. (1986). The vicissitudes of autonomy in adolescence. *Child Development, 57*, 841-851.

Vaughn, B., Egeland, B., Waters, E., & Sroufe, L.A. (1979). Individual differences in infant-mother attachment at 12 and 18 months: Stability and change in families under stress. *Child Development, 50*, 971-975.

Violato, C., & Genuis, M. (1993). Problems of research in male child sexual abuse: A review. *Journal of Child Sexual Abuse, 2*, 33-44.

Weiss, R.S. (1991). The attachment bond in childhood and adulthood. In C. M. Parkes, J. Stevenson-Hinde, & P. Marris (Eds.), *Attachment across the life cycle.* London: Routledge.

13

Anger and Sadness Experiences in Late Adolescence

Mark Atkinson

There is something very basic and 'real' about our feelings. We can all recall times when we were exceedingly angry or weighed down by sadness. Often these negative emotions arise when events challenge deeply personal desires or expectations regarding our achievements or relationships. Yet, if we look around us, our feelings are not unique. We share with others common emotional experiences that, from infancy to old age, form the basis of our social context and weave us together into human communities.

This chapter documents a recent research project which assessed the types of situations and thoughts occurring during students' experiences of anger and sadness. The data for this project were based on the narrative and psychometric information provided by 149 university students about the emotional events in their daily lives. The next section introduces recent theoretical perspectives in order to illuminate what are perhaps some of the most fundamental experiences of our lives, our emotional states.

Background Research

Biological theorists, and indeed, most psychological theorists recognize that emotional expression and experience perform two extremely basic and necessary functions. Emotions communicate meaning and they motivate us. Since individuals of a species are endowed with a set of universal emotional traits or characteristics, even the most dissimilar people experience many similar emotions.[1] These emotional universals provide the vast majority of humans with a common ground for meaningful communication and social understanding (cf., Booth-Butterfield & Booth-Butterfield, 1990). Such commonalities act as a currency for parent-infant interaction and attachment, and also provide the foundations for numerous cognitive and social achievements occurring over the life-span (Fridlund, 1991).[2]

Secondly, although somewhat of a truism, emotion motivates people. The qualities of positive emotion are inherently attractive, while those of negative emotion are aversive. Mammals and humans, in particular, typically try to prevent or minimize aversive emotional states, while maximising pleasurable ones (Izard, 1979; Giblin, 1986; Tomkins, 1981). Thus, negative emotional experiences will usually result in efforts aimed at reducing the source of aversive stimulation. Conversely, positive emotions tend to result in activities which further pleasurable experience(s).

Darwin (1872) was one of the earliest theorists to speculate on the evolutionary significance of emotions and motivational states. He suggested that emotional states prepare the body's physiological systems for adaptive action.[3] Supporting this hypothesis, fear and anger are typically accompanied by elevations in epinephrine, blood pressure, heart rate, peripheral blood flow, and muscle tension, all of which are useful when coping with situations which require quick action and increased physical activity (Bandura, Reese & Adams, 1982; Levenson, 1992). Conversely, emotions related to sadness reduce or suppress normal activity and functioning. Depression and loneliness, for example, have been linked to decreases in smooth muscle contraction, decreased appetite, and feelings of lethargy (Schwartz, 1982).

Plutchik and Kellerman (1983) have proposed that emotions and their accompanying physiological states can be classified according to the biological function(s) each promotes. Within their affective taxonomy, the functions of negative emotions are as follows: (a) *disgust* – rejection of distasteful or foreign experiences, (b) *fear* – the protection of the self and other loved ones by avoidance and flight, (c) *anger* – the destruction of situations which threaten one's well being, and (d) *sadness* – the reintegration of the self after personal loss.

Emotionally induced states of physiological motivation and behavior are usually accompanied by complementary changes in the thoughts of individuals. A correspondence has been observed between individuals' emotional states and their mental preparation for certain behavioral responses (Frijda, 1987). Anger has been associated with a psychological preparation for antagonistic, excited, dominant, or disapproving types of behavior. Sadness has been associated with thoughts regarding inhibited, submissive, antagonistic, avoidant, and helpless behavior.

The role thought plays in people's emotional experiences has been a topic of particularly heated debate (cf., Lazarus, 1984; Zajonc, 1984 for discussions about the primacy of cognition versus emotion). Theorists advocating a biological epistemology have tended to view conscious thought processes as secondary to people's more basic emotional characteristics. Conversely, certain cognitive theorists suggested that emotion does not exist without some form of conscious or preconscious cognition.

Cognitive Perspectives on Emotion

Cognitive theorists view emotions as products of the ways in which individuals think about themselves and their world. They try to understand how particular patterns of thought cause individuals to experience specific types of emotion. Two broad and overlapping perspectives exist regarding the cognitive antecedents of emotion; these are the constructivist and structural explanations of emotion.

Constructive theories and emotion

Constructivists consider cognition as a mental construction of reality. The ways in which individuals construe themselves, others, and their world cannot be separated from how they feel within situations. Emotions are the physiological accompaniment to the activation of central schema (e.g., beliefs, values and anticipations) (cf., Harter, 1988; Mahoney, 1988, 1990).

Kelly (1955), often called the father of constructivism, proposed that individuals construct a consistent, meaningful, and relativistic world view through repeated interactions with significant people. Kelly maintained that individuals anticipate and are able to control events in their lives "by construing their replications" over time. In other words, people know about their present situation by having thought about a similar event in the past. Thus, an individual's sense of a coherent and predictable world view occurs as a result of constructs built on repeated experiences. More recently, Epstein (1985, 1990) has elaborated on this idea, by suggesting that an individual discovers orderliness in the world by assembling emotionally significant experiences into preconscious beliefs.

Like the biological theorists mentioned earlier, constructivists maintain that all individuals possess a common set of motivational states (i.e., prototypical constructs). They believe that these prototypical constructs are consistent aspects of human nature. Fisher (1990) proposed that such constructs impart three basic characteristics to human's motivational systems: approach-avoidance, arousal-quiescence, and attachment-separation. Moreover, these prototypical thought processes form the foundations on which individuals learn to evaluate themselves and their environment (Kelly, 1955; Mascolo & Mancuso, 1990).

Over the life cycle, and particularly during childhood, these prototypical constructs act as a basis on which beliefs about self (i.e., self-schema) become organised into complex evaluative systems (cf., Harter, 1990; Markus, 1990). Stable self-schema, which include personal beliefs, values, and goals, are acquired through repeated socio-emotional interactions. Later, these self-schema serve as guides, organizing individuals' actions and directly impacting on their emotional experiences (Lazarus, 1984; Shotter, 1982). According to constructivists, self-schema, guides and personal constructs form the stable and enduring foundation of personality.

Structural Theories of Emotion

Whereas constructivists focus on personal history and the uniqueness of individuals, structuralists maintain that certain classes of cognition, if exercised, will inevitably lead to particular types of emotional experiences.[4] As a result, structural theorists have concerned themselves with the specific types of cognition which determine emotional responses.

Early research in the area of self-attribution theory led to an understanding of how interpretive processes influence the valence, quality, and intensity of emotional experience (cf., MacDowell & Mandler, 1989). Notable research by Schachter and Singer (1963) demonstrated that drug induced arousal could be experienced as pleasurable or aversive, depending on subjects' thoughts regarding the cause(s) of their arousal. These early theorists adopted an extreme and somewhat untenable position that all emotion arises out of a person's interpretation of their state of arousal or quiescence. Although the majority of current theorists do not subscribe to such a radical perspective (Truax, 1984), most have acknowledged the important effects of attribution on the subjective experience of emotion.

Epstein (1984) has suggested that individuals view themselves and their response options in characteristic ways. These cognitive styles explain why individuals differ with regards to their emotionality. Several theoretically oriented psychotherapists, most notably Aaron Beck and Albert Ellis, have suggested that the relationship between cognitive styles and emotional distress is the source of emotional and behavioral disturbance.[5] Individuals who report greater subjective intensity of moods also tend to personalize events and over generalise experiences to a greater extent than individuals who report less extreme moods. Moreover, the relationship of self-focus and over generalisation with emotional intensity appears to hold for both negative and positive emotions (Larsen, Diener & Cropanzano, 1987).

Causal Attributions: Anger and Sadness

Three attributional dimensions are often used to describe differences between emotions; these are *personal agency, emotional valence,* and *outcome expectancy*. Personal agency refers to individuals' beliefs about their own ability to shape, control or manage life circumstances. Emotional valence refers to the experientially aversive or attractive value of emotional states (i.e., pleasure versus pain). Outcome expectancy refers to the anticipations which individuals hold regarding the outcome of a particular event.

Table 13.1 summarizes three structural models of emotion which have employed various subtypes of the dimensions of agency, valence, and expectancy to explain emotional reactions.

Table 13.1
A Comparison of the Agentic, Valence and Outcome
Dimensions Within Three Structural Models of Emotion

	Weiner (1988)	Ellsworth & Smith (1988)	Ortony et al. (1988)
AGENCY	Locus of Control Controllability Intentionality Responsibility	Power Intentionality	Approval vs Disapproval
VALENCE	Positive vs Negative	Reward Value	Pleasure vs Displeasure
OUTCOME EXPECTANCY	Permanence Certainty Stability	Legitimacy Certainty Desirability	Liking vs Disliking Consequences for Self and Others

With some variation, each of these theorists would generally agree that anger is associated with high levels of personal agency, a negatively valenced experience, and a negative expectancy regarding the outcome of events. Ortony, Clore and Collins (1988) proposed that we feel angry when actions (performed by self or others) have a negative impact on ourselves and elicit our disapproval (i.e., agency). Similarly, Ellsworth and Smith (1988) suggested that we feel angry when we attribute the imposition of an undesirable barrier or harmful outcome to the intentional and unjust actions of others (i.e., agency). Cognitively oriented practitioners have suggested that clients having problems with anger management often use these types of attributions to excess in their thought lives (Ford, 1991; Hart, Turner, Hittner, Cardozo & Paras, 1991).

Structural theorists have proposed that feelings of sadness, on the other hand, are the product of low self-agency, negative experience and negative outcome expectancy. The primary difference, according to structural theorists, is that anger is associated with a belief in one's effectiveness, abilities and control, whereas sadness is not. Beck (1987) noted that individuals who attribute failure to internal and stable causes are more likely to suffer from chronic sadness and cognitive depression.[6] It is not a coincidence that advocates of both the Cognitive and Modified Learned Helplessness theories of depression have included the constructs of helplessness and hopelessness within their discussions on the etiology of sadness and depression (Beck, 1987; Abramson, Metalsky & Alloy, 1989).

Subjects and Data Collection Methods

Subjects for the present research were recruited from an undergraduate course in the faculty of education. Of the 149 participants, 86% (n = 129) were undergraduates, 12% (n = 17) were in the B.Ed. after degree program, and 2% (n = 3) were unclassified students. The majority of subjects (70%, n = 104) were between the ages of 18 and 24 (mean age = 21.2 years). Females made up 78.5% (n = 117) of the sample, while 21.5% (n = 32) were male. Finally, most subjects were single (75%, n = 112), approximately one quarter (n = 37) were married or had been married in the past.

Participants were asked to keep a written journal in which they were to record *five* angering and *five* saddening emotional events which they experienced over the course of the semester. Although participants could choose any emotional event to report on, they were asked to select events which were as different from each other as possible.[7] For each emotional situation, subjects recorded (a) the type of emotion experienced (i.e., anger or sadness), its intensity, and duration, (b) the importance of the situation, and (c) their thoughts about the causes of the emotional experience[8] (*Causal Dimension Scale*, Weiner, 1986).

Information from the most recent journal entry was summarized by the students each week using computerized data entry forms. At the end of a ten week period, participants had completed ten forms, five for anger experiences and five for sadness experiences. Their log books were also collected for later reading and classification.

Results of the Study

In order to determine the types of *people* and *situations* associated with students' anger and sadness experiences, each of the 1490 journal entries were read and coded as to the relationship of people involved in the emotional event with the subject (i.e., the *Involved Persons Coding Protocol*) and the type of situations which gave rise to the emotional experiences (i.e., *Issues/Tasks Coding Protocol*).

The Relational Context of Emotional Experiences

Table 13.2 presents the frequency of anger and sadness events classified according to subjects' relationships with the people involved.

Table 13.2
Frequency of Incidents by Persons Directly Involved With Subjects' Emotional Experiences

Person Classification**	Anger Incidents	Sadness Incidents	Totals
1. No Persons Involved (e.g., personal thoughts, response to visual or written media)	68 (9.1%)	147 (19.7%)	215 14.4%)
2. Primary Relatives: living or having lived together (not spouses or children)	123 (16.5%)	99 (13.3%)	222 (14.9%)
3. Secondary Relatives (e.g., aunts, uncles, cousings)	11 (1.5%)	64 (8.6%)	75 (5.0%)
4. Spouses/Lovers	98 (13.2%)	127 (17.0%)	225 (15.1%)
5. Professionals or Service Providers	133 (17.8%)	37 (5.0%)	170 (11.4%)
6. Associates	118 (15.8%)	65 (8.7%)	183 (12.3%)
7. Close Friends and Pets	85 (11.4%)	142 (19.1%)	227 (15.2%)
8. Own Children	22 (3.0%)	19 (2.6%)	41 (2.8%)
9. Others' Children and Own Students or Pupils	11 (1.5%)	12 (1.6%)	23 (1.5%)
10. Persons Unknown or Not Well Known (not associates)	76 (10.2%)	33 (4.4%)	109 (7.3%)
Totals	745	745	1490

**Primary person(s) responsible for, or involved with the emotion. The percentages are proportions of column values.

It is interesting to note from Table 13.2 that the persons most frequently involved in subjects' anger experiences were professionals and service providers, while sadness experiences most often occurred when subjects were alone.

Table 13.3 presents the categories of involved persons according to the degree to which subjects were familiar or acquainted with them. Three reclassification categories were used: situations which did not involve any other people, situations involving people who were distantly acquainted with subjects, and situations occurring within close or intimate relationships.

Table 13.3
Frequency of Incidents According to Subjects'
Familiarity With the Persons Involved**

	Anger	Sadness	Totals
I. Personal Thoughts and Response to Media	68 (31.6%)	147 (68.4%)	215 (100%)
II. Less Familiar Persons			
1. Professionals and Service Providers	133	37	170
2. Associates	118	65	183
3. Unknown Persons	76	33	109
Totals	327 (70.8%)	1335 (29.2%)	462 (100%)
III. Intimate Relationships			
1. Primary Relatives	123	99	222
2, Secondary Relatives	11	64	75
3. Spouses/Lovers	98	127	225
4. Close Friends/Pets	85	142	227
5. Own Children	22	19	41
6. Own Pupils/Others' Children	11	12	23
Totals	350 (43%)	463 (57%)	813 (100%)

**X^2 (df 2) = 124, p < .001.

A chi-square analysis of differences in the number of anger and sadness experiences between each of the three (involved person) categories was significant (X^2 (df 2) = 124, p < .001). Inspection of the cell frequencies revealed that anger, as opposed to sadness, was more likely when experiences involved persons who were less familiar to subjects. The proportion of anger and sadness experiences was more equally balanced when experiences involved better known persons. Situations in which no people were directly involved tended to accompany reports of sadness.

The Situational Context of Emotional Experiences

Through a recursive reading of journal entries, it became apparent that an important situational aspect of emotional events was the *types of issue and/or task* which the student was coping with at the time. Thus an *Issues/Tasks Coding Protocol* was designed and each of the 1490 journal entries was classified. The frequencies of anger and sadness experiences within each coding category are reported in Table 13.4.

Table 13.4

Frequency of Incidents by Situational Issues and Task Classification

Situational Class*	Anger Incidents	Sadness Incidents	Totals
1. Mass Media/Entertainment	15 (2%)	45 (6%)	60 (4%)
2. Transportation (occurring while driving)	30 (4%)	1 (<1%)	31 (2%)
3. School Work and Other Form of Achievement	132 (18%)	94 (13%)	226 (15%)
4. Social Coordination (primarily task focused and includes caring for others)	256 (34%)	41 (6%)	297 (20%)
5. Family Members' Involvement and Participation	57 (8%)	108 (14%)	165 (11%)
6. Personal Thoughts, Dreams, Realizations, and Empathic Exchanges	14 (2%)	230 (31%)	244 (16%)
7. Employment, volunteer and Financial Tasks or Environment	62 (8%)	17 (2%)	79 (5%)
8. Maintenance, Repair, Purchase, and Accident Situations or Tasks	67 (9%)	24 (3%)	91 (6%)
9. Social Involvement and Participation (outside of the family)	112 (15%)	185 (25%)	297 (20%)
Totals	745	745	1490

**Situations are defined by the tasks and issues facing subjects within the emotional incidents. The percentages are computed from column totals.

Table 13.5 presents the Issues/Tasks categories reduced into three issue/task clusters: Familial and Social Involvement, Instrumental and Achievement-Related Tasks, and Reflective or Empathic Situations.

A chi-square analysis of the frequency of anger and sadness experiences between each of the three issues/task categories was significant (X^2 (df 2)=419, $p < .0001$). Inspection of cell frequencies revealed that instrumental and achievement-oriented situations were more likely to be reported for anger than sadness. In contrast, sadness occurred more frequently in situations involving issues of social or familial unity and participation. Sadness especially predominated during empathic exchanges and reflective moments.

Table 13.5

Frequency of Incidents According to Three Broad Issues/Tasks Categories**

	Anger	Sadness	Totals
I. Familial and Social Involvement			
1. Family Involvement and Participation	57	108	165
2. Social Involvement and Participation	112	185	297
Totals	169 (36.6%)	293 (63.4%)	462 (100%)
II. Instrumental Tasks			
1. Transportation	30	1	31
2. Scholastic and Other Achievement	132	94	226
3. Social Coordination and Organization	256	41	297
4. Employment and Finances	62	17	79
5. Maintenance, Accident and Repair	67	24	91
Totals	547 (75.6%)	177 (24.4%)	724 (100%)
III. Empathic or Reflective Experiences			
1. Media and Entertainment	15	45	60
2. Personal Thoughts and Empathic Experiences	14	230	244
Totals	29 (9.5%)	275 (90.5%)	304 (100%)

**X^2 (df = 2) = 419, p < .0001

Subjects' Causal Attributions about Emotional Situations

Participant thoughts about the causes of situations were collected using the Causal Dimension Scale (Weiner, 1986). Differences in how students thought about the causes of angering and saddening situations are reported in Table 13.6.

A comparison of the means for anger and sadness experiences by CDS variables suggested that within angering situations, subjects' thoughts were characterized by views of cause(s) as being more (a) situationally determined (rather than self-caused), (b) controllable by self or others, (c) temporary, (d) intentionally caused, (e) externally caused, (f) variable over time, (g) involving others, (h) amenable to change, and (i) where blame or responsibility could be laid. In other words, subjects tended to become angry (as opposed to sad) when they considered an incident to be more situationally determined, controllable, temporary, intentionally but externally caused, variable, changeable, and involving others on whom blame could be laid.

Table 13.6
Mean Causal Attribution Ratings by Emotion

Causal Dimension Scale Item (Causal Attributions)**			Anger Experiences	Sadness Experiences
Low Scores to High Scores 1 2 3 4 5 6 7 8 9			Means ++ (n + 750)	Means (n = 750)
Aspect of the Situation	vs	Aspect of Yourself	3.4	4.0
Uncontrolable	vs	Controllable	6.9	4.3
Temporary	vs	Permanent	3.1	5.2
Unintended	vs	Intentional	4.1	2.3
Outside of Self	vs	Inside of Self	3.0	3.9
Variable Over Time	vs	Stable Over Time	4.7	5.6
Something About Others	vs	Something About Self	3.4	4.4
Changeable	vs	Unchanging	3.3	5.7
No One is Responsible	vs	Someone is Responsible	7.5	4.4

**The CDS employs a bipolar rating scale, high scores endorse the righthand side of the bipolar item, with low scores the left side of the dimension.
++ The means are the mean CDS item response across all participants within a particular emotional state.

Sadness experiences were thought to be caused more by (a) aspects of one's self (than by situations), (b) factors outside of human control, (c) more permanent causes, (d) unintentional events, (e) causes arising from inside of oneself, (f) stable factors, (g) causes which involve self, (h) things not ameliorable to change, and (i) causes for which no responsibility or blame could be laid. In contrast, subjects tended to become sad when they attributed the cause of an incident to themselves, believing it to arise from (internal) causes which were outside human control, which were permanent in nature, unintentional, stable, and unchangeable and for which no one was responsible.

A discriminant analysis was used to examine the degree to which subjects' thoughts about the causes of the situations could be used to predict the type of emotion they experienced. To clearly separate anger from sadness situations, reports for which subjects indicated that their emotional state changed during the experience (blended emotional experiences) were considered separately from those which consisted of a unitary or non-blended emotion.[9]

Each of the CDS variables (CDS v1-v9) passed the tolerance criteria for entry (p < .001), and all CDS variables were entered simultaneously into the discriminant analysis. The discriminant classification of reports was accomplished using the pooled within-group covariance matrix. The overall discriminant equation was significant and included all CDS items (Wilk's Lambda = .62, X^2 (df 9) = 560, p < .0001).

The percentage of emotional reports correctly classified, based on the derived discriminant function for non-blended emotional experiences, was 78.9% (X^2 (df 9) = 561, p < .00001). The percentage of correctly classified blended experiences was much lower (57.8%). For both blended and non-blended analyses, correct assignment to the anger experience group was better predicted (non-blended = 89%, blended = 72%) than assignment to the sadness group (non-blended = 71%, blended = 47%). This finding was most obvious for the blended sadness group, in which correct classification was no better than chance.

Results from this discriminant analysis suggest that knowledge of subjects' attributions about an emotional situation can be used correctly to discriminate between unitary anger and sadness experiences 79% of the time. Discrimination between blended or complex emotional states, however, was much weaker. These findings support Roseman et al.'s (1990) theorizing regarding the existence of discrete emotions and their accompanying attributional structures. It is also likely that a knowledge of how a person feels within a situation allows a listener to form some fairly good hypotheses about the thought processes involved.

Discussion

As noted by developmental psychologists, anger occurs in early childhood as a response to thwarted needs and wants, notably the frustration due to externally imposed barriers to exploration and gratification. Over time, children learn to control their tempers and, with the diminution of egocentrism, take the needs and wants of others into account. Nevertheless, the hallmarks of anger across the lifespan continue to be personal agency, physical action and situational control (Ellsworth & Smith, 1988).

Supporting this view, subjects reported more anger when their experiences were task and achievement oriented. They were three times as likely to report anger than sadness when dealing with pragmatic and task-oriented problems in their lives. Moreover, angering situations were twice as likely to involve less familiar persons. It is likely that instrumental and achievement-oriented tasks within the lives of students tended to include persons who were less intimate, possibly since the majority of subjects had not yet formed procreative familial relationships. These less familiar persons, such as employers, coworkers, and professors were more likely to be seen as imposing external and possibly unjust limitations on subjects' activities and aspirations.

Subjects' beliefs about the causes of angering experiences complemented the necessities inherent within instrumental or achievement oriented situations. Subjects tended to view the causes of angering situations as external to themselves, placing blame for personal harm or impediment on the intentional actions of others. These findings provide yet further support for theoretical positions that describe anger as an active (e.g., defensive or territorial) orientation towards an external threat, harm or impedance to self and one's own (e.g., Lazarus, 1991).

It is interesting to note that psychological constructs of identity, autonomy and status are also linked to individuals' ability to direct and control their lives. Erickson (1950) described identity as emerging from a relatively individualistic process, as young adults come to grips with personal choice and pursuit of a chosen life purpose (i.e., autonomy) (Marcia, 1980). From this perspective, it might be expected that a good measure of anger, assertion and competition would be characteristics of individuals with a clear sense of their identity and purpose in life. This leaves an important question unanswered. Have psychologists and society as a whole over-emphasized individual mastery while overlooking an equally important socially integrative force which exists within each of us?

The lethargy and introspection associated with sadness may provide individuals with time to come to cope with personal loss. Plutchik and Kellerman (1983) suggested that following a personal loss, sadness and introspection are necessary in order to reestablish a coherent and stable sense of self. Consistent with this process of 'inward turning', these subjects tended to view the causes of their sadness as internally situated, involving central aspects of themselves, and relatively stable and unchangeable.[10]

In addition to facilitating an intrapsychic (re)integration, some theorists have suggested that sadness performs a socially integrative function, namely that the expression of sadness may foster interpersonal understanding and the formation of social coalitions (Nesse, 1992; Plutchik, 1992). Most of us are aware that the expressions of sadness by others elicits feelings of sympathy and acts of compassion. Sadness, as opposed to anger, may provide a communicative channel through which individuals' needs are recognized without recourse to interpersonal confrontation or challenge. A communicative mechanism able to elicit assistance while managing to minimize confrontation may have had adaptive significance in primate evolutionary history (Nesse, 1992; Sloman, 1992).

This speculation aside, the results of this study have provided clear evidence for an association between sadness and issues of social connection. Sadness was reported twice as frequently as anger when subjects were dealing with issues of social and familial unity. Furthermore, sadness was ten times more frequently reported than anger when subjects were either responding to others' emotion (empathy) or when reflecting on life. These observations support proposals regarding the dual function of sadness, promoting social reflection and deepening our understanding of interpersonal values.

Individuals' reflections on personal and social meaning during times of disappointment, loss and loneliness may provide an opportunity for personal growth, awareness and social connection. Beck (1987) noted that an equally important, yet often devalued facet of identity, involves individuals ability to align their social needs with their social experiences. Moreover, an important developmental task during this period of life is the formation and sustenance of close interpersonal (particularly intimate heterosexual) relationships. Coming to grips with the loss of relationships re-emphasizes their importance to us. Experiences of loss, separation, and loneliness may provide a balance to self-preoccupation, and give place to social responsibility and meaningful community.

In summary, we arrive in the world with an innate capacity to recognize and experience basic human emotion. It is our ability to recognize the emotional experiences in others which, from the first weeks of life, provides a basis for our relationships. As a result of our common emotional heritage, we can better appreciate the motivations and experiences of others. Additionally, emotion nudges, and at times drives us toward specific types of behavioral responses. When expressed appropriately, these emotional behaviors help provide us with the safety, nurturance and awareness which we all need. Finally, emotions affect and are affected by, our thoughts. They form the foundation for both the ways in which we understand ourselves and the ways in which we interpret life events.

Notes

1. It should be noted that evolutionary principles and biological determinism aplly most directly to primary as opposed to secondary emotions. Seconday or social emotions are complex blends of primary emotions and are heavily influenced by the socialization process (e.g., Izard, 1979; Plutchik & Kellerman, 1983).

2. Evidence to support the genetic universality of primary emotion and accompanying experience have been supported by nuimerous cross-cultural studies examining the relationship between emotionsl atates, facial expression and physiologic experience (e.g., Ekman, 1992; Rime, Philippot & Cisamolo, 1990).

3. Adaptive function refers to any behavior or thought process which has contributed to the survival and reproduction of the members of a species.

4. An example of a structural approach within the current studyy was the use of causal attributions to discriminate between the two types of emotional expperience (c.f., Mandler, 1990 for further discussion).

5. Beck, for example, suggests that clients make themselves depressed by utilizing faulty logic such as personalizing, overgeneralization, selective abstraction, or cognitive amplification (Beck, 1976).

6. Sadness is characterized by most structural theories as a complex and subtle emotion. In fact, descriptions of sadness often encompass states of loneliness, dejection, disappointment, failure, and disillusionment. While each of these emotional states are

accompanied by similar physiological experineces, the attributional structures of each varies slightly (Roseman, Spindel & Jose, 1990).

7. There were two reasons for this diversity. First, it was desirable to collect information on as diverse a sample of emotional incidents as possible. Secondly, I did not want associations between thoughts and emotions to be artifically large due to similarities between situational types.

8. Monroe (1982) noted that as much as 60% of situational specifics may be under-reported bby subjects when asked to spontaneously recall events occurring within the last two months. Moreover, the effects of current mood may attenuate recalll of past events in different emotional states (e.g., Bowers, 1981). I stressed the importance of taking notes soon after the emotional experience, since a journal serves to reduce the effects of recall bias and memory loss between the experience and the time of actual data collection.

9. This distinction was made so that statistical rules regarding the mutual exclusivity of group membership (i.e., not belonging to both anger and sadness grouping simulttaneously) were not violated in discriminant analysis (Kleinbaum, 1978; Stevens, 1986). Since exclusion of the blended subset resulted in an unbalanced number of reports within each emotion group (655 anger and 533 sadness experiences), the prior probability of group membership was set by the proportion of cases analyzed within each emotional class.

10. The patterns of causal attribution provides some evidence for the idea that an attributionally mediated continuum exists between cognitve depression and milder experiences of sadness (Beck, 1987; Hunsley, 1989). Both deporession and sadness appear to be associated with internal, global and stable attributions towards aversive life situations. More recently, however, theorists have challenged the central importance of cognitive factors in the etiology of biological or clinical depression (Haaga, Ernst & Dyc, 1991 for example). Nevertheless, the present results favor a cognitive attributional interpretation of sadness among normal individuals.

References

Abramson, L.Y., Metalsky, G.I. & Alloy, L.B. (1989). Hopelessness depression: A theory-based subtype of depression. *Psychological Review, 96*, 358-372.

Bandura, A., Reese, L. & Adams, N.E. (1982). Micro-analysis of action and fear arousal as a function of differential levels of perceived self-efficacy. *Journal of Personality and Social Psychology, 43*, 5-21.

Beck, A. (1976). *Cognitive therapy and emotional disorders.* New York: International University Press.

Beck, A. (1987). Cognitive models of depression. *Journal of Cognitive Psychotherapy: An International Quarterly, 1*, 5-37.

Booth-Butterfield, M. & Booth-Butterfield, S. (1990). Conceptualizing affect as infor- mation in communication. *Human Communication Research, 16*, 451-476.

Bower, G.H. (1981). Mood and memory. *American Psychologist, 36*, 129-148.

Darwin, C. (1872). *The expression of emotions in man and animals.* London: Murray.

Ekman, P. (1992). Facial expressions of emotion: New findings, new questions. *Psychological Science, 3,* 34-37.

Ellsworth, P. & Smith, C. (1988). From appraisal to emotion: Differences among unpleasant feelings. *Motivation and Emotion, 12,* 271-302.

Epstein, S. (1984). Controversial issues in emotion theory. In P. Shaver (Ed.), *Review of Personality and Social Psychology: Emotions, Relationships, and Health* (pp. 64-88). Beverly Hills, CA: Sage.

Epstein, S. (1985). The implications of Cognitive-experiential Self-theory for research in social psychology and personality. *Journal for the Theory of Social Behavior, 15,* 283-310.

Epstein, S. (1990). Comment on the effects of aggregation across and within occasions on consistency, specificity, and reliability. *Methodika, 9,* 95-100.

Erikson, E. (1950). *Childhood and society.* New York: W.W. Norton.

Fisher, D. (1990). Emotional construing: A psychobiological model. *International Journal of Personal Construct Psychology, 3,* 183-203.

Ford, D. (1991). Anger and irrational beliefs in violent inmates. *Personality and Individual Differences, 12,* 211-215.

Fridlund, A. (1991). Evolution and facial action in reflex, social motive, and paralanguage. *Biological Psychology, 32,* 3-100.

Frijda, N. (1987). Emotion, cognitive structure, and action tendency. *Cognition and Emotion, 1,* 115-143.

Giblin, P.T. (1986). Methodologies of affective classification. *The Journal of Genetic Psychology, 146,* 217-226.

Haaga, D., Dyck, M. & Ernst, D. (1991). Empirical status of cognitive theory of depression. *Psychological Bulletin, 110,* 215-236.

Hart, K. (1991). Coping with anger-provoking situations: Adolescent coping in relation to anger-reactivity. *Journal of Adolescent Research, 6,* 357-370.

Hart, K., Turner, S., Hittner, J., Cardozo, S. & Paras, K. (1991). Life stress and anger: Moderating effects of type A irrational beliefs. *Personality and Individual Differences, 12,* 557-560.

Harter, S. (1988). Psychotherapy as a reconstructive process: Implications of integrative theories for outcome research. *International Journal of Personal Construct Psychology, 1,* 349-367.

Harter, S. (1990). Developmental differences in the nature of self-representations: Implications for the understanding, assessment, and treatment of maladaptive behavior. *Cognitive Therapy and Research, 14,* 113-142.

Hunsley, J. (1989). Vulnerability to depressive mood: An examination of the temporal consistency of the reformulated learned helplessness model. *Cognitive Therapy and Research, 13,* 599-608.

Izard, C.E. (1978). On the ontogenesis of emotion and emotion-cognition relationship in infancy. In M. L. Lewis & L. A. Rosenblum (Eds.), *The Development of Affect*. New York: Plenum Press.

Izard, C.E. (1979). *Emotions in personality and psychopathology*. New York: Plenum Press.

Kelly, G. (1955). *The psychology of personal constructs*. New York: Norton.

Larsen, R., Diener, E., & Cropanzano, R. (1987). Cognitive operations associated with individual differences in affect intensity. *Journal of Personality and Social Psychology*, *53*, 767-774.

Lazarus, R.S. (1984). On the primacy of cognition. *American Psychologist*, *39*, 124-129.

Lazarus, R. (1991). *Emotion and adaptation*. New York: Oxford University Press.

Levenson, R. (1992). Autonomic nervous system differences among emotions. *Psychological Science*, *3*, 23-27.

MacDowell, K. & Mandler, G. (1989). Constructions of emotion: Discrepancy, arousal, and mood. *Motivation and Emotion*, *13*, 105-124.

Mahoney, M. (1990). Representations of self in cognitive psychotherapies. *Cognitive Therapy and Research*, *14*, 229-240.

Mandler, G. (1990). A constructivist theory of emotion. In N.S. Stein, B.L. Leventhal & T. Trabasso (Eds.), *Psychological and biological approaches to emotion*. Hillsdale, NJ: Lawrence Erlbaum Associates.

Marcia, J.E. (1980). Identity in adolescence. In J. Adelson (Ed.), *Handbook of adolescent psychology*. New York: Wiley.

Markus, H. (1990). Unresolved issues of self-representation. *Cognitive Therapy and Research*, *14*, 241-253.

Mascolo, M. & Mancuso, J. (1990). Functioning of epigenetically evolved emotion systems: A constructive analysis. *International Journal of Personal Construct Psychology*, *3*, 205-222.

Monroe, S. (1982). Assessment of life events: Retrospective vs. concurrent strategies. *Archives of General Psychiatry*, *39*, 606-610.

Nesse (1992). Mood as a communication medium (#3.1.1.2). In Harnad (Mediator), *PSYCOLOQUY*. A refereed electronic journal of peer discussion. harnad@princeton.EDU: APA.

Nesse (1992). Social functions of mood (#3.1.1.4). In Harnad (Mediator), *PSYCOLOQUY*. A refereed electronic journal of peer discussion. harnad@princeton.EDU: APA.

Ortony, A., Clore, G. & Collins, A. (1988). *The cognitive structure of emotions*. Cambridge: Cambridge University Press.

Plutchik, R. (1992). What is mood for? (#3.2.1.5). In Harnad (Mediator), *PSYCOLOQUY*. A refereed electronic journal of peer discussion. harnad@princeton.EDU: APA.

Plutchik, R. & Kellerman, H. (1983). *Emotion: Theory, research, and experience, Vol. 2*. New York: Academic Press.

Rime, B., Philippot, P. & Cisamolo, D. (1990). Social schemata of peripheral changes in emotion. *Journal of Personality and Social Psychology, 59,* 38-49.

Roseman, I., Spindel, M. & Jose, P. (1990). Appraisals of emotion-eliciting events: Testing a theory of discrete emotions. *Journal of Personality and Social Psychology, 59,* 899-915.

Schachter, S. & Singer, J. (1963). Cognitive, social and psychological determinants of emotional states. *Psychological Review, 69,* 379-399.

Schwartz, R.M. (1982). Cognitive-Behavior modification: A conceptual review. *Clinical Psychology Review, 2,* 267-293.

Shotter, J. (1982). Understanding how to be a person: An ecological approach. In E. Shepherd & J. P. Watson (Eds.), *Personal Meanings: Th First Guy's Hospital Symposium on the Individual Frame of Reference.* New York: John Wiley & Sons.

Sloman (1992). How mood regulates aggression (#3.1.1.3). In Harnad (Mediator), *PSYCOLOQUY.* A refereed electronic journal of peer discussion. harnad@princeton.EDU: APA.

Tomkins, S. (1981). The quest for primary motives: Biography and autobiography of an idea. *Journal of Personality and Social Psychology, 41,* 306-329.

Truax, S. (1984). Determinants of emotion attributions: A unifying view. *Motivation and Emotion, 8,* 33-54.

Weiner, B. (1986). *An attribution theory of motivation.* New York: Springer.

14

Mass Media Use and Beliefs About Youth

Ewen (1977) has suggested that a concept or symbol of youth has become central to business thought in today's consumer oriented society. At the turn of this century, as entrepreneurs were developing means for the mass production of goods and services, they came to realize that children and adolescents formed a lucrative market for these goods and services. Through their advertising media, businessmen began to treat young people as a consumer market. As a result, youth became a powerful tool in the ideological framework of business. Symbols or images of youth which were useful in selling products and services were created.

Business, with its astonishing array of advertisers and mass media resources, has since developed and cultivated the worship of youth by unremittingly associating its wares with virtue, wisdom and all things "valuable" including "youth" (Travis, 1975, p. 185). Mass media have created and given wide-spread and durable visibility to stereotypes of youth through their entertainment, advertising, and information dissemination activities. In a wider sense, youth has become incorporated into modern liberal ideology as a "broad cultural symbol of renewal, of honesty, and criticism against injustice" (Ewen, 1977, p. 139). Youthfulness, as manifested in the broad cultural symbol and more specifically, in mass media stereotypes, has made youth a desirable and saleable commodity (Ewen, 1977). Although some of the basic characteristics of the cultural symbol of youth seems to remain constant over time (Ewen, 1977), specific changes in the mass media stereotype can be discerned.

In the mid-sixties, Adelson (1964) observed that mass media evaluations of youth as manifested in their treatment of it in stereotypes had undergone change. The earlier mass media portrayals indicated that the adolescent was evaluated as a figure "of little substance" who was stereotyped as a "fool," a "figure of fun: callow, flighty, silly, given to infatuations, wild enthusiasms and transient moodiness." As a ... sensitive, emotionally afflicted, overly sentimental" figure, the adolescent was nevertheless "lovable, though sometimes exasperating and not to be taken seriously" (Adelson, 1964, p. 1).

The replacement for the "adolescent as fool" image in the mid-sixties, attributed much more value to youth. Adelson (1964) claimed that during the 1960s an image of youth which was given high visibility characterized the young person as a "visionary." The visionary was distinguished by a purity of moral vision. Furthermore, in the way of the prophets he was also a victim: he was betrayed, exploited, coerced, neglected and otherwise maltreated by a venal adult world which perpetuated corruption through insidious manipulation of the perceptive, insightful, knowledgeable, morally precocious but powerless young. Faithfully reproduced in the stereotype was the simple but time-honored formula consisting of a saint-like creature battling heroically against the immense forces of evil which surround him. Moreover, the elements shared buy this stereotype and its more passive counterpart (often referred to as the anti-hero; a kind of passive visionary victim) were youth, moral superiority, precociousness, powerlessness and victimization.

Other studies reported by Bandura (1964), Jahoda and Warren (1965) and Musgrove (1964a, b) have also drawn attention to the stereotypes or images of youth which have been given massive and sustained visibility in the mass media. These writers have argued that one of the effects of the high visibility of these images may well be that of making the mythical stereotype come true. Since both young people and adults are part of the mass media audience, the young people themselves are bombarded with the fashionable definitions inherent in the images. All the ingredients of the self-fulfilling prophecy are present (e.g., Bandura, 1964). As Jahoda and Warren (1965 , p. 40) have argued, the widespread and sustained visibility of the images "may [have made] the mythical stereotype based on it come true, owing to acceptance . . . of this stereotype by the very object of the stereotyped perception."

A study by Meisels and Canter (1971) reveals evidence which indicates that some young people have been affected by the flattering stereotype: when they asked students to indicate the extent to which they, their parents and their peers agreed with statements about contemporary issues, Meisels and Canter found that on political issues like the Vietnam war, students "shared perceived parental values but were significantly different from perceived peer values" (1971, p. 528). However, their data suggested that students' judgments of peer attitudes were systematically distorted in the progressive direction and that the students were far less progressive than they, or others imagined. Similarly, a study by Blair and Pendleton (1971) produced evidence which suggests that at least teachers like those involved in their study (of teacher estimates of adolescents' attitudes about certain contemporary issues) apparently were affected as well: the teachers consistently over-estimated the extent of students' opposition to the U.S. involvement in Vietnam, the draft, police and other adult expressions of authority. Indeed, this sample of teachers apparently had a consistently exaggerated sense of the extent to which deviant and progressive attitudes are held by students.

Although the image or stereotype of youth as visionary-victim does not seem to be enjoying the sustained and widespread visibility in recent years that it did in the past, both the broad cultural symbol of youth and mass media stereotypes portray youth as possessing virtuous qualities and progressive attitudes (Adelson, 1979; Ewen, 1977). Six basic components of the youth stereotype can be identified. In comparison to their elders, young people have been represented as being (1) more knowledgeable, (2) less hypocritical, (3) not as conservative, (4) more progressive, (5) wiser, and (6) more virtuous (Travis, 1975) even though this depiction is erroneous (Adelson, 1979).

Teachers, like other groups of people, form part of the mass media audience and, like other people, share the social ideology of the times. Accordingly, it should not be surprising if teachers as well as other professional and non-professional people come to believe that youth, as a group, possess qualities which are attributed to them by mass media stereotypes and the symbols of youth in the culture in general. Moreover, teachers' perceptions and beliefs about those they would teach may influence how teachers interact with the young people with whom they have intercourse. And since a major proportion of teachers' professional activities involves interactions with children and adolescents, it is important to discover what perceptions teachers share with regard to young people.

The foregoing discussion suggests that there may be some advantage in ascertaining mass media usage habits of teachers and would-be teachers. It would also be useful to discover what relationships, if any, exist between habits of mass media use and beliefs about youth. In addition, it may also be useful to discover which sources are perceived as providing trustworthy and adequate ideas about social and other matters, since such perceptions might be taken as indicative of the user's credulity *viz a viz* different sources (Roper, 1975). Such information would be useful because, despite the distorted and over-simplified treatment of social, political, economic and other matters which is characteristic of television (Mankiewicz & Swerklow, 1978) and other mass media sources (Funkhouser, 1973), some studies (e.g., Finlay, 1979) indicate that users place high degrees of confidence in mass media sources.

The foregoing general considerations form the basis upon which the present study was conceived. The major purpose of this study was to collect three classes of data from Canada's would-be teachers: (1) information pertaining to their beliefs about and perceptions of youth, (2) data about their patterns of mass media usage, and (3) information bearing on their perceptions about what sources provide reliable and trustworthy ideas about social, political and economic matters as well as other world affairs. The present study is embedded in a larger national survey of students enrolled in teacher preparation programs at universities across Canada. The larger study is broader in scope and is designed to collect information about the background, habits, and outlook of Canadian would-be teachers (Violato & Travis, 1990). Three major hypotheses were tested in the present study: (1) A majority of prospective teachers believe that, in comparison to their elders, today's youth are wiser, more virtuous, more knowledgeable, more progressive (and not more conservative), and less hypocritical; (2) Mass media (television, radio, newspapers, and magazines) are more often perceived, or judged to be, reliable and trustworthy sources of information and ideas about social, political, and economic matters as well as other world affairs than are all other possible sources; (3) Heavier users of light (culturally and intellectually insubstantial) mass media will tend to place more credence in the dimensions of a youth stereotype than will the less heavy users of such mass media.

Method

Subjects.

Subjects were drawn from the students enrolled in teacher preparation programs at eight Canadian universities (Dalhousie, Mount Allison, McGill,

Saskatchewan, Regina, Alberta, British Columbia, Victoria). The total sample size of 488 was made up of 166 males (34.0% of the sample) and 322 females (66.0% of the sample) enrolled in both pre-baccalaureate programs (B.Ed.) and post-baccalaureate programs (those who held at least one degree and were enrolled in a teacher training program). Three hundred and fifty-three subjects (72.3%) were studying for their first degree while 135 (27.6%) subjects held at least one degree. Of those who held degrees, six subjects (1.2% of the total sample) held advanced degrees as well as bachelor degrees, while 129 (26.4%) held bachelor degrees only. A larger proportion of males (43.4%; n = 72) held degrees than did females (19.6%; n = 63). The numbers and proportions of subjects in each academic year were as follows: 83 in first year (17.0%), 85 in second year (17.4%), 154 in third year (31.6%), 34 in fourth year (7.0%, and 132 in fifth year (27.0%). Two hundred and eighty-five (58.4%) subjects were in programs which are preparatory for work in elementary schools (elementary program), 174 (35.7%) were preparing to teach in secondary schools (secondary programs), and 10 (2.0%) were in an "others" category (e.g., Special Education). Nineteen subjects (3.9% of the sample) failed to indicate what program of study they were in.

Respondents ranged in age from 18 to 49 years with a mean age of 23 years (S.D. = 2.44; mode = 20). For age comparisons the subjects were classified into three age categories as follows: (1) 20 or younger (n = 174; 35.7%), (2) 21-25 (n = 208; 42.6%), and (3) 26 or older (n = 106; 21.7%).

Procedure.

Questionnaires were mailed to contacts (faculty members) at the eight universities included in this study and were administered to the subjects by the contacts during the 1977-78 and 1978-79 academic sessions according to standardized procedures. These administrative procedures entailed the following: (1) respondents were told that they were participating in a national survey that was designed to collect information about Canada's future teachers and accordingly, their candid and honest responses were being solicited; (2) respondents were apprised that the purpose of the study was to acquire information which would help bring about improvement in teacher preparation programs; (3) subjects were instructed not to put their names or any identification on the questionnaire so that anonymity could be guaranteed; (4) subjects were informed that no one other than the researchers would see their questionnaires. They were instructed to complete the questionnaire in the classroom and then return the completed form to the administrator who would, in their presence, seal the questionnaire in a pre-addressed envelope. Completion of the task took approximately 40 minutes. The completed questionnaires were subsequently returned to the authors via mail.

To derive an index of the proportions of program types shown on television, a content analysis of *TV Guide* for the week of November 10-16, 1979, was conducted. All programs with the exception of programs on the French language channel, cartoons, children's programs, and religious programs, aired between 6:00 p.m. and 12:00 midnight from Monday through Friday, and 12:00 noon and

12:00 midnight on Saturday and Sunday, were included in the analysis. Each program was coded into one of seven types: (1) situation comedy/variety/game/talk shows, (2) cops/medics/lawyers/adventure, (3) sports, (4) public affairs documentaries, (6) national and local news, and (7) serious drama. For further analysis, the original seven categories were reduced to three as follows: (1) entertainment (combined categories 1,2 and 3), (2) information (combined categories 4,5 and 6), and (3) serious drama (category 7).

The Questionnaire

The questionnaire was composed of a variety of question types (open-ended, multiple choice, yes-no, rank order, and check lists) which were designed to gather data on the backgrounds, habits, and outlooks of the respondents. In addition to some background data (i.e., age, sex, year of program, present program of study, and degrees held – if any), two items on television viewing habits, two items about newspaper usage, a checklist of 69 widely circulated periodicals, and two items on source of reliable information and ideas were analyzed.

Mass Media Use

Television. On the first item about television viewing habits, respondents were asked to check the category which best represented how many hours per week they spent watching television: (a) 0, (b) 1-7, (c) 8-14, (d) 15-21, (e) 22-29, (f) 30+. the second item was open-ended and read as follows: "List the television programs you watch: (a) regularly, (b) occasionally." The programs listed were subsequently classified as belonging to one of the seven categories reported in the Results section of this chapter (see Table 14.2). These seven categories were then classified as denoting (1) entertainment, (2) information, and (3) serious drama for further analysis.

Newspapers. Respondents were asked to indicate (yes or no) whether or not they read a daily newspaper. If they answered yes, they were then asked to indicate how many times per week (on the average) they read the newspaper.

Periodicals. Subjects were presented with a check list of 69 widely circulated periodicals which were arranged in random order with respect to subject matter or content, and they were asked to indicate (check) which ones they read regularly (at least once per month for weeklies and at least once every two months for others except dailies). An "others" category was provided so that periodicals which were not listed might be included.

Sources of information and ideas.

The first of these two items was the open-ended question: "From what source or sources do you get trustworthy ideas and adequate information about social, economic and political matters? (list in order from most to least important.)" The second item asked respondents to indicate the relative importance of media they rely upon for information about wold affairs by ranking them from most to least important. The media categories included were: television, newspapers, radio, magazines and "others."

Beliefs about youth.

The following item was put to the respondents: "Compared with their elders, do you believe that the majority of today's youth are:

(a) more knowledgeable	YES	NO	(circle)
(b) wiser	YES	NO	(circle)
(c) more virtuous	YES	NO	(circle)
(d) less hypocritical	YES	NO	(circle)
(e) more conservative	YES	NO	(circle)
(f) more progressive	YES	NO	(circle).

Results

A breakdown of the sample by sex and program of study reveals that most of the females (78.1%) were in elementary programs while more than half of the males (59.2%) were in secondary programs. Accordingly, the analysis of results begins with an explanation of how sex differences with regard to the variable of interest were treated.

Sex differences.

The present sample included a disproportionate number of females (66.0%). Furthermore, only 19.6% of the females held degrees while 43.4% of the males did so. Any analysis of sex differences in the variables that were tapped therefore, might tend to be confounded by level of education. Accordingly, the sample was broken down into two groups on the basis of possession and non-possession of a degree. Each variable was analyzed for sex differences for each group separately. For the group made up of 63 female and 72 male degree holders, no sex differences were found on any of the variables. Sex differences appeared however, for the group made up of 259 females and 94 males who did not possess degrees, in hours/week watching television, types of television programs preferred, newspaper reading frequency and types of magazines read, but not in perceived sources of reliable information and ideas and beliefs about youth. Within this group, it was still suspected however, that these apparent sex differences were again influenced by level of education since most of the females (61.7%) were in either the first or second year of study in their program. Therefore, for the people who did not possess degrees, each variable was analyzed for sex differences by year cohorts from first year through to fifth year. The ensuing result was that no sex differences emerged on any of the variables. Thus it can be concluded that in the present sample, there were no sex differences on any of the variables when level of education was controlled.

For program of study (i.e., elementary or secondary), the level of education was similarly controlled on all variable since most of the subjects in the elementary program were females who did not possess degrees. Accordingly, it was suspected that any apparent program of study differences which emerged would be confounded by level of education. This suspicion was borne out by further analyses. When level of education was controlled, no program of study differences emerged as they had on several variables (hours/week watching television, types of television programs preferred, frequency of newspaper reading, and types of magazines read) in the uncontrolled situation. Thus no further discussion of sex or program of study differences is included in this paper. The rest of the results are presented in four sections: (1) description of mass media usage, (2) presentation of results about sources of information and ideas, (3) presentation of data on beliefs about youth, and (4) evaluation of hypotheses.

Mass Media Use

Television. The sample distribution by time categories in watching television is shown in Part A of Table14.I. From this it can be seen that only a small proportion (8.2%) watch no television at all, while 76.9% are "Medium" users and 12.7% are "High" users.

The proportions of types of programs watched are summarized in Table 14.2. Also summarized in this table are the results from the content analysis of *TV Guide*. Very similar patterns emerge in the types of programs watched regularly and occasionally. An obvious exception is the national or local news which respondents tend to watch regularly more often than occasionally. The percentages of programs watched are very similar to the percentages of programs that are aired on television according to our analysis of *TV Guide*, particularly if the superordinate categories (entertainment, information, serious) are compared. The greater proportion of programs are of the entertainment variety, while only a very small percentage consist of serious drama programs. The viewing patterns of the present sample (as indicated by proportions of time devoted to each of the program categories) very closely resemble the proportions of time devoted to the

Table 14.1
Television Viewing and Newspaper Reading Habits

Part A. Hours per week spent watching television

Time (hours)	Percent of Sample n = 477	Category	Percent of Sample
0	8.2	Zero	8.2
1 - 7	49.2		
8 - 14	27.7	Medium	76.9
15 - 21	9.2		
22 - 29	2.3	High	12.7
30 +	1.2		

Part B. Breakdown of average time per week newspaper is read

	Times per Week						
	1	2	3	4	5	6	7
Percent of sample	5.2	11.3	12.1	9.6	8.2	22.1	8.8

Mean = 3.53, Mode = 6, Variance = 5.93, S.D. = 2.44

telecast of each program category. This suggests that the respondents may not be vary discriminating in their viewing since they generally seem to watch whatever happens to be offered. Another indication of this is given by a more fine-grained analysis. For example, such analyses reveal that one of the most frequently watched programs was "Mork and Mindy," a situation comedy which has large audiences but little merit – even as entertainment.

Cross-tabulation of age with program types shows significant differences both in regularly watched programs (X^2 (df 4) = 51.84; $p < .01$) and occasionally watched programs (X^2 (df 4) = 20.55; $p < .01$). The under 20 and 21-25 year groups watch significantly more entertainment programs and less information and serious programs than the 26 or older group. the general pattern clearly indicates an increasing use of information and serious programs with increasing age. Such between-age differences are probably due to differences in maturity, educational level and interests.

Newspapers. 77.3% of the sample (n = 488) reported that they read a daily newspaper while 19.9% said they do not and 2.8% failed to respond to the question. The proportions of the sample associated with their frequencies of newspaper reading is summarized in Part B of Table 14.I. The overall mean number of times per week that newspapers are read is 3.53 while the mode is 6.

Periodicals. Table 14.3 (Part A) summarizes the percentages of the sample that indicated that they read each of the listed periodicals regularly. The top and bottom ten periodicals (determined by the magnitude of the proportion reading them regularly) are shown in rank order. It is interesting to note that none of the top ten could conceivably be called quality magazines. Indeed, all of them are insubstantial in content, style and tone. All of the bottom ten are either "political" or "quality." (There were 22 periodicals that had a 0.1% readership, all of which were "political," "quality" or "business" but for space reasons, only ten are listed here.)

Eleven categories of periodicals (formed on the basis of the quality of content and its treatment – see Part B of Table 14.3) were represented in the list. A coefficient of reading was calculated by summing the total percentage in each category and dividing this sum by the number of periodicals in each category and then dividing that ratio by ten. This formula may be expressed as follows.

$$C_j = \frac{\sum_{i=1}^{n} P_i}{n_j \times 10}$$

where:
C is the coefficient of reading for category j;
P is the percentage reading periodical i regularly;
n is the number of periodicals in category j.

The maximum value that C can take then, is 10 while the minimum is 0.

Since there were unequal numbers of periodicals in each category, this standardization allows for a comparison to be made across categories. The magnitude of the coefficients of reading gives an indication of the relative frequency with which the 11 periodical types are read. The results from this analysis are summarized in Part B of Table 14.3. The eleven periodical categories were then reduced to three categories as follows: (1) entertainment (light, sport, women's, skin and humor); (2) information (news, arts and crafts, alternate press); and (3) serious (quality, business, political). The distribution of regular readership for the three categories is shown in Part A of Table 14.4. A comparison of the distributions in Tables 14.2 and 14.4A reveals that television viewing and periodical reading habits resembled one another. Light fare was used most regularly; and serious material was used least frequently – in both cases.

Table 14.2

Comparison of Percentages of Types of Programs Watched by
Respondents and Percentages of Program Types Aired
on Television According to TV Guide

	Percent of Program Types Watched by Respondents		Percent of Program Types on Television According to TV Guide
	Regularly	Occasionally	
1. Sitcoms/variety/game /talk shows	54.7%	55.8%	46.1%
2. Cops/medical/lawyer /adventure	4.4 Entertain- ment = 66.0%	8.4 Entertain ment = 73.8%	13.3 Entertain- ment = 68.5%
3. Sports	6.9	9.6	9.1
4. Nonpublic affairs docu mentaries	5.1	6.7	8.3
5. Public affairs documentaries	5.3 Informa- tion= 27.4%	4.3 Informat ion = 20.6 %	6.5 Information = 28.3%
6. National or local news	17.0	9.6	13.5
7. Serious drama	6.6 Serious = 6.6%	6.6 Serious = 6.6%	3.2 Serious = 3.2%

From Part B of Table 14.4, it can be seen that very clear age differences (X^2 9df 4) = 84.94; $p < .01$) emerge in periodical reading. As age increases, reading of entertainment periodicals decreases while there is an increase in information and serious magazine reading. These between-age differences probably reflect differences in educational level, interest, maturity and so forth.

Some relationships between television, newspaper and periodical use are summarized in Table 14.5. Part A of this table shows that the heavier users of television prefer entertainment magazines and read less information and serious periodicals (X^2(df 4) = 24.43; $p < .01$). For newspaper reading, the high frequency users read less entertainment and more information and serious periodicals (X^2 (df 4) = 13.99; $p < .01$)). From Table 6, it can be seen that there is a clear relationship between types of periodicals preferred and types of television programs preferred (X^2 (df 4) = 75.23; $p < .01$). Those who read relatively more serious magazines watch relatively less entertainment television programs and more information and serious television programs. Similarly, those who tend to prefer entertainment magazines also prefer entertainment television and watch less serious and information programming.

Table 14.3
Periodical Reading Habits

Part A Top ten and bottom ten periodicals read regularly

Top Ten	Percent of Sample Reading Regularly	Bottom Ten	Percent of Sample Reading Regularly
1. Time	47.1	1. Atlas World Press Review	0.1
2. Weekend Magazine	41.8	2. Christian Science Monitor	0.1
3. Macleans	34.4	3. Phi Delta Kappan	0.1
4National Geographic	34.0	4. The Canadian Forum	0.1
5. Reader's Diggest	32.2	5. The New Republic	0.1
6. Chatelaine	31.6	6. Canadian Dimension	0.1
7. T.V. Guide	24.6	7. Encounter	0.1
8. People	23.4	8. The New Yorker	0.1
9. Woman's Day	18.4	9. Manchester Guardian	0.1
10. Newsweek	17.4	10. Intellectural Digest	0.1

Part B Rank order of categories of periodicals as determined by a "coefficient of reading."

Category	Coefficient
1. Light (e.g., People, TV Guide)	3.98
2. News (e.g., Time, Newsweek	3.88
3. Sport (e.g., Sports Illustrated)	2.76
4. Women's (e.g., Vogue, Chatelaine)	2.75
5. Skin (e.g., Playboy, Penthouse)	1.31
6. Humor (e.g., Mad, National Lampoon)	0.95
7. Arts and Crafts (e.g., Popular Mechanics, Photography)	0.86
8. Quality (e.g., Harper's, N.Y. Review of Books)	0.86
9. Alternate Press (e.g., Rolling Stone, L.A. Free Press)	0.45
10. Business (e.g., Fortune)	0.20
11. Political (e.g., Encounter, Vanguard)	0.12

Sources of ideas and information.

Table 14.7 summarizes the data on the "sources of ideas" items. Part A of this table shows the proportions of the sample listing each source as one which provides adequate and reliable information and ideas. These categories encompass all responses to the open-ended item that asked respondents to list, in order of importance, those sources which they perceived as providing "trustworthy ideas and adequate information about social, economic and political matters." The sources which were listed most frequently as providing such a function were television (18.8%) and newspapers (24.2%). Books, on the other hand, were listed only 9.9% of the time, while professors were listed only 6.3% of the time. A somewhat surprising finding is that 15.9% apparently relied upon parents, relatives and/or friends. Furthermore, 22.6% of the sample felt that these people were the most important source of trustworthy information and ideas, while

Table 14.4
Periodical Reading Habits

Part A   Proportions of "regular" readership associated with periodical types

Periodical Type	Percent Read Regularly
Entertainment	46.7
Information	32.6
Serious	20.7

Part B   Age differences in periodical reading

	Periodical Type		
Age (Years)	Entertainment	Information	Serious
20 or younger	65.9%*	28.2%	5.9%
21 - 25	51.9%	35.9%	12.2%
26 or older	43.5%	40.4%	16.1%

*Numbers represent percentage of each age category in each periodical type category.
$X^2 = 84.94$; df = 4; $p = .0000$

Table 14.5
Relationships Between Use of Television, Newspaper, and Periodicals

Part A   Time spent watching television by types of periodicals read

	Periodical Type		
Time Watching T.V. (hours/week)	Entertainment	Information	Serious
1. Zero (0)	42.7%*	36.6%	20.7%
2. Medium (1 - 14)	55.8%	34.0%	10.2%
3. High (15 - 30+)	59.8%	31.5%	8.7%

*Numbers represent percentage of people in each time category that read the associated magazine types regularly.
$X^2 = 24.43$; df = 4; $p = .0001$

Part B   Frequency of newspaper reading by types of periodicals read

Frequency of Newsspaper Reading (time per week)	Entertainment	Information	Serious
1. Low (1, 2)	58.9%*	33.1%	8.0%
2. Medium (3, 4, 5)	57.6%	31.2%	11.2%
3. High (6,7)	50.7%	37.7%	11.6%

*Numbers represent percentage of people in each time category that read the associated magazine types regularly.
$X^2 = 13.99$; df = 4; $p = .0073$

another 9.7% felt that these people were at least the *second most* important source (Part B, Table 14.7). Only the proportion designating newspapers as the most important source of trustworthy information was a larger percentage of the sample (23.1%). Again, professors fared rather badly in this analysis as they were nominated by only 6.6% of the sample as being *the most* important source of reliable information (about socioeconomic and political matters).

Table 14.6

Relationship Between Types of Television Programs Watched Regularly and Types of Periodicals Read Regularly

| | Television Programs | | |
Periodical Type	Entertainment	Information	Serious
Entertainment	68.8%*	25.4%	5.8%
Information	57.8%	34.7%	7.5%
Serious	49.9%	41.2%	8.9%

*Numbers represent the percentage of people watching the television program types regularly according to the periodical type read regularly.
$X^2 = 75.23$; df = 4; $p = .0000$

Table 14.7

Sources of Ideas and Information About Social, Political, and Economic Matters

Part A	Percentage of respondents listing items as being important sources of ideas and information about social, political and economic matters

Source	Percent of Sample*
1. Newspapers	24.2
2. Television	18.8
3. Parents/Relatives/Friends	15.9
4. Radio	12.4
5. Periodicals/Magazines	11.4
6. Books	9.9
7. Professors	6.3
8. Religious Literature	0.7
9. Clergy	0.4

Part B	Percentage of respondents listing items as being the most or second most important source of ideas and information about social, political, and economic matters

Source	Most Important (%)*	Second Most Important (%)*
1. Newspapers	23.1	24.4
2. Parents/Relatives/Friends	22.6	9.7
3. Radio	16.7	10.3
4. Television	12.5	26.9
5. Books	11.1	6.9
6. Professors	6.6	6.7
7. Periodicals/Magazines	5.4	13.9
8. Religious Literature	1.5	0.6
9. Clergy	0.5	0.6

*n = 407

Table 14.8 shows the results from the "forced-choice" item wherein respondents were asked to rank order television, magazines, radio, newspapers and "other" in terms of their efficacy in providing reliable information about world affairs. Television was ranked first by 29.9% of the sample and second by 24.6%. Television then, was ranked as the first or second most important source of adequate information by 54.5% of the sample.

Table 14.8
Rank Order of Mass Media Sources in Order of Relative Importance for Providing Information About World Affairs

	Rank Order				
Mass Media Source	1	2	3	4	5
Television	29.9%*	24.6%	19.7%	8.8%	2.0%
Newspapers	27.3	28.5	25.4	6.6	1.6
Radio	26.0	24.0	19.5	16.0	1.4
Magazines	9.6	16.6	18.2	33.6	2.5
Others	5.5	3.9	2.7	2.9	5.1

*Numbers represent percentages of sample giving the source of that particular ranking.

A comparison of the data in Part B of Table 14.7 and Table 14.8 reveals some interesting patterns. While Part B of Table 14.7 reveals 11.5% felt that of *all possible sources*, television was *the most* important in providing adequate information, Table 14.8 indicates that 29.9% rated TV as the most important of *mass media* sources. Overall, mass media in general, and television in particular, are deemed as being important sources of ideas and information by the present sample. This result is congruent with Finlay's (1979) data which indicate that among 17 societal institutions, television news, TV and radio commentators and newspapers were among the top five which inspire a "great deal of confidence" or a "fair amount of confidence" in his respondents. Only medical doctors and consumer activists ranked higher. Scientists were eighth on the list and 56% of the sample had "no confidence at all" in them (Finlay, 1979, p. 40).

Perhaps the patterns of credulity and trust which respondents in the present study manifested are related to the extent to which they make use of and are on intimate terms with the various sources of ideas and information. For it seems they use and are on less intimate terms with books, serious periodicals, and professors (which are less trusted) than is the case with regard to the allegedly more reliable television, radio and newspapers – and parents, relatives and friends.

Beliefs about youth.

Table 14.9 (Part A) reports the proportions of respondents who agreed or disagreed with the statements which compared youth with their elders. Notably large proportions of the sample felt that today's youth when compared to their elders are more knowledgeable (77.1%), less hypocritical (39.4%), more progressive (60.6%), but not more conservative (83.7%). Somewhat smaller proportions reported beliefs that these youth are more virtuous (12.2%) and wiser

(16.4%) than their elders. Further analysis reveals that beliefs about wisdom, conservatism and progressiveness are related to types of periodicals read; and beliefs about hypocrisy are related to age. This is apparent in Table 14.9, Part B.

Compared with regular readers of serious fare, a significantly greater proportion of those who read insubstantial magazines regularly, agreed that today's youth are wiser than their elders (X^2 (df 2) = 6.02; $p < .05$). A larger proportion of readers of serious and information magazines said today's youth *are more* conservative than those who read entertainment magazines. Meanwhile, the proportion of light fare (entertainment) readers who said youth are *not* more conservative than their elders was significantly less than their counterparts who read high quality fare (X^2 (df 2) = 11.58; $p < .01$). Significantly larger proportions of entertainment magazine readers suppose today's youth are more progressive than their elders, than is the case with readers of higher quality periodicals (X^2 (df 2) = 18.81; $p < .01$). The overall pattern suggests that those who use magazines which contain little or no durable or serious intellectual content (those periodicals which trade in superficial treatments of content and rely on the categorical style) tend to believe the flattering attributions of the youth stereotype. Conversely, those who read better quality magazines seemed to subscribe to these stereotyped mythical attributes less frequently.

Additionally, beliefs about hypocrisy are related to age (Part C, Table 14.9). Interestingly, it is the older (26 or older) and mid-range (21-25-year-olds) respondents who tend to feel today's youth are less hypocritical than their elders while generally the younger subjects (20 or younger) are less likely to concur with this view (X^2 (df 2) = 9.73); $p < .01$). The younger subjects, may be less familiar with this notion about young people which was given greater salience in mass media several years ago when the older respondents were younger.

The overall results indicate that youth is, for the most part, construed by the bulk of the present sample, as possessing qualities and attitudes which are deviant in a progressive direction. Furthermore, some of these beliefs are associated with some patterns of mass media use and age.

Evaluation of hypotheses.

Hypothesis 1: The first hypothesis predicted most would-be teachers believe that youth in comparison to their elders are more knowledgeable, wiser, more virtuous, more progressive (and not more conservative) and less hypocritical. As can be seen from the foregoing data, this hypothesis is not uniformly supported. The proportions of the respondents which said that youth, compared with their elders, are more knowledgeable, wiser, more virtuous, more progressive, less hypocritical and not more conservative were 77.1%, 16.4%, 12.2%, 60.6%, 39.4%, and 83.7% respectively. Data with respect to only three of the six components of the stereotype met the criterion of the prediction. (However, the adopted criterion was arbitrary and perhaps unnecessarily stringent).

Table 14.9

Number and Percentage of Respondents Answering Yes or No to Statements About Youth When Compared to Their Elders and Relationships to Types of Periodicals Read Regularly and Age

Part A Beliefs about youth when compared to their elders

	Yes		No		
	N	Percent	N	Percent	Total N
1. More knowledgeable	363	77.1	108	22.9	471
2. Wiser	73	16.4	371	83.6	444
3. More virtuous	53	12.2	380	87.8	433
4. Less hypocritical	175	39.4	269	60.6	444
5. More conservative	72	16.3	370	83.7	442
6. More progressive	263	60.6	171	39.4	434

Part B Relationships between periodical types read regularly and beliefs about youth wisdom, conservatism, and progressiveness

	Beliefs about Youth					
	Wiser*		More Conservative**		More Progressive***	
	N	Percent	N	Percent		
	Yes (%)	No (%)	Yes (%)	No (%)	Yes (%)	No (%)
Entertainment	19.5[a]	80.5	14.8	85.2	66.7	33.3
Information	16.8	83.2	17.6	82.4	61.2	38.8
Serious	13.3	86.7	23.7	76.3	52.4	47.6

[a]Numbers represent percentage of respondents that read the particular periodical type answering Yes or No to statements about youth.

$*X^2 = 6.02$; df = 2; $p = .0494$

$**X^2 = 11.85$; df = 2; $p = .0027$

$***X^2 = 18.81$; df = 2; $p = .0001$

Part C Age differences in beliefs about youth hypocrisy

	Belief About Youth	
	Less Hypocritical	
Age (Years)	Yes (%)	No (%)
20 or less	29.1	42.4
21 - 25	44.6	40.5
26 or older	26.3	17.1

$X^2 = 9.73$; df = 2; $p = .0077$

Hypothesis 2: This hypothesis predicted that mass media are more frequently perceived as being reliable and trustworthy sources of information and ideas about social, political, economic and other world affairs than all other sources. The data presented above indicated strong support for this hypothesis. Of *all* possible sources of adequate information and trustworthy ideas about world affairs, newspapers, television, radio and magazines were listed by over 2/3 of the respondents, whereas books and professors were listed by only 16.2%. Of mass media sources, television was considered *the most* important by the largest proportion of respondents.

Hypothesis 3: This hypothesis predicted that heavier users of light media fare (culturally and intellectually insubstantial material) would tend to place more credence in stereotyped beliefs about youth than those who tend to use this type of material less. Although some strong support for this hypothesis is indicated in the data, the patterns are not completely clear. While beliefs about wisdom and progressiveness were clearly related to types of periodicals read as were beliefs about conservatism, no such cllear relationships emerged for beliefs about conservatism, knowledgeability, hypocrisy and virtuosity. Perhaps it is because the myths that youth are more knowledgeable and less hypocritical than their elders are so wide-spread both in the "cultural symbol" and mass media stereotypes that it is difficult to make discriminations among people on these beliefs based on specific mass media usage habits. In addition, other factors such as intelligence, educational background, maturity, political beliefs and so forth, may also be confounding the relationships. Although there was not absolutely clear support for the third hypothesis, there are some indications that relationships between beliefs about youth and some patterns of mass media usage exist.

Discussion

The major findings of this study may be summarized as follows: (1) unrealistic beliefs about youth that are implicated both in the wider North American cultural symbol (Ewen, 1977; Hodgson, 1976) and specific mass media stereotypes (Adelson, 1964; Jahoda & Warren, 1965; Meisels & Canter, 1971) are fairly widespread among Canadian would-be teachers; (2) some of these beliefs are related to mass media usage habits; (3) respondents tend to place high degrees of confidence in mass media as sources or reliable and trustworthy information about social, political, economic and other world affairs.

Of the six dimensions of the youth stereotype, two (virtuosity and wisdom) were subscribed to by relatively small proportions of the sample (12.2% and 16.4% respectively) and a third (hypocrisy) was accepted by 39.4%. However, three dimensions of the stereotype (pertaining to knowledgeability, progressiveness and conservativism) were accepted by large proportions of the sample as representing actual characteristics of youth. This may indicate that mass media evaluations of youth as manifested in stereotypes have undergone changes since the earlier work in this area was carried out (e.g., Adelson, 1964; Jahoda & Warren, 1965; Meisels & Canter, 1971). As Adelson (1964) pointed out, the stereotypes of youth in mass media do change over time. From the present study it can be seen that it was the older subjects who tended to place more credence in the hypocrisy dimension of the stereotype. Perhaps this belief was a carry-over from exposure to earlier mass media stereotypes. In any case, there appears to be a need for a re-assessment of the dimensions of the stereotype of youth as it is currently displayed in mass media (see chapters 4 and 7).

Although it may be premature at this point to attempt to establish cause and effect relationships between beliefs, attitudes, behavior and mass media usage, recent studies (Beuf, 1974; Gerbner & Gross, 1976; Tan, 1979) show that mass media, particularly television, can have a "cultivator" effect. According to this hypothesis, mass media cultivates audience beliefs about social reality through selective presentations and by emphasizing certain themes. Audience perceptions about such matters then, become distorted and over-simplified views of social reality. For it has been amply demonstrated that this selection and emphasis in mass media produces systematically distorted and over-simplified accounts of social, political, economic and other world affairs (e.g., Becker, McCombs & McLeod, 1975; Ellul, 1973; Epstein, 1973; Funkhouser, 1973; Kraus, 1973; Liebert & Schartzberg, 1977; Mankiewicz & Swerklow, 1978). In Funkhouser's words, "bias does not have to involve opinions and viewpoints, but can occur as a sort of sampling bias – that is, as systematic deviations from reality" (1973, p. 74).

It may very well be that the unrealistic beliefs held by a great many of the respondents in the present study, have been cultivated by the mass media. Regardless of the fact that there is not a completely clear connection between these beliefs and patterns of mass media use, there are strong indications that it is those people who have placed trust in and rely on those media which characteristically resort to extreme simplification devices such as stereotypes that subscribe to the unrealistic, categorical beliefs about youth. One could, of course, argue that it is people with these unrealistic beliefs that are attracted to this kind of media fare anyway. Although this may be the case, reliance on and credulity with regard to such mass mediated material may congeal these beliefs as suggested by the so-called cultivator hypothesis. The difference between the older and younger respondents suggests this possibility. However, the matter is not settled here – only further research can clarify the issue.

Additional implications arise from the findings of this study. Large proportions of Canadian teachers-in-training hold unrealistic beliefs about the nature of the youth that they will teach – whether or not these beliefs are cultivated by mass media dissemination of stereotypes. Such unrealistic beliefs about the young people they would teach are probable impediments to reasonable intercourse between them and their students. The daily realities of the classroom may not force changes in these beliefs about youth even though the teacher receives repeated exposure to youth. Certainly, this state of affairs seems to have been the case in the Blair and Pendleton (1971) study. Perhaps these beliefs are commonly subscribed to by many veteran teachers whose mentality is often depicted in unflattering terms. Further research which focuses on experienced teachers' beliefs about youth, may help clarify these matters as well (see chapter 15).

In sum, it is clear that unrealistic beliefs about youth are widespread among Canadian would-be-teachers. Furthermore, these beliefs may have been cultivated by stereotypes of youth given sustained and widespread visibility in mass media. Finally, large proportions of the respondents in this study perceived mass media as being trustworthy and adequate sources of ideas and information about world affairs. Perhaps the most important implication of these findings is that they suggest it may be incumbent on those who teach would-be-teachers to make systematic efforts to disabuse their students of these unrealistic notions; and that they make substantial provision for the critical study of mass mediated culture. Such studies might enhance the literacy and reduce the credulity of prospective teachers. The data reported herein, together with studies of the character and functioning of mass media suggest this is an urgent matter (Ellul, 1973; Epstein, 1973; Funkhouser, 1973; Hodgson, 1976; Mankiewicz & Swerklow, 1978; Schrank, 1977; Travis, 1975; Tuchman, 1974; Williams, 1968). Moreover, books and courses on adolescent psychology have not met this challenge very adequately. Indeed, many may have exacerbated the problem. As Adelson (1979) has observed:

> The established truth about the young consists of fictions designed to serve purposes other than the clear apprehension of reality. We seem to need a simple manageable set of images that will allow us to make sense out of what (is) . . . complex . . . various . . . (and) changeable . . . (p. 33).

The mass media and adolescent psychologists have fostered "the illusion that there is one single adolescent psychology, timeless and universal" (Adelson, 1979, p. 37) even though we know that cultural, demographic, and economic forces are critical influences on the experience of adolescence (p. 37) and that they probably preclude the possibility of a universal adolescent psychology. Accordingly, books and courses on adolescent psychology might well incorporate the critical study of mass mediated culture which has herein been recommended for prospective teachers.

References

Adelson, J. (1964). The mystique of adolescence. *Psychiatry, 27,* 1-5.

Adelson, J. (1979). Adolescence and the generalization gap. *Psychology Today, 12*(9), February, 33-37.

Bandura, A. (1964). The stormy decade: Fact or fiction? *Psychology in the Schools, 1,* 224-231.

Becker, L., McCombs, M., & McLeod, J. (1975). The development of political cognitions. In H. Chaffe (Ed.), *Political communication.* Beverly Hills: Sage, pgs 21-63.

Beuf, A. (1974). Doctor, lawyer, household drudge! *Journal of Communication, 24,* 142-145.

Blair, G., & Pendelton, C. (1971). Attitudes of youth toward current issues as perceived by teachers and adolescents. *Adolescence, 24,* 424-428.

Ellul, J. (1973). *Propaganda: The formation of men's attitudes.* Toronto: Vintage.

Epstein, E. (1973). *News from nowhere.* New York: Random House.

Ewen, S. (1977). *Captains of consciousness: Advertising and the social roots of consumer culture.* Toronto: McGraw Hill.

Finlay, R. (1979). The strange sceptical mood of the campus. *Saturday Night,* October, 35-40.

Funkhouser, R.G. (1973). The issues of the sixties: An exploratory study in the dynamics of public opinion. *Public Opinion Quarterly, 37,* 62-75.

Gerbner, G., & Gross, L. (1976). Living with television: The violence profile. *Journal of Communication, 26,* 172-179.

Jahoda, M., & Warren, N. (1965). The myths of youth. *Sociology of Edcuation, 38,* 2.

Kraus, S. (1973). Mass media and political socialization: A re-assessment of two decades of research. *Quarterly Journal of Speech, 59,* 390-400.

Liebert, R., & Schwartzenberg, N. (1977). Effects of mass media. *Annual Review of Psychology, 28,* 141-173.

Mankiewicz, F., & Swerklow, J. (1978). *Remote conrol: Television and the manipulation of American life.* New York: Times Book, Co.

Meisels, M., & Canter, F. (1971). A note on the generation gap. *Adolescence, 6,* 523-529.

Musgrove, F. (1964a). *Youth and social order.* London: Routledge.

Musgrove, F. (1964b). Why youth riot: The adolescent ghetto. *The Nation, 199,* 137-140.

Roper, B.W. (1975). *Trends in public opinions toward television and other mass media, 1959-1974.* New York: Televison information office.

Schrank, J. (1977). *Snap, crackle and popular taste.* New York: Delta.

Tan, A.S. (1979). TV beauty ads and role expectations of adolescent female viewers. *Journalism Quarterly, 56,* 283-287.

Travis, L.D. (1975). Political economy, soical learning and activism: Toward a theory of educational turmoil. Unpublished Ph.D. dissertaion, University of Alberta.

Tuchman, G. (ed.) (1974). *The TV establishment.* Englewood-Cliffs: Prentice-Hall.

Violato, C., & Travis, L.D. (1990). A national survey of education students: Some data on background, habits and reasons for entering education. *Canadian Journal of Education, 15,* 277-292.

15

Teacher Beliefs About Youth

"What's wrong with our teachers?" This question on the cover of a widely circulated newsmagazine (Solorzano, 1983) illustrates a genre of question which greets the browser at newstands with great regularity today. A sense of urgency pervades these signs of renewed interest in teacher quality (Gallup, 1982; Kirst, 1981; Zumwalt, 1982). The urgency seems to arise from alarming indications of declines in pupil performances on achievement tests (e.g., Astin, 1979; Atkin, 1981; Eurich & Kraetsch, 1982; Jones, 1981; Kirst, 1981; McGregor, 1984; McQuaid, 1984), declines in the abilities scores for would-be teachers (e.g., Solorzano, 1983; Vance & Schlechty, 1982; Watts, 1980) and deterioration of public confidence in and support for education (e.g., Gallup, 1982; *Newsweek*, 1983; Weiler, 1982). Government bodies, foundations and universities are making concern about the quality of teachers, and selection and preparation practices which affect same, salient (e.g., Berliner, 1983; McGregor, 1984; McQuaid, 1984; Santinelli, 1983; Spitzberg, 1983; Travis, 1983a, 1983b). If the rhetorical signs of rejuvenated interest in teacher quality follow past patterns, they portend, and we should anticipate, changes in teacher education (Cogan, 1975, p. 209; Zumwalt, 1982). In such circumstances, evidence bearing on specific issues of selection and preparation should be made available to and made salient for those who will make decisions about reform.

The present report provides evidence which is pertinent to the general issue of what we might expect teachers to gain from their practice of teaching, including everything from preservice practicums and internships to years of subsequent practice. Indirectly, it is therefore pertinent to selection and other preparation questions such as what should be studied in preparation.

Some people might suppose (quite reasonably) that the practices of teaching or instruction are best learned in the settings of teaching and instruction. Accordingly, such people sometimes urge a new or renewed emphasis on practice teaching, internships or on-site learning for intending teachers (e.g., Cogan, 1975). However, competent teaching entails more than the arts of organization, management and instruction which can be learned and refined on-site. Among the characteristics which we might, with reason, expect to see exhibited by our teachers (in addition to those practical matters already mentioned) are (1) a realistic understanding of human beings generally and youngsters particularly, (2) a cultivated or informed critical capacity to assess the merits of information and ideas (i.e., and educated capacity to discriminate between higher and lower quality cultural objects, conditions and events); and (3) a discerning or discriminating comportment in relation to organs, agencies or sources of information, ideas and images (i.e., a set of refined cultural habits and sensibilities). The adequacy of a teacher's orientations to the subjects, objects and interactions, to the pupils, content and experience for which he or she is responsible is greatly affected by such understanding and cultivation (e.g., Turner, 1975). Accordingly, the present study addresses the general question of whether we have reason to expect teachers to acquire these characteristics in the same manner, at the same time, and in the same settings as they acquire their other practical knowledge (i.e., internship-practice; on site *in situ*). The answer to this question is not obvious or settled. However, some might assert otherwise – especially when financial stringency might urge the attractiveness of supposing that all practical knowledge is best acquired, and can be expected to be acquired, where and when practice is done. Such assertions invite a reminder of the distinction between logic and psychologic: Evidence is pertinent here.

The availability of data on education students' habits of mass media use, credulity and beliefs about youth (Travis & Violato, 1981) and the instrumentation by which same was gathered, made a pertinent comparative study feasible. Accordingly, parallel (corresponding) data from veteran (experienced) teachers were sought for comparisons with those for the relatively inexperienced education students of the Travis and Violato (1981) study. Comparisons of the data for the two groups were made to discover the extent to which the experienced teacher differed significantly from the inexperienced students with regard to their habits of mass media use, credulity and beliefs about or perceptions of youth.

Such comparisons were assumed to yield some modest but specific indications of the impact of teaching experience on beliefs about perceptions of youth, patterns of mass media use and credulity with respect to mass mediated information and ideas. Significant differences between the responses of the veteran teachers and those of the inexperienced education students were interpreted as indices of the influence of teaching experience. Since Travis and Violato (1981) had studied the nature of covariations of these variables with age, any systematic differences between the comparison groups on these variables were subject to assessment.

The items used to assess beliefs about youth were taken to be items which sampled respondents' understanding of children and adolescents. Affirmation of beliefs which entailed inaccurate or unwarranted attributions to young people was very frequent in the Travis and Violato (1981) sample of inexperienced education students. Apparently, large proportions of Canadian students preparing to be teachers hold unrealistic beliefs about the nature of the young people they would teach (Adelson, 1979, 1980; Springhall, 1983-1984). Such unrealistic beliefs are probable impediments to reasonable interaction between pupils and teachers. However, one might argue that since these education students have not had protracted or substantial experience with young people in classrooms, as have veteran teachers, they may have less realistic beliefs about them than do experienced teachers. In sum, experience with daily realities of teaching may force adjustments in beliefs as teachers become more experienced with youth. (Indeed, in the light of their findings that their education students were very frequently unrealistic in their perceptions of young people, Travis and Violato [1981] suggested studies of teachers' beliefs about youth.) Accordingly, if the teachers' beliefs about youth were found to be significantly different from those of the education students and the difference was that the teachers were more realistic, this difference would suggest an experience effect. The first hypothesis for the present study, then, predicted that there would be no significant differences between the two samples with regard to their beliefs about youth as indicated by their affirmations and rejections of five dimensions of a six dimensional youth stereotype described by Travis and Violato (1981). On five of the six beliefs or dimensions of the youth stereotype, Travis and Violato found increases in age were not correlated with affirmation or rejection of the beliefs. However, on the sixth dimension, increases in age were associated with more unrealistic beliefs in the inexperienced student group. With regard to the sixth dimension on which Travis and Violato found an age effect (which consisted of the fact that the older members of the inexperienced student sample were significantly more unrealistic than the younger ones), the veteran teacher group (which was both older and experienced) was predicted to differ from the inexperienced group. That is, members of the former would more frequently affirm the belief that, compared with their elders, young people are less hypocritical. This is in accord with the findings of Travis and Violato (1981).

In addition to the comparisons made to gain evidence on the possible influence of teaching experience on belief indicators of understanding young people, other useful comparisons were suggested. These yield evidence pertaining to the question of whether gains in teaching experience are accompanied by increases in informed critical judgment, discernment and discrimination in relation to organs, agencies or sources of ideas, images and information. Comparisons of the two groups' orientations to mass media serve this purpose. Specifically, comparisons of the teachers and intending teachers with regard to their credulity or their trust in and reliance upon mass media provides another check on, or indicator of, possible changes which arise from or accompany the acquisition of teaching experience. Similarly, comparisons of the two groups' patterns of mass media use throw more light on the same question of cultural comportment. Moreover, since virtually nothing is known about this, it would be useful to gain information about veteran teachers' habits of mass media use (Cortes, 1983; Schalock, 1979). Accordingly, two more predictions were made: The first of these (the second prediction) was that the experienced teachers would not differ from those who aspire to teach in their trust of and reliance on mass media. That is, they would rely upon and trust mass media (for adequate information on and ideas about world affairs) more than they trust and rely upon all other possible sources. The final or third prediction was that veteran teachers and inexperienced education students differ significantly with regard to the patterns of mass media use. Specifically, the former were predicted to be more selective and discriminating than the latter in their use of television and magazines, with the veterans using serious and informational fare more than their inexperienced counterparts; and the students using entertainment fare more than the veteran teachers. The latter prediction is in accord with the evidence which indicates that age and usage patterns are so related. Accordingly, observed differences of the sort predicted will not be interpretable as simple expressions of effects from experience in teaching.

The purpose of the present study, then, was to discover whether a sample of veteran teachers on specific indicators would demonstrate greater understanding of young people, less credulity with regard to mass mediated information, and more discernment and discrimination in their use of mass media fare, than a sample of inexperienced education students. The comparisons were made to obtain evidence pertaining to the question of whether teaching experience is an efficient and sufficient developer of human understanding, as well as informed critical judgment and refined or at least discriminative habits and sensibilities in relation to sources of information, images and ideas.

Method

Subjects

The group of veteran teachers consisted of volunteers from the population attending recent spring and summer sessions of the University of British Columbia. The total sample (n = 122) was made up of 50 male (41.0 percent) and 72 female (59.0 percent) teachers. Eighty-nine (73.0 percent) respondents held at least one degree while 33 (27.0 percent) did not possess a degree. Nine respondents (7.4 percent of the total sample) held advanced degrees as well as bachelor's degrees. Seventeen teachers (13.9 percent) had taught for two years or less, while the bulk of the sample (81 subjects or 66.4 percent) had taught for 3-10 years and 24 (19.7 percent) had taught for more than ten years. The mean number of years of teaching experience for the sample was 7.6. More than half of the subjects taught in elementary schools (60.2 percent) while 39.8 percent taught in secondary schools. subjects ranged in age from 22 to 55 years with a mean age of 35.6 years (SD = 9.01; mode = 35). The inexperienced student (comparison) groups consisted of those described by Travis and Violato (1981).

Procedure

Questionnaires were distributed in classes by course instructors who administered the questionnaires and adhered to the procedures described by Travis and Violato (1981). There were, however, two departures from that procedure. First, potential respondents were told that the survey project was designed to collect information about practicing teachers (rather than education students). Second, respondents were instructed to complete the questionnaire outside of class time (but they were urged to return the forms, within two days, in sealed envelopes provided by the course instructors). Course instructors subsequently sent the completed questionnaires to the investigators.

The procedure which Travis and Violato used for deriving an index of the proportions of program types shown on television was used: a content analysis of *TV Guide* was conducted. Accordingly, their scheme for the classification of programs was used: (1) sitcoms / variety / game / talk shows; (2) cops / medics / lawyers / adventure; (3) sports; (4) public affairs documentaries; (5) non-public affairs documentaries (6) national or local news; and (7) serious drama. Again, following Travis and Violato, the original seven categories were reduced for further analysis, to three as follows: (1) entertainment (combined categories 1,

2 and 3); (2) information (combined categories 4, 5, and 6); and (serious drama (category 7).

The Questionnaire

The questionnaire used by Travis and Violato was modified slightly. Items which were designed for inexperienced teachers were eliminated and others which asked respondents to indicate the extent and nature of their teaching experience were added. Thus, in addition to the latter, respondents provided information about their backgrounds, habits and outlooks. Accordingly, their responses were comparable to those of the 488 education students described by Travis and Violato (1981).

Results

The data are presented under three main headings: (1) Mass Media Use, (2) Sources of Ideas and Information, and (3) Beliefs About Youth.

Mass Media Use

Television. With regard to their reports about amount of time spent watching television, the present sample of veteran teachers did not differ from the education students described by Travis and Violato: a small proportion (8.5 percent) watched no television at all, while 73.1 percent were "medium" users (1-14 hours/week) and 7.4 percent were "high" users (15+ hours/week). However, this sample differed from the Travis and Violato sample in that male teachers tended to log more viewing time per week than did female teachers $(X^2 = 7.73; df = 2; p = 0.0209)$.

The programs which teachers said they watched were classified according to type of programs as were programs listed in *TV Guide*. The proportions of viewing associated with each program type and the proportions of television programs available for each program type are reported in Table 1. Very similar patterns emerge in the types of programs watched "regularly" and "occasionally" with the exception of national or local news. The teachers, like the students, tended to watch news more regularly than occasionally. However, the percentages of teachers' viewing associated with program types are not very similar to the percentages derived from content analysis of programs in *TV Guide* that are telecast. This is in contrast with the student's viewing patterns reported by Travis and Violato: the students tended to watch whatever was offered. The proportions of viewing associated with each program type watched regularly by teachers and students were compared (see Table 15.2, Part A). These data indicate that the teachers, on a regular basis, watched less entertainment and more informational and serious program fare than did the Travis and Violato students $(X^2= 59.72; df = 2; p = 0.000)$. This same contrast between the two groups exists for programs that are watched occasionally $(X^2 = 36.24; df = 2; p = 0.0000)$. The teachers seemed to be more discriminating in their viewing in that they watched more serious and informational programs than was the case with the education students.

Following the procedure described by Travis and Violato, the teachers' periodicals reading was analyzed to discover the relative popularity of different types of periodicals. The magnitudes of reading coefficients indicated that for the teacher sample, the popularity of different periodical types rank (from high to low) as follows: (1) News (e.g., *Time*); (2) Light (e.g., *People*); (3) Sport (e.g., *Sports Illustrated*); (4) Women's (e.g., *Vogue*); (5) Skin (e.g., *Playboy*); (6) Arts and Crafts (e.g., *Photography*); (7) Quality (e.g., *Harper's*); (8) Humor (e.g., *National Lampoon*); (9) Alternate Press (e.g., *Rolling Stone*); (10) Political (e.g., *Encounter*); and (11) *Business (e.g., Fortune*). The rank order of these periodical types for teachers differs little from that which Travis and Violato reported for their sample of education students. The rank of "news" periodicals is higher for the teachers than for students and "light" periodicals rank higher for students than for teachers. The only difference between the first five elements in the two rank orders is that the "light" and "news" categories change places. However, when the periodicals were regrouped into three categories (i.e., Entertainment, Information and Serious) the reading patterns of teachers differed from those of the students (see part B of Table 15.2).

Table 15.1

Comparison of Percentages of Types of Programs Watched by Teachers and Percentages of Program Types Aired on Television According to TV Guide

	Percent of Program Types Watched by Respondents				Percent of Program Types on Television According to TV Guide	
	Regularly		Occasionally			
1. Sitcoms/variety/ game/talk shows	20.4%		29.4%		46.1%	
2. Cops/medics	2.7%	Entertainment = 31.8%	8.1%	Entertainment = 45.6%	13.3%	Entertainment = 68.5%
3. Sport	8.7%		8.1%		9.1%	
4. Nonpublic affairs documentaries	5.4%		5.6%		8.3%	
5. Public affairs documentaries	16.2%	Information = 55.4%	16.3%	Information = 32.5%	6.5%	Information = 28.3%
6. National or local news	33.8%		10.6%		13.5%	
7. Serious drama	12.8%	Serious = 12.8%	21.9%	Serious = 21.9%	3.2%	Serious = 3.2%

Newspapers. A daily newspaper was read by 75.4 percent of the present sample (n = 122) while 19.7 percent said they did not read a daily newspaper, and 2.5 percent failed to respond to the question. The overall mean number of times per week that daily newspapers were read was 4.11 while the mode was 6. When these data were compared to the corresponding data for the Travis and Violato sample of education students, no between-group differences emerged (X^2 = 0.57; df = 2; p = 0.7533).

Periodicals. Members of the teacher sample were asked, as were the Travis and Violato respondents, to indicate which periodicals they read regularly. Their responses indicated that the ten periodicals listed below (each followed by the sample proportion which read it) were the most popular: (1) *Time* (57.4 percent), (2) *National Geographic* (50.0 percent), (3) *Macleans* (38.5 percent), (4) *Weekend Magazine* (33.6 percent), (5) *Reader's Digest* (22.3 percent), (6) *Newsweek* (20.5 percent), (7) *TV Guide* (19.7 percent), (8) *Chatelaine* (18.8 percent), (9) *Sports Illustrated* (15.6 percent), and (10) *Playboy* (12.3 percent). These data closely resemble the data for education students which Travis and Violato reported. *Time* was the most popular in both instances; and the bottom ten periodicals for both groups belonged to the "political" or "quality" categories. Both the veteran teachers group and the student group preferred magazines which are insubstantial in content, style and tone and showed very little interest in better quality periodicals.

Table 15.2
Comparison Between Types of Television Programs Watched Regularly and Magazine Types Read Regularly by Teachers and Education Students

Part A: Comparison between types of television programs watched regularly

| | Television Programs | | |
Group	Entertainment	Information	Serious
Education Students	66.0*	27.4	6.6
Teachers	31.8	55.4	12.8

*Numbers represent the percentage of people watching the associated program types regularly.
$X^2 = 59.72$; df = 2; $p = 0.0000$

Part B: Comparison between types of periodicals read regularly

| | Periodical Type | | |
Group	Entertainment	Information	Serious
Education Students	54.4*	34.8	10.8
Teachers	42.1	45.7	12.2

*Numbers represent percent of people reading the associated periodical type regularly.
$X^2 = 27.10$; df = 2; $p = 0.0000$

An analysis comparing these distributions shows that teachers tend to read more informational and serious magazines while the education students showed a comparatively greater preference for entertainment periodicals and read less informational and serious materials ($X^2 = 27.10$; df = 2; $p = 0.0000$). The older (veteran teacher) group seem to be more discriminating in that they tended to read better quality magazines (just as within the inexperienced group, Travis and Violato found that older students were more discriminating than younger students).

Sources of Ideas and Information

Data about sources of ideas and information are summarized in Table 15.3. Part A of this table shows the proportions of the sample, listing each source as one which provides adequate and reliable information and ideas about social, economic and political matters. Newspapers and television were listed most frequently (22.6 percent and 21.5 percent respectively) and while professors were listed least frequently (9.7 percent), books were not listed by anybody. Meanwhile, 13.6 percent listed parents, relatives and/or friends as providing such a function. Moreover, 17.4 percent felt that these people were *the most* important source of trustworthy information and only the proportion designating newspapers as the most important such source was higher proportion (30.6 percent). Of the six sources listed by respondents, professors ranked behind four as the most important source of trustworthy information. These data indicate that teachers tend to accord magazines more importance as sources of trustworthy information than do education students (see Travis & Violato, 1981); but neither group seems to think that books or professors are very important as sources of information and ideas.

The data from the rank ordering of mass media sources which provide information about world affairs do not differ much from the parallel data for the education students reported by Travis and Violato. Television was ranked first by 32.6 percent of the sample and second by 23.8 percent. Newspapers were ranked first by 30.5 percent, radio by 24.6 percent, magazines by 8.2 percent and "other" by 4.1 percent. Television was ranked as the first or second most important source of adequate information by 56.4 percent of the sample. Overall then, television was regarded as "the most important" mass media source; and it was clearly a very important source when all possible sources for providing adequate information about world affairs were considered. This result is congruent with the Travis and Violato data for education students as well as the data from other studies of university students (Finlay, 1979). In sum, even though it is well known that television and other mass media sources provide systematically distorted views of reality (e.g., Epstein, 1973; Funkhouser, 1973; Lapham, 1981; Mankiewicz & Swerklow, 1978) both the present sample of veteran teachers and the Travis and Violato sample of would-be teachers seem to be trusting and credulous with respect to mass media in general and television in particular.

Beliefs About Youth

Large proportions of the sample (that responded to the question) indicated that today's youth, when compared to their elders, are more knowledgeable (n = 90; 78.6 percent), less hypocritical (n = 60; 52.5 percent), more progressive (n = 67; 60.4 percent) and not more conservative (n = 89; 81.7 percent). Smaller proportions reported beliefs that these youth are more virtuous (n = 9; 8.0 percent) and wiser (n = 13; 11.6 percent) than their elders. The results of the comparison of the beliefs about youth of teachers and education students are summarized in Table 15.4. From this data, it can be seen that there are no between-group differences on the beliefs regarding five of the six dimensions of the stereotype (knowledgeability, wisdom, virtuosity, conservatism and progressiveness). None of the corrected chi-square statistics (for a 2x2 contingency table) for the cross-tabulations on these dimensions is significant at the $\alpha = .05$

Table 15.3
Teachers' Sources of Ideas and Information About
Social, Political and Economic Matters

Part A:	Percentage of teachers listing items as being important sources of ideas and information about social, political and economic matters.	

Source	Percent of Sample
1. Newspapers	22.6
2. Television	21.5
3. Periodicals/Magazines	18.3
4. Radio	14.3
5. Parents/Relatives/Friends	13.6
6. Professors	9.7

Part B: Percentage of teachers listing items as being the most or second most important source of ideas and information about social, political and economic matters.

Source	Most Important (%)	2nd Most Important (%)
1. Newspapers	30.6	18.6
2. Parents/Relatives/Friends	17.4	8.1
3. Periodicals/Magazines	14.2	25.7
4. Television	13.3	29.0
5. Professors	13.3	8.1
6. Radio	11.2	10.5

level of significance.

However, teachers did tend to place more credence in the hypocrisy dimension of the stereotype ($X^2 = 5.590$; df = 1; $p = 0.0181$). A larger proportion of teachers than education students asserted that today's youth are less hypocritical than their elders (Table 15.4). Overall, the results from the teacher data indicate that youth is, for the most part, construed by many in the sample as possessing qualities and attitudes which are deviant in a progressive direction.

Beliefs about three dimensions of the stereotype covaried with sex, teaching level and degree of educational attainment. Females more than males indicated that youth are less hypocritical than their elders ($X^2 = 4.75$; df = 1; $p = 0.0361$). Moreover, subscription to this dimension was more characteristic of those who had no degree than those who held one or more degrees ($X^2 = 4.75$; df = 1; $p = 0.0293$). Females also tended to subscribe to the conservatism dimension more than did males ($X^2 = 9.47$; df = 1; $p = 0.0021$). We see then, that there are some sex, educational level and teaching level differences in some of the beliefs about youth.

Table 15.4
Comparison of the Beliefs About Youth of Teachers and Education Students

Group	More Knowledgeable[1]		Wiser[2]		More Virtuous[3]		Less Hypocritical[4]		More Conservative[5]		More Progressive[6]	
	yes	no	yes	no	yes	no	yes	no	yes	no	yes	no
Teachers	(90)* 79.6	(23) 20.4	(13) 11.6	(99) 88.4	(9) 8.0	(103) 92.0	(60) 52.2	(55) 47.8	(20) 18.3	(89) 81.7	(67) 60.4	(44) 39.6
Education Students	(363) 77.1	(108) 22.9	(73) 16.4	(371) 83.6	(53) 12.2	(380) 87.8	(175) 39.4	(269) 60.6	(72) 16.3	() 83.7	(263) 60.6	(171) 39.6

$^{1}X^2 = 0.215$; df = 1; $p = 0.6427$	$^{2}X^2 = 1.250$; df = 1; $p = 0.2635$
$^{3}X^2 = 1.17$; df = 1; $p = 0.2792$	$^{4}X^2 = 5.590$; df = 1; $p = 0.0181$
$^{5}X^2 = 0.139$; df = 1; $p = 0.7092$	$^{6}X^2 = 0.003$; df = 1; $p = 0.9499$

*Numbers in parentheses indicate the number of respondents in that group who responded yes or no to the beliefs about youth. The other figure in the cell is the percentage of the group that gave that response.

Evaluation of Hypotheses

Hypothesis 1. The first hypothesis predicted that the veteran teachers would not differ from the education students with respect to beliefs about five dimensions (knowledgeability, wisdom, virtuosity, progressiveness, and conservatism) of the youth stereotype. Moreover, it was predicted that teachers would place more credence than did the education students in the hypocrisy dimension. As can be seen from the foregoing data, this hypothesis is unequivocally supported. The only difference in beliefs which emerged between the two groups was on the hypocrisy dimension wherein teachers placed more credence in this than did education students ($X^2 = 5.590$; df = 1; $p = 0.0181$).

Hypothesis 2. This hypothesis predicted that, with regard to perceived reliability and trustworthiness of all possible sources of information and ideas about social, political, economic and other world affairs, teachers would favor mass media over all other possible sources. The data in the present study indicate strong support for this hypothesis. When asked on which of all possible sources of adequate information and trustworthy ideas about world affairs they relied, only 23.3 percent of the teachers designated sources other than mass media. Moreover, designations of parents, relatives and friends constituted the bulk of nominated sources (other than mass media) which were relied upon and trusted for adequate information and ideas about world affairs. Meanwhile, 76.7 percent of the teachers indicated that they relied upon and trusted mass media for adequate information and ideas. Furthermore, the mass media source which was considered to be the most important source of adequate ideas and information was television (which was so designated by 32.6 percent of the sample).

Hypothesis 3. This hypothesis predicted that the veteran teachers would watch more informational and serious television programs and read more serious and informational periodicals than did the Travis and Violato sample of education students. From the data presented in Tables 15.1 and 15.2, it can be seen that this hypothesis is uniformly supported. The teachers overall seemed to be more discriminating than the education students in their television viewing and periodical reading habits.

Discussion

The major findings from this study may be summarized as follows: (1) The veteran teachers' beliefs about youth were not much different from those of the students; untenable beliefs were subscribed to by both groups. Indeed, the veteran teachers seemed to have an even less realistic perception of youth than did the education students in the proposition that today's youth are less hypocritical than their elders. (2) The second major finding was that the veteran teachers tended to be more discriminating and selective than the students with respect to the types of television programs watched and the types of periodicals read, though there were no between-group differences on amount of time spent watching television and the frequency with which newspapers are read. (3) The third major finding was that veteran teachers tended to place high degrees of confidence in mass media as sources of reliable and trustworthy information about social, political, economic and other world affairs as did the Travis and Violato (1981) sample and others (Finlay, 1979; Roper, 1975).

A majority of the teachers in the present sample subscribed to four of the six dimensions of the youth stereotype (knowledgeability [79.6 percent], hypocrisy [52.2 percent], conservatism [81.7 percent], progressiveness [60.4 percent] while smaller proportions subscribed to the other two (wisdom [11.5 percent], virtuosity [8.0 percent]). It seems likely then, that protracted and continued exposure to young people in the classroom has not made this sample of teachers' beliefs about youth any more realistic than those of the relatively young (mean age was 23 years) and inexperienced education students. As Travis and Violato suggested, these beliefs may have been cultivated by mass media dissemination of stereotypes of young people. This assertion gains further support from the present study as it was the teachers (who are older) that tended to put more credence in the hypocrisy dimension of the stereotype. Perhaps this belief was congealed when, some years ago, the then younger teachers encountered an image of youth which was then given widespread and sustained visibility in mass media (Adelson, 1964). The education students (who are younger) have received less exposure to this hypocrisy-free youth notion since it has been less prominent in mass media in recent years. Most significant for the purpose of the present study however is the fact that teaching experience did not stimulate the development of greater understanding of youngsters, represented by the belief indicators, than that of the inexperienced students.

It should also be pointed out that while the teachers did tend to be more discriminating and selective in their television program viewing and magazine reading than were the education students, the greatest difference was in the use of what was called "information" material. For television programs, this includes national or local news and documentaries while for magazines this includes *Time, Newsweek, Macleans,* and the like. It is well known, however, that television news documentaries hardly reflect an accurate portrayal of reality (e.g., Epstein, 1973; Mankiewicf & Swerklow, 1978; Tuchman, 1974) and that such widely circulated magazines as *Time* (bought by scores of millions) provide superficial and systematically distorted accounts of social, political and economic matters (Felder, Meeske, & Hall, 1979; Funkhouser, 1973; Lapham, 1981; Merril, 1965). For the present sample, national or local news constituted the greatest proportion (33.8 percent) of television programs watched regularly (see Table 15.1). Of magazines, *Time* was the most widely read (57.4 percent of the sample), while *Macleans* and *Newsweek* were among the ten most widely used. Clearly, the teachers in the present sample are receiving fairly heavy doses of highly stylized accounts and misinformation about young people and other subjects (Lapham, 1981). It is somewhat unsettling that they so frequently abandon the task of constructing their own beliefs about youth based on their own observations. For the prefabricated depictions of youth supplied by organs dominated by style, format and economic considerations are not only inaccurate: they can contribute to misperception, misunderstanding and maladroit behavior.

The results of the present study once again underscore the merit of reiterating the suggestions which Travis and Violato (1981) made. Teacher educators have reason to make systematic efforts to disabuse their students of unrealistic notions about young people. This might well be done best within the context of the critical study of mass mediated culture and the impact of such culture on young people. A logical place for such efforts in teacher preparation programs is the usual adolescent or developmental psychology component. Unfortunately, many textbooks on adolescent psychology may be implicated in fostering unrealistic notions about young people and creating the illusion of a universal adolescent psychology (Adelson, 1979; Springhall, 1983-1984; Travis & Violato, 1981). However, critical appraisal of what is read in any context is desirable; and as Piaget said, one of the most useful strategies for improving our constructions and apprehensions of reality is that which entails a foil which one attacks (Bringuier, 1980). Of course this presumes that such things can be taught-and taught, moreover, to a group of people who are typically not inclined toward intellectual pursuits let alone noteworthy accomplishment. Perhaps without serious efforts to select candidates who are more fond of learning (as an end), too many teachers will continue to show the signs of a gravely limited human understanding, undeveloped critical judgment and rather primitive orientation to information and its sources, irrespective of experience in teaching and/or instruction which might be given to them.

In sum, the evidence from this comparative study did not support the proposition that all matters of practical importance in teaching are accrued in teaching practice. On the contrary, experienced teachers showed no more human understanding as represented by beliefs about youth than did inexperienced education students. Moreover, they seemed to be as credulous with regard to mass media as the students; and finally, though they seemed to be more discriminating in their patterns of mass media use, this discernment is not clearly a gain from teaching experience.

References

Adelson, J. (1964). The mystique of adolescence. *Psychiatry*, 27, 1-5.

Adelson, J. (1979). Adolescence and the generalisation gap. *Psychology Today*, 12(9), 33-37.

Adelson, J. (Ed.). (1980). *Handbook of adolescent psychology*. New York: Wiley Interscience.

Astin, A. (1979). *Four critical years*. San Francisco: Jossey Bass.

Atkin, J.M. (1981). Who will teach in high school? *Daedalus* 110, 3, 91-103.

Barzun, J. (1946). *We who teach*. London: Victor Gallancz.

Berliner, W. (1983, December 30). Closer scrutiny of teacher training planned. *The Guardian*, p.5.

Beuf, A. (1974). Doctor, lawyer, household drudge. *Journal of Communication*, 24, 142-145.

Bringuier, J.C. (1980). *Conversations with Jean Piaget*. Chicago: University of Chicago Press.

Cogan, M. (1975). Current issues in the education of teachers. In K. Ryan (Ed.), *Teacher education: The seventy-fourth yearbook of the National Society for the Study of Education*, Part II (pp.204-229). Chicago: University of Chicago Press.

Cortes, C. (1983). The mass media: Civic education's public curriculum. *Journal of Teacher Education*, 34(6), 25-29.

Ellul, J. (1973). *Propaganda: The formation of men's attitudes*. Toronto: Vintage.

Epstein, E. (1973). *News from nowhere*. New York: Random House.

Eurich, A.C., & Kraetsch, G.A. (1982). A 50 year comparison of University of Minnesota freshman's reading performance. *Journal of Educational Psychology*, 74(5), 660-665.

Ewen, S. (1977). *Captains of consciousness: Advertising and the social roots of consumer culture*. Toronto: McGraw-Hill.

Felder, F., Meeske, M., & Hall, J. (1979). *Time* magazine revisited: Presidential stereotypes persist. *Journalism Quarterly*, 56, 353-359.

Finlay, R. (1979, October). The strange skeptical mood of the campus. *Saturday Night*, 35-40.

Funkhouser, R.G. (1973). The issues of the sixties: An exploratory study in the dynamics of public opinion. *Public Opinion Quarterly*, 37, 62-75.

Gallup, G.H. (1982). The 14th annual Gallup Poll of the public's attitudes toward the public schools. *Phi Delta Kappan*, 64(1), 37-50.

Gerbner, G., & Gross, L. (1976). Living with television: The violence profile. *Journal of Communication*, 26, 172-179.

Hodgson, G. (1976). *America in our time.* New York: Doubleday.

Jones, L. (1981). Achievement test scores in mathematics and science. *Science 213,* 412-416.

Kirst, M. (1981). Loss of support for public secondary schools: Some causes and solutions. *Daedalus 110,* 3, 45-68.

Lapham, L.H. (1981, July). Gilding the news. *Harper's* 263, 1574, pp.31-39.

Mankiewicz, F., & Swerklow, J. (1978). *Remote control: Television and the manipulation of American life.* New York: Times Book Co.

McGregor, I. (1984, January 20). France launches reading campaign. *The Times Higher Education Supplement,* p. 8.

McQuaid, E . (1984, January 13). US concern over slipping standard. *The Times Higher Education Supplement,* p. 9.

Merril, J.C. (1965). How *Time* stereotyped three US presidents. *Journalism Quarterly,* 43, 563-570.

Newsweek. (1983, May 9). Can the schools be saved? pp.50-54, 56-58.

Roper, B.W. (1975). *Trends in public opinions toward television and other mass media, 1959-1974.* New York: Television Information Office.

Santinelli, P. (1983, December 30). Controlling the quality: Teacher training. *The Times Higher Education Supplement,* (Review of 1983), p. iii.

Schalock, D.R. (1979). Research on teacher selection. In D.C. Berliner (Ed.), *Review of research in education.* Chicago: American Educational Research Association.

Solorzano, L. (1983, March 14). What's wrong with our teachers? *US News and world Report* 94, 10, pp. 37-40.

Spitzberg, I.J., Jr. (1983, September 2). The problem with dealing with problems. *The Times Higher Education Supplement,* p. 22.

Springhall, J. (1983/1984). The origins of adolescence. *Youth and Policy,* 2(3), 20-24, 33-35.

Tan, A.S. (1979). TV beauty ads role expectations of adolescent female viewers. *Journalism Quarterly,* 56, 283-287.

Tan, A.S., & Tan, G. (1979). Television use and self-esteem of Blacks. *Journal of Communication,* 29, 283-287.

Travis, L.D. (1983a, June). *Personal attributes and education: Issues and directions* Paper presented to the Learned Societies of Canada Conference, CAEP/CSSE, at Vancouver.

Travis, L.D. (1983b, September). *Teacher as content and the metaphor problem: Teacher selection and preparation revisited.* Paper presented to the European Association for Research and Development in Higher Education at Frankfurt am Main, F.R.G.

Travis, L.D., & Violato,C. (1981). Mass media use, credulity and beliefs about youth: A survey of Canadian education students. *The Alberta Journal of Educational Research,* 27 (1), 16-34.

Tuchman, G. (Ed.). (1974). *The TV establishment.* Englewood Cliffs, NJ: Prentice-Hall.

Turner, R. (1975). An overview of research in teacher education. In K. Ryan (Ed.), *Teacher education: The seventy-fourth yearbook of the National Society for the Study of Education*, Part II (pp. 87-110). Chicago: University of Chicago Press.

Vance, V.S., & Schlechty, P.C. (1982). The destruction of academic ability in the teaching force: Policy implications. *Phi Delta Kappan*, 64 (1), 22-27.

Watts, D. (1980). Admission standards for teacher preparatory programs: Time for a change. *Phi Delta Kappan*, 60, [Special Issue], 120-122.

Weigel, R.H., & Jessor, R. (1973). Television and adolescent conventionality: An exploratory study. *Public Opinion Quarterly*, 37, 79-90.

Weiler, H.N. (1982). Education, public confidence and the legitimacy of the modern state: Do we have a crisis? *Phi Delta Kappan*, 64 (1), 9-14.

Zumwalt, K. (1982). Research on teaching: Policy implications for teacher education. In A. Lieberman & M. McLaughlin (Eds.), *Policy making in education: The eighty-first yearbook of the National Society for the Study of Education* Part I (pp. 215-248). Chicago: University of Chicago Press.

16
Disposition and Achievement

For every person wishing to teach
there are thirty not wanting to be taught
(Anon.)

On achievement, learning and teaching

One might suppose that scholastic achievement is all about teaching and learning. One might also suppose that learning, like teaching, is all about truth, beauty and goodness. Certainly, great scientists (e.g., Chandrasekhar, 1987) tell us that the truths that are good in science derive from sensed beauty. Similarly, the poet Keats and the Grecian urn tell us

"Beauty is truth, truth beauty" that is all
Ye know on earth, and all ye need to know.

However, in school, if you can fake that you've got it made. For educational achievement is, by formal definition, a specified level of attainment in scholastic or academic work – as assessed by teachers who may or may not utilize standardized tests or measures in making such assessments (Chaplain, 1968, p. 5). This definition only raises the question of what teachers take to be academic or scholastic work as well as what they consider as standards. Apparently, more than 20% of Canadians are illiterate (Maynard, 1989).

The degree of success or educational achievement entails comparisons of observed manifestations of what the teacher regards as learning with some criteria, some standards or norms which the teacher regards as pertinent and adequate for assessing levels of attainment. Of course, this implies that the teacher's judgement of what are pertinent and adequate signs of learning depends upon his or her sense and understanding of what concrete or manifest truth, beauty and goodness entail in, say, grade four composition, grade seven geometry, or grade ten history. Unfortunately, ineptitude (e.g., Nickerson, 1988, p. 34) and even corruption (e.g., *Time* 3 April, 1989) are not unknown.

Even so, this seems fairly simple: Teachers teach; pupils learn. Teachers observe pupils grapple with specific matters and reflect upon what they assume are pertinent and adequate signs of progress. Degree of success is judged through comparison of performance and standards.

The foregoing characterization of achievement is simple and superficial. Matters below the surface complicate life in general and achievement in particular. Thus, disposition complicates achievement. While a person's attainments are affected by his abilities, many other factors matter too. His goals, his plans, his striving, his sense of what matters in the achievement of success, as well as how those who assess degree of success are disposed to evidence and pertinent standards, all affect his attainments.

At the outset, dispositional matters call for consideration of the fact that scholarship or devotion to truth, beauty and goodness is not painless and easy. As the poet Housman (Wells, 1988, pp. 723-724) said, "the faintest of all human passions is the love of truth." Nor is studiousness an instinctive tendency or a quality that appeals to popular taste. The latter place a premium on freshness rather than on truth (which is always old). Scholastic achievement then, insofar as it entails devotion to learning or erudition; and, insofar as it also entails experience and standards which are unattractive to many in schools, evokes feelings of ambivalence for many – pupils and teachers alike. In sum, not everyone is well disposed to scholarly activity or to refinements which embody what is enduringly true, beautiful and good.

The second factor which complicates the matter of scholastic achievement – its conceptualization, pursuit and assessment is directly connected with the first. But the second factor is seldom mentioned – perhaps because reflection on the subject can evoke serious discomfort. As Freud (1963, pp. 104-115) said, we are naturally disposed to protect ourselves from such reflective experience through repression. That is, we unconsciously avoid, forget, disguise or deny matters which, if taken up in contemplation, are extremely painful or threatening. Indeed, as Jacoby (1975) showed, when a given matter is widely repressed, a society can forget insights or truths which are important for the very reason that they warn the society of serious danger. Repression and "social amnesia" are mentioned here because few will remember what Bernfeld (1973) described nearly 65 years ago: "the limits of education" which comprise the second complication.

Bernfeld's argument turns on the notion that there are irreconcilable facts and forces in education which set the character of what can occur. Accordingly, a working relationship between irreconcilables is all we should hope for because "no theory of education can resolve the antinomy between the justified will of the child and the justified will of the teacher; on the contrary, education consists in this antinomy." (Bernfeld, 1973, p. xxviii). Little is to be found in the literature of education and educational psychology on the subject of will and the clash or conflict of wills.

Bernfeld represents the eternal situation faced by man in education with Sisyphus, a mythical figure who, we should remember, was condemned to the eternal repetition of rolling a large rock to the top of a steep hill. Since the rock, immediately, rolled back to the bottom whenever it reached the hilltop, Sisyphus had to follow it and, from the base, repeat his pushing with the knowledge that the cycle of his toil would never end. In the ancient myth, failure to act in accord with an adequate calculation of his own limits and with respect for the dominion of other forces in realms destined to lay outside his control, won Sisyphus his eternal situation in Hades.

For every human, difficulty and error, to say nothing of inadequate wisdom, are eternal renewers of the burdens we must bear as, through every life, we grope for the line of action which marks the limits of our control or freedom of action. There is no map which charts the line that divides the world of self-made troubles into those arising from under-estimation and those arising from over-estimation of one's own powers or control and freedom.

With the ancient Greeks, Bernfeld recognized that there are certain constants or regularities in life; and these givens are often hard to discern and understand. Such difficulties often arise in the presence of conflicts which are, themselves, regular features of life.

Inter-personal conflicts are so ubiquitous no reader will be short of experience of such conflicts, and the limits they place on us and our actions. Similarly, reflective readers will recognize the common-place conflicts that arise from our unavoidable condition of being, simultaneously, the locus of multiple roles. Certainly, anyone familiar with the sensibilities of professional callings knows work-roles conflict with care-giving roles at home and in the family. In addition, socio-cultural conflicts can be seen in institutions, like schools, where incompatible demands are made on the institution. In the case of schooling, there is an inherent conflict between the demands for academic learning and custodial demands which consist of the insistence that young people be kept in school for as long as possible and the practices entailed in such "warehousing" (e.g., see Frye, 1988, p. 130). So at work, the teacher's ambit of influence is limited by ubiquitous interpersonal role and socio-cultural conflicts as well as the inevitable psychological conflicts and limitations that nobody escapes.

Psychological conflict, as Freud (1961) showed so well, arises from the opposition of culture and instinct. The individual, for example, feels the tension between work and biological pleasure; and so his strength is sapped. His energy and concentration are diverted by this conflict. Humans are caught in a losing struggle between these two realms of experience from which we cannot escape. Accordingly, much that we do consists in, or is given to maneuvering. Much energy is invested in efforts to gain room for manoeuvre between the cultural life and its demands on the one side and the biological life which is hostile to cultivation and the denial of somatic urges which culture requires on the other.

Achievement then takes place, is conceptualized, and is assessed in the midst of difficulties and trouble; in the midst of interpersonal, role, socio-cultural and psychological conflicts. Such conflicts, said Bernfeld (1973) along with fear, frustration, cruelty and the outbreak of adult emotions, comprise "eternal constants in education" which limit what can be accomplished by teaching and schooling (pp. 35-36). So the oft-seen personal withdrawal and apathy among teachers which have been interpreted as work effects (e.g., Hargreaves, 1978, pp. 540-541) should surprise nobody.

Certainly, the too much neglected topic of the psychology of teachers warrants examination when one considers pupil disposition and scholastic achievement. In a time when there is much presumption about and discussion of school and teacher "effectiveness" (e.g., Hirsch, 1989; O'Neill, 1988; Westbury, 1988); "skills" (e.g., Bloom, 1987; Chipman, Segal and Glaser, 1985; Hirsch, 1989; Skinner, 1984); "management" (e.g., Coleman, 1986; Barker, 1986; Slavin, 1986) and other such signs of "technification" (Marton & Saljo, 1984) and "tool-thinking" (Bettelheim, 1980, pp. 142-168) we would be well served by observation and thought about the psychology of teachers. For it is teachers who conceptualize and assess achievement; and it is teachers who may forget about or repress thought concerning their limits and their manner of handling the inevitable conflicts discussed above.

Again, Bernfeld's (1973) observations are to the point. He said educators can have a "lust for omnipotence" (p. 94), and deceive themselves by conferring exaggerated importance on technique and methods which give them "the flattering feeling of being active and at the very centre of things" (p. 96). All the while "the educational process itself occurs within the individual" pupil (p. 96) not as effects of curriculum implementation, treatments or methods but as a concomitant of the individual's effort, perseverance, "sweat, renunciation and . . . sense of guilt . . . " (p. 55).

Bernfeld seems to have agreed with the poet who said the "faintest of all human passions is the love of truth." For he argued that the school concerned with learning is "compelled to act counter to the children's inherited urges and against their spontaneous desires and interests. Whether methods are brutal or humane, it (the school) is forever in opposition to the powers of nature" (p. 55).

Thought about this requirement is so unpleasant that those who aggressively deny it while glorifying childhood suggest to Bernfeld, the presence of "repressed passionate and violent urges" (p. 22). These teachers represent what Meehl (1977, p. 228) calls "the tradition of exaggerated tenderness" which countenances substantive absurdities in the name of lofty ideals. Bernfeld aimed some of his most pointed remarks at all who, whether of technological or tenderminded enthusiasm, would not recognize the limits of pedagogy:

> All educational measures for changing the child in accordance with (the loftiest) . . . aim are suspiciously simple and banal. . . . None of them is new, and perhaps it is impossible to think up any new educational method. The greatest educators certainly did not succeed. They have run the gamut from love to harsh discipline, from verbal instruction to teaching by personal example. They have recommended that teachers play an active part, and that they practice restraint . . . They have demanded free expression for the child's impulses and their repression. The whole scale has been tried . . . and millions of children . . . exposed to every imaginable combination of means and methods. And the result? Humanity as it is today and always was. The distance between empirical man and ideal man remains essentially unchanged. (p. 27)

So far then, we see that scholastic achievement (as conceptualized, nurtured or pursued and assessed) is complicated by two classes of trouble. The first consists of the difficulties and unpleasantness that accompany studious devotion to learning and erudition. The work and sacrifices that are entailed in the development of skills, refinement of sensibilities, acquisition of knowledge and enhancement of understanding in the content domains of genuine (serious) culture, are not trivial investments or commitments – for anyone. When there is little manifest care for such content on the part of parents, teachers or society as it is known; where there is an absence of devotion to, and a palpable presence of ambivalence toward, standards of cultivation, the development of the disposition to work and sacrifice, as required, is troublesome. The second set of troubles which we considered consists of conflicts of several sorts that, along with frustration, fear, cruelty and adult emotion, are "eternal constants in education." Since teachers face and must cope with these conflicts, they are affected by them. Patterns of repression in the face of these conflicts can affect not only the demeanor and reactions of teachers who, after all, are agenda-setters, organizers, adjudicators and are in other respects, major features of each school child's educational situation. Such patterns of repression through, for example, sustained and intense concern about instructional methods, or through expression of an elaborate sentimentalism with regard to children, can complicate achievement for children.

In Canada, the classroom is not merely the official site for the apprenticeship of scholars or the place where pupils and teachers interact. It is these things and more – including a focus and locus for conflict between various people who expect to have influence over what is found therein.

In the clamor of claims and conflict, subject matter, procedures and even what comprises achievement itself, can become subject to negotiation – especially when teachers have weak academic principles or weak Principals. Of course, negotiated standards of this sort merely express the triumph of a political expression localized in time and place. Standards so secured are not secure. The mass media of popular culture make a mockery of the notion of standards. For standards are always "out of date." That is, what makes them standards. Accordingly, when "norms" are just local prejudice that changes with the climate of opinion on "information radio" or other instruments of commercial culture, scholastic achievement is complicated. Under these conditions, evidence for consideration of achievement in relation to non-local standards may be unavailable to, for example, those who move to a new school. These confusing circumstances breed fear, frustration, cruelty and emotional outbreaks.

Given such circumstances, one can understand, even as one disapproves of, the inclination or disposition of some teachers to simplify the situation through the adaptation of fashions of the moment (otherwise called "trends"). However, this adaptation suggests the presence of a frivolous sensibility which can claim little credit for the nurturance of academic learning or the dispositions and interests which are vital to such learning. Under these circumstances pupils can indeed "fake" truth, beauty and goodness since the throw-away mode of fashion prevails while concern for what is serious or durable has been lost or repressed by the would-be custodians of the cultural heritage. Even more disturbing is the realization that some children will not know that their learning is "fake" in the absence of a presence who cares for the concision in language, for the depth and nuances of feeling, for the richness and range of interests, for the sharpness of wit, for the aesthetic sensibilities, for the empathic capacity, for the sharpness of perception, for the daring and critical powers, for the depth of understanding, for the distinctions that adorn the "house of intellect" (Barzun, 1961).

The knowledge of range in human achievement, the critical capacity to spot weakness and flaw, the detachment of judgement that encourages a civilized tolerance are central to what Northrop Frye (1963) calls "the educated imagination." Dispositions to fake achievement might be discouraged in the presence of such imagination. And if more teachers were in possession of an educated imagination, the dispositions necessary for genuine achievement might be more readily discerned.

The physicist, Paul Dirac, is credited with the observation that while the quest of the physicist is to make plain and simple what is obscure and difficult, the poet's effort is to achieve the opposite: to make complex and difficult what seems simple and obvious. Teachers must do both. When matters obscure and difficult are the object of children's curiosity; or when they stand between a goal and the present condition and position of her children, the teacher strives to make the obscure and difficult plain and simple for them. Indeed, most people probably suppose that this is the teacher's principal function. However, in the degree of their immaturity, children's puerile understanding and inexperience requires that teachers must also regularly make complex and difficult what seems simple and obvious to the relatively innocent mind. They must upset or perturb a state of balance that an established, but inadequate, sense of reality provides for a child. One rarely sees this side of teaching discussed in the literature on education or educational psychology. On the contrary, the exaggerated emphasis on quelling or reducing the child's trouble and the neglect of trouble-making by teachers, suggests the presence of a shared defense that looks like repression. In any event, teachers must simplify and complicate to bring benefit to pupils in their charge. In both cases, they may affect the disposition of their pupils toward matters at hand.

Teachers address pupils' dispositions to matters at hand because they presumably want to aid and abet educational development, to help pupils achieve as well and as much as they are able. However, as we have seen, this is no simple matter since the context of scholastic achievement is laced with difficulties, conflicts, and troubles.

Since the subject of disposition and achievement is complicated and problematical, the foregoing discussion of achievement questions and issues is intended as preparation for a consideration of dispositions. In the next section, a conceptual analysis of dispositions precedes an exploration of the concept of achievement in relation to disposition. Thereafter, we turn to a pair of studies of dispositional phenomena and achievement. This examination of evidence and its significance in relation to current work brings this chapter to its end.

Disposition as a Factor in Achievement

Disposition is a complex concept that denotes a dynamic but enduring organization of a person's whole mind (affection, cognition and conation) and its orientation to given classes of objects, conditions and events. Disposition, says Chaplin (1968, p. 141) is "the organized totality of the individual's psychophysical tendencies to react in a certain way." Thus, when we notice that somebody is generally unflappable and cheerful, we say the person has "a happy disposition." The studious and critical frame of mind is said to be that of a person with "a serious disposition"; or the perseverant and purposive person may be said to have "a stubborn disposition." These instances of commonly recognized dispositions highlight the continuities, patterns or regularities in the orientations of others. By themselves, they are both illustrative and misleading in that while they highlight the characteristic, enduring qualities of disposition, they fail to underscore the complicating dynamics of dispositions. Accordingly, the dynamic nature of a psyche gives disposition the quality of a firefly. That is, the person of unflappable disposition can be seen to lose composure under some circumstances. Similarly, nobody is immune to unhappiness; and those of serious disposition are, at times and with particular matters, uncritical or whimsical. In sum, the attributes that are the signature of a given enduring orientation or disposition do not always shine or glow or show themselves.

Accordingly, while one may have a disposition to think before one acts, some circumstances call for a reversal of order; so we find deliberative or reflective people acting first and considering later, when the press of events precludes conscious consideration of alternatives in anticipation of action. The disposition construct is, then, more able to encompass situation sensitivity and flexibility than are other constructs like habit, set, drive and motive which also connote regularity and continuity in behavior but which suggest greater rigidity or less dynamic complexity. In this light, dispositions are tendencies to feel, think and strive in particular ways that are relatively predominant over other emotional, cognitive and connotive propensities. However, enduring dispositional tendencies can be moderated by transient states which situations evoke.

Frequently, psychologists distinguish between traits and states which dispose us to behave in particular ways. This distinction allows us to make sense of the occasional calm behavior of people who are usually labile or anxious, and the occasional "nervous behavior" of people who are generally calm. Accordingly, the reader may sense the kinship of the trait concept with the notion of disposition.

Similarly, psychologists often distinguish between intrinsic and extrinsic motivation to contrast differential effects of external incentive and consequence conditions on behavior, with effects of desires, needs, self-direction, anticipation, aspirations, worries, fears, and so forth. The disposition construct also connotes motivation; and in particular, it places emphasis on the significance of continuities that arise from memory, aesthetic sensibilities, aspirations, knowledge – the range of conative, emotional and cognitive resources that give direction and spirit, feeling and meaning to one's attentions, intentions and actions.

In any case, dispositions like intrinsic motivation energize behavior; and if pupils' sates and dispositions organize and direct the behavior so energized, the simplifications and complications which teachers try to arrange may or may not affect such states and dispositions of any given pupil toward matters at hand. A major reason for this indeterminate situation is that all humans, at any time, are simultaneously in a number of states (of arousal, anxiety, contentedness, deprivation, interest, anticipation and so forth). These states can moderate, or mediate the more enduring and characteristic dispositions (that, in a class, exist simultaneously in great variety and number). In their turn, dispositions affect the quality and intensity of states. As William James said long ago, "My experience is what

I choose to attend to." So choices reflect dispositions; and accordingly, predispositions order experiential states, since we can choose to attend to internal matters like worry, fantasies, plans and so forth, and exclude those features of the world external that don't suit our fancies, pique our curiosity, play on our vanity or otherwise tantalize, scare or amuse us.

In summary, the dispositions which teachers address represent continuities of the inner life which are situation sensitive, dynamic, selective, directive and propulsive or motivational. They are not merely cognitive, affective or conative: they constrain and express all these mental functions in confluence – and more. So cultural matters that take up continuous residence in the mental life also influence dispositions.

Only two examples of the principal cultural influences on disposition can be briefly discussed here. They are language and the reality principle.

Language and Disposition

To the extent that Vygotsky and his followers are correct, language has an important influence on self-regulation (Luria, 1979). Without it, the disposition to direct self by foresightful, planful and critically analytical thought would not develop fully. Language, according to Whorf (see Bruner, 1979, p. 137) also predisposes us to think along certain lines. The givens of syntax and lexicon orient us in the world of both thought and action. Indeed, as Lakoff and Johnson (1980) say "we live by" metaphors that are at the centre of "systems" of thinking. They "commit" us, for example, to treat "argument as war" and "time as a resource."

The importance of language as a dispositional factor in education warrants special attention here before we turn to a brief consideration of the other major cultural factor that can be considered here: the reality principle.

Generally, the education of children, and more particularly, the teaching of children, are conventionally thought of as something adults do to children. Both expressions turn on transitive verbs. Both imply a subject that acts on the object – children. So something is done to children by adults (presumably because educators or teachers are all adults). The active agent is the adult. Implicitly, the object or child upon whom the action is performed is passive. Obviously, the observant and thoughtful among us by now must suspect syntax of serious and many metaphysical sins. What is taken as truth can be just the inventions of predatory organizations.

This rude subject-object manner of thought, about education and teaching, entails or makes manifest a deterministic view which is evident in the favorite metaphors one finds in educational discourse. For example, one finds process or activity metaphors, like "moulding," whereby raw material is transformed into a desired shape. Moreover, the process of transformation, the moulding that determines the eventual shape of the child-object, is mechanical. This leaves aside any question about resistance or active participation on the part of the object. The process term, the metaphor, lacks capacity to incorporate questions about the nature of the object-child and the impact of its variability on the moulder and moulding process.

A current and widely-used metaphor in the educational discourse of what may become known as the Age of Nixon reflects the educators' alliance with the ethos (and lucre) of business. So we find the process-product conception which, again, takes children to be raw material that is subjected to refining. The process is assumed to be an efficient cause of effects which are presumed to be predictable products of the process. The presumption is that schools and teachers are producers. This leaves little room for products to claim responsibility for the degree of their own refinement or lack of same. This is objectionable, misleading and is probably harmful to some children and their achievement insofar as they locate the critical forces in achievement outside themselves.

In sum, the language of education predisposes us to think about teaching and learning along certain lines that warrant critical analysis. One such line of thought has been called "tool thinking" (Bettelheim, 1980; pp. 142-168) and its importance is examined further below. Meanwhile, another major cultural influence on dispositions requires attention.

Human Tendencies and the Reality Principle

Some dispositional qualities are given by the fact of our species characteristics. As humans, we are all predisposed to feel, think, imagine and compare. Each human is, at once, both sensuous and given to formalize with symbols (Schiller, 1965). So we all know that

the eye of man hath not heard,
the ear of man hath not seen,
man's hand is not able to taste,
his tongue to conceive
nor his heart to report
what my dream was. (Alexander, 1988, p. 15)

At the same time, we share the innate capacity (in degree) to see the look of one thing in another. While we all live in details, in particulars, we think in generalities. So we see the look, feel the touch, hear the sound, taste the flavor and smell the aroma of one thing in another. We are disposed to make meaning through drawing similarities and differences. As someone has said, the fine thing about poems, plays and novels is that they show you what it is like to have feelings other than your own. So in hearing, seeing and reading them we can gain a basis for the comparisons that are necessary for us to achieve some concision of thought about this essentially private world, man's inner life of dreams, feelings and imagination (e.g., see Frye, 1963, 1988).

However, the achievement of greater concision and other refinements (of sensibility, knowledge, understanding, and skill) requires that he who would become more cultivated must work. Although those who have chosen their parents and circumstances with care may have to work less diligently than their more carefree fellows, cultivation always costs work – an undertaking to which nobody is predisposed.

Most work is unpleasant and generally unattractive. Moreover, there is no sign of progress in this regard. Indeed, close examination of evidence suggests that the situation is, and has been, deteriorating for some time (e.g., Jones, 1982). Generally, people work because they must. For only a few can work be a source of meaning as well as the exchange of living energy and time for money. Even for the blessed few, much work is pointless. So much of the necessary toil is so remote from that which might confer meaning on the activity that the connection is lost on the worker (Jones, 1982). Unfortunately, much of school work is of this sort – for both teachers and pupils. Moreover, the pupils who work do so in the absence of pay. The common disinclination to work under these conditions is regrettable but understandable. Since the authority and coercive powers of teachers have been seriously eroded, declines in achievement that are reported regularly, especially in the USA (see, for example, Hirsch, 1989; Jones, 1988; Partington, 1987) may to some degree reflect a decline in work. Certainly, those who celebrate the pay-off from time-on tasks celebrate a banality rather than a discovery.

We all may be predisposed to make sense of things even when, as in inkblots or nonsense verse, no sense is to be made. However, there are notable limits to the efforts we will voluntarily invest to make that sense. Accordingly, the natural disinclination to suffer or tax ourselves has to be countered if society is to be well-ordered and civilized and if the individual is to cultivate or achieve the refinements on which civility, social order and culture depend. In effect, the "primary" or first "sovereign tendency" to maximize pleasure and minimize unpleasure must be countered with what Freud (1983, p. 22) called the "reality-principle" which insists that present pleasure must be largely forgone for greater advantage or gains in the future.

Bettleheim (1980) reminds us that "all genuine education," all achievement "is based on this principle" which "is not learned on a rational basis" (p. 31). The disposition described by the reality principle which is so fundamental to scholastic achievement is, says Bettelheim, developed or acquired from the example of parental behavior and from the experience of anxiety instilled by parents and significant others in the child's life. The significance of example and the importance of such social anxiety can be readily seen in Simon's (1987) portrayal of modern Japanese mothers ("kyoiku mamas") and their devotion to the education of their dependent children.

Simons (1987) says that the kyoiku teaches her child, from an early age, that he must do well or people will laugh at him – and at his mother too (p. 48). Motherhood is regarded as a profession that is demanding and prestigious. The social perception of a woman's success as a mother depends in large part on how well her children do in school. In their turn, mothers, says Simons, believe it is their responsibility to see that the child fulfills his responsibility. In his turn, the child sees vivid signs of the care and effort invested by the mother on the child's behalf. Accordingly, in a country which has regular competitive exams, and where test scores are the keys that open doors, children's striving is energized by social anxiety about the standing of oneself and one's mother and the laughter that might accompany noted failure or inadequacy. The diligence, concentration and perseverance which visitors to Japan see in Japanese students, express both the consequences of respect for caring parents and the superego anxiety that Freud (1930) showed us, long ago, is the price one must pay for culture and civilization. Since "most learning gives no immediate pleasure" (Bettleheim, 1980, p. 132) and "solid knowledge requires . . . prolonged hard work for a distant purpose" (p. 131) the reality principle that is based on example and anxiety is a disposition which serves achievement well in Japan as elsewhere (see also Doi, 1981).

In those individuals and groups that recoil from the harsh truths about our condition, one discerns an irrational keenness for the civilizing power of the pleasure principle. Thus, one readily finds a refusal to acknowledge the merits of that gentle fear which informs the reality principle and concentrates the mind. Rather, one finds a following for a faith in the importance of contentedness with self as a necessary disposition for scholastic achievement in spite of the fact careful scrutiny has repeatedly shown that measures of self and achievement yield only low correlations at best (e.g., Hamford and Hattie, 1982; Scheirer and Kraut, 1979). Since results of careful investigations indicate that there is "not . . . a causal relationship between self-concept and achievement" (Pattebaum, Keith and Ehly, 1986, p. 140), the explanation for persistent faith in the importance of self-contentment as a disposition which enhances achievement might well entail patterns of repression in educators as well as the impact of the custodial or warehousing demands that are made on schools and teachers. Those who are prone to glorify children and indulge in rescue fantasies may have guilt-induced repression of violent urges and desires toward the adults who suppressed their infantile rages. The nurturance of self-contentment in children would be attractive to such persons. Since the mind is an instrument for arranging the world according to its own desires and needs, its arrangements can have the quality of fiction. Moreover, emphasis on the nurturance of self-contentment reduces friction, strife and antagonisms. But let us not forget the price that is paid for such peace.

When parents and teachers abandon the reality principle and insist that learning be "fun," they give up their grounds for claiming any credit for aiding and abetting children's achievements. Only the fortunate few children who are blessed with either (better yet both!) very exceptional brightness or a home rich in cultural capital (discussed below) can achieve, by serious standards, in spite of a school given over to monotonous fervor or one infused with solemn frivolity. Such observations are not made to argue for grim teaching or for velleity of imagination and feeling in the tone of schooling. They are merely offered to bolster the chances of victory of honesty over hope in that unhappy struggle against illusion and self-deception.

The play of the market-place on the eyes of consumer society celebrates possessions and the sybaritic type of happiness made visible in commercials. The good life so seen is a life of carefree ease and "fun." The parabolic world of celebrities, entertainment and relaxation is a world wherein differences between consumers are de-emphasized. The "dictatorship of the commonplace" against which Ortega Y Gasset warned us, the mass attitude of the consumer ethos, is readily discerned in schools. The commercial culture carries with it the unspoken message "if you bore me you die." In a world where there is a tendency to "live now" by the line of polling, there is a tendency to accept nice nonsense over bleak sense; and a teacher's freedom to displease disappears where teachers serve the empire of demand.

Non-trivial achievement is the reward of one's own diligence, concentration and perseverant efforts. Celebrity and riches often seem to require nothing more than a fetching face; and to the puerile eye and ear the apparent fun and trapping of a hockey or pop-music fame are readily contrasted with vague and comparatively stuffy promises of future usefulness to which educators too frequently resort as incentives for attentiveness or work. Appeals to usefulness or economic advantage to be seen in the remote future are not merely ineffectual as incentives (Skinner, 1984). Such appeals are "barbarous" and degrading to both the pupil and culture. For the pupil is implicitly being told that he is moved only by greedy expectations (Powell, 1985), and scholarship or culture is being debased with the implicit message that it lacks inherent worth and requires the disguise of instrumental or "tool" value (Bettelheim, 1980, pp. 143-145).

If disadvantaged youth are to achieve well, they probably need to have first-hand experience of the superiority of the reality-principle over the pleasure principle. As James (1962) said long ago, "the fighting impulse must often be appealed to" (p. 28). For, frequently, they have not been prepared to act on the basis of long-term goals. Accordingly, what James called "soft pedagogics" which assumes the nonsense "that every step in education *can* be interesting" may be more harmful in the long term than the experience of some fear or shame which can be concomitants of pedagogics that embrace the reality principle. The enduring advantages that arise from the discovery of what one can win with one's perseverant and energetic effort can far outweigh transient discomfort. So James (1962) advised teachers to:

> Make the pupil feel ashamed of being scared at fractions, of being 'downed' by the law of falling bodies; rouse his pugnacity and pride, and he will rush at the difficult places with a sort of inner wrath at himself that is one of his best moral faculties . . . The teacher who never rouses this sort of pugnacious excitement in his pupils falls short of . . . his best . . . (p. 28).

Such advice seems especially pertinent when one encounters underachievement that reflects deficits not of ability or affect but of conation or striving. While care and tact (sensitivity to the possibilities and limitations inherent in evolving situations) are always crucial teacher attributes when fear and shame are part of the situation, one can consider and approach such exercises as analogues to the experience of inoculation. The irritation and discomfort that are entailed in both cases are signals of a strengthening of a capacity to cope with future troubles. The puffery of popcorn curricula does not merely fail to immunize children whose lives are ordered by the pleasure principle only; it punishes them and stunts them over the long term because it deprives them of opportunities to form and incorporate the cultural capital (including such intellectual possessions as organized knowledge, social acumen, aesthetic refinements, moral sensibilities, concision of thought and speech) which seriously affects the range of choices available in life. Perhaps their orientation to choices in general is affected adversely.

In any event, a child that behaves in accordance with the pleasure principle only has no conscience worth mentioning (Freud, 1930). Bettelheim (1980) sets forth the significance of this state of affairs for those considering disposition, achievement and teaching:

> ... the modern view of morality ... does not prepare the young to act on the basis of long range goals. It takes mature judgement to be able to 'do the right thing' when one is no longer motivated by fear, and to do it even though one knows how relative all human values are. Before the age of reason, conscience (or the superego) operates on the irrational basis on which it was originally formed ... fear (not ... reasoned judgement). Only later does mature ego apply reason to ... do's and don't's ...

> One primary motive for learning is the wish first to satisfy and later to modify an irrationally demanding superego ... But if there is no excessive superego anxiety to reduce, a most important motive for learning is absent ... If we do not fear the forces of nature, why learn about them? The detachment that permits hard study out of sheer curiosity ... is a stance arrived at only by very few, and even by most of them only in maturity.

> Thus, while conscience originates in fear, any learning that is not immediately enjoyable depends on the prior formation of a conscience. ... True ... too much fear interferes with learning, but for a long time any learning that entails serious application does not proceed well unless also motivated by some manageable fear. (Bettelheim, 1980, pp. 129-130)

In summary, evidence suggests that "a certain degree of anxiety is necessary for an individual to be fully motivated to give of his best" (Gammage, 1982, p. 177). And while one should avoid trying to explain anything as complex as human behavior through the use of a single concept, we have reason to wonder about the extent to which deficits are entailed in underachievement. Since there is reason to believe that underachievement is, to some extent, disguised through a theory-begging manoeuvre that renames the underachiever as one afflicted with a "learning disability" (e.g., Haring, 1982), we can wonder again about the ways in which the psychology of teachers can be implicated in the mystification of achievement and in the success of faking in school. The vagueness and ill-defined character of the learning disability concept seems to reflect political experiences more than intellectual honesty. Given that state of affairs, beauty, truth and goodness might sometimes be in danger.

Similarly, the tendency to generate and rely on local norms for assessment of abilities and achievement may mislead too. For example, Himelfarb (1977) has shown that there are some socio-cultural characteristics in the common one-industry towns of Canada which are inhospitable to learning. His description of indifference to or lack of concern about the quality of schooling in such towns suggests that the low level of education which is characteristic of the populations of these towns will be incessantly reproduced – especially if local performances are not seen in relation to provincial and national norms. While learning and cultivation have seldom been at the centre of life in such towns, a recognition of the importance of a genuine education for the youth of such towns whose future there is, at best, precarious, would be helpful. If the teachers, who Himelfarb said were very like those they teach, could clearly see how far local performances fall below norms from beyond their niche, they might link the heavy use of alcohol and drugs and the exaggerated resignation that is typical, with the poor school achievement that is seen.

Disposition and Achievement: Some Recent Work

In the final portion of this chapter, data from two studies receive attention. The first study focused on high school students in academic and nonacademic programs. These two groups were compared on a variety of matters that are pertinent to the present topic. Results reported earlier (Travis, 1987) indicated their orientations to teachers are also pertinent to this consideration of disposition and achievement. The second study examined the relationships between standardized achievement scores and ability measures as well as such dispositional indicators as behavioral persistence and several measures of narcissism. This study was one in a series of studies that focus on the assessment of individual differences in educational personality. In this instance, a sample of private school children in the sixth and seventh grades were studied.

Recent Work and Directions

In our studies of people in education, we have tried to discover, among other things, whether and what differences exist between youngsters in academic programs as opposed to those in nonacademic programs on a range of variables which can be taken as indicative of dispositional characteristics. In one such study, a sample consisting of 259 senior secondary pupils from three metropolitan centres (two Canadian and one American) provided us with questionnaire data on personal and family backgrounds, interests, plans, orientation to the future; their sense of what is important and notions about what brings success; their reading habits and background; their preferences among and use of information sources; their fears and sense of trouble in the world; and their orientation to teacher qualities. Table 16.1 summarizes the distributions of the sample and the academic and non-academic sub-sets of the sample across four socio-cultural classes which reflect differences in principal source of family income: (1) entrepreneurial (ENTR), (2) professional (PRO), (3) skilled (licensed) labor (SKL), and (4) unskilled labor (UNSKL).

Clearly, youngsters from households headed by professionals are over-represented in the academic (university preparation) programs and their cohorts from both labor groups are under-represented. This fact is mentioned because a number of interesting differences between the two program groupings, not seen when parallel contrasts were made between classes, were discovered. First, while the members of both academic and non-academic groups (about 80%) ranked subject matter knowledgeability as the teacher quality of greatest importance, the academic students differed significantly from non-academic pupils in their rankings of several other teacher qualities. Friendliness was far more important as a teacher quality for the non-academic pupils than it was for the academic students. Similarly, teacher attractiveness mattered more to non-academic than academic youngsters. Further, these program groups differed with respect to how a demanding teacher is regarded. The tendency to require high quality work was clearly more out of favor with the non-academic pupils than with their academic counterparts. While less than 58% of the academic group placed "demanding" as a teacher quality in the lower half of the rankings, 77% of the non-academic pupils did so.

Table 16.1

Distributions of Proportions for Whole Sample and Program Sub-sets
Across Occupational Classes of Fathers (n = 243)

Group	Occupational Classes				
	ENTR.	PRO.	SKL.	UNSKL.	TOTAL %
Academic	11.6	50.0	16.3	22.1	35.4
Nonacademic	8.9	22.9	28.7	39.5	64.6
Total Sample	9.9	32.5	24.3	33.3	100.0

X^2 = 21.49; df = 3; $p < 0.001$

These findings suggest that among non-academic pupils there may be a greater appreciation of custodial care from teachers that make their stay in school pleasant, than of an academic or scholastic emphasis from teachers that are disposed to make demands of pupils. While the reader is cautioned against making the mistake of assuming that a comparison of a given individual from one group with one from the other will yield the same contrasts as drawn here between the groups, there is reason to look further for evidence of differences in disposition to teachers and school experience. For there was other evidence from the same study that indicates the students in the academic programs were significantly different from the non-academic people in other matters that suggest dispositional differences.

Accordingly, members of the academic group were more inclined than were the others, to think about the future, be optimistic about it and make plans. On the other hand, they were less inclined to say that having much money mattered a great deal to them than were the members of the non-academic group. Similarly, the latter people were more disposed to reliance on their friends and relatives for information about current affairs and were more inclined to believe that connections with "the right people" is important in gaining success than were the academic youngsters. At the same time, the groups did not differ regarding the belief (widely held in both groups) that good grades and a university education were very important in gaining success. When one considers these findings together with the fact that the academic pupils, more than the others, planned to undertake further studies after high school, one has reason to suspect that significant differences exist between the two groups with respect to their dispositions to matters at hand. One might also suspect that in their turn, teachers might be disposed to perceive and treat such pupils differently.

This last conjecture has a bearing on the final matter which can be considered in this chapter. The subject of dispositional differences in the elementary school years has also received our attention. In one project, from which Mah (1988) reported data on private school pupils, we have tried to gain a sense of how behavioral persistence and achievement are affected by differences in cultural capital, narcissism and abilities (as they covary). In effect, we have reason to expect that Freud's (1914, 1931, 1963) narcissism construct is pertinent to the study of achievement in that he (Freud, 1914, 1931) made an important distinction between narcissism that interferes with or inhibits striving and persistence and a type of narcissism that disposes one to "obsessive" and tenacious striving, that is, perseverant effort to meet high standards for achievement.

This theoretical basis for studying individual differences in conation has been overlooked. Accordingly, we have been developing procedures and devices for studying individual differences in conation as found in educational settings. This has entailed development of a projective procedures and device (e.g., see Travis & Mah, 1986; Mah, 1988) and other psychometric and behavioral measures. Given the early stage of this work, the data available are spare but provocative and encouraging.

Moreover, the data reported by Mah (1988) comes from a very unrepresentative sample which consisted primarily of females (54 out of 56) from families of privilege; and these children are generally higher achievers and brighter than those in a random sample of Canadian pupils from all Canadian schools. Not surprisingly, underachievers were virtually non-existent in the sample. The sample was not large and the range of percentile ranks for the abilities measure was 25 to 99 (mean = 82; SD = 17.6). Even so, the over-achievers and those whose narcissism was judged to be of the obsessive type (in clinical tests) had very much more consistent striving patterns (as indicated by several behavioral persistence measures) than did the other members of the sample. Alpha coefficients for the judged obsessionals (across three situations, n = 5) was $\alpha = .70$, whereas for non-obsessionals $\alpha = .13$ (n = 31). When overachievement was used as the index for obsessional narcissism, $\alpha = .55$ (n = 5) and the nonobsessionals (n = 31) had an $\alpha = .38$.

An inventory measure of narcissism (The Narcissistic Personality Inventory – NPI) was also used to explore how narcissism might moderate persistence and affect achievement. When comparisons were made between those with scores in upper and lower quantities of the NPI, the striving patterns for those with the higher scores were clearly more consistent than were those in the lower quartile ($\alpha = 50$, n = 11 versus $\alpha = .07$, n = 10). The same contrasts were seen in the data from the projective procedure ($\alpha = .55$ for top quartile n = 8; versus $\alpha = .15$, n = 8, for the bottom).

In sum, while little evidence of the debilitating or inhibitory narcissism which might be associated with low persistence and underachievement was seen, the signs of an advantageous obsessional narcissism were seen in association with high achievement. This latter dispositional factor is certainly not to be regarded as the same species of narcissistic disposition which is associated with the avoidance of challenge, exhibitionistic display, acting out and so forth. On the contrary, the observed behavior of those pupils who scored, and were judged to have been, high on manifestations of narcissism, was exemplary. Accordingly, this dispositional construct deserves further attention in studies that incorporate large numbers of pupils from a wide diversity of socio-cultural backgrounds. For while this early exploratory work has yielded some correspondence between measures that suggest the possible presence of some coherence of theory, we do not yet know whether or to what degree we are on an investigatory trajectory that is good enough, and true enough to arrive at the beauty of knowing and understanding the full complexities of disposition and achievement.

References

Alexander, M. (1988, 16 September). Homer, sweet Homer . . . *The Times Higher Education Supplement*, No. 828, p. 5.

Barker, R. (1986, 4 April). Rise of the great pretenders. *The Times Higher Education Supplement*. No. 700, p. 13.

Barzun, J. (1961). *The House of Intellect*. New York: Harper.

Bernfeld, S. (1973). *Sisyphus or the Limits of Education*. Berkeley, CA: University of California Press.

Bettelheim, B. (1980). *Surviving and Other Essays*. New York: Vintage.

Bloom, A. (1987). *The Closing of the American Mind*. New York: Simon & Schuster.

Bruner, J.S. (1979). *On Knowing: Essays for the Left Hand*. (Expanded Edition). Cambridge, MA: Belknap/Harvard U. Press.

Bruner, J.S. (1983). *In Search of Mind: Essays in Autobiography*. New York: Harper and Row.

Chandrasekhar, S. (1987). *Truth and Beauty: Aesthetics and Motivations in Science*. Chicago: University of Chicago Press.

Chaplin, J. (1968). *Dictionary of Psychology*. New York: Dell.

Chipman, S., Segal, J., & Glaser, R. (Eds.) (1985). *Thinking and Learning Skills, Volume 2: Research and Open Questions*. Hillsdale, NJ: Erlbaum.

Coleman, P. (1986). School districts and student achievement in British Columbia: A preliminary analysis. *Canadian Journal of Education*, *11*, 4, 509-521.

Doi, T. (1981). *The Anatomy of Dependence*. Tokyo: Kondansha International.

Freud, S. (1914). On narcissism: An introduction. *The Standard Edition*, 14, 69-102.

Freud, S. (1930). *Civilization and Its Discontents*. New York: Norton.

Freud, S. (1963). *General Psychological Theory: Papers on Metapsychology.* New York: Collier/Macmillan.

Frye, N. (1963). *The Educated Imagination.* Toronto: CBC (The Massey Lectures).

Frye, N. (1988). *On Education.* Toronto: Fitzhenry & Whiteside.

Gammage, P. (1982). *Children and Schooling.* London: George Allan and Unwin.

Hamford, B., & Hattie, J. (1982). The relationship between self and achievement/performance measures. *Review of Educational Research, 52,* 123-142.

Hargreaves, D. (1978). What teaching does to teachers. *New Society,* 9 March, 540-541.

Haring, N. (1982). *Exceptional Children and Youth* (Third Edition). Toronto: Charles E. Merrill.

Himelfarb, A. (1977). *The Social Characteristics of One-Industry Towns in Canada: A Background Report.* (Royal Commission on Corporate Concentration, Study No. 30). Ottawa: Government of Canada, Ministry of Supply and Services.

Hirsch, E. (1989). The primal scene of education. *The New York Review of Books. 36* (2 March), 29-35.

Jacoby, R. (1975). *Social Amnesia.* Boston: Beacon Press.

James, W. (1962). *Talks to Teachers on Psychology and to Students on Some of Life's Ideals* (originally 1899). New York: Dover.

Jones, B. (1982). *Sleepers, Wake! Technology and the Future of Work.* Brighton, UK: Wheatsheaf Books.

Jones, L. (1988). School achievement trends in mathematics and science, and what can be done to improve them. In E. Rothkopf (Ed.), *Review of Research in Education,* Vol. 15, 1988-1989. Washington, D.C.: American Educational Research Association.

Lakoff, G., & Johnson, M. (1980). *Metaphors We Live By.* Chicago: University of Chicago Press.

Luria, A.R. (1979). *The Making of Mind: A Personal Account of Soviet Psychology.* Cambridge, MA: Harvard University Press.

Mah, T. (1988). Narcisstic Personality and Academic Underachievement in School Age Children. (Unpublished M.A. thesis). Vancouver, BC: University of British Columbia.

Marton, F., & Saljo, R. (1984). Approaches to learning. In F. Marton, D. Hounsell, and N. Entwistle (Eds.), *The Experience of Learning.* Edinburgh, UK: Scottish Academic Press.

Maynard, R. (1989). Look Jane, Dick can't read. *Report on Business Magazine, 5,* 11 (May), 87-96.

Meehl, P. (1977). *Psychodiagnosis.* New York: Norton.

Nickerson, R. (1988). On improving thinking through instruction. In E. Rothkopf (Ed.), *Review of Research in Education.* Vol. 15, 1988-1989.

O'Neill, G.P. (1988). Teaching effectiveness: A review of the research. *Canadian Journal of Education, 13,* 1, 162-185.

Partington, G. (1987). The disorientation of western education. *Encounter, 68,* 1, 5-15.

Pattebaum, S., Keith, T., & Ehly, S. (1986). Is there a causal relationship between self-concept and academic achievement? *Journal of Educational Research, 79,* 140-144.

Powell, E. (1985, 13 January). The heresy that education must be useful. *The Manchester Guardian Weekly, 132,* 2, p. 10.

Scheirer, M., & Kraut, R. (1979). Increasing educational achievement via self-concept change. *Review of Educational Research, 49,* 1, 131-149.

Schiller, F. (1965). *On the Aesthetic Education of Man: In a Series of Letters* (originally 1793). New York: Frederick Ungar.

Simons, C. (1987). They get by with a lot of help from their kyoiku mamas. *The Smithsonian, 17,* 12, 44-53.

Skinner, B.F. (1984). The shame of American education. *American Psychologist, 39,* 9, 947-954.

Slavin, R. (1986). *Educational Psychology: Theory into Practice.* Toronto: Prentice-Hall.

Time. (1989, April 3). Foul! pp. 40-47.

Travis, L.D. (1987). Secondary pupils and teacher qualities: Contrasts in appraisals. *Canadian Journal of Education, 12,* 1, 152-176.

Travis, LeRoy D., & Mah, T. (1986). Narcissism, education and debasement through elevation. *Proceedings of the Pacific Region Association for Higher Education.* Seattle, WA: PRAHA.

Wells, R. (1988, 15 July). Holding out alone. *The Times Literary Supplement.* No. 4450, 723-724.

Wesbury, M. (1988). The science and art of teacher effectiveness: An examination of two research traditions. *Canadian Journal of Education, 13,* 1, 138-161.

Introduction
Section Four: Problems in Adolescence

The last section of this book, section four, contains four chapters dealing with topics that are commonly regarded as difficulties that adolescents experience. These include suicide, delinquency, childhood sexual abuse (CSA), intergenerational differences, and emerging intellectual processes such as creativity. These topics can be all profitably combined in this section since they all deal with "problems" in adolescence. Indeed, many theorists regard these topics as the fundamental manifestation adolescence. It is very common, if not universal, to see chapters or sections in adolescent psychology textbooks dealing with delinquency, suicide, and more recently, sexual abuse. These may be regarded as the "hot" topics of adolescence along with drugs, sex and rock and roll.

These topics, of course, also find widespread visibility and sustained exposure in mass media such as television, film and newspapers. Indeed, these are the staples of both entertainment and "information" depictions in mass media (see also chapters 7 and 9). The mass media depictions have a basis in psychological theory. Anna Freud, for example, regarded adolescence as a time of "normative crises," as did Erik Erickson who saw it as a time of "identity crisis." The tone for acceptance of such views had been set by G. Stanley Hall at the turn of this century who, we may recall, had characterized adolescence as a period of *sturm und drang*. Cognitively, Jean Piaget regarded adolescence as a time of emerging new abstract logical processes that can create a crisis of understanding for the young person. David Elkind has theorized that these new cognitive processes also gives rise to adolescent egocentrism – a special and disorienting form of self-perception.

All of these and many other theorists as well, encourage the belief that adolescence is "normally" or universally a time of deviance, angst, confusions, idealism, madness and bizarre behavior. Accordingly, deviant behavior such as delinquency and suicide are normalized for the period of adolescence.

Suicide, whenever in the life-span it occurs, is intriguing, macabre, fascinating and the ultimate form of self-annihilation. During the period of adolescence, suicide holds special interest for researchers, psychologists and many others perhaps because it appears in measurable prevalence for the first time in the life-span. Moreover, it begs the question, "What can possibly lead a young person with their whole life and future ahead of them to take their own life?"

Chapter 17 focuses on adolescent suicide. In this chapter we focus on epidemiology, factors related to suicide (e.g., depression, hopelessness and helplessness, interpersonal conflict and isolation, etc.), a causal model of suicide and implications for treatment and prevention. We present empirical evidence from recent studies that implicate the importance of early loss and emotional isolation as causal factors for the development of suicidality.

In chapter 18, "Delinquency," we examine both theories of causes of delinquency and intervention and treatment programs of it. In the first part of this chapter we review and evaluate the validity of biological and health theories, as well as social control, strain and family systems theory. We conclude this section of chapter 18 favoring the validity of family systems theory as it is currently one of the most accepted with some supportive empirical evidence.

In the second section of chapter 18 we review and evaluate a variety of treatment and intervention programs for delinquents that have been implemented and tried on a widespread basis. These include diversion programs, family interventions, community programs, those in correctional institutions and multi-systems interventions. None of these programs have been notably successful on their own in "rehabilitating" delinquents, although multisystems intervention holds some promise.

One of the most recent concerns and issues for psychologists, researchers and policy makers is the sexual abuse of children and adolescence. In chapter 19, we discuss the significance and definition of CSA, we review current data on prevalence rates of CSA and discuss the implications of it for developmental psychopathology. Given the currently available data, our best estimate of the prevalence of CSA for girls is 20% and for boys is 14%. There are reasons to believe, however, that the two prevalence rates may be essentially the same but it is somewhat overstated for girls because they tend to report as CSA some behaviors that males would not (e.g. salacious comments). Moreover, males tend to underreport even very intrusive CSA (e.g. anal penetration) compared to girls for fear of being considered a homosexual (most perpetrators of CSA are male) or "mentally ill." In any case, more conclusive statements on the prevalence, type and impact on psychological development of CSA will have to await further research.

The final chapter (20) of this section and the book deals with the relationship between creativity, intelligence and achievement in preadolescents. In effect, we test the "threshold hypothesis" using hierarchical confirmatory factor analysis. What is the relationship between intelligence and creativity? Between intelligence and achievement? Achievement and creativity? These are some the questions we posed and addressed in the research reported in chapter 20. Using 201 subjects we tested the full model that examines the relationships between the three latent variables (IQ, Creativity, Achievement). In accordance with the threshold hypothesis that there is a zero correlation beyond a threshold level of IQ (perhaps 120), our results showed a near zero correlation between intelligence and creativity in our high IQ children (125). There was (as expected) a high correlation between intelligence and achievement, however.

The foregoing five chapters, then, comprise this final section of the book, "Problems in Adolescence."

17
Adolescent Suicide

The increased rates of suicide among young people world wide in the last 40 years (Diekstra, 1989; Garland & Zigler, 1993) have alarmed many and have inspired a number of studies dealing with children and adolescent suicide. Despite these efforts, however, the nature and causes of suicide generally and of suicide in adolescents specifically are not well understood. The main purpose of the present chapter is to explore suicide in adolescence further by an analysis of causes and possible prevention of adolescent suicide.

Epidemiology

In most industrialized countries, the rate of suicide among 15-19 year-olds has tripled since 1950 (Diekstra, 1989; Garrison, et al., 1991). In the United States, the rate among males has increased 295% but only 67% for females with similar increases in Canada (Grossi & Violato, 1992; Thompson, 1987). In a recent study of adolescent suicide in Manitoba, Thompson (1987) found the rate to be 15 completed suicides per 100,000 population with a similar incidence rate in Alberta, although in 1990 the rate was slightly higher at 18.8 in the latter case (Office of the Chief Medical Examiner, 1990).

Adolescent suicide victims are predominantly male with the current rate for males in the United States being nearly five times compared to females (Centres for Disease Control, 1986; Diekstra, 1987). Similar patterns pertain in most industrialized countries including Canada (Diekstra, 1987). Interestingly, females greatly exceed suicide attempts and ideation compared to males (Allberg & Chu, 1990; Hawton, 1986). It is generally believed that this gender difference in completed suicides versus attempted ones is that males use far more lethal means than females. Males tend to prefer firearms (50 – 60% of suicides) but females tend to prefer self-poisoning involving analgesics and other pharmacological agents (Hoberman & Garfinkel, 1988) for about 30 – 40% of attempts. Medical resuscitation is, of course, much more probable from self-poisoning of analgesics than it is from fatal gun shot wounds.

Marked racial differences also characterize adolescent suicide victims in the United States and Canada, with Caucasians committing suicide at twice the rate of most other minority youth (C.D.C., 1986; Thompson, 1987). Suicide rates are especially high among certain groups of Native American and Canadian aboriginal people, however, with the rates among 15-19 year-olds nearly five times greater than the general population (Hoberman, 1989; Thompson, 1987). In marked contrast to industrialized countries, the suicide rate in general in developing countries such as Mexico, New Guinea and the Philippine Islands drops to about 1.1 per 100,000 (Coleman, et al., 1980; Diekstra, 1987). Among some groups of aborigines of the Australian western desert, the suicide rate drops to zero, possibly as a result of the strong fear of death (Kidson & Jones, 1968).

There are no currently conclusive explanations of the marked differences of suicidal incidence cross-culturally, within cultures and between the sexes, though socio-cultural differences, economic variation, religious beliefs, different political systems, societal norms, and so on are probably implicated (Diekstra, 1987; Hoberman, 1989). Individual factors such as genetic variation, homelessness, psychopathology, substance abuse, and so on, insofar as these vary cross-culturally, may also be at the root of the incidence of suicidal variation (Van Egmond & Diekstra, 1987). There are also no compelling explanations in general of suicide, notwithstanding current research efforts. There are, however, a number of factors which have been found to be related to, or implicated in, suicide. These are reviewed in the following sections beginning with depression.

Depression

Depression is perhaps the most prominent symptom that has been found in attempted and completed adolescent suicide (Allberg & Chu, 1990; Holden, 1986). Indeed, some theorists (e.g., Beck et al., 1993; Mauk & Leopold, 1992) believe that depression is a key ingredient in all suicides. Tishler et al. (1981) concurred with this when they stated that most adolescent suicide attempters had clear somatic signs of depression such as sleep disturbance, appetite problems, restlessness, aggression and inappropriate laughter. Shaffi et al. (1985) in their study of psychological autopsies of adolescent suicide found that 76% of their sample showed clear signs of depression. Hoberman and Garfinkel (1988) reported that 50% of adolescent suicide victims showed clear evidence of depressive disorders. Additionally, some researchers have claimed that many suicidal adolescents show symptoms of "masked" depression in behaviors such as social withdrawal, complaints of boredom, impairment in school work, pathological guilt, mood fluctuations, and so on (Greuling & DeBlassie, 1980; Lesse, 1979; Poznanski, 1982).

Despite the apparently high prevalence of depressive symptomology in some studies of adolescent suicide, not all researchers have found similarly high rates. Golombek and Garfinkel (1983) in an archival study, for example, found that only 25% of their sample exhibited depressive disorders. Poteet (1987) found that only 33% of her sample of decedents showed depressive symptoms. Similarly, Morrissey et al. (1991) did not find that depression was a prominent symptom in hospitalized suicidal adolescents. Finally, in a comparative study, Grossi and Violato (1992) found that there were no differences in depressive symptoms between adolescent suicide attempters and a matched clinical non-suicidal sample though depression was evident in both groups.

The conflicting findings reviewed above may indicate that depression is not a simple "cause" or even a precipitate of suicide. It is obviously implicated, however, in psychopathology generally and probably does play some important role in suicide specifically. Clearly, much more research is required to explicate further the role of depression in suicide.

Hopelessness and Helplessness

Two other factors that are frequently related to both depression and suicide are hopelessness and helplessness. Hoberman and Garfinkel (1988), for example, found that many of their suicidal adolescents were withdrawn, lonely, hopeless and helpless. Schaffer (1974) identified 30% of his sample as exhibiting characteristics that suggested hopelessness and helplessness. Shaffi et al. (1985) demonstrated that 70% of their sample had "inhibited personalities" indicating hopelessness and helplessness. The presence of such affect and behavior of these adolescents suggests that they may experience extreme emotional reactions to events and/or may have difficulty regulating or modulating these reactions. Their social withdrawal indicates that they are uncomfortable with others and may be deficient in social skills (Blumenthal, 1988; Pfeffer, 1989). Particularly under conditions of stress, they may isolate further, leading to exacerbated hopelessness and helplessness, rather than employing social support to mediate their distress.

Several studies have indicated that suicidal adolescents have exceptionally poor school records, chronic behavior problems, and hopeless attitudes toward academic attainment as well as helpless behavior in achievement situations. Rohn et al. (1977), for example, concluded that suicidal adolescent subjects demonstrated many of the above characteristics. In a more recent study, Lewis et al. (1988) found that young suicide attempters had lower school achievement and motivation than nonattempters and had mothers who had lower educational goals for them than nonattempters. Similarly, Pettifor et al. (1983) also noted lower grades in school, hopelessness in future academic attainment as well as negative attitudes towards school and teachers. The poor academic achievement of many suicidal adolescents is probably not due to poor intellectual abilities as many researchers have found these subjects to have normal range IQ's (Garrison et al., 1991; Grossi & Violato, 1992; Shaffer, 1974). Rather, their poor school performance is probably due to a hopeless outlook, and helpless behavior related to achievement situations.

Interpersonal Conflicts and Isolation

In addition to feelings of hopelessness, helplessness, pessimism and unhappiness, suicide attempters become increasingly isolated from important people in their lives and experience intense feelings of isolation shortly before their suicide attempt (Hart & Keidel, 1979; Pfeffer, 1986). Suicide rates have also been found to vary inversely with the stability and durability of social relationships – suicide completers and attempters have unstable and transitory relationships (Houter, 1981; Van Egmond & Diekstra, 1988). Because adolescence is a time of identity formation and the development of autonomy, interpersonal frictions and difficulties may be particularly pronounced at this time in the life cycle. Thus interpersonal conflict which may be manageable at other times in the life cycle may precipitate suicide in an already at risk adolescent. Both Shaffer (1974) and Poteet (1987), for example, indicated that the vast majority (90% and

64% respectively) of their subjects had encountered a negative interpersonal event prior to their death. In Thompson's (1987) investigation, 48% of the subjects had relationship break-ups or family disputes prior to their death. Hoberman and Garfinkel (1988) noted that 56% of their sample had experienced interpersonal conflict prior to suicide and Brent et al. (1988) found that 70% of young suicides had the same experience. Finally, Hoberman and Garfinkel (1988) noted that arguments were the most common precipitant and occurred within twelve hours of the suicide. Arguments were typically with a lover or parent.

The foregoing studies suggest that social isolation and interpersonal conflicts are common among suicidal adolescents. The interplay of isolation and conflict probably lead up to a suicide attempt in an already at risk adolescent. A problematic romance or a perceived rejection may serve as catalysts to push the isolated adolescent to the desperate edge of suicide. The loss of a parent through death, divorce, or abandonment may also trigger suicide in a high risk adolescent (Flanagan, 1985). The adolescent, because they have not yet stabilized their identity and developed adequate autonomy, may be incapable of coping with these interpersonal losses other than through desperate means such as self annihilation.

Family Background

Suicidal adolescents tend to come from families which are characterized by instability, disorganization, substance abuse, violence, sexual abuse, psychiatric disorders, and general chaos (Allberg & Chu, 1991; Violato & Genius, 1993; Wozencraft et al., 1991). Friedman, Corn, and Hart (1984) compared suicidal, depressed adolescents to matched nonsuicidal depressed adolescents. They found that chronic illness of a parent during adolescence and pre-adolescence characterized the suicidal subjects, as well as a history of family suicide behavior and life time psychiatric illness. Similarly, Hawton, Osborn and O'Grady (1982) found a relationship between the severity of family disorganization and the severity of behavioral disturbances and suicide ideation in their subjects (children) as did Velez and Cohen (1988). Rohn et al. (1977) concluded that their suicidal adolescent subjects were socially isolated, described themselves as loners, and had parents who were divorced or separated with a large number being alcoholics. In the Lewis et al. (1988) study, suicide attempters had mothers who had lowered educational goals for them than mothers of nonattempters. In a meta-analysis of 81 published studies on the predictability of suicidal behaviors, Van Egmond and Diekstra (1988) concluded that suicide attempters were characterized by an "unstable way of life" (frequent change of residence, unemployment, coming from a broken home, substance abuse) compared to nonattempters. Finally, substantial proportions of suicidal adolescents have been sexually, physically and/or emotionally abused within the home environment (Grossi & Violato, 1992; Wozencraft et al., 1991).

Early Loss

There is considerable evidence that suicidal behavior and disturbances in attachment and early loss are closely related (Diekstra, 1987; Pfeffer, 1989; Shafi, Carrigan, Whittinghill & Derrick, 1985). Epidemiological studies of attempted and completed suicide have frequently shown a higher incidence of single status and marital failure than in control groups and many clinical studies have shown that these people experience major difficulties in their interpersonal relationships (Maris, 1981; Pfeffer, 1989). Adam (1980) has suggested that clinical studies of people immediately following suicide attempts indicate a striking resemblance to the behavior of infants and children following brief separation and loss from the mother. The actual suicide episode is usually preceded by clear communication of intent to a significant other person, and often takes place where discovery is almost certain. Significant others and caretakers are often subject to angry, hostile behavior intermingled with pleading and clinging alternating with aloofness and detachment (Pfeffer, 1986). Such behavior is remarkably similar to that of insecurely attached children and infants following brief separations from the mother (Ainsworth, 1979, 1989; Bowlby, 1977). In their study, Grossi and Violato (1992) found that disturbed attachments and early loss (of mother or significant others) were the most powerful discriminants between the suicidal and nonsuicidal adolescents. These results suggest the importance of early loss in subsequent psychopathology, including suicide.

Emotional and Other Disorders

In addition to the major symptoms of depression, hopelessness and helplessness, an amazing array of other disorders have been identified among suicidal adolescents. Finch and Poznaski (1972) identified impulsive character disorder as a major feature of their adolescents who exhibited suicidal behavior. Thompson (1987), Hoberman and Garfinkel (1988) and Holden (1986) all noted that many of their suicide victims had alcohol and substance abuse disorders. Moreover, Holden (1986) reported that there were high rates of eating disorders (anorexia nervosa, bulimia) among female decedents. Many of the subjects in the above studies also demonstrated anti-social behaviors. Brent et al. (1988) in a detailed analysis, found that 93% of adolescent completed suicide victims had at least one major emotional disorder at the time of death. These included the following: dysthymic disorder (22%); manic or hypomanic episodes (7%); attention deficit disorder (26%); conduct disorder (22%); and overanxious disorder (15%). Additionally, 11% had recurrent unipolar depression and 22% had bipolar affective disorder.

In an electroencephalographic study, Sabo et al. (1991) showed that suicidal subjects had a variety of sleep disorders including increased sleep latency, lowered sleep efficiency, reduced late-night delta wave counts, and reduced rapid eye movement time and activity. Some researchers (Finch & Poznanski, 1972) have reported a significant number of psychotics (16%) among suicidal victims and others have identified some schizophrenics in the group (Coleman et al.,

1980). Hoberman and Garfinkel (1988) found that 10% of their sample had pathologic anger, 8% were lonely and 5% could only be described as "bizarre." Finally, sexual deviations and perversions have also been noted in some adolescent suicide victims (Hendin, 1991; Wozencraft et al., 1991).

Major factors that are associated with adolescent suicide and their manifestations are summarized in Table 17.1.

Table 17.1
Major Factors and Their Manifestations in Adolescent Suicide
(Mauk & Leopold, 1992)

Factors	*Manifestatiion*
Apparent or Masked Depression	Overt: Sleep disturbance, appetite disturbance; inappropriate affect (e.g., unwarranted happiness, sulkiness, grouchiness, restlessness, aggression, inappropriate laughter); social withdrawal; complaints of boredom and fatigue; academic problems; pathological guilt; a lack of spontaneity; anhedonia (incapacity for experiencing pleasure); feelings of hopelessness/despair, low self-esteem and/or self-efficacy; *Covert:* Sexual promiscuity; delinquency; drug/alcohol use; anorexia/bulimia; colitis; various psychosaomatic illnesses.
Interpersonal Conflicts, Stress, and Alienation	Loss of meaningful relationships (e.g., break up of a romantic relationship, death of a close friend/relative, divorce); lack of meaningful social relationships; overwhelming achievement/athletic pressure; feelings of alienation/isolation.
Family Dynamics	Faimly is characterized by high levels of conflict and low levels of support/cohesion; Lack of affection/nurturance/ Economic stress; Impaired communication networks marked by a lack of productive communication; frequent conflict in communication styles; impaired problem-solving ability; more frequent use of negative comments; parental separation, divorce, or death; parental neglect/abadonment; physical/sexual abuse by parent; parental substance abuse; parental psychopathology.
Psyopathology	Impulsive character disorders; depressive tendencies; anti-social/conduct disorders with concomitant drug use; anxiety disorders; borderline perrsonality disorder; psychosis.
Hopelessness and Helplessness	Feelings that tthe future is hopeless and no good will come from it; Feliefs that failure is inevitable; Beliefs that "I will never make friends"; lack of concentration and effort; Inability to persist in an achievement situation.

A Model of Risk Factors to Suicide

Figure 17.1 is an attempt to integrate the various factors described in this section of adolescent suicide into a pathway from risk factors to attempted and completed suicide. Overall, the picture of the adolescent at risk for completed suicide is one of a young person with multiple problems and a limited and maladaptive repertoire of coping skills. As can be seen in Figure 17.1, long standing conditions of psychological disorders, family discord and early loss, deficits in emotional and impulse control, social skills, problem solving skills and motivation are all potential vulnerabilities which interact with immediate stressors to elicit a state of emotional distress. In the absence of effective attempts to resolve the current crisis, hopelessness and helplessness ensues. An interpersonal crisis together with the availability of reason-impairing alcohol or drugs is the final link to attempted suicide. The presence and lethality of life-threatening agents are the final determinants in completed suicide.

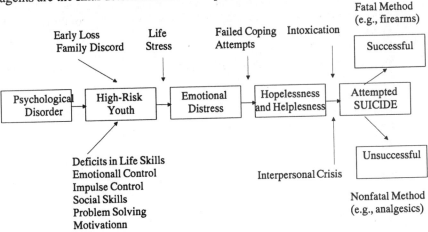

Figure 17.1: The Pathway from Risk Factors to Attempted and Completed Suicide.

An Empirical Test of A Causal Model

We have seen that despite a substantial research effort in the last several decades, little is understood about the causes of suicide generally and of adolescent suicide specifically. Accordingly, in a recent study we focused on a causal analysis of adolescent suicide employing structural equation modelling techniques.

The underlying causal model was developed based on the theory of disrupted childhood attachments leading to early loss and subsequent developmental psychopathology. It is now generally believed that childhood attachments to principal caregivers can play a critical role in affective and psychosocial development (Ainsworth, 1979; Bowlby, 1977; see also chapter 12). Severely disrupted attachments due to loss, neglect or abuse can result in psychopathology (Bowlby, 1977) and poor social integration (Ainsworth, 1979).

In the research by Grossi and Violato (1992), it was found through stepwise discriminant analysis that a single function labelled "stability/attachment" successfully discriminated between suicidal and non-suicidal adolescents. Grossi and Violato (1992) concluded that disrupted attachments lay at the core of the adolescents' suicide attempts. Similarly, de Jong (1992) found that insecure attachment characterized her suicidal subjects (undergraduates with mean age = 18.5 years). She concluded that disrupted childhood attachments underlay suicidality of the subjects. These findings are consistent with results from studies that have shown a relationship between family instability and serious suicidal ideation or suicide attempt (Adam, 1980).

In addition to disrupted attachments, depression, hopelessness, helplessness, health problems, self-esteem disturbances, poor peer relations and drug abuse have been consistently linked to adolescent suicide (Beck et al, 1993; Grossi & Violato, 1992). The present study therefore, attempted to incorporate all of these variables (as well as others) into a causal model to probe further the etiology of adolescent suicide. Accordingly, a latent variable path model (LVPA) was developed and is depicted in Figure 17.2.

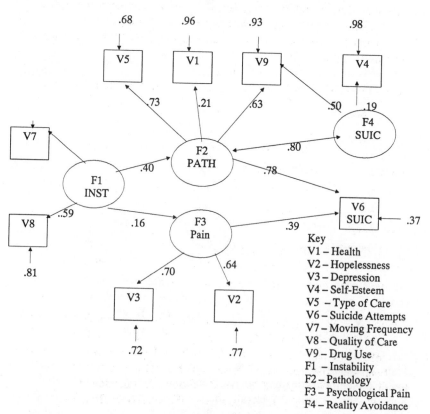

Figure 17.2. Latent Variable Model of Antecedents of Suicide Attempts Estimated with the Maximum Likelihood Method

Four latent variables have been named and identified: F1 (Instability/Attachment), F2 (Pathology), F3 (Psychological Pain), and F4 (Reality Avoidance). Direct paths are drawn from F1 to F2 and F3 which in turn are linked to suicide attempts (V6). The fourth latent variable (F4) is correlated with Pathology (F2) which is directly linked to suicide attempts (V6). We then fit the model depicted in Figure 17.2 to a data set.

Data were collected from 260 (62 females, 198 males) institutionalized (Young Offender Centre) adolescents (mean age = 15.7 years), some of whom had attempted suicide (n=82) and some who had not (n=178). The suicide attempts had been officially documented in the subjects' medical files and included shooting, jumping, wrist slashing, drug overdose, and hanging. Ethnicity of subjects included Caucasian (n=60; 73.2%), Aboriginal (n=15; 18.3%), Black (n=2; 2.4%), and Asian (n=5; 6.1%).

The following data were obtained from the subjects: (a) demographic, (b) life history data, and (c) psychological variables. Interrater reliability for coding a random sample of 10% of the data was 95% while intrarater reliability with a one month interval was 98%. Accordingly, reliability of data coding was very high.

In order to fit the model depicted in Figure 17.2 to the data, all nine relevant variables were intercorrelated (phi, point-biserial and product-moment coefficients as required by the nature of the variables – categorical or continuous). This correlation matrix together with the standard deviations of each variable is summarized in Table 17.2.

Table 17.2
Correlation Matrix of Nine Variables and Their Standard Deviations

Variable	1	2	3	4	5	6	7	8	9
1. Health	1.0								
2. Hopelessness	0.10	1.00							
3. Depression	0.13	0.44	1.00						
4. Self-esteem	0.02	0.07	0.09	1.00					
5. Type of Care	0.13	0.25	0.14	0.12	1.00				
6. Suicide Attempt	0.26	0.33	0.29	0.16	0.30	1.00			
7. Moving Frequency	0.00	0.14	0.19	0.12	0.34	-0.21	1.00		
8. Quality of Care	0.01	-0.09	-0.16	0.03	-0.08	0.07	-0.59	1.00	
9. Drug Use	0.00	011	0.02	-0.10	0.20	-0.15	0.24	-0.01	1.00

Using the EQS computer program (Bentler, 1992), the model was fit to the data. The LVPA model provided an overall good fit to the data (Comparative Fit Index = .89; Residual Mean Square = .07; 84% of the residuals were near zero). As can been seen from Figure 17.2, large path coefficients were found for the predicted paths (F1F2; F2V6; F3V6) and although the coefficient F1F3 was not large (.16), it is statistically significant (p < .05). Moreover, Reality Avoidance

(F4) was strongly correlated (r=.80) with Psychopathology (F2), and thus indirectly influenced suicide attempts (V6) through F2.

As expected, Psychological Pain (F3) was identified by hopelessness (V3) and depression (V2) while Reality Avoidance (F4) was identified by Self-esteem (V4) and drug use (V9) although V9 also loaded on Pathology (F2) as did health problems (V1) and type of childhood care (V5). Instability (F1) in early childhood or attachment problems was identified by quality of care received (V8) and family moving frequency (V7). The coefficients (both path and residual) could not be estimated for V7 (see Figure 17.2) because of Heywood cases (out of range values) probably due to the error involved in these categorical variables.

Further analyses were undertaken using stepwise discriminant analysis to identify a function which may separate the suicidal and non-suicidal groups. Eight variables from Table 17.2 were entered as discriminating variables and the ninth variable (suicide attempts) as the criterion variable. A single discriminant function was formed from the eight variables that successfully separated the groups (Wilks' lambda = 0.75; df=7; p < .001). In rank-order of importance, the variables entered were (1) hopelessness, (2) quality of care, (3) depression, (4) health problems, (5) frequency of moves, (6) self-esteem, (7) drug use, and (8) type of care. Using the discriminant function, 76.92% of the subjects were correctly classified into group membership (suicidal vs. non-suicidal). The canonical correlation of the independent variables to suicidal status was approximately 0.50.

These results provide strong support for the proposed four-factor LVPA causal model of attempted suicide. The overall fit of the model to the data was very good – it clearly shows that attachment/instability as proposed by Grossi and Violato (1992) may be at the root of subsequent developmental psychopathology such as suicidality as did the result of the discriminant analysis. The present results are concordance with many previous studies which have found hopelessness, helplessness, health problems, self-esteem disturbances, and drug abuse to be related to suicidality (Beck et al, 1993; de Jong, 1992; Hoberman, 1989; Grossi & Violato, 1992). The major strength of the present study was the use of latent variable path analysis where (1) important latent variables were identified and confirmed, and (2) "causal" paths were specified and supported from early childhood attachment to adolescent suicidality. Accordingly, it appears clear that disrupted childhood attachments may be important antecedents to subsequent suicide attempts.

Two limitations of the foregoing study should be noted: (1) many of the variables were only assessed categorically and thus introduced error of measurement (probably resulting in the Heywood cases around V7), and (2) the data were based on incarcerated young offenders. In future research the first limitation may be overcome by better psychometric measurement and the second by employing non-offender suicidal samples. Previous research, however, indicates that prison suicides are similar in most respects to non-offender suicide (Liebling, 1992). Accordingly, we may expect the present results to generalize to other samples.

Notwithstanding these limitations, the above results clearly support the attachment /stability disruption hypothesis of suicidality and more generally developmental psychopathology. Disrupted childhood attachment is clearly confirmed in the etiology of suicide in the present study.

Implications for Suicide Prevention

Suicide prevention programs in general have not made a significant impact on the rate of suicides (Garland & Zigler, 1993; Pfeffer, 1989). In recent years, a number of suicide curricula have been developed and implemented in junior high and high schools (Zinner, 1987). As Garfinkel (1986) has noted, however, these curricula tend to focus on the circumstances and means surrounding suicides but include little on the relationship between psychopathology and suicide. It is obvious that a focus on precipitants, signs of premeditation or planning is likely to be unproductive given the developmental history of at-risk adolescents and the impulsive nature of the actual suicidal act. The probability of preventing a particular suicide at the time of the act is low.

Suicide Prevention Centres or "Hot Lines" which have gained widespread notice, serve primarily as crises facilities. There are currently more than 250 centres in the United States and some 20 in Canada whose main purpose is crisis intervention, usually via 24-hour-a-day telephone contact. The main purpose of these centres is to help people who are experiencing acute suicidal ideation and impulses, forestall suicidal attempts until the crisis passes within minutes or hours. The effectiveness of Suicide Prevention Centres, however, is questionable. First, the rate of suicide generally has increased as we have seen, since the first centre was established in 1958 in Los Angeles (Farberow, 1974) and they have become widespread. Second, only a small portion of suicidal adolescents ever contact such crises centres (Hawton, 1986). Third, the majority of people who do contact these centres never follow-up by seeking additional help for their suicidal impulses. Sawyer et al. (1972), for example, in a follow-up of 53 people who committed suicide after initial contact with a prevention centre, found that none had recontacted the centre just prior to their death. Additional problems of the centres include poorly trained staff and unmanned telephones (Bridge et al., 1977).

The emphasis in youth suicide prevention programs must be on early identification and appropriate treatment of the episodes of psychopathology which underlie and precede most instances of suicide in adolescents. Parents are generally inaccurate judges of the presence of depression and suicide ideation in adolescents (Leon et al., 1980) as are professionals such as teachers, physicians and clergy (Lefkowitz & Tesiny, 1984; Murphy, 1975; Sacco & Graves, 1985). Conversely, peers or siblings are often the persons most likely to be informed of suicidal ideation or threats (Brent et al., 1988). Yet peers so informed often respond inappropriately to the possibility of suicide and fail to inform others to allow intervention (Mishara, 1982). It is often asserted (e.g. Hoberman, 1989) that programs are needed to train parents, teachers, physicians, and peers to recognize depressive disorders, alcohol and substance abuse in adolescents, and make appropriate referrals. Such suggestions are little more than platitudes, however, as such "programs" whether for general public education or formal schooling are both unlikely to be implemented or to be successful.

More likely candidates than the above mentioned people for suicide ideation detection and suicidal intervention, are school counsellors and school psychologists. This is because these mental health professionals come into contact with a great many if not all children and adolescents and are, therefore, in a position as primary professional identifiers. Unfortunately, *most* school counsellors and psychologists currently have little training in suicide detection and prevention (Allberg & Chu, 1991) but such information could be included in their professional education. Khuri and Akisal (1983) have argued that energetic treatment and ongoing follow-up of people with primary and secondary affective disorders will prove to be an effective method of preventing suicide. School psychologists and school counsellors are both in an excellent position to do primary screening of these disorders in children and adolescents. An effective treatment of these youth who would be at an elevated risk for suicide, is a combination of multi-dimensional counselling and appropriately administered medication. These interventions may involve several mental health professionals such as psychologists, psychiatrists, social workers, counsellors, and so on. The targets of intervention are indicated by the characteristics of the at-risk youth: containing or reducing psychiatric symptomatology; increasing the ability to modulate emotional distress and impulsivity; reducing conflict in and facilitating the utilization of social relationships for support; to effectively problem-solve; and to change dysfunctional family patterns. Nevertheless, considerably more research is needed to better understand the most effective treatment for adolescents experiencing affective disorders or alcohol and substance abuse.

Summary and Conclusions

The rate of adolescent suicide has increased at an alarming rate world wide in the last four decades, tripling in most of the industrialized world. While the causes and nature of suicide generally are not fully understood, several factors have been identified which are strongly related to adolescent suicide. These include overt or masked depression, interpersonal conflicts, stress, alienation, hopelessness and helplessness, disorganized and dysfunctional families, a variety of psychopathology, and the availability of suicidal means (e.g. firearms, self-poisoning). In our LVPA model, we found that early attachments are clearly implicated in the etiology of adolescent suicide.

A variety of attempts at suicide prevention have not been markedly successful. These have included school based curricula and suicide prevention centres. Neither of these approaches generally treat the underlying causes of suicide but rather have focused either on the circumstances surrounding suicide or an immediate acute crisis. It is suggested that school based mental health professionals might act as useful primary identifiers of high risk children and adolescents.

References

Adam, K. (1980). Interpersonal factors in suicidal attempts. A pilot study in Christ Church. *Australian and New Zealand Journal of Psychology, 12,* 59-63.

Ainsworth, M.D. (1979). Infant-mother attachment. *American Psychologist, 34,* 932-937.

Allberg, W.R., & Chu, L. (1990). Understanding adolescent suicide: Correlates in a developmental perspective. *The School Counsellor, 37,* 343-350.

Beck, A.T., Steer, R.A., Beck, J.S., & Newman, C.F. (1993). Hopelessness, depression, suicidal ideation, and clinical diagnosis of depression. *Suicide and Life-Threatening Behavior, 32,* 139-145.

Bentler, P.M. (1992). *EQS program manual.* Los Angeles: BMDP Statistical Software.

Blumenthal, S.J. (1988). A guide to risk factors assessment and treatment of suicidal patients. *Medical Clinics of North America, 72,* 937-971.

Bowlby, J. (1977). The making and breaking of affectional bonds. *British Journal of Psychiatry, 130,* 201-210.

Brent, D.A., Perper, J.A., Goldstein, C.E., Cole, D.J., Allan, M.J., Allman, C.J., & Zelenak, J.P. (1988). Risk factors for adolescent suicide. *Archives of General Psychiatry, 45,* 581-588.

Bridge, T.P., Potkin, S.D., Sung, W.W.A., & Soldo, B.J. (1977). Suicide prevention centres. *Journal of Nervous Mental Diseases, 164,* 18-24.

Centres for Disease Control (1986). *Youth suicide in the United States, 1970-1980,* Washington: US government.

Coleman, J.C., Butcher, J.N., & Carson, R.C. (1980). *Abnormal psychology and modern life* (6th ed.). Palo Alto, CA: Scott, Foresman and Company.

de Jong, M.L. (1992). Attachment, individuation, and risk of suicide in late adolescence. *Journal of Youth and Adolescence, 21,* 357-372.

Diekstra, R.F. (1987). The complex psychodynamics of suicide. In R.F. Diekstra, & K. Hawton (Eds.), *Suicide in adolescence* (pp. 30-35). Dordrecht/Boston: Nijhoff.

Diekstra, R.F. (1989). Suicidal behavior in adolescents and young adults: The international picture. *Crisis, 10,* 16-35.

Faberow, N. (1974). *Suicide.* Morristown, NJ: General Learning Press.

Finch, S.M., & Poznanski, E.O. (1972). Adolescent suicide. *Hospital and Community Psychiatry, 23,* 130.

Flanagan, W. (1985). By their own young hands. *Forbes, 136,* 162-166.

Friedman, R.C., Corn,R., & Hart, S. (1984). Family history of illness in the seriously suicidal adolescent: A life-cycle approach. *American Journal of Orthopsychiatry, 54,* 390-397.

Garland, A.F., & Zigler, E. (1993). Adolescent suicide prevention: Current research and social policy implications. *American Psychologist, 48,* 169-182.

Garrison, C.Z., Lewinsohn, P.M., Marsteller, F., Langhinrichsen, J., & Lann, I. (1991). The assessment of suicidal behavior in adolescents. *Suicide and Life-Threatening Behavior, 21,* 217-230.

Golombeck, H., & Garfinkel, B.D. (1983). *The adolescent and mood disturbances.* New York: International Universities Press.

Grossi, V., & Violato, C. (1992). Attempted suicide among adolescents: A stepwise discriminant analysis. *Canadian Journal of Behavioral Science, 24,* 185-187.

Hart, N., & Keidel, G. (1979). The suicidal adolescent. *American Journal of Nursing, 79,* 80-84.

Hawton, K. (1986). Suicide in adolescents. In A. Roy (Ed.), *Suicide* (pp. 135-150). Baltimore: Williams and Wilkins.

Hawton, K., Osborn, J., & O'Grady, J. (1982). Classification of adolescents who take overdoses. *British Journal of Psychiatry, 140,* 124-131.

Hendin, H. (1991). Psychodynamics of suicide, with particular reference to the young. *American Journal of Psychiatry, 148,* 1150-1158.

Hoberman, H.M. (1989). Completed suicide in children and adolescents: A review. *Residential Treatment for Children and Youth, 7,* 61-88.

Hoberman, H.M., & Garfinkel, B.D. (1988). Completed suicide in children and adolescents. *Journal of the American Academy of Child Adolescent Psychiatry, 27,* 689-695.

Hoberman, H.M., & Garfinkel, B.D., (1988). Completed suicide in youth. *Canadian Journal of Psychiatry, 33,* 494-504.

Holden, C. (1986). Youth suicide: new research focuses on a growing social problem. *Science, 233,* 839-841.

Houter, D.K. (1981). To silence one's self: A brief analysis of the literature on adolescent suicide. *Child Welfare, 60,* 1-9.

Khuri, R., & Akiskal, H.S. (1983). Suicide prevention: The necessity of treating contributory psychiatric disorders. *Psychiatric Clinics of North America, 6,* 193-207.

Kidson, M., & Jones, J. (1968). Psychiatric disorders among aborigines of the Australian Western Desert. *Archives of General Psychiatry, 19,* 413-422.

Lefkowitz, M.M., & Tesiny, E.P. (1980). Assessment of childhood depression. *Journal of Consulting Clinical Psychology, 8,* 221-235.

Liebling, A. (1992). *Suicide in prisons.* London: Routledge.

Leon, G.R., Kendall, P.C., & Garber, J. (1980). Depression in children: Parent, teacher, and child perspectives. *Journal of Consulting and Clinical Psychology, 8,* 221-235.

Lewis, S.A., Johnson, J., Cohen, P., Garcia, M., & Belez, C.N. (1988). Attempted suicide in youth: Its relationship to school achievement, educational goals, and socioeconomic status. *Journal of Abnormal Child Psychology, 16,* 459-471.

Maris, R.W. (1981). *Pathways to suicide.* Longon: John Hopkins University Press.

Mauk, G.W., & Leopold, G.D. (1992, May). Adolescent suicide and aspects of school-based postvention with survivors. Paper presented at the 72nd Annual convention of the Western Psychological Association, Portland, OR.

Mishara, B. (1982). College students' experiences with suicide and reactions to suicidal verbalizations: A model for prevention. *Journal of Community Psychology, 10,* 142-150.

Morrissey, R.F., Dicker, R., Abikoff, H., Koplewicz, H.S., DeMarco, A. (1991, August). Paper presented at the 99th Annual Convention of the American Psychological Association, San Francisco, CA.

Murphy, G.E. (1975). The physician's errors of omission. *Annals of International Medicine, 82,* 305-309.

Office of the Chief Medical Examiner (1990). Suicide rates in Alberta, 1990.

Pettifor, J., Perry, D., Plowman, B., & Pitcher, S. (1983). Risk factors predicting childhood and adolescent suicides. *Journal of Child Care, 1,* 17-47.

Pfeffer, C.R. (1989). Studies of suicidal preadolescent and adolescent inpatients: A critique of research methods. *Suicide and Life-Threatening Behavior, 19,* 58-77.

Poteet, D.J. (1987). Adolescent suicide: A review of 87 cases of completed suicide in Shelby County, Tennessee. *American Journal of Forensic Medical Pathology, 8,* 12-17.

Rohn, R.D., Sartes, R.M., Kenny, T.J., Reynolds, B.J., & Heald, F.P. (1977). Adolescents who attempt suicide. *Journal of Paediatrics, 90,* 636-638.

Sabo, E., Reynolds, C.F., Kupfer, D.J., & Berman, S.R. (1991). Sleep, depression, and suicide. *Psychiatry Research, 36,* 265-277.

Sacco, W., & Graves, D. (1985). Correspondence between teacher ratings of childhood depression and self-ratings. *Journal of Clinical Child Psychology, 4,* 353-355.

Sawyer, J.B., Sudak, H.S., & Hall, S.R. (1972). A follow-up study of 53 suicides known to a suicide prevention centre. *Life-Threatening Behavior, 2,* 227-238.

Schaffer, D. (1974). Suicide in childhood and early adolescence. *Journal of Child Psychology and Psychiatry, 15,* 275-291.

Shafi, M., Carrigan, S., Whittinghill, J.R., Derrick, A. (1985). Psychological autopsy of completed suicide in children and adolescents. *American Journal of Psychiatry, 149,* 1061-1064.

Thompson, T.R. (1987). Childhood and adolescent suicide in Manitoba: A demographic study. *Canadian Journal of Psychiatry, 32,* 264-269.

Tisher, C.L., & McKenry, P.C. (1981). Parental factors related to adolescent suicide attempts. *Proceedings from the Fourteenth Annual Association Suicidology.* Albuquerque, New Mexico.

Van Egmond, M., & Diekstra, R.F. (1988). The predictability of suicidal behavior: The results of a meta-analysis of published studies. In R.F. Diekstra, R.A. Mavis, S. Platt, A. Schmidtke, & G. Sonneck (Eds.), *Suicide prevention: The role of attitude and imitation.* Leiden: Brill.

Velez, C.N., Cohen, P. (1988). Suicidal behavior and ideation in a community sample of children: Maternal and youth reports. *Journal of American Academy of Child and Adolescent Psychiatry, 27,* 349-356.

Violato, C., & Genuis, M. (1993). Problems of research in male child sexual abuse: A review. *Journal of Child Sex Abuse, 3,* 37-50.

Wozencraft, T., Wagner, W., Pellegrin, A. (1991). Depression and suicidal ideation in sexually abused children. *Child Abuse & Neglect, 15,* 505-511.

Zinner, E.S. (1987). Responding to suicide in the schools. *Journal of Counselling and Developing, 65,* 499-501.

18
Delinquency

Delinquency is a major social and mental health problem in modern society. Every year millions of people are victimized by delinquency, property is stolen or destroyed and people are injured or killed. Delinquency includes acts which are considered criminal whether they are perpetrated by adults or juveniles as well status offenses (e.g., truancy, alcohol consumption, sexual promiscuity). This latter category applies to people who are not adults so that the same behavior by an adult would not be considered a crime. In discussions of delinquency, therefore, it is important to distinguish between status offenses and more serious crimes such as assault, robbery and murder. This chapter deals with both theories of causes of delinquency and intervention and treatment programs of it. Several types of theories have been proposed to explain delinquency. These are briefly reviewed in the first section of this chapter, followed by an examination of other variables which are related to delinquency. Many treatment and intervention programs for delinquents have also been tried and implemented. These are discussed in the second section of this chapter as is an evaluation of their efficacy.

Biological, Health and Psychological Theories

Some theorists believe that individual characteristics, whether inherited, developed or learned, contribute to delinquency. These characteristics are thought to include deficits in intellectual functioning, learning disabilities, personality traits, and some genetic disorders like the XYY chromosome syndrome.

It is now widely recognized that many unincarcerated and most incarcerated young offenders are probably learning disabled (Sawicki & Schaeffer, 1979). Moreover, delinquents often score below their non-delinquent peers on intelligence and achievement tests and have attentional problems associated with learning disabilities (Grande, 1988; Meltzer et al., 1986). These young people with perceptual learning disabilities are slow to develop language skills; as a result they experience early and repeated failure which creates a sense of inadequacy that may lead to delinquency as a compensatory mechanism.

In addition to intelligence deficits and learning disabilities, several personality traits and disorders have been identified in incarcerated males. In a recent study in England and Wales, for example, Gunn and Swinton (1991) surveyed 406 male young offenders and 1478 adult male prisoners. They found that 652 (37%) subjects had been diagnosed with psychiatric disorders, of which 15 (0.8%) had organic disorders, 34 (2%) psychosis, 105 (6%) neurosis, 177 (10%) personality disorder, and 407 (23%) substance misuse. Gunn and Swinton (1991) estimated that nearly 40% of male prisoners (both adults and young offenders) in England and Wales require urgent psychological treatment. They concluded that psychological disorders, whether learned, developed, or innate, are an important source of criminal and delinquent behavior.

In an American study, Guze (1976) using standardized testing, labelled 78% of his sample of male prisoners as "sociopaths." The substantial differences between this study and the Gunn and Swinton (1991) one, may be attributable to the much more rigorous inclusion criteria used in the latter. Other studies in Canada and Finland have indicated that the prevalence rate of serious psychological disorders among young offenders fall somewhere between the British and American estimates in the range of 50 – 60% (Jaffe et al., 1985; Karkkainen, 1989; Thompson, 1988). In any case, whatever the precise estimates, there is clearly a large prevalence of serious psychological disorders among young offenders, whether the disorders are innate, learned or a result of developmental psychopathology. These data seem to support the health and psychological theories of delinquency.

Throughout the 1960s, it was widely believed that XYY syndrome was linked to aggression, antisocial and criminal behavior. These conclusions were based on early studies of highly select males in prisons or mental institutions. Subsequently more carefully designed and executed studies, however, indicated that the typical characteristics of XYY males are not violence and criminality, but above-average height, large teeth and in some cases, severe acne. The combined results in which 59 XYY boys were followed through childhood indicated that their intelligence was normal and that the incidence of behavior problems among them was no different than XY males (Netley, 1986; Stewart, 1982).

Another biological explanation of delinquency is the yet unproven field of nutriophysiologic criminology, which focuses on the role of nutrition in criminal behavior. Substances such as lead, mercury, cadmium and sugar are known to affect behavior. With the many thousands of chemical additives used in foods, it is possible that some foods and chemicals may affect the brain and nervous system to cause violence and criminal behavior. While there is no evidence to support this contention, at least one researcher is very enthusiastic in advocating nutriophysiologic criminology as an exciting possibility in explaining and preventing crime (Geary, 1983).

Social Control Theory

Control theorists posit that socialization is the process by which people become bonded to family, school, and law (Hirschi, 1969). In this theory, conformity is explained through socialization and bonding between the individual and society (Wiatrowski et al., 1981). This is a process whereby individuals develop commitment to society leading to some form of internal control (Segrave & Hastad, 1985). This bonding consists of four main elements: attachment, commitment, involvement, and belief. The stronger the bond, the less likely the person (a juvenile in this case) will demonstrate delinquent behavior (Wiatrowski et al., 1981).

Social control theory maintains the importance of conventional values; attachments are seen as instrumental in the prevention of juvenile delinquency. The weakening of such attachments is likely to induce involvement in delinquent behavior (Segrave & Hastad, 1985).

The first area, attachment, is related to the bonding between a person and his or her significant others. Hirschi's (1969) findings indicated that for males "attachment to conventional peers, parents, and school, is conducive to the development of conventional attitudes, forming a bond between the juvenile and society, hence preventing delinquency" (p. 27). The family environment was noted by Rosenbaum (1989) and Wiatrowski et al. (1981) to be a main source of attachment, as it is the parents who act as role models for their children and teach them socially appropriate behavior.

Social control theory has been tested with rather positive results and thus has received much support from researchers since the seminal work of Hirschi in 1969. It has not, however, been without shortcomings. Numerous authors made the claim that social control theory, although relevant, cannot claim to be sufficient in understanding the reasons behind delinquency in juveniles. Segrave and Hastad (1985) found a negative association between conventional values and juvenile delinquency, as well as a positive relation between 'subterranean' values and delinquency. Their data indicated that adherence to conventional norms tends to insulate juveniles from delinquency.

Wiatrowski et al. (1981) found a strong negative correlation between the attachment of the juvenile to his or her parents and delinquency. They also found that the commitment variable did not hold in comparison to the predictions made by Hirschi in his study. Wiatrowski et al., concluded that "large correlations with Hirschi's four bond elements do exist, with the exception of the element of commitment to college and a high-status career" (1981, p. 537). Hirschi (1969) wrote of attachment being the critical family concept in the prediction of delinquency; and Simons, Robertson, and Downs (1989) found in their analysis that "the predominant causal flow is from parental rejection to delinquency" (p. 297).

Subculture Theory

From a sociological perspective, subculture theory seems to have a very strong base of support. Many researchers who find social control theory to be lacking, often to find refuge in the concepts of subculture theory.

In subculture theory juveniles are socialized into violating the law as a result of their exposure and affiliation with deviant influences. The greater the youth's association with his delinquent peers, the greater the possibility of differential association with them, and therefore with definitions conducive to delinquency. The most commonly stressed variables in subculture formulations are delinquent associates and peer approval for delinquency (Segrave & Hastad, 1985). It follows that if delinquency is committed in accordance with values and attitudes learned from peers, such behavior should be exhibited by individuals whose friends approve of such illegal activity.

Segrave and Hastad (1985) found delinquent behavior to be positively associated with both delinquent associates and peer approval for delinquency. Like the social control data, the subculture data in Segrave and Hastad's (1985) work accounted for a significant, but small, portion of the variance in delinquency, and as well, accounted for the highest portion of variance in all three of the theories that were considered (social control, subculture, and strain). The actual figures were 25.4 percent for males, and 14.9 percent for females. These two specific reports seem to verify each other to some extent, and allow one group of researchers to write "that delinquent companions are fundamentally related to committing delinquent acts, regardless of the level of attachment or of conventional attitudes for females and, especially for males" (Thompson et al., 1984, p. 18). The apparent overpowering strength of peer involvement is disputed in the findings of Williamson (1978), who found that lack of appropriate activities for youth is a major determinant of delinquency.

Looking at the findings of Williamson (1978), in combination with the results obtained by Thompson et al. (1984) and Segrave and Hastad (1985), it seems as though the development of delinquency approving friends may be the result of prior occurrences in the life of the youth involved and not a random occurrence. This being the case, peer relations would become more of an antecedent to delinquency than a cause, forming an advanced stage in the development toward delinquent actions.

Strain Theory

Strain theory postulates the greatest amount of juvenile delinquency among people of lower socioeconomic status (Cernkovitch, 1978). Such a position states that there is a perception within the individual that sees only limited access to legitimate opportunities. The motivation to deviate is enhanced when individuals accept and internalize culturally formulated goals of success and perceive legitimate avenues for achieving them as severely limited (Allan & Steffensmeier, 1989; Segrave & Hastad, 1985). Thus delinquent individuals see themselves, more so than their middle or upper class contemporaries, as being blocked from reaching goals they wish to attain. This theory postulates that such members of society are "forced" to deviate in order to achieve goals they are not able to attain through legitimate channels (Cernkovich, 1978).

Segrave and Hastad's (1985) findings support the major proposition of the strain model, although they account for only 7 percent for females. This was less significant than either the social control or subculture theories. In the work by Cernkovich (1978) the strain model accounted for 8 percent of the variance in delinquency: a finding which, though significant, is weak. Williamson (1978) discussed the fact that many youth make a rational decision to take the delinquent route because of the relative low risk and high gain involved, as compared to their perceived chances when considering a legitimate route.

It is apparent that internalized views of opportunity play a part in the movement of a juvenile toward delinquency. This, however, appears to be somewhat limited and unclear, as strain theory is often associated with low socioeconomic status, and the reports on the influence of socioeconomic status are conflicting. Although some researchers have claimed a definite relation between low socioeconomic status and delinquency in juveniles (Wiatrowski et al., 1981; Williamson, 1978), others strongly refute such findings, calling them correlations which "fall out" in rigorous analysis, and are not actual causes (Cernkovitch, 1978; Segrave & Hastad, 1985).

Family Systems Theory

There are two basic emphases in family-systems: 1) Learning in the family focusing on modelling, child-rearing and dysfunctional relationships within the family, and 2) Lack of affectional bonds, especially between parent-child.

In the first variant of family systems, the parents themselves model dysfunctional and criminal behavior. In these families, one or more parent may be a criminal and thus pass this on to their children. Moreover, these parents have difficulty in their child-rearing practices employing harsh, punitive, and violent discipline strategies. These children have little opportunity to model self-control, restraint and moral reasoning (Stott, 1982). Patterson (1981) identified four aspects of delinquency in parents that have failed to provide to their children: 1) house rules, 2) adequate parental monitoring of behavior, 3) proper effective contingencies, and 4) adequate crises and problem solving.

The second variant of family-systems revolves are around the endemic difficulty of parent-child relationships (Anolik, 1983; Gold & Petroni, 1980). These weak attachments are thought to create rejection in the children as well as a lack of responsibility, lack of concern for consequences, impulsive behavior and failure to learn from experience. Stott (1982) in a five-year longitudinal study of 102 delinquents, and a 10-year follow up of 700 juvenile delinquents, concluded that 93 percent of delinquent acts stemmed from a "breach of affectional bond between parent and child" (p. 318). The insecure attachment had been communicated to the adolescent by threatened rejection, loss of the preferred parent with no substitute, the mother was undependable, and the adolescent feared the loss of the preferred parent. Stott (1982) concluded that it was both failure of parental control and delinquency that were caused by breach of affectional bonds in the parents.

A further complicating factor in family systems is stress that can happen due to break-down: illness, death, unemployment, abandonment, poverty, and difficulties of general living. These stresses create discord that threaten family existence and lead to maladaptive emergency response, including delinquency.

Other Correlates of Delinquency

Several general factors appear time and time again in research on the characteristics of delinquents. These include individual characteristics, peer relations, school and academic performance and ecological variables.

Individual characteristics

There are three main individual characteristics that are correlated with delinquency: antisocial tendencies, aggression and poor self-control.

The antisocial tendencies of juvenile delinquents is pronounced and manifests itself early by age 10 (Farrows & French, 1986; Hundleby, 1986, 1987). They are less honest, more hedonistic, sexually preoccupied, violent, smoke, drink, gamble and use drugs. Generally delinquents tend to be less conforming and less socially restrained than nondelinquents in all aspects of their lives.

The single most prominent and destructive antisocial attitude and behavior associated with delinquency is aggression (Goldstein, 1980; Prothow-Stith & Spivak, 1992). Delinquent adolescents prefer to settle conflicts with fights rather than discussion, to steal to gain desired goods, act tough and are distrustful of others. Finally, they maintain aggressive attitudes, commit violent offenses, and engage in destructive vandalism.

Delinquents generally have poor self-control. Consequently, they tend to score high on measures of impulsiveness, external locus of control, and low on measures of conscience and morality (Gold & Petroni, 1980). They tend to blame others and external events for their problems, and express no guilt and remorse over antisocial and delinquent behavior (Henggeler, 1989; Quay, 1987).

Peer Relations

Association with deviant peers has been the most powerful and most consistent correlate of delinquency (Henggeler, 1992). Deviant peers model deviant behavior and provide social support for it. This deviant behavior is typically part of the conforming process that occurs in adolescent friendship groups. Nevertheless there is evidence emerging that an adolescents susceptibility to negative peer pressure is attenuated by positive family relations. Thus youths who associate with deviant peers and who also have poor family relations are especially at high risk for delinquency (Henggeler, 1992).

School and Academic Performance

As we have already seen, researchers have consistently found that delinquency is associated with poor school performance. This might be a result of the association that delinquency and school performance have with IQ, learning disabilities and family relations. In addition, as delinquent behavior begins to emerge, school personnel such as teachers and principals may react weakly, inconsistently and ineffectively to the emerging delinquent.

Ecological Variables

A number of variables related to the environment called ecological variables have been persistently found to be related to delinquency. These include chronic poverty and unemployment, and participation in neighborhood groups. Also, religious commitment has been associated to delinquency (high commitment reduces delinquent acts) although this is mediated through family relations. That is, it is the quality of family relations that is central and not religious commitment. Finally, there is emerging evidence that neighborhood characteristics, such as the existence of a criminal subculture are linked with delinquency (Henggeler, 1987).

Summary and Conclusions

Numerous theories and correlates of delinquency have been proposed. These theories include biological, health and psychological theories which focus on individual characteristics whether inherited, developed or learned. This brand of theory includes characteristics such as deficits in intellectual functioning, learning disabilities, personality traits, and some genetic disorders.

Social control theory posits that socialization is the process by which people become bonded to family, school and law. This theory maintains the importance of conventional value attachments as instrumental in the prevention of juvenile delinquency. The weakening of these attachments is likely to induce involvement in delinquent behavior.

In subculture theory it is posited that juveniles are socialized into violating the law as a result of their exposure and affiliation with deviant influences. The greater the youth's association with these delinquent peers, the greater the possibility of differential association with them. While some evidence supports subculture theory, it appears that in many cases, peer relations are more of a consequent of delinquency than a cause of it.

Strain theory postulates that juvenile delinquents come disproportionately from lower socioeconomic status. Such poverty status persons are thought to see only limited possibilities to legitimate opportunities and thus are motivated to deviant and delinquent behavior as means to economic advancement. Many theorists strongly refute such findings claiming that these correlations fall out in rigorous analysis and are not actual causes.

There are two emphases in family systems theory: learning in the family focusing on modelling, child-rearing and dysfunctional relationships within the family, and lack of affectional bonds between parent and child. Empirical support for both foci of family systems theory has been demonstrated. Future work in this area is likely to bring further causal links in family functioning and delinquent behavior.

Several other correlates of delinquency have been identified. These include individual characteristics such as antisocial tendencies and aggression, association with deviant peers, chronic depressed school and academic performance, and ecological factors such as poverty, exposure to neighborhood gangs and criminal subculture.

The major theories of delinquency and their relative validity are summarized in Table 18.1. Each theory is briefly explained and is given a rating from 0-5 to indicate a numerical value of its validity based on current data and research evidence. A value of 5.0 indicates overwhelming support while 0 suggests that there is no validity whatsoever for that theory. From Table 18.1 it can be seen that family systems theory received the highest rating (4.0) because current data and evidence provide strong support for it. Strain theory received the lowest rating (1.5).

Table 18.1
Summary of Major Theories of Delinquency and Their
Relative Validity Based on Current Data

Theory	Explanation	Validity
1. Biological, Health and Psychological	Delinquency is caused by individual characteristics which might be inhereted, developed or learned (e.g., genetic disorders, psychiatric problems, learning disabilities).	There is little doubt that most delinquents and criminals have some of these problems. These characteristics are probably related to and mediate criminality rather than cause it, however. (rating = 3.0)*
2. Social Control	Delinquency is caused when the individual fails to become properly socialized to accept the values of family, school, law and morality.	Substantial evidence supports this view, though critics argue that this theory is not sufficient to fully explain delinquency by itself. (rating = 3.5)
3. Subculture	Juveniles are socialized into violating the law as a result of exposure to and affiliation with deviant influences.	Evidence indicates that delinquent behavior is positively associated with delinquent associates and peer approval for delinquency. These, however, probably reflect antecedents to delinquency rather than its cause. (rating = 2.0)
4. Strain	Delinquency is caused by chronic poverty and low socioeconomic status.	There is a definite relation between poverty and delinquency but this is probably a correlation rather than a cause. (rating = 1.5)
5. Family Systems	Children learn dysfunctional criminal behavior from their parents and/or endemic difficulties of parent-child relationships which create developmental pathology in children such as criminality.	This view is one of the most currently accepted causes of delinquency although substantial empirical work is still required. (ratiing = 4.0)

*Ratings are given for each theory on a scale from 0 -5 based on current data and thinking. A value of 0 indicates no validity whatsoever in the theory, while a value of 5.0 indicates overwhelming support.

From the foregoing discussion it can be concluded that delinquency is associated with numerous variables and is explained by several theories. Given the plethora of explanations and variables, complex causal models will undoubt-edly be required to delineate the factors that are central to delinquency. Such results from complex studies may demonstrate the multidimensional nature and causality of delinquency and thus support the social-ecological model of behavior. Family, peer, and school factors which consistently contribute to delinquency either directly or indirectly may be explicated. Thus a viable model of delinquency is one that includes multiple pathways from the key systems in which youths are embedded.

Treatment and Intervention Approaches

The Role of Mental Health Services in Dealing with Young Offenders

The multidimensional nature of delinquency among adolescents requires the intervention of many agencies. Prothrow-Stith and Spivak (1992) have suggested that overemphasis on the criminal justice system in dealing with young offenders has failed to address a number of issues. Among the most critical of these is the observation that current criminal justice systems are not prevention oriented. Instead, they are limited to responding to delinquent acts after they have occurred. For the most part the focus is on blame and punishment. Moreover, criminal justice strategies are not useful in the case of unplanned violence, for example, between acquaintances and family members that accounts for a significant portion of violent crimes.

Despite the desirability of the high amount of contact that young offenders should have with public health agencies (e.g., Jaffe et al., 1985), the role of these agencies has not been central. Their primary role has been characterized as a band aid solution without any systematic attention being given to factors which underlie delinquency and which are likely to continue it. Both criminal justice and public health agencies appear to deal with delinquency itself rather than attempt to address it within the broader context of the delinquent's life. If effective intervention is to occur it must include acknowledgement of the factors which are thought to contribute both the initial criminal acts and its recidivism. Among the most critical factors are individual characteristics, family relations, peer relationships and school and academic performance, and ecological variables.

The way in which the adolescent views themselves and the manner in which he or she functions within family, peer and school systems, has a profound impact on the possible emergence of delinquent behavior. Because mental health professionals have expertise in family systems and/or behavioral treatment approaches and specialize in the treatment of children and families, their contribution to the effort of reducing violence among adolescents can be great. Many of the unsuccessful interventions to date have failed to address these issues adequately.

In Canada, direct involvement by mental health professionals within the juvenile court process was mandated through the *Juvenile Delinquents Act*, which was proclaimed into law over 80 years ago. Despite this long history, however, little is known about psychological service to the court, and what is known suggests outdated practice (Haynes & Peltier, 1983; Thompson, 1988).

The proclamation of the *Young Offenders Act* in April of 1984, has brought with it the potential for an increased emphasis on mental health services for young offenders. Some recent studies though, indicate that only a minimal amount of young offenders receive mental health services. In a study in Ontario of the London Family Court Clinic, for example, Jaffe et al. (1985) found that only about 10% of all juveniles coming before that court receive psychological assessments in the clinic. While the percentage seems to be somewhat higher in Alberta, it is still rather small. In a recent study of 2539 individuals charged under the *Young Offenders Act* over a one year period, Thompson (1988) found that only 18% had been on the caseload of Alberta Mental Health services subsequently. Similar proportions of juvenile offenders receive mental health services in the United States (Pabon, 1980; Rich, 1982). All of these estimates may be low, however, as they deal with archival information within public agencies. Many young offenders may be receiving treatment from others (private practice psychiatrists and psychologists, hospitals, school counsellors and psychologists). Even so, there is unquestionably a need for further involvement of mental health services with young offenders.

Figure 18.1 indicates an ideal relationship between public health (Mental Health) and the criminal justice systems in dealing with delinquency. Public health strategies are aimed at understanding, reducing, and preventing risk factors to delinquency not merely to responding to specific episodes. Multi-institutional and multidisciplinary models that change behavior, knowledge and attitudes are central to such an approach. Mass media, health care institutions, public schools, businesses and health fairs, are all sources of education, information and intervention. Once delinquency is understood as a health problem, effective interventions will emerge.

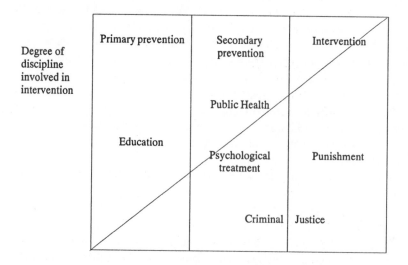

Figure 18.1: Ideal Relationship Between Public Health and Criminal Justice Systems for Preventing Delinquency

In what follows a number of programs aimed at dealing with young offenders and their families will be reviewed. Anyone who wishes to replicate a particular program in their own jurisdiction must be certain that their clients are similar to those involved in the initial implementation of the intervention. Moreover, care must be taken to secure the services of the appropriate practitioners and resource allocations. Failure to do so will not only lead to unsuccessful implementation, but may be a disservice to the clients as well (Ross & McKay, 1980).

The discussion surrounding intervention has frequently been characterized by the belief that "nothing works" when dealing with young offenders. This incorrect depiction of the effects of intervention has been a serious barrier to the implementation of successful intervention. If practitioners and politicians believe that nothing can be done, the drive for conceptualizing effective service delivery for young offenders is lost and the problems continue unabated. In what follows we will attempt to briefly describe a number of interventions which have demonstrated substantial success. In the following sections a review of various types of interventions including Diversion Programs, Intervention with Families of Delinquents, Community Based Programs, Programs for Juveniles in Correctional Institutions and Multisystem Intervention will be presented.

Diversion Programs

The need for effective diversion programs – which divert juveniles from the justice system – to help the juvenile offender has led to many innovative approaches to reduce juvenile recidivism. One of the more successful diversion programs is the Dallas Police Department Youth Services Program (YSP) which involves police officers and mental health practitioners working together. YSP was developed to deal with traditional methods of handling juveniles, from release with a warning, through referral to the juvenile court, as these methods have not alleviated the problem of delinquency (Collingwood, Douds & Williams, 1980). The two major goals of the programs were (1) to divert juveniles from the juvenile justice system, and (2) to reduce recidivism.

The YSP is staffed by officers and mental health professionals with a lieutenant of police as director. Fourteen counsellors supervised by a counselling psychologist make up the counselling unit. The program serves arrested youth between the ages of 10 and 16. The clients for this voluntary program include felons and misdemeanants, first offenders, and repeat offenders. Before beginning the program a youth and his or her parents are required to sign a statement of participation.

The two main components of the YSP include the First Offender Program which consists of a 3-hour lecture dealing with such topics as the law, implications of future illegal acts, and drug abuse. The second component, the Counselling Unit Program, is designed for more serious offenders, such as repeaters, assault offenders and other felons. A strength of the program rests in its teaming of a police investigator and a mental health professional in making the determination of need and providing subsequent therapy.

The procedures involved in YSP begin with the police investigator conducting an interview at the point of arrest to determine the young offenders needs.

After the interview is complete, the officer may choose to (1) send the youth home, (2) refer him or her to juvenile court, (3) refer the youth to a First Offender lecture program, or (4) refer the individual to the counselling unit. The decision that the officer makes is based on established criteria.

In the case of first time minor offenders, the most frequent disposition is referral to the First Offender lecture program while the most serious repeat offenders are referred to the juvenile court. The middle range youth (described as one who has committed a moderate to severe offense such as theft or burglary, or who has less than six previous arrests) is enrolled in the YSP. Referral to YSP is also a function of whether the youth and his parents could actually benefit from the relatively short-term YSP alternative. If the youth is referred to the First Offender Program he or she will attend the 3-hour lecture given by police officers. It should be noted that both police officers and the mental health professionals are given special training in inter-personal counselling and problem-solving skills to increase their effectiveness.

A youth referred to the Counselling Unit will have greater involvement over a longer period time with the program's resource individuals. In fact he or she will participate in a three stage program lasting approximately 6 months. At the intake stage the counsellor assesses the youth's physical, intellectual, and emotional functioning. The assessment period is followed by a direct treatment skill development phase. Over a 16 hour period of instruction the youth is provided with a set of skills which putatively will keep the youth out of further trouble. The specific skill areas focus on physical fitness, inter-personal skill and study/learning skills. Physical skills are taught to help provide the youth with energy, self-respect and awareness of self. Inter-personal skills focus on strategies to deal effectively with peers and methods which would foster positive relationships with parents. Study/learning skills are aimed at increasing the youth's participation and success in the school setting. Those students requiring remedial reading assistance are offered a reading program which includes 24 hours of instruction over a 2-month period. The goal of this component of the program is to keep the youth in school, thereby reducing opportunities to become involved in trouble. Moreover, the consolidation of basic literacy skills may assist the youth to be engaged in more constructive activities and result in more employment opportunities.

A significant cost factor associated with the program was the actual training of the staff. Sixty-six police officers from the Youth Section received 40 hours of training on interpersonal skills and problem solving skills in order to enhance their interviewing and communication skills with the youth and their parents. Initial training for counselling personnel included 80 hours of training, again in interpersonal and problem solving skills plus 24 hours on physical fitness training and 24 hours on program development skills. In addition, on-going training for the counselling staff is provided dealing with such topics as behavioral contracting, community referral use and program review and revision.

A review at the end of the first year of the program revealed a number of encouraging findings. The repeat arrest rate for youth who participated in the First Offender Program was 9.6% as opposed to the non-participating comparison group (n = 445) at 15.5%. The repeat rate for the Counselling Unit youths was 10.7% compared to a comparison group (n = 196) rate of 50.5%.

The results of a follow-up questionnaire to determine the impact of the Counselling Unit program on such factors as (1) communication with parents, (2) obedience to parents, (3) responsibility at home, (4) school attendance, (5) study time, (6) grades, (7) trouble in schools, (8) part-time job, (9) career planning, (10) recreation participation, and (11) hobby participation was administered. The results showed that 72% of parents indicated improved communication, 74% noted a greater obedience to parental requests, 54% of parents indicated that there was an increased tendency to assume responsibility, 63% of the youth were found to increase their school attendance, 54% of the youth were seen to study more, 52% actually achieved better grades, and 60% got into less trouble in school. In addition, parents reported that the youth expressed a positive self-concept and a more positive attitude toward police.

The results from the Dallas Police Youth Services Program indicated a significant reduction of recidivism for the middle-range offender. The combination of police and mental health professionals is clearly a combination worth examining, as is the inclusion of a skills approach to training and treatment. Other researchers have found that many diversion programs substantially reduce recidivism and re-arrest rates for young offenders (Quay, 1987; Quay & Love, 1977; Seidman et al. 1976).

Intervention with Families of Delinquents

Increasingly, interventions dealing with young offenders have involved members of the entire family. A basic assumption of family therapy is that youth problems are closely associated with dysfunctional family interactions and consequently, treatment must ameliorate problematic family relations.

The two most promising approaches to family therapy for young offenders include Behavioral Parent Training and Functional Family Therapy. The aim of Behavioral Parent Training is to assist parents in accurately monitoring child behavior and to provide consistent reinforcement for positive behavior and punishment (e.g., loss of privileges) for negative behavior (Henggeler, 1992). To date, such approaches have tended to be more effective with young adolescents.

Consistent with family systems approaches, Functional Family Therapy assumes that delinquency reflects maladaptive interactions with the family. A variety of techniques are used with this approach including contingency contracting and training in communication skills among family members. To this point this type of intervention appears to be most effective with more moderate young offenders.

Wade et al. (1977) described an intensive family crisis intervention program and its evaluation. The intervention strategies included five components: (1) immediate referrals to capitalize on the motivation of the family crises situation, (2) intensive but time-limited outreach services in the young offender's home, (3) a focus on the family as a system which was functioning maladaptively, (4) both male and female counselling teams of the same ethnic origins of the family, and (5) reliance on adjunct agencies and professionals as needed. Half of the 153 families served over a two year period had experienced some degree of family disorganization such as divorce, separation, remarriage, adoption or death of a natural parent.

The program was considered a success based on both recidivism data and goal attainment data (Wade et al., 1977). After one year, the recidivism rate was low (14.75%), and only 1 of 66 adolescent siblings came before the court during the one year follow-up. A number of goals were also assessed and found to improve substantially, including improved family communications, increased school attendance, reduced runaways, and increased acceptance of responsibility in the family.

In a family preservation program called Homebuilders, Haapla and Kinney (1988) found that 87% of 687 high-risk status offenders avoided out-of-home placement for 12 months after service intake. The program included a multiplicity of treatment orientation including behavior modification in the natural environment, crisis intervention theory, client-centred therapy, values clarification, assertiveness training, and multiple-impact therapy. As the program evolved over a 15 year period, additional treatment interventions such as Rational Emotive Therapy were added as well as concrete and tangible services to clients as transportation, house cleaning, and cooking. This program has been considered so successful that by 1987, 28 state programs based on the Homebuilder model which began in Washington state in 1974, had been developed.

Over the past decade it has become increasingly clear that the treatment of choice for most juvenile delinquents is family therapy (Gordon & Arbuthnot, 1987). Family therapy is usually delivered by professionals who have graduate training in mental health (M.S.W., M.D., Ph.D., M.A., R.N.). These professionals are most often in private practice and are very expensive to employ in family therapy. Therefore, there is an emerging trend to use paraprofessionals (those without graduate training) such as caseworkers, teachers, ministers, probation officers, students, parents and volunteers. Because the use of paraprofessionals is much less expensive than professionals, family based intervention can be expanded. In a systematic review of the literature comparing the effectiveness of paraprofessionals to professionals, Gordon and Arbuthnot (1988) concluded that paraprofessionals achieve results equal to or superior to those achieved by professionals. Obviously, the use of paraprofessionals should be explored further given these positive results.

Community Based Programs

Although the stress is on including the family of the offender in the treatment program, for many delinquents it is unrealistic to expect that it will be possible to involve the family. Correctional workers know only too well that there are many families with whom they cannot work either because of major personal shortcomings of some of the members or because of the gross instability of the family relationships or, equally common, because they adamantly refuse to cooperate with any attempt to involve them in any program effort. Clearly, there is a need for an effective program which can be applied in a community setting which does *not* necessitate direct intervention with the delinquent's home.

"Community based programs" is a general phrase which encompasses a plethora of activities and projects. These include placing delinquents in individual foster homes, establishing group homes for delinquents, establishing community centres which provide athletic, recreation and cultural activities, and public works projects (tree trimming, litter removal, playground maintenance, etc.). Skills based programs involve vocational training and job placement, tutoring, and educational upgrading. Social support includes the buddy system as well as discussion and support groups. Finally, community based prevention measures include mass media campaigns and the development and implementation of school based curricula.

The Violence Prevention Project of the Health Promotion Program for Urban Youth (Boston Department of Health Hospitals), represents an effort to reduce the incidence of delinquent behavior and associated social and medical hazards for adolescents at the community level (Prothrow-Stith, Spivak, & Hausman, 1987). This program is based on individual behavior modification through risk communication and education. In consultation with a host of individuals from various therapeutic services, a curriculum was developed and became the central material for a grade 10 health class. An evaluation of the material revealed changes in knowledge and attitudes regarding such activities as fighting. One school principal employing the curriculum, indicated a 50% reduction in the number of fights over a three year period. The program offers support for the value of education in attempting to reduce delinquency in one of the most demanding communities for the adolescent: the community school.

Other programs based within the school setting and supported by mental health resource individuals have also proven effective. For example, a program designed to prevent violence had the following goals:

1. Provide statistical information on adolescent violence and homicide

2. Present anger as a normal, potentially constructive emotion

3. Create an awareness in students of alternatives to fighting by discussing potential gains and losses from such behavior

4. Have students analyze situations preceding a fight and practice avoiding fights by using role-play and videotape

5. Create a classroom ethos that is nonviolent and values violence prevention behavior (Prothrow-Stith, 1986)

The key to this program was that anger was not denied but presented as a normal, essential and potentially constructive emotion. What is critical in this case is an acceptable alternative to dealing with anger through some delinquent act. Other techniques instruct the students to appreciate some of the dynamics of confrontation. For example, students are taught to recognize the escalation phase of the fight, at which point it is easier to prevent further confrontation. Many schools have initiated peer and teacher mediation programs that acknowledge the value of recognizing the critical point at which a confrontation escalates.

Taken together, programs which are educationally oriented and focused on prevention can and do have a significant impact on the prevention of delinquency.

In another innovative community program, O'Donnell et al. (1979) employed a "buddy system" where adult paraprofessionals were paired with juvenile offenders who had been referred by public schools for behavior and academic problems. The main tasks of the buddies were to help reduce the presenting behavior problems and to help increase the adolescents' school attendance and academic performance through contingency management using praise, social support, and money as reinforcers. The primary purpose of this buddy system, however, was the prevention and remediation of delinquent behaviors. All of the subjects had committed major criminal offenses.

Results of the O'Donnell et al. (1979) study showed that of 335 offenders in the buddy system group, they experienced 22.3% fewer arrests after three years than did those in a control group. The overall arrest rate was 20.7%, though the overall rate ranged form 10.8% to 81% when recent offense history, sex, and type of crime committed was considered. There were no data provided on school attendance information or achievement in the study, though O'Donnell et al. (1979) pronounced the buddy system a success solely on re-arrest rates.

Many other community based programs have been shown to be successful in reducing re-arrest rates and generally improving the conduct and behavior of the young offenders. Walter and Mills (1989), for example, described a successful program where delinquents were placed in jobs and monitored both by professionals and employers. A study conducted over 20 years ago but which yielded impressive results, employed behavior modification techniques, group discussion and social support groups (Thomas et al., 1971). The recidivism rate of the treatment group of delinquents dropped to 10% while in the control group it was 50%. Henggeler (1989) has described a number of community based programs including public works projects, group homes and vocational training which have been successful with young offenders. Finally, Fabiano et al. (1990) have described skills based programs (knowledge and social) which has reduced recidivism in offenders, and Quigley et al. (1992) have attempted to implement a computer-assisted vocational life skills program for offenders in Newfoundland in hopes to reduce recidivism rates.

Programs for Juveniles in Correctional Institutions

Among the most frequently used intervention programs in correctional institutions are token economies based on behavior modification principles. These programs provide opportunities to earn tokens for a wide range of adaptive positive behaviors. The tokens are later exchanged for a variety of secondary reinforcers such as food, television time and other privileges. While the efficacy of such programs has been demonstrated in a number of settings (Quay, 1987), their success is dependent on a number of factors. First, the staff overseeing the program must have an understanding of behavior modification principles and must be consistent in their adherence to the principles. One of the main factors which can result in the failure of such programs is related to how thoroughly the staff members understand the specific program, and the principles of reinforcement. Moreover, there exits a fine line between using such programs as constructive means to develop appropriate behavior and turning such devices into tools of control.

Again based on reinforcement theory, Ross and Mckay (1980) developed the peer intervention strategy for adolescent offenders. These researchers trained a group of "unmanageable" delinquent adolescent girls with chronic and severe behavior problems to essentially serve as therapists for each other. Although the training component was time consuming, the results of the program were quite impressive. The results indicated that major institutional problems were eliminated including such behaviors as assault, vandalism, self-inflicted injuries, and suicide gestures. Moreover, these results held over a three month follow-up period. In an extension of conventional behavior modification techniques, Saranson and Ganzer (1980) added modelling and group discussion for the treatment of incarcerated juveniles. They concluded that the modelling and structured discussion approaches had greater concurrent and long-term effects on adolescent delinquents than the normal program of a high-quality institution. Further extending this approach to group counselling strategies also has benefits for the inmates (Lewis, 1989).

A wide variety of other interventions (vocational training, community works, token economies, buddy systems, bibliotherapy, etc.) have been used with incarcerated adolescents. In a highly structured residential setting, it is possible to substantially reduce rates of problem behavior. Unfortunately, such positive changes are rarely maintained when the youth is returned to the community. This finding is not surprising when one considers that little therapeutic attention is devoted to altering problems with the youth's family, peer groups, and neighborhood which created the problem in the first place and is likely to continue it.

Multisystem Interventions

At the centre of multisystem interventions is the recognition that there are multiple determinants of adolescent antisocial behavior. The context of intervention from this perspective is the various systems in which the adolescent functions including the family, peers and school. One type of intervention which this orientation has spawned is Multisystemic Therapy. This type of intervention is a family-based approach which emphasizes adolescent cognitive variables and the youth's and family's relations with extrafamilial systems. To date several studies have shown that multisystemic therapy is effective in changing the types of family interactions which are associated with delinquency, decreasing the youth's association with deviant peers and reducing the overall rate of adolescent behavior problems.

Vocationally oriented psychotherapy is another form of multisystem intervention in which the therapist provides both intensive psychotherapy and assistance in obtaining educational and vocational placement. Follow-up studies indicate that adolescents receiving this approach evidenced better social adaptation to family life, employment success, and legal difficulties than did comparison boys (Henggeler, 1992).

Another form of multisystems intervention is Child Advocacy Treatment which uses paraprofessionals (e.g., university or college students) as intervention agents with juvenile offenders. Nonprofessionals use behavioral contracting techniques and child advocacy to intervene in a wide range of problem areas (e.g., peer, family, school). Preliminary outcome data suggest that this approach is very promising (Gordon & Arbuthnot, 1987).

Effective treatments of delinquency must recognize the multiple determinants of adolescent antisocial behavior. Consistent with this conclusion, broadbased treatment approaches such as multisystem interventions, intervene at multiple levels of the youth's ecology (e.g., with family, peers, and school). Although approaches in this area are based on different theoretical models, they share several communalities. All three interventions described above address individual and systemic characteristics, are pragmatic and problem-focused, are conducted in a variety of community settings, and are as flexible and intensive as necessary.

Summary and Conclusions

By way of summary, the treatment and intervention approaches together with their relative efficacy are compiled in Table 18.2. The relative efficacy of each approach is assigned a value 0-5 with 5 indicating great efficacy and 0, complete ineffectiveness. As can be seen from Table 18.2, family interventions and multisystems intervention (which includes family therapy) are given the highest rating (4.0) while programs in institutions are given the lowest ratings (1.0).

Table 18.2
Summary of Treatment and Intervention Approaches for
Delinquents and Their Relative Efficacy

Treatment or Intervention	Explanation	Efficacy
1. Diversion Programs	The two major goals of these is to (1) divert juveniles from the justice system, and (2) to reduce recidivism.	Several outcome studies have shown substantial success of both goals as well as improving school attendance and achievement, and improving family and peer relations. (rating = 3.5)*
2. Family Intervention	Since the families of delinquents are frequently dysfunctional, this approach seeks to ameliorate this and reduce recidivism and improve family relations.	Well implemented and executed family interventions have proven to be highly successful in most of their goals. Unfortunately, families of some delinquents will simply refuse to participate in any program. (rating = 4.0)

3. Community Programs	These include a plethora of activities and projects such as group homes, public works, vocational training, educational upgrading, community centre activities, etc.	The success of these has been mixed. It depends largely on the type of program, the needs of the juveniles, and the resources of the program. (rating = 2.5)
4. Programs in Correctional Institutions	A number of such programs have been implemented but the most common are token economies based on behavior modification principles. The main goals are to reduce undesirable behaviors and increase desirable ones.	Many token economy and behavior modification programs have been very successful in institutions. The desirable behavior rarely generalizes outside the institution and previous delinquent behavior re-emerges. (rating = 1.0)
5. Multisystem Interventions	Multisystemic therapy (family based), vocationally oriented psychotherapy, and child advocacy treatment are the main types. These are broad-based treatment approaches which intervene at multiple levels of the youth's ecology (e.g., school, family, peers, etc.).	Preliminary outcome studies indicate that well implemented and intensive programs show promising results. More research is required to establish efficacy, however. (rating = 4.0)

*Ratings are given for each intervention based on a scale of 0 - 5. A value of 0 indicates no efficacy whatsoever, while a value of 5.0 indicates unquestionable efficacy.

By the mid-1970s researchers and policy makers had become pessimistic about the efficacy of correctional treatment in general. Research and outcome studies since that time, however, have shown that many carefully designed and executed programs have been successful. Perhaps the most successful and promising are family based interventions and multisystem interventions, though other interventions such as diversion programs, community based programs, and even some in correctional institutions have demonstrated success. Some of these programs can be very expensive because of the intensive use of professionals in direct contact with the offender, the family, peers and so on. Fortunately, an emerging trend has been to use paraprofessionals under the supervision of professionals. More fortunately still, outcome studies and evaluations have shown that paraprofessionals are generally as effective or more effective than professionals in dealing with adolescent offenders (Gordon & Arbuthnot, 1988).

As the above program descriptions indicate, there are a variety of interventions which have been successfully implemented with young offenders. The key to successful implementation is to determine the specific needs of a young offender and then to match those needs to the appropriate program. Failure to do this will likely result in the failure of the intervention (Reitsma-Street, 1984).

References

Allan, E.A., & Steffensmeier, D.J. (1989). Youth underemployment, and property crime: Differential effects of job availability and job quality on juvenile and young adult arrest rates. *American Sociological Review, 54*, 107-112.

Anolik, S.A. (1983). Family influences upon delinquency: Biosocial and psychosocial perspectives. *Adolescence, 18*, 489-498.

Berman, A.L., & Carroll, T.A. (1984). Adolescent suicide: A critical review. *Death Education, 8*, 53-64.

Cernkovich, S.A. (1978). Evaluating two models of delinquency causation. *Criminology, 16*, 335-352.

Collingwood, T.R., Douds, A., & Williams, H. (1980). Juvenile diversion: The Dallas Police Department Youth services Program. In R.R. Ross, & P. Gendreau (Eds.), *Effective correctional treatment*. Toronto: Butterworths.

Fabiano, E., Robinson, D., & Porporino, F. (1990). *A preliminary assessment of the cognitive skills training program pilot project*. Ottawa: Correctional Service of Canada.

Farrow, J.A., & French, J. (1986). The drug-abuse delinquency connection revisited. *Adolescence, 21*, 951-960.

Garrison, C.Z., Lewinsohn, P.M., Marsteller, F., Langhinrichsen, J., & Lann, I. (1991). The assessment of suicidal behavior in adolescents. *Suicide and Life Threatening Behavior, 21*, 217-230.

Geary, D.P. (1983). Nutrition, chemicals and criminal behavior: Some physiological aspects of antisocial conduct. *Juvenile and Family Court Journal, 34*, 9-13.

Gold, M., & Petroni, R.J. (1980). Delinquent behavior in adolescence. In J. Adelson (Ed.), *Handbook of adolescent psychology*. New York: Wiley.

Goldstein, A.P., Sprafkin, R.P., Gershaw, N.J., & Klein, P. (1980). *Skill-streaming the adolescent*. Champaign, IL: Research Press.

Grande, C.G. (1988). Delinquency: The learning disabled student's reaction to academic school failure? *Adolescence, 23*, 209-219.

Greuling, J.W., & DeBlassie, R. (1980). Adolescent suicide. *Adolescence, 15*, 589-601.

Gunn, J., Maden, A., & Sweinton, M. (1991). Treatment needs of prisoners with psychiatric disorders. *British Medical Journal, 303*, 338-341.

Guze, S.B. (1976). *Criminality and psychiatric disorders*. New York: Oxford University Press.

Haapala, D.A., & Kinney, J.M. (1988). Avoiding out-of-home placement of high-risk status offenders through the use of intensive treatment. *Criminal Justice and Behavior, 15*, 334-348.

Hawkins, J.D., & Fraser, M.W. (1981). Theory and practice in delinquency prevention. *Social Work Research and Abstracts, 17*, 3-13.

Henggeler, S.W. (1989). *Delinquency in adolescence*. Newbury Park, CA: Sage.

Hirschi, T. (1969). *Causes of delinquency*. Berkeley: University of California Press.

Hundleby, J.D. (1986). Personality and the prediction of delinquency and drug use. A follow-up study of training school boys. *British Journal of Criminology, 26,* 129-146.

Jaffe, P.G., Leschied, A.W., Sas, L., Austin, G.W. (1985). A model for the provision of clinical assessments and service brokerage for young offenders: The London Family Court Clinic. *Canadian Psychology, 26,* 54-61.

Karkkainen, H. (1989). Treatment of Delinquent Youth in Finland. *Child Welfare, 68,* 183-188.

Lewis, W.B. (1989). Correctional counselling: What, why, how much, and who? *Child & Youth Services, 11,* 71-81.

Lesse, S. (1979). Behavioral problems masking depression: Cultural and clinical survey. *American Journal of Psychotherapy, 33,* 41-53.

Meltzer, L.J., Roditi, B.N., & Fenton, T. (1986). Cognitive and learning profiles of delinquent and learning-disabled adolescents. *Adolescence, 21,* 581-592.

Netley, C.T. (1986). Summary overview of behavioral development in individuals with neonatally identified X and Y aneuploidy. *Birth Defects, 22,* 293-306.

O'Donnell, C.R., Lydgate, T., & Fo, W.S. (1979). The buddy system: Review and follow-up. *Child Behavior Therapy, 1,* 161-169.

Pabon, E. (1980). Mental health services in the juvenile court: An overview. *Juvenile & Family Court Journal, 31,* 23-29.

Patterson, G.R. (1981). *Coercive family processes.* Eugene, OR: Castalia.

Poznanski, E.O. (1982). The clinical phenomenology of childhood depression. *American Journal of Orthopsychiatry, 52,* 308-313.

Prothrow-Stith, D. (1989). Interdisciplinary interventions applicable to prevention of violence and homicide in black youth. In Surgeon General's Workshop on Violence and Public Health DHHS (pp. 35-43). Pub. No. HRS-D-MC 86.1. Washington, DC.

Prothrow-Stith, D., & Spivak, H.R. (1992). In S.B. Friedman, M. Fisher, & S.K. Schonberg (Eds.), *Comprehensive Adolescent Health Care* (pp. 806-811). St. Louis: Quality Medical Publishing.

Prothrow-Stith, D., Spivak, H., & Hausman, A.J. (1987). The violence prevention project: A public health approach. *Science, Technology and Human Values, 12,* 67-69.

Quay, H.C. (1987). *Handbook of juvenile delinquency.* New York: John Wiley.

Quay, H.C., & Love, C.T. (1977). The effect of a juvenile diversion program on rearrests. *Criminal Justice and Behavior, 4,* 377-396.

Quigley, M., Jeffery, G.H., & McNutt, M. (1992). Computer-assisted vocational life skills program for offenders. *Canadian Journal of Counselling 17,* 28-36.

Reitsma-Street, M. (1984). Differential treatment of young offenders: A review of the Conceptual Level Matching Model. *Criminology, 26,* 199-215.

Rich, P. (1982). The juvenile justice system and its treatment of the juvenile: An overview. *Adolescence, 27,* 141-152.

Rosembaum, J.L. (1989). Family dysfunction and female delinquency. *Crime and Delinquency, 35*, 31-44.

Ross, R.R., & McKay, H.B. (1980). Behavioral approaches to treatment in correction: Requiem for a panacea. In R.R. Ross & P. Gendreau (Eds.), *Effective correctional treatment*. Toronto: Butterworths.

Sarason, I.G., & Ganzer, V.J. (1980). Modeling and group discussion in the rehabilitation of juvenile delinquents. In R.R. Ross & P Gendreau (Eds.), *Effective correctional treatment*. Toronto: Buttersworth.

Sawicki, D., & Schaeffer, B. (1979). An affirmative approach to the LD/JD link. *Juvenile & Family Court Journal, 30*, 11-16.

Seidman, E., Rappaport, J., & Davidson, W.S. (1976, September). Adolescents in legal jeopardy. Paper presented at the American Psychological Association Convention, Washington, DC.

Segrave, J., & Hastad, D. (1985).Evaluating three models of delinquency causation for males and females: Strain theory, subculture theory, and control theory. *Sociological Focus, 18*, 1-17.

Simons, R., Robertson, J., & Downs, W. (1989). The nature of the association between parental rejection and delinquent behavior. *Journal of Youth and Adolescence, 18*, 297-310.

Stewart, D.A. (1982). *Children with sex chromosome anenploidy: Follow-up studies.* New York: Alan R. Liss.

Stiffman, A.R. (1989). Suicide attempts in runaway youth. *Suicide and Life-Threatening Behavior, 19*, 147-159.

Stott, D. (1982). *Delinquency: The problem and its prevention.* New York: SP Medical and Scientific Books.

Thompson, T.R. (1987). Childhood and adolescent suicide in Manitoba: A demographic study. *Canadian Journal of Psychiatry, 32*, 264-269.

Thompson, W.E., Mitchell, J., & Dodder, R.A. (1984). An empirical test of Hirschi's control theory of delinquency. *Deviant Behavior, 5*, 11-22.

Wade, T.C., Morton, T.L., & Lind, J.E., & Neuton, R.F. (1977). A family crisis intervention approach to diversion from the juvenile justice system. *Juvenile Justice Journal, 28*, 43-51.

Walter, T.L., & Mills, C.M. (1989). A behavioral-employment intervention program for reducing juvenile delinquency. In J.S. Stumphauzer (Ed.), *Progress in behavior therapy with delinquents*. Springfield, Il: Charles C. Thomas.

Wiatrowski, M.D., Griswold, D.B., & Roberts, M.K. (1981). Social control theory and delinquency. *American Sociological Review, 46*, 525-541.

Williamson, H. (1978). Choosing to be a delinquent. *New Society, 9*, 333-336.

19
Childhood Sexual Abuse and Adolescence

It is now suspected by many that the current incidence and prevalence of child sexual abuse (CSA) may be alarmingly high (Violato & Genius, 1993b). Notwithstanding some excellent reviews of CSA which have been published recently (Beitchman, Zucker, Hood, da Costa, Akman, & Cassavia, 1992; Browne & Finkelhor, 1986; Finkelhor, 1990; Kendall-Tackett, Williams, & Finkelhor, 1993; Violato & Genius, 1993b), however, the effects, sequelae and prevalence of CSA are still not very well understood. Much more work is urgently required into all aspects of CSA, including a clearer understanding of prevalence and the possible implications of this for child development and psychopathology. The main purpose of the present chapter is to review the major studies of the prevalence of CSA and to discuss its implications for developmental psychopathology. Accordingly, aspects of CSA that are reviewed in the present paper include a) definitions, b) effects, c) possible mechanisms of how CSA effects the victims, d) prevalence rates, and e) implications for psychopathology into adolescence and beyond.

Definitions of Child Sexual Abuse

One of the main problems in the area of sexual abuse is the variation in the definitions used by different researchers. Browne and Finkelhor (1986), Beitchman et al. (1992), and Kendall-Tackett et al. (1993) in their respective reviews, noted that few studies in this area employ incompatible definitions. Some focus on experiences with older partners only, excluding coerced sexual experiences by peers, while others narrow in on CSA occurring solely within the family. These differences in the samples make it difficult to compare relevant studies.

Many studies leave the definition of CSA up to the subjects. Such studies frequently ask the subjects to indicate whether they were sexually abused as children, and if so how frequently and by whom (e.g., Briere, Henschell, & Smiljanieh, 1992). Other studies include definitions involving intercourse, touching, exposure of the sexual organs, showing pornographic material, or talking about sexual matters in an erotic way (Finkelhor, 1984; Finkelhor & Hotaling, 1984; Finkelhor, Hotaling, Lewis, & Smith, 1990; Fromuth & Burkhart, 1989; Reinhart, 1987). Systematic comparisons across these studies are exceedingly difficult because of both the vagueness and inclusivity of the definitions.

A more rigorous definition was provided by Pierce and Pierce (1985) after examining the records of 205 cases of CSA (25 cases of abuse of males and 182 females). They defined sexual abuse as "exposure, fondling the child's genitals, masturbation, intercourse, and attempted intercourse" (p. 192). While this definition is more precise than the foregoing ones, it also remains unsatisfactory because it included exposure. It is difficult to determine if this constitutes abuse in all cases.

Condy, Templar, Brown, and Veaco (1987) allowed for only contact abuse in their definition. In a study where the data were gathered from adolescent male runaways, Janus, Burgess, and McCormack (1987) included both contact and non-contact acts within their definition of CSA. They did, however, explicitly state in their questioning that the acts, contact or not, had to be unwanted. Asking if the sexual acts were unwanted adds to the clarity of the definition as it removes any suggestion of consent or mutual sexual action. Faller (1989) in a study of 87 incidents between 1979 and 1986, however, failed to use the criterion of consent in her report of cases taken from medical records of both girls and boys who had been sexually abused. Faller's (1989) criteria were that the perpetrator had to be at least five years older than the victim, and that sexual contact had to have taken place.

In another study relevant to a definition of CSA, Fritz, Stoll, and Wagner (1981) administered a 45-item questionnaire to 952 college students (both male and female) who were older than 18 years. While no specific definition of sexual abuse was given, the authors indicated that questions were asked about the salient components of molestation, all of which included sexual contact. included both contact and non-contact experiences.

Violato and Genius (1993b) have proposed that CSA is any unwanted approach or action of a sexual nature involving a child and/or which causes the child (anyone younger than 17 years old) psychological discomfort or pain having more than transitory effects. Having employed this definition, Bagley (1988), for example, questioned 935 Canadian males in a national survey about "unwanted" sexual acts prior to their 17th birthday: 8.2% of the sample reported at least unwanted genital fondling while they were children or adolescents and one-third of these assaults involved attempted or achieved anal penetration of the victim. For 19% of the male victims, the assaults resulted in "significant emotional hurt." Eighty percent of victims had not told anyone about the assaults. Violato and Genuis (1993a) also employed this definition of CSA when they interviewed 200 university males between the ages of 18 and 27 years. Twenty-eight subjects (14%) reported unwanted sexual contact prior to the legal age of adulthood (18 years in the Province of Alberta).

From the criteria presented above, we propose that the clearest and least restrictive definition is provided by unwanted contact. The criterion of unwanted sexual contact is a better method of eliminating cases of consensual sex play among peers than some arbitrary age criterion, as was used by Faller (1989) for example. Therefore we recommend that for research and discussion purposes, CSA be operationalized as unwanted sexual contact (genital touching and fondling to penetration) while the victim is considered a child by legal definition and the perpetrator is in a position of relative power vis a vis the victim (e.g., parent, adult, babysitter, guardian, older child, etc.).

Effects of Child Sexual Abuse

Sexual abuse has at least three types of results: initial effects (those exhibited within two years after the ending of the sexual abuse), initial effects found to last and become long-term effects, and long-term effects (those exhibited more than two years after the ending of the sexual abuse which were not necessarily present initially).

Initial Effects

Initial effects related to the self-esteem of the victim have been found to vary and the evidence on this point is scanty and conflicting. Many researchers have reported diminished self-esteem as initial effects following sexual abuse (Bolton et al., 1990; Conte & Shuerman, 1987a; 1987b; Steele, 1986). At least one study, however, reported no differences in self-esteem between sexually abused and control subjects (Tong et al., 1987). These researchers did, however, report a diminished confidence in the CSA victims.

Other initial effects of CSA include depression, guilt, feelings of inferiority, dissociation, initial fear, homosexual impulses, suicidal feelings, learned help-lessness, distrust and shock, and surprise leading to anger and resentment (Adams-Tucker, 1986; Beitchman, Zucker, Hood, da Costa, & Akman, 1991; Conte & Shuerman, 1987a, 1987b; Grossi & Violato, 1992; Steele, 1986; Woods & Dean, 1984). Outcomes associated with CSA also include self-destructive behavior, increased suicide attempts, eating disorders, delinquency, interpersonal problems, substance abuse, prostitution, failing grades in school, school dropout, anger and hostility, acting out, inappropriate sexual behavior, running away, victim/perpetrator cycle, increased aggression, and increased sexual awareness (Briere & Runtz, 1986; Janus, Scarlon, & Price, 1984; McCormack, Janus, & Burgess, 1986; Silbert & Pines, 1983).

Initial Effects Lasting Into the Long Term

Numerous writers have noted that many of the initial effects of the sexually abused child become long-term (Beitchman et al., 1992; Bruckner & Johnson, 1987; Freeman-Longo, 1986; Kendall-Tackett et al., 1993; Vander-Mey, 1988). These lasting effects are alienation, a desperate and often ineffective search for nurturing, distrust, low self-esteem, depression, guilt, and self-harm (Briere, 1992).

Long-Term Effects

Briere (1992) has proposed that in the long-term, victims of CSA show a "postsexual abuse syndrome" which includes social withdrawal, chronic fear, uncontrollable anger, and deliberate self-harm. Other factors that have been identified as long-term sequelae of CSA include confused sexual orientation, distrust, homosexual tendencies, difficulties with interpersonal relationships, becoming a neglectful and/or abusive caretaker, multiple personality disorder, sexual masochism and eating disorders (Beitchman et al., 1992; Finkelhor, 1984; Freeman-Longo, 1986; Inderbitzen-Pisaruk, Sawchuck, & Hoier, 1992; Janus et al., 1987; Johnson & Schier, 1987; Krug, 1989; Roane, 1992; Steele, 1986;

Woods & Dean, 1984). Indeed, in a recent comprehensive review, Kendall-Tackett et al. (1993) concluded that there is virtually no general domain of psychopathologic symptomatology that has not been associated with a history of sexual abuse. In many of the studies which have identified these factors, however, CSA has occurred within the context of disturbed family systems, alcoholism, drug abuse, poverty and violence, and thus may be due to these latter factors rather than CSA *per se* (Ciccheti & Howes, 1991; Wolfe & Wolfe, 1988). A recent well-designed study wherein 17 CSA victims were matched to a group of 17 nonabused community children on age, sex, socioeconomic level and living situation, may help disentangle the effects of CSA from other deleterious factors. In this research, Inderbitzen-Pisaruk et al. (1992) found that CSA children compared to the matched control group had increased depression, dysphoria, sex-behavior problems, were more disobedient, aggressive and felt more hopeless. Similarly, Violato and Genuis (1993a) found that their CSA adult males also had disturbed sexuality as indicated by paedophilia ideation. Even so, there is as yet little understanding of the *specific* abuse-related variables on long-term outcomes. Accordingly, we concur with Beitchman et al. (1992) that it is probably premature to confirm a history of CSA with a long-term "postsexual abuse syndrome."

Another possible serious consequence of sexual abuse experiences is the victim/perpetrator cycle for males and revictimization for females. Steele (1986) noted however, that the type of abuse perpetrated does not necessarily transmit from one generation to the next. But abuse (whether sexual, physical, or psychological) can often be traced back through three or four generations in the history of the perpetrator (Steele, 1986; Wolfe & Jaffe, 1991). Gilqun and Reiser (1990) suggested that sexual abuse can result in subsequent disturbed sexual identity and the possibility of abnormal sexual ideation and activity such as paedophilia. This victim/perpetrator cycle potential is a particularly important problem for CSA of males since males constitute the vast majority of offenders of CSA. Females who have been victims of CSA appear to be at a high level of risk for revictimization for rape, battering, physical abuse and various forms of sexual assault (Alexander & Lupfer, 1987; Beitchman et al., 1992).

The foregoing results point to a trend where the initial effects of CSA remain steady and worsen throughout the lives of the victims. What mechanisms might account for the psychopathologies summarized above?

Possible Mechanisms of How Sexual Abuse Affects Victims

Most researchers in the field of CSA agree that such maltreatment can cause harm to the victim, but researchers disagree as to the nature and severity. Bolton et al. (1990) indicated that the single most important variable in reducing trauma associated with a sexually abusive event for both sexes was the availability of a support system for the child. Victims from families which demonstrated significant problems and pathology did worse than those who have supportive relationships with nonoffending adults and siblings.

If the social support in the child's life is lacking, then the effects of the sexual abuse may be magnified. One of the reasons for CSA having deleterious effects on the victims is that through such abuse, there is a disregard by the abuser for the child's level of development and needs. The corollary of this disregard of the child is that the interactions between the caregiver and child are excessively oriented toward the caregiver's own whims, needs and satisfactions. Inconsistency of caregiving, where the caregiver is the perpetrator, also adds to the confusion for the child. No caregiver, even the most devoted, can be completely consistent in child care, but children can adapt to these "normal" inconsistencies. Extreme inconsistencies, however, such as is shown through CSA, may leave the child in a state of confusion and disarray leading to disrupted attachment, deficits in emotional regulation, confusion in the autonomous self, and defective peer relations (Cicchetti & Howes, 1991; Steele, 1986; Wolfe & Jaffe, 1991).

Children, both boys and girls, who have felt inadequately cared for by their parents, and have also been sexually abused by other family members, seem to have an especially difficult time while growing up. They have a low self-esteem and a poor sense of identity which is particularly evident in the sphere of sexuality (Gilqun & Reiser, 1990). They continue to feel exploited and may have the same tendency to exploit others. Males tend to feel much more ashamed, embarrassed and denigrated by their past experiences, whereas girls seem to feel more degraded and dirty or despoiled. Both carry a deep lasting, although often unconscious, sense of fear, anger, and hatred toward authorities and against those whom they feel have exploited them in the past and fear they will do so again in the future (Wolfe & Wolfe, 1988). A significant number of such youngsters of both sexes eventually get into prostitution but most have other types of sexual problems, and intimacy is difficult for them to attain (Steele, 1986).

Kempe and Kempe (1984) also noted the severity of the consequences of abuse by a family member when they concluded that "a single molestation by a stranger . . . may cause only transitory harm to normal children living with secure, reassuring parents" (p. 188). Repeated molestations by a relative, however, may have profound and lasting effects. The degree of social support, then, may be a critical variable in determining the extent of both the initial and lasting effects of CSA (Wolfe & Jaffe, 1991).

Prevalence of the Sexual Abuse

Several studies have now been published which provide useful estimates of prevalence rates of CSA. Even so, extreme caution must be exercised in selecting studies for establishing these rates because they vary dramatically from study to study. Fritz, Stoll, and Wagner (1981), for example, employing a community sample estimated a CSA prevalence rate of 4.8% while Condy et al. (1987) estimated it at 57.0% in their sample of rapists. Obviously, both the definition of CSA employed and the nature of the sample in the study will have a large impact of estimated CSA prevalence rates. Nevertheless, several studies have been conducted which are valuable in estimating CSA prevalence rates. Table 19.1 contains a list of these studies and some relevant characteristics of them.

Only studies of nonclinical samples were included for analysis because other sorts of samples (psychiatric, child molesters, rapists, prostitutes, runaways, etc.) might provide gross overestimates in the general population. Accordingly, such studies (e.g., Janus, Burgess, & McCormack, 1987; Johnson & Shrier, 1987; Roane, 1992) have not been included in the present analysis in Table 19.1.

Table 19.1
Prevalence of Child Sexual Abuse of
Nonclinical Samples in Published Studies

Study	Type of Sample	N	Prevalence (%)
1. Alexander & Lupfer (1987)	American university students	586F	24.4
2. Bagley (1988)	Canadian national survey	935M	8.2
3. Bagley & Ramsay (1986)	Canadian community sample	377F	21.8
4. Barker & Duncan (1985)	British national survey	969M	12.0
		1050F	12.0
5. Briere et al. (1992)	American university students	106M	20.8
		212F	22.2
6. Condy et al. (1987)	American college men	359M	16.0
7. Finkelhor (1979)	American university students	266M	9.5
		520F	19.6
8. Finkelhor et al. (1990)	American national survey	1145M	16.0
		1481F	27.0
9. Fritz et al. (1981)	American community sample	952M	4.8
10. Fromuth (1986)	American university students	299F	21.9
11. Fromuth & Brukhart (1989)	American university students	582M	14.0
12. Gundlach (1977)	American community sample	458F	25.1
13. Mullen et al. (1988)	American community sample	314F	13.1
14. Murphy et al. (1988)	American communitty sample	391F	9.7
15. Runtz (1987)	American university students	291F	25.1
16. Runtz & Briere (1986)	American university students	152F	26.9
17. Russell (1986)	American university students	930F	16.3
18. Sedney & Brooks (1984)	American college students	301F	16.00
19. Stein et al. (1988)	American community sample	1473M	12.2
		1307F	26.6
20. Violato & Genuis (1993a)	Canadian university students	200M	14.0

Male Prevalence = 12.4% Female Prevalence = 20.5% (unweighted means)

As can be seen in Table 19.1, we analyzed the prevalence rates of males and females separately. Taking the simple unweighted mean of the prevalence rates from the studies of males (Bagley, 1988; Baker & Duncan, 1985; Condy et al., 1987; Finkelhor et al., 1990; Fritz et al., 1981; Fromuth & Burkhart, 1989; Stein, Golding, Siegel, Burnam, & Sorensen, 1988; Violato & Genuis, 1993a), we estimated the prevalence rate of male sexual abuse to be 12.4 % (low = 4.8%; high = 20.8%). For studies of females (Alexander & Lupfer, 1987; Bagley & Ramsay, 1986; Barker & Duncan, 1985; Briere et al., 1992; Finkelhor, 1979; Finkelhor et al., 1990; Fromuth, 1986; Gundlach, 1977; Mullen et al., 1988; Murphy et al., 1988; Runtz, 1987; Runtz & Briere, 1986; Russell, 1986; Sedney & Brooks, 1984; Stein et al., 1988), the prevalence rate is 20.5% (Table 19.1).

From the above results, it appears that the rate of male CSA is significantly lower than that of female CSA. Several researchers, however, believe that the rates between the sexes may be the same but that the male rate appears lower because of underreporting (Beitchman et al., 1992; Bolton, Morris, & MacEachron, 1990; Pettis & Hughes, 1985; Violato & Genuis, 1993b). Pettis and Hughes (1985) estimated that, typically, there were about three to four times as many cases of abuse than is disclosed. Possible reasons for the lack of disclosure by males of their sexually abusive experiences include shame, fear of ridicule and rejection, fear of being considered mentally ill, and fear of being considered a homosexual (Beitchman et al., 1992; Bolton et al., 1990). Underreporting for males, for whatever reason, appears to be a significant problem. Prevalence rates then, need further study.

Using what must be a conservative estimate of a 10% prevalence rate of male CSA, 2.1, 1.0 and 8.0 million adult men (older than 17 years) in Great Britain (population = 57 million), Canada (population = 27 million), and the United States (population = 253 million) respectively, have been sexually abused. Similarly, if we use a conservative estimate of a 15% prevalence rate of female CSA, 3.2, 1.5, and 12.0 million adult women have been sexually abused in those respective countries. This also means that 1.7, 0.9, and 7.2 million children in these respective countries will be sexually abused before age 18. If we further assume that the prevalence rate of very serious CSA (repeated assaults over a prolonged period of time involving penetration, force and actual or threatened violence) is roughly 5% (Baker & Duncan, 1985; Beitchman et al., 1992; Finkelhor, 1990), then about 17 million people in Great Britain, Canada and the United States have been seriously abused. These calculations indicate that the number of people who are subjected to CSA is astounding. Moreover, the implications of this for the development of psychopathologies is profound.

Implications of CSA for Psychopathology

While as we have seen it may be premature to confirm a postsexual abuse syndrome in the long term, and while there have not been definitive abuse specific factors associates with sequelae, it is clear that CSA is associated with a number of pathological outcomes (Kendall-Tackett et al., 1993). At the very least, CSA is associated with disturbed sexual identity and ideation, prostitution, suicidal impulses, difficulties in interpersonal relationships, and possibly multiple personality disorders.

It is noteworthy that several recent epidemiological studies have suggested that the prevalence rates of psychopathology in young adults (18-24 years old) is approximately 20% (Gatz & Smyer, 1992; George, Blazer, Winfield-Laird, Leaf, & Fishbach, 1988; Robins, Helzer, Weissman, Orvaschel, Gruenberg, Burke, & Reiger, 1984), and is between 17% and 22% for adolescents (under 18 years of age) (Kazdin, 1993). In the George et al. (1988) study, for example, results were based on the Diagnostic Interview Schedule (DIS), a structured interview used to collect information about symptoms on which diagnoses are based. While categories of various psychopathologies such as anxiety disorders, depression, dysphoria, phobias, cognitive impairments, and personality disorders was included, an overall DIS diagnoses was arrived at producing a prevalence rate of precisely 20.0% (George et al., 1988, p. 205). While other sources may not produce a precise estimate of 20.0%, it is probably reasonable to estimate that perhaps one-fifth of young adults and adolescents suffer from at least one serious psychological disorder.

The foregoing review of the long-term sequelae, and prevalence rates of CSA suggests that a large proportion of the pathologic young adults and adolescents have CSA as the etiology of their disorders. As we have seen, CSA is probably implicated in affective, anxiety and personality disorders which may lead to a long-term postsexual abuse syndrome. If 5-6% of CSA may be considered very severe (repeated incidents involving penetration, violence and threats), this may result in more than 17 million people developing psychopathology. CSA, therefore, may be involved in 1/3 to 3/4 of all psychopathologies (6-15% prevalence rate) (George et al., 1988; Kazdin, 1993; Kendall-Tackett et al., 1993).

Even if not all CSA leads to psychopathologies, it can typically lead to disturbed sexual identity and ideation in adolescence. Since many adolescents face disturbances and stress in identity formation (Erikson, 1950; Nurmi, 1992); those who have experienced CSA will have particular difficulties in gender and sexual identity formation. This, in turn, may lead to prostitution, sexual dysfunction, and difficulties in achieving intimacy and satisfactory interpersonal relationships. Such problems are likely to continue into adulthood and indeed, to become exacerbated. The long-term effects of CSA, then, are likely to be profound.

The specific mechanisms of how CSA results in both initial and long-term effects are not yet fully understood. It may be, for example, that a postsexual abuse syndrome with a multiplicity of pathologies develops and continues to worsen. Alternatively, it is possible that CSA may also have a "sleeper effect" (Beitchman et al., 1992) producing problems later in life during adolescence and adulthood. These difficulties may include disturbed identity, lack of intimacy, and problems in interpersonal relationships. In any case, much more research and work is urgently required into all aspects of CSA as this is clearly a social, developmental and psychological issue of a large magnitude.

Summary and Conclusions

From the foregoing review, the following findings may be summarized: (1) a universal definition of CSA has not yet been arrived at; (2) the actual prevalence of CSA appears to be around 10-20%; (3) we are beginning to understand the effects, both initial and long-term, of CSA; and (4) CSA has profound implications of developmental psychopathologies.

The study of CSA, while expanding, is characterized by research whose methodologies are questionable and whose results are difficult to compare, and when they are compared, may be contradictory and confusing. Few definitive conclusions can be made based on research on CSA. Several tentative conclusions and some suggestions for future study, however, may be appropriate at this time.

First, future researchers may profitably define sexual abuse as unwanted sexual contact, genital touching and fondling to penetration while the victim is considered a child by legal definition and the assailant is in a position of power vis-a-vis the victim (e.g., parent). This will provide a practical and simple operational definition of CSA. Thus, it will become easier to compare the information accrued from different studies. Second, multivariate analyses may be very helpful to researchers studying CSA since these methods have not been widely used in the area. They will allow researchers to further examine factors such as those which may increase children's vulnerability to sexual abuse. Such analyses may also provide for a clearer understanding of direct effects of CSA and clarify abuse-specific outcomes (Wolfe & Jaffe, 1991). Third, replication of the findings that separation from a parent and intra-familial instability during childhood are related to CSA (Finkelhor et al., 1990; Violato & Genuis, 1993b) may provide further insight into the factors which put a child at risk of such abuse. Finkelhor's (1984) model in which four preconditions to sexual abuse are required may be pertinent here: (1) The potential perpetrator must overcome external inhibitors to abuse; (2) there must be the motivation to sexually abuse; (3) intrapersonal inhibitors to sexually abuse a child must be overcome; and (4) the perpetrator must overcome the resistance of the child). Separation from a parent during childhood may eliminate necessary external inhibitors (a parent watching over and protecting the child from possible abuse simply through his or her presence), and therefore leave the child more vulnerable to sexual abuse than when the child is not separated from a parent for a long period of time. Fourth, some empirical data indicates that significantly more young adult males who have been victims of CSA are interested in having sex with male children than are young adult males who have not been sexually abused as children (e.g., Violato & Genuis, 1993a). Such findings require replication in further well designed research. Fifth, further work is required to clarify the prevalence rate of CSA. The estimate for males may be low due to underreporting and still needs to be clarified for females. Even using the current prevalence rate, however, we can estimate that about 12 million males and 17 million females are victims of CSA combining the populations of Great Britain, Canada and the U.S.A. This astounding figure clearly has profound implications for mental health research and therapy. Sixth, there is considerable confusion in the data about gender differences in sexual abuse, prevalence, frequency and severity of abuse, types of abuse, and relationship to the perpetrator. It is clear, however, that most assailants of both male and female victims are male. Seventh, there appears to be a definite risk of a victim/perpetrator cycle. Male victims of sexual abuse may themselves subsequently become abusers. Eighth, and finally, the implications for developmental psychopathology of CSA are profound. A large proportion of the prevalence rate of current psychopathology may be due to the effects of CSA.

While the area of CSA is relatively new and still requires further exploration, some intriguing possibilities have been raised in the present review. The possibility of a postsexual abuse syndrome may provide a theoretical framework for future thought and research. This syndrome, especially in the long-term, may be characterized by confused sex-roles, homosexuality, prostitution, paedophilia, deliberate self-harm, depression, and problems with anger. Researchers theoretically grounded in the postsexual abuse syndrome, however, must be careful to employ research designs which disentangle abuse-specific variables from the many other deleterious factors that commonly characterize the environments of CSA children. Future research might also be designed to investigate the gender-specific effects of CSA since it is possible that such trauma may be more harmful for males than for females. Finally, CSA may profit by a more theoretically sophisticated analysis, possibly within the context of developmental psychopathology generally. Thus, future work may be more focused, theoretically oriented, and involve hypothesis-testing studies. Some ground work has been laid but much more research is urgently required.

References

Adams-Tucker, C. (1986). Defence mechanisms used by sexually abused children. In D.C. Haden (Ed.), *Out of harm's way: Readings on child sexual abuse, its prevention and treatment*, (72-80). Phoenix, AZ: The Onyx Press.

Alexander, P.C., & Lupfer, S.L. (1987). Family characteristics and long-term consequences associated with sexual abuse. *Archives of Sexual Behavior, 16*, 235-245.

Bagley, C. (1988). *Child sexual abuse in a national Canadian survey*. Ottawa: Department of Health and Welfare.

Bagley, C., & Ramsay, R. (1986). Sexual abuse in childhood: Psychosocial outcomes and implications for social work practice. *Journal of Social Work and Human Sexuality, 4*, 33-47.

Baker, A.W., & Duncan, S. P. (1985). Child sexual abuse: A study of prevalence in Great Britain. *Child Abuse and Neglect, 9*, 457-467.

Beitchman, J.H., Zucker, K.J., Hood, J.E., da Costa, G.A., & Akman, D. (1991). A review of the short-term effects of child sexual abuse. *Child Abuse and Neglect, 15*, 537-556.

Beitchman, J.H., Zucker, K.J., Hood, J.E., da Costa, G.A., Akman, D., & Cassavia, E. (1992). A review of the long-term effects of child sexual abuse. *Child Abuse and Neglect, 16,* 101-118.

Bolton, F., Morris, L., & MacEachron, K. (1990). *Males at risk: The other side of child sexual abuse.* London: Sage.

Briere, J. (1984). *The effects of childhood sexual abuse on later psychological functioning: Defining a post-sexual-abuse syndrome.* Paper presented at the Third National Conference on Sexual Victimization of Children, Washington, D.C.

Briere, J.N. (1992). *Child abuse trauma: Theory and treatment of the lasting effects.* Newbury Park: Sage.

Briere, J.N., Henschell, D., & Smiljanieh, K. (1992). Attitudes towards sexual abuse: Sex differences and construct validity. *Journal of Research and Personality, 26,* 398-406.

Briere, J., & Runtz, M. (1986). Suicidal thoughts and behaviors in former sexual abuse victims. *Canadian Journal of Behavioral Science, 18,* 413-423.

Browne, A., & Finkelhor, D. (1986). Impact of child sexual abuse: A review of the research. *Psychological Bulletin, 99,* 1, 66-77.

Bruckner, D., & Johnson, P. (1987). Treatment for adult male victims of childhood sexual abuse. *Social Casework, 68,* 1-9.

Cicchetti, D., & Howes, P.W. (1991). Developmental psychopathology in the context of the family: Illustrations from the study of child maltreatment. *Canadian Journal of Behavioral Science, 23,* 257-281.

Condy, S., Templar, D., Brown, R., & Veaco, L. (1987). Parameters of sexual contact of boys with women. *Archives of Sexual Behavior, 16,* 379-394.

Conte, J., & Shuerman, J. (1987a). Factors associated with an increased impact of child sexual abuse. *Child Abuse and Neglect, 11,* 201-211.

Conte, J., & Shuerman, J. (1987b). The effects of child sexual abuse on children: A multidimensional view. *Journal of Interpersonal Violence, 2*(4), 330-390.

Davis, C., & Leitenberg, H. (1987). Adolescent sex offenders. *Psychological Bulletin, 101,* 417-427.

De Jong, A.R., Hervada, A.R., & Emmett, G.A. (1983). Epidemiologic variations in childhood sexual abuse. *Child Abuse and Neglect, 7,* 155-162.

Erikson, E. (1950). *Childhood and society.* New York, NY: Norton.

Faller, K. (1989). Characteristics of a clinical sample of sexually abused children: How boy and girl victims differ. *Child Abuse and Neglect, 13,* 281-291.

Farber, E.D., Showers, J., Johnson, C.F., Joseph, J.A., & Oshins, L. (1984). The sexual abuse of children: A comparison of male and female victims. *Journal of Clinical Child Psychology, 13*(3), 294-297.

Finkelhor, D. (1979). *Sexually victimized children.* New York, NY: Free Press.

Finkelhor, D. (1984). *Child sexual abuse: New theory and research.* New York: The Free Press.

Finkelhor, D. (1990). Early and long-term effects of child sexual abuse: An update. *Professional Psychology: Research and Practice, 21*, 325-330.

Finkelhor, D., & Hotaling, G.T. (1984). Sexual abuse in the national incidence study of child abuse and neglect: An appraisal. *Child Abuse and Neglect, 8*, 23-33.

Finkelhor, D., Hotaling, G., Lewis, I., & Smith, C. (1990). Risk factors for sexual abuse in a national survey of adult men and women. *Child Abuse and Neglect, 14*, 19-28.

Freeman-Longo, R. (1986). The impact of sexual victimization on males. *Child Abuse and Neglect, 10*, 411-414.

Fritz, G., Stoll, K., & Wagner, N. (1981). A comparison of males and females who were sexually molested as children. *Journal of Sex and Marital Therapy, 7*, 54-59.

Fromuth, M.E. (1986). The relationship of childhood sexual abuse with later psychological and sexual adjustment in a sample of college women. *Child Abuse and Neglect, 10*, 5-15.

Fromuth, M., & Burkhart, B. (1989). Long-term psychological correlates of childhood sexual abuse in two samples of college men. *Child Abuse and Neglect, 13*, 533-542.

Gatz, M., & Smyer, M.A. (1992). The mental health system and older adults in the 1990s. *American Psychologist, 47*, 741-751.

George, L.K., Blazer, D.F., Winfield-Laird, I., Leaf, P.J., & Fishbach, R.L. (1988). Psychiatric disorders and mental health service use in later life: Evidence from the epidemiologic catchment area program. In J. Brody & G. Maddox, (Eds.), *Epidemiology and aging*. New York: Springer.

Gilqun, J. F., & Reiser, E. (1990). The development of sexual identity among men sexually abused as children. *The Journal of Contemporary Human Services*, (November), 515-523.

Gomes-Schwartz, B. (1984). Juvenile sexual offenders. In *Sexually exploited children: Service and research project*. Washington, DC: U.S. Department of Justice.

Gordon, M. (1990). Males and females as victims of childhood sexual abuse: An examination of the gender effect. *Journal of Family Violence, 5*, 321-333.

Greenburg, N.H. (1979). The epidemiology of childhood sexual abuse. *Paediatric Annals, 8*(5), 289-299.

Grossi, V., & Violato, C. (1992). A stepwise discriminant analysis of suicidal and non-suicidal adolescents. *Canadian Journal of Behavioral Sciences, 24*, 410-413.

Gundlach, R.H. (1977). Sexual molestation and rape reported by homosexual and heterosexual women. *Journal of Homosexuality, 2*, 367-384.

Inderbitzen-Pisaruk, H., Sawchuck, C.R., & Hooier, T.S. (1992). Behavioral characteristics of child victims of sexual abuse: A comparison study. *Journal of Clinical Child Psychology, 21*, 14-19.

Janus, M., Burgess, A., & McCormack, W. (1987). Histories of sexual abuse in adolescent male runaways. *Adolescence, 22*, 405-417.

Janus, M., Scarlon, B., & Price, V. (1984). Youth prostitution. In A. Burgess & M. Lindequist-Clark (Eds.), *Child pornography and sex rings*. Toronto: Lexington Books.

Johnson, R., & Shrier, D. (1987). Past sexual victimization by females of male patients in an adolescent medicine clinic population. *American Journal of Psychiatry, 144*, 650-652.

Kazdin, A.E. (1993). Psychotherapy for children and adolescents: Current progress and future research directions. *American Psychologist, 48*, 644-657.

Kempe, R.S., & Kempe, C.H. (1984). *The common secret: Sexual abuse of children and adolescents*. New York: W.H. Freeman & Company.

Kendall-Tackett, K.A., Williams, L.M., & Finkelhor, D. (1993). Impact of sexual abuse on children: A review and synthesis of recent empirical studies. *Psychological Bulletin, 113*, 164-180.

Krug, R. (1989). Adult male report of childhood sexual abuse by mothers: Case descriptions, motivations and long-term consequences. *Child Abuse and Neglect, 13*, 111-119.

McCormack, A., Janus, M., & Burgess, A. (1986). Runaway youths and sexual victimization: Gender differences in an adolescent runaway population. *Child Abuse and Neglect, 10*, 387-395.

Metcalfe, M., Oppenheimer, R., Dignon, A., & Palmer, P. (1990). Child sexual experiences reported by male psychiatric patients. *Psychological Medicine, 20*, 925-929.

Mullen, P.E., Romans-Clarkson, S.E., Walton, V.A., & Herbison, G.P. (1988). Impact of sexual and physical abuse on women's mental health. *Lancet, 1*, 841-845.

Murphy, S.M., Kilpatrick, D.G., Amick-McMullen, A., Veronen, L.J., Paduhovich, J., Best, C.L., Villeponteaux, L.A., & Saunders, B.E. (1988). Current psychological functioning of child sexual assault survivors. *Journal of Interpersonal Violence, 3*, 55-79.

Nurmi, J.E. (1991). How do adolescents see their future? A review of the development of future orientation and planning. *Developmental Review, 11*, 1-59.

Pettis, K., & Hughes. (1985). Sexual victimization of children: A current perspective. *Behavioral Disorders, 10*(2), 136-143.

Pierce, R., & Pierce, L. (1985). The sexually abused child: A comparison of male and female victims. *Child Abuse and Neglect, 9*, 191-199.

Reinhart, M. (1987). Sexually abused boys. *Child Abuse and Neglect, 11*, 229-235.

Roane, T.H. (1992). Male victims of sexual abuse: A case review within a child protective team. *Child Welfare, 71*, 231-239.

Robins, L.N., Helzer, J.E., Weissman, M.M., Orvaschel, H., Gruenberg, E., Burke, J.D., & Reiger, D.A. (1984). Lifetime prevalence of specific psychiatric disorders in three sites. *Archives of General Psychiatry, 41*, 949-958.

Rogers, C., & Terry, T. (1984). Clinical intervention with boy victims of abuse. In I. Stuart & J. Green, (Eds.), *Victims of sexual aggression*, New York: Van Nostrand.

Russell, D.E. (1986). *The secret trauma: Incest in the lives of girls and women*. New York: Basic Books.

Sedney, M.A., & Brooks, B. (1984). Factors associated with a history of childhood sexual abuse experience in a nonclinical female population. *Journal of the American Academy of Child Psychiatry, 23*, 215-218.

Silbert, M.H., & Pines, A.M. (1981). Sexual child abuse as an antecedent to prostitution. *Child Abuse and Neglect, 5,* 407-411.

Silbert, M.H., & Pines, A.M. (1983). Early sexual exploitation as an influence in prostitution. *Social Work, 28,* 285-289.

Steele, B. (1986). Notes on the lasting effects of early child abuse throughout the life cycle. *Child Abuse and Neglect, 10,* 283-291.

Stein, J.A., Golding, J.M., Siegel, J.M., Burnam, M.A., & Sorenson, S.B. (1988). Long-term psychological sequelae of child sexual abuse: The Los Angeles Epidemiologic Catchment Area Study. In G.E. Wyatt & G.J. Powell (Eds.), *Lasting effects of child sexual abuse.* Newbury Park: Sage.

Summit, R. (1983). The child sexual abuse accommodation syndrome. *Child Abuse and Neglect, 7,* 177-193.

Tong, L., Oates, K., & McDowell, M. (1987). Personality development following sexual abuse. *Child Abuse and Neglect, 11,* 371-383.

Vander-Mey, B. (1988). The sexual victimization of male children: A review of previous research. *Child Abuse and Neglect, 12,* 61-72.

Violato, C., & Genuis, M. (1993a). Factors which differentiate sexually abused from nonabused males: An exploratory study. *Psychological Reports, 72,* 767-770.

Violato, C., & Genuis, M. (1993b). Problems of research in male child sexual abuse: A review. *Journal of Child Sexual Abuse, 2,* 33-54.

Wolfe, D.A., & Jaffe, P. (1991). Child abuse and family violence as determinants of child psychopathology. *Canadian Journal of Behavioral Science, 23,* 282-299.

Wolfe, V.V., & Wolfe, D.A. (1988). Sexual abuse of children. In E. J. Mash & L. G. Terdal (Eds.), *Behavioral assessment of childhood disorders* (2nd ed.), (pp.670-714). New York: Guilford.

Woods, S.C., & Dean, K.S. (1984). *Final report: Sexual abuse of males research project (NCCA Report No. 90-CA-812).* Washington, DC: National Center on Child Abuse and Neglect.

20
Creativity, Intelligence and Achievement

Despite substantial research into the relationship between intelligence and creativity in the last several decades, the nature of this relationship is still not well understood (Haensly & Reynolds, 1989; Runco, 1991; Sternberg, 1992; Wakefield, 1991). Various researchers have explored this relationship during this past century (e.g., Cattell, 1963; Guilford, 1981; Terman, 1955; Torrance, 1962, 1988). The general conclusion from this work is that creativity and intelligence are each normally distributed human traits but that they have limited overlap or are somewhat correlated. The correlations between measures of creativity (e.g., Torrance Tests of Creative Thinking – TTCT) or divergent thinking and intelligence (e.g., IQ tests as the Wechsler Intelligence Scale for Children – Revised – WISC-R) or convergent thinking for the general population are between .20 and .40 (Haensly & Reynolds, 1989; McCabe, 1991; Wakefield, 1991).

Getzels and Jackson (1962) have proposed a curvilinear relationship between creativity and intelligence (also known as the "threshold hypothesis"). Here it is posited that above a certain threshold of intelligence, creativity and intelligence are orthogonal (there is no correlation). Getzels and Jackson (1962) reasoned that a minimal level of intelligence is required for creative production (somewhat above average) but beyond that, further increases in IQ do not correspond to increases in creativity. Barron (1969) and Torrance (1962) have provided precise minimum cutoffs of IQ of 120 as the threshold of the relationship between IQ and creativity. Essentially, the threshold theory holds that a minimum level of intelligence is required to recognize that a meaningful problem exists, to select and integrate the relevant information, and to generate an applicable and perhaps original solution (Haensly & Reynolds, 1989; Runco, 1992; Sternberg, 1992). The main purpose of the present study was to undertake a direct test of the threshold hypothesis employing structural equation modelling techniques of divergent thinking, IQ and achievement tests with a sample of gifted children. Specifically, the threshold theory was conceptualized as a second-order hierarchical confirmatory factor analysis so that measured variables (e.g., achievement tests) as well as latent variables (e.g., IQ) and second-order latent variables (e.g., convergent thinking) could be identified and included in the model of the theory to be tested.

There has been a substantial amount of empirical evidence to support the proposition that intelligence and creativity are related to some degree. Guilford (1968), for example, using a battery of divergent production tests and a group intelligence test (California Test of Mental Maturity – CTMM), found correlations between divergent test scores and CTMM scores to range between $r = .10$ and $r = .40$. The correlation between total divergent thinking scores and IQ was $r = .22$. In another study, Guilford and Christensen (1973) administered five divergent thinking tests to elementary school children. From school records they secured Lorge-Thorndike IQ scores for some of the children and estimated IQ for others (from achievement test scores). They found that intelligence scores were correlated with divergent thinking scores at $r = .25$. In a similar vein, McCabe (1991) in her study of 126 adolescent Australian girls found a correlation between TTCT-Form B subtest scores and the Australian Council for Educational Research IQ test total score ranging between $r = .29$ and $r = .47$. Employing a Venezuelan university sample of science freshmen (mean age = 17.7), Niaz and de Nunez (1991) found small correlations ($r = .30$) between the Raven Progressive Matrices Test (IQ) scores and the TTCT – Figural Form scores. Similar correlations have been found between IQ and divergent thinking scores by Anastasi and Schaefer (1971), Crockenberg (1972), and Getzels and Jackson (1962) as well as others (Ausubel, 1978; Nichols, 1972; Ripple & May, 1962; Runco, 1986, 1991; Thorndike, 1963; Torrance, 1962, 1979; Wakefield, 1991; Wallach & Kogan, 1972).

While the foregoing research generally supports a moderate correlation between IQ and creativity in the general population, some scanty data can also be found in support of the threshold hypothesis. Guilford and Christensen (1973) generated scatterplots from their data and concluded that the pattern between IQ and creativity scores supported the threshold hypothesis. Similarly, the Niaz and de Nunez (1991) data indicated that the correlation between creativity and IQ scores diminished as IQ increased beyond one standard deviation above the mean. Similarly, Weinstein and Bobko (1980) found no correlations between creativity and IQ (as well as androgyny) beyond an intelligence threshold. In a rare longitudinal study, Hall (1985) demonstrated complex interrelationships among intelligence, creativity and achievement scores. She studied this interrelationship in eighth and later in the same twelfth grade pupils. Hall (1985) found that in a gifted sample, there was no correlation between IQ and creativity. The work of Guilford and Hoepfner (1966), Richards (1976) and Schubert (1973) all lends further support to the threshold view.

Notwithstanding these supportive data, several investigators have reported findings contrary to the threshold hypothesis. Runco and Albert (1986), for example, using Stanford-Binet or WISC-R IQs and the Wallach and Kogan (1965) divergent thinking battery, not only failed to support the threshold hypothesis, but produced contrary results. The correlations between creativity and intelligence (for grades 5, 6, 7 and 8 public school pupils) were nonsignificant in a low intelligence group (average $r = -.03$), for example, and significant in the high intelligence group (average $r = .35$). In another study, Runco and Pezdek (1984) found nonsignificant relationships between achievement and three divergent thinking indices using various linear and non-linear computational techniques. Mednik and Andrews (1967) also uncovered evidence contrary to the threshold hypothesis. Using the Remote Associates Test (RAT) as a measure of creativity and the Scholastic Aptitude Test (SAT) to estimate intelligence, they found overall correlations of $r = .43$ between the RAT and the SAT verbal scale and $r = .20$ between the RAT and the SAT math scales, but there were no differences in the size of the correlations between these variables for the low and high SAT groups. These findings contradict the threshold hypothesis as does the work of Ripple and May (1962) who generally failed to find significant correlations between IQ and divergent thinking tests in all three samples of grade seven high (116 to 133), average (96 to 110), and low (72 to 90) IQ groups.

The empirical evidence for the relationship between intelligence and creativity generally and for the threshold hypothesis specifically, is conflicting and equivocal. This may be due to at least four interrelated problems in this area of research. First, a great variety of divergent thinking tests have been employed in different studies. These have included the Torrance Tests, Remote Associate Tests, the Wallach and Kogan tests, the Guilford Tests and the Welsh Figure Preference Test which have varying degrees of reliability and validity (Crockenberg, 1972; Haensly & Reynolds, 1988; Sternberg, 1992; Wakefield, 1991). Moreover, some researchers have invented their own "homemade" tests (e.g. Runco & Okuda, 1988; Ripple & May, 1962) with unknown reliability and validity.

Second, a great variety of IQ measures such as the WISC-R, Lorge-Thorndike, CTMM, Stanford-Binet, Raven Progressive Matrices, and so on have been employed in different studies. Some of these tests are group administered while some are individually administered. Additionally, sometimes only verbal sub-scales are employed to estimate IQ, while at other times non-verbal estimates are employed and still other times composite verbal and non-verbal estimates are derived. These different practices obviously introduce variability in results.

Third – and a far more serious problem than using different IQ tests – is the questionable practice of "estimating" intelligence using achievement scores (e.g. Guilford & Christensen, 1973; Mednick & Andrews, 1967; Runco & Albert, 1986). It is well established that IQ and achievement are overlapping but distinct constructs and should not be treated as interchangeable (Anastasi, 1988; Cronbach, 1984; Violato, McDougall & Marini, 1992). IQ is a predictive measure which tends to focus on general intellectual ability, while achievement tests tend to reflect more specific learning experiences. Goh and McElheron (1992) in their further examination of this aptitude-achievement distinction, concluded that IQ and achievement tests are ordered along a continuum of skills and abilities. Achievement and IQ measures undoubtedly reflect distinct underlying cognitive processes (Gustafsson & Undheim, 1992) and their distinction is crucial. The practice by some researchers of using achievement scores to estimate IQ has no doubt introduced considerable confusion and error into the creativity research.

Fourth, samples employed by various researchers have been highly varied. Subjects have been very heterogeneous by age, IQ, socioeconomic status, ethnicity, and sex composition. These widely different and incomparable populations have been sampled thus undermining the generality and stability of the findings.

Taken together it is not surprising that these four major problems – varied divergent thinking tests, widely different IQ measures, confusing achievement and IQ, incomparable samples – have resulted in conflicting, confusing and equivocal results. Accordingly, the present study was undertaken to directly test the threshold hypothesis while at the same time mitigating at least some of the problems addressed above. In concordance with the threshold hypothesis, it was posited that intelligence and creativity are distinct cognitive processes in high IQ children. Moreover, it was assumed that achievement is independent of creativity but is related to intelligence and that both of these cognitive processes (intelligence and achievement) arise from an underlying latent variable, convergent thinking. Since both intelligence and achievement are themselves latent variables as is creativity, convergent thinking is a second-order latent variable. The full model to be tested, therefore, is a second-order hierarchical confirmatory factor analysis and is detailed in Figure 20.1. The present study was an attempt to test this structural equation model.

Subjects

A total of 201 elementary school pupils (109 females, 96 males) in grades five (n = 73), six (n = 60) and seven (n = 68) participated in the present study. All of these children were enrolled in a program for the gifted in six different schools. The inclusion criteria for the program included: (1) achievement data, (2) aptitude/interest measures, (3) reading test scores, and (4) IQ scores. The mean IQ (Full Scale WISC-R) for this sample was 132 (SD = 11.7). The mean age of the subjects was 11.2 years with a standard deviation of 0.68 years.

Procedures and Instruments

Subjects' IQs were retrieved from permanent records. (All IQs had been measured no longer than 2 years prior to the present study.) These included WISC-R Verbal, Performance and Full Scale scores. Over a two week period, four subtests (Vocabulary, Reading, Math Concepts, Math Problems) of the Canadian Tests of Basic Skills (CTBS) were administered to all subjects as were the Torrance Tests of Creative Thinking – Figural Form. Accordingly, all subjects had scores on ten measures. These included creativity scores from the TTCT (fluency, flexibility, originality, elaboration), achievement (vocabulary, reading, math concepts, math problems), and intelligence (Verbal IQ, Performance IQ). All these variables were intercorrelated (Table 20.1).

Results

In order to test the threshold hypothesis in the model depicted in Figure 1, structural equation modelling (SEM) techniques were employed. SEM is a collection of statistical procedures (e.g., multiple regression, factor analysis, path analysis) which allows the depiction and testing of complex models of psychological processes. Both measured and latent variables can be included in these models and the structural relations (i.e., correlations) between latent variables can be determined. Accordingly, data can be fit simultaneously to the model in

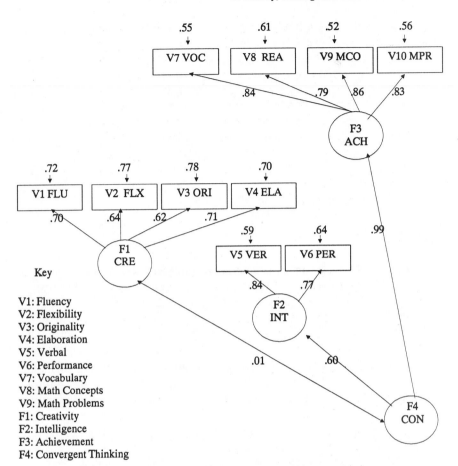

Figure 20.1: Structural Model of Achievement (ACH), Intelligence (INT), Creativity (CRE) and Convergent Thinking (CON).

order to evaluate the theory. As we have seen, the present problem required the use of a second-order hierarchical confirmatory factor analysis. Thus as a preliminary step, all ten measures were intercorrelated using Pearson product-moment correlations. The resulting matrix represented in Table 1 contains all of these correlations as well as the standard deviations of each variable.

As a next step, the intercorrelation matrix was converted to a variance-co-variance matrix in preparation for a confirmatory factor analysis. For the final step, these data were then fit to the proposed model (Figure 20.1) employing the algorithms from EQS (Bentler, 1992).

The overall fit of the data to the model was very good resulting in a Comparative Fit Index (CFI) of 0.93 (Normed Fit Index = 0.89; Nonnormed Fit Index = 0.92) based on 40 degrees of freedom. This solution resulted in a Residual Mean Square (RMS) of 0.04. Almost ninety percent (89.1%) of the standardized residuals (49) of the covariance matrix (S-sigma) were less than ±

.10. To re-iterate, these results indicate that the overall fit of the data to the model was very good.

Table 20.1
Intercorrelations and Standard Deviations
of Ten Cognitive Variables

Variable	Intercorrelations										S.D.
Fluency	1.00										4.1
Flexibility	0.56	1.00									4.6
Originality	0.38	0.37	1.00								4.3
Elaboration	0.45	0.50	0.43	1.00							3.8
V-IQ	0.04	0.12	0.10	0.05	1.00						14.7
P-IQ	0.02	0.01	0.01	0.09	0.62	1.00					15.4
Vocabulary	0.08	0.06	0.05	0.02	0.44	0.42	1.00				25.1
Reading	0.07	0.09	0.11	0.08	0.47	0.40	0.74	1.00			27.3
Math Con	0.06	0.01	0.07	0.02	0.32	0.30	0.73	0.64	1.00		24.6
Math Prob	0.10	0.06	0.09	0.13	-.41	0.47	0.61	0.63	0.776	1.00	24.5

Closer inspection of the model (Figure 20.1) clearly shows that three first-order latent variables were confirmed (F1, F2, F3) as was the second-order latent variable (F4). The factor loadings for all four measures of creativity (fluency, flexibility, originality, and elaboration) were high ranging from .62 to .71. The factor loadings for both measures of intelligence (Verbal IQ, Performance IQ) were very high (.84 and .77 respectively) on F2. Finally, the four achievement measures (vocabulary, reading, math concepts, math problems) all loaded very heavily on the achievement factor (.79 to .86).

Two first-order latent variables (F2 and F3) have very large (.60 and .99 respectively) path coefficients (i.e. correlations) from the second-order latent variable (F4), while the remaining first-order latent variable (F1) shows a near zero (.01) correlation coefficient with F4. The results clearly show that intelligence (F2) and achievement (F3) arise from a common underlying latent variable, convergent thinking (F4). Moreover, convergent thinking is heavily identified by achievement measures as indicated by a very large coefficient (.99). Conversely, it is evident that creativity (F1) is independent of convergent thinking (F4) given the correlation coefficient of .01. These correlations between these latent variables, then, strongly support the theory of the independence of creativity and convergent thinking, and the interrelatedness of achievement and intelligence.

Discussion

The results of the present study strongly support the threshold hypothesis of intelligence and creativity. The major results indicate that (1) achievement (CTBS scores) was related to but separate from IQ, (2) IQ (WISC-R Verbal and Performance subtest scores) identified an underlying convergent thinking process together with achievement, and (3) divergent thinking variables (fluency, flexibility, originality, elaboration) loaded on an underlying creativity factor which was unrelated to convergent thinking.

The major strength of the present study is that it employed a complete model specification of the threshold hypothesis and used confirmatory techniques to test it. Previous researchers have generally failed to identify basic underlying latent variables (e.g. intelligence, convergent thinking) but have focused instead on interpreting simple correlations. Ripple and May (1962), for example, merely interpreted simple correlations in samples of different IQ groupings as did Runco and Albert (1986). In this latter study, simple correlations between IQ and divergent thinking tests were averaged and compared between low and high IQ groupings. Similar analytic approaches were used by Runco and Pezdek (1984) and Mednick and Andrews (1967). The failure to both identify underlying latent variables through factor analytic or latent variable path analytic approaches, and to study the relationships between these latent variables, has been a serious shortcoming of this research which has produced results contradictory to the threshold hypothesis. Moreover, none of this work was confirmatory in the sense that the present study is. All of these previous researchers (Mednick & Andrews, 1967; Ripple & May, 1962; Runco & Albert, 1986; Runco & Pezdek, 1984) have employed exploratory techniques (e.g., simple correlations or regression procedures) and therefore failed to provide an adequate test of the threshold hypothesis by identifying relevant latent variables (e.g., convergent thinking) and determining their structural relations. Accordingly, contradictory findings may be the result, in part, of both inadequate research designs and data analytic procedures.

Achievement, IQ and divergent thinking were also identified and measured separately in the present study so that no confounding was possible of these factors as has been the case in some previous research (Guilford & Christensen, 1973; Mednick & Andrews, 1967; Runco & Albert, 1986). It is evident from the present results, that IQ and achievement, while correlated, are different latent variables which in turn identify a second-order latent variable, convergent thinking. In turn this second-order latent variable is orthogonal to creativity. The highly questionable practice of previous researchers of using achievement measures (e.g. SAT scores) to "estimate" intelligence has resulted in confounding effects with divergent thinking variables (Anastasi, 1988; Cronbach, 1984; Gustafsson & Undheim, 1992; Violato, et al., 1992).

Notwithstanding the generally clear support of the threshold theory of the present results, some cautions are in order. Measuring creativity is no simple task. The Figural Form of the TTCT was used in the present study and while the TTCT is regarded as having generally the most adequate psychometric properties of divergent thinking tests (Wakefield, 1991), it is by no means widely regarded as an entirely valid measure of creativity (Haensly & Reynolds, 1989; Runco, 1992; Sternberg, 1992). Indeed, Sternberg (1992) regarded this and other conventional creativity measures (Guilford, 1986; Wallach & Kogan, 1965) as essentially trivial and quite remote from the kind of creativity relevant to actual disciplines. There may be some truth to this so that the present clear and parsimonious results should not be taken as construct validation of the TTCT. Clearly an adequate theory of creativity and the assessment and measurement of divergent thinking remain as central problems although in a recent review, Runco (1992) concluded that divergent thinking tests such as the TTCT have "selective validity" (i.e. reflecting content validity) as well as discriminant validity.

Another limitation of the present study is the relative homogeneity of the sample composition by age (and educational level). It is possible that older subjects (and more educationally advanced ones) may demonstrate a different relationship between the latent variables. This might be the case, for example, if increased cognitive maturity and educational experience may effect performance on the TTCT (Haensly & Reynolds, 1986; Runco, 1992; Wakefield, 1991). Further research should be designed to address this present limitation.

A final limitation of the present study is that "gifted" children were employed as subjects in accordance with a test of the threshold hypothesis. The structural relationships between creativity, intelligence and achievement should also be studied further in samples which more adequately reflect the general population. Such research would better explicate not only the threshold theory, but increase our understanding of these various cognitive processes in general.

In conclusion, while the present study has several limitations, it is nevertheless a strong test of the threshold theory. The present results clearly support the theoretical proposals of Getzels and Jackson (1962) that there is a curvilinear relationship between creativity and intelligence. The full model specification and the theory confirmation approach are the primary strengths of the present study. As explicated above, further research is required for a fuller explication of the relationships between creativity, intelligence and achievement. The present study provides a good example of a useful approach to this problem.

References

Anastasi, A. (1988). *Psychological testing* (6th ed.). New York: Macmillan.

Anastasi, A., & Schaefer, C.E. (1971). Notes on the concepts of creativity and intelligence. *Journal of Creative Behavior, 5*, 113-116.

Ausubel, D.F. (1978). The nature and measurement of creativity. *Psychologia, 21*, 179-191.

Barron, F. (1963). *Creativity and psychological health: Origins of personality and creative freedom*. Princeton, NJ: Van Nostrand.

Bentler, P.M. (1992). *EQS: Structural Equations Program Manual*. Los Angeles: BMDP Statistical Software, Inc.

Cattell, R.B. (1963). The personality and motivation of the researcher from measurements of contemporaries and from biography. In C.W. Taylor & F. Barron (Eds.), *Scientific creativity: Its recognition and development.* (pp. 119-131). New York: Wiley.

Crockenberg, S.B. (1972). Creativity tests: A boon or boondogle for education? *Review of Educational Research, 42,* 27-45.

Cronbach, L. J. (1990). *Essentials of psychological testing.* (5th ed.). Cambridge: Harper & Row.

Getzels, J.W., & Jackson, P.W. (1962). *Creativity and intelligence: Explorations with gifted students.* New York: Wiley.

Goh, D.S., & McElheron, D. (1992). Another look at the aptitude-achievement distinction. *Psychological Reports, 70,* 833-834.

Guilford, J.P. (1968). *Intelligence, creativity and their educational implications.* San Diego, CA: Robert Knapp.

Guilford, J.P. (1981). Potentiality for creativity. In J.C. Gowan, J. Khatena, & E.P. Torrance (Eds.), *Creativity: Its educational implications* (2nd ed., pp. 1-5). Dubuque, IA: Kendall/Hunt.

Guilford, J.P. (1986). *Creative talents: Their nature, uses and development.* Buffalo, NY: Bearly Limited.

Guilford, J.P., & Christensen, P.R. (1973). The one-way relation between creative potential and IQ. *Journal of Creative Behavior, 1,* 247-252.

Guilford, J.P., & Hoepfner, R. (1966). Creative potential is related to measures of IQ and verbal comprehension. *Indian Journal of Psychology, 41,* 7-16.

Gustafsson, J., & Undheim, J.O. (1992). Stability and change in broad and narrow factors of intelligence from ages 12 to 15 years. *Journal of Educational Psychology, 84,* 141-149.

Haensly, P.A., & Reynolds, C.R. (1989). Creativity and intelligence. In J.A. Glover, R.R. Ronning & C.R. Reynolds (Eds.), *Handbook of creativity.* New York: Plenum Press.

Hall, E.G. (1985). Longitudinal measures of creativity and achievement for gifted IQ groups. *The Creative Child and Adult Quarterly, 10,* 7-16.

Mednick, M.T., & Andrews, F.M. (1967). Creative thinking and level of intelligence. *Journal of Creative Behavior, 1,* 428-431.

McCabe, M.P. (1991). Influence of creativity and intelligence on academic performance. *Journal of Creative Behavior, 25,* 116-122.

Niaz, M., & de Nunez, G.S. (1991). The relationship of mobility-fixity to creativity, formal reasoning and intelligence. *Journal of Creative Behavior, 25,* 205-217.

Nicholls, J.G. (1972). Creativity in the person who will never produce anything original or useful: The concept of creativity as a normally distributed trait. *American Psychologist, 27,* 717-727.

Richards, R.L. (1976). A comparison of selected Guilford and Wallach-Kogan creative thinking tests in conjunction with measures of intelligence. *Journal of Creative Behavior, 10,* 151-164.

Ripple, R.E., & May, F. (1962). Caution in comparing creativity and IQ. *Psychological Reports, 10*, 229-230.

Runco, M.A. (1991). *Divergent thinking*. Norwood, NJ: Ablex Publishing.

Runco, M.A. (1992). Children's creative thinking and creative ideation. *Developmental Review, 12*, 233-264.

Runco, M.A., & Albert, R.S. (1986). The threshold theory regarding creativity and intelligence: An empirical test with gifted and nongifted children. *Creative Child and Adult Quarterly, 11*, 212-218.

Runco, M.A., & Pezdek, K. (1984). The effect of television and radio on children's creativity. *Human Communications Research, 11*, 109-120.

Runco, M.A., & Okuda, S.M. (1988). Problem-discovery, divergent thinking, and the creative process. *Journal of Youth and Adolescence, 17*, 211-220.

Schubert, D.S. (1973). Intelligence as necessary but not sufficient for creativity. *Journal of Genetic Psychology, 122*, 45-47.

Sternberg, R.J. (1992). Ability tests, measurements and markets. *Journal of Educational Psychology, 84*, 134-140.

Terman, L.M. (1955). Are scientists different? *Scientific American, 192*, 25-29.

Thorndike, R.L. (1963). Some methodological issues in the study of creativity. *In Proceedings of the 1962 invitational conference on testing problems*. Princeton, NJ: Educational Testing Services.

Torrance, P.E. (1962). *Guiding creative talent*. Englewood Cliffs, NJ: Prentice-Hall.

Torrance, P.E. (1979). *The search for satori and creativity*. Buffalo: Creative Education Foundation, Inc.

Torrance, P.E. (1988). The nature of creativity as manifest in testing. In R.J. Sternberg (Ed.) *Nature of creativity*. Cambridge: Cambridge University Press.

Violato, C., McDougall, D., & Marini, A. (1992). *Educational measurement and evaluation*. Dubuque, IA: Kendall/Hunt.

Wakefield, J.F. (1991). The outlook for creativity tests. *Journal of Creative Behavior, 25*, 184-193.

Wallach, M.A., & Kogan, N. (1972). Creativity and intelligence in children. In A. Rothenberg & C.R. Hausman (Eds.), *The creativity question*. Durham, NC: Duke University Press, (pp. 208-217).

Wallach, M.A., & Kogan, N. (1965). *Modes of thinking in young children*. New York: Holt, Rinehart & Winston.

Weinstein, J.B., & Bobko, P. (1980). The relationship of creativity and androgyny when moderated by an intelligence threshold. *The Gifted Child Quarterly, 24*, 162-165.

Index